THE HOOAH SCHOOLS

U.S. ARMY SPECIAL OPERATIONS COURSES & UNITS
PREREQUISITES

DELTA FORCE
JUMPMASTER
AIRBORNE
RANGER
SNIPER
SERE
RIP
SPECIAL FORCES
COMBAT DIVER
AIR ASSAULT
PATHFINDER
SOTIC
HALO
LRS

D1361908

Compiled By
Robert S. Bertrand

THE HOOAH SCHOOLS
U.S. ARMY SPECIAL OPERATIONS COURSES & UNITS
PREREQUISITES

Copyright © 2000 by Robert S. Bertrand

ISBN 0-9703000-0-X

FIRST EDITION
FIRST PRINTING

All Rights Reserved: No part of this book may be reproduced by any means without the expressed written consent of the author.

This book is not an official publication of the United States Government, Department of Defense, United States Special Operations Command, Department of the Army, or the United States Army Special Operations Command; nor does its publication in any way imply its endorsement by these agencies. However, most of the information in this book has been derived from these sources and has been checked for accuracy.

PRINTING HISTORY
First Printing 2000

Printed in the United States of America

DISCLAIMER

It is <u>not</u> the intention of this reference guide to provide an alternative to Field Manuals and other relevant Army publications. Information is constantly being revised and incorporated into an increasingly sophisticated, rapidly changing Army. Even as you read this paragraph information is becoming obsolete and publications are being updated. It is important for persons planning to attend any of the courses outlined in this guide to obtain their own copies of required manuals, form, pamphlets, and other Army publications pertaining to the course.

Likewise, it is important for the reader to understand that the information contained herein is constantly changing, and thus training schedules, packing lists, and even uniforms included in this book may have changed since the date of publication. However I feel that the information is the most accurate and up to date information currently available to the public.

In closing, it is duly important for the reader to understand the nature of Special Operations; due to the extreme sensitivity of units' missions, training information is highly classified. Therefore, not all information pertaining to special operations courses and training are available to the public. The information contained in each section is the extent of information available without security clearance, and thus some sections of highly sensitive nature contain very little information outside of prerequisite information to attend the course.

ACKNOWLEDGEMENTS

This reference guide was compiled through the exhaustive research of Technical Manuals, Field Manuals, Pamphlets, and a diversity of other US Army publications. A list of references is provided in the end of each chapter. If any acknowledgements have been inadvertently omitted, I would appreciate receiving full information so that proper credit may be given in future editions. As for myself, I accept credit only for the research and time-consuming compilation of the material contained herein.

I would like to extend my sincere thanks to Jacqueline M. Pearlman and William C. Peterson of Pearlman Publishing Company. For the time and effort you have put into this project. Without your assistance, this book would not have been possible. Also many thanks to Timothy P. Dunnigan of Tyler Enterprises Inc., Keith Goodrum, Jason P. Polaski and Eric George; your contributions made this book a reality

TABLE OF CONTENTS

HALO

AIR ASSAULT

PURPOSE:

The purpose of the Air Assault Course is to prepare soldiers to participate in a lead combat air assault operation. At the end of the course soldiers will be able to demonstrate the skills required to make maximum use of the helicopter in combat to support their units' operations.

OVERVIEW:

The Air Assault course employs three types of learning environments.

Mental Skill:

Using the nondependent training devices approach, soldiers develop mental skills and study relevant principles and procedures. The classroom contains instructional materials, media, and a few training devices.

Hands On:

Soldiers develop physical skills using the actual training devices.

Combination:

Soldiers develop mental and physical skills simultaneously.

Training Outline:

The Air Assault Course is a 10 day course (11 days, including "Zero Day"). The course consists of prerequisite test (which soldiers must pass to continue the course) known as Zero Day, three phases of instruction (Combat Air Assault, Slingloading and Rappelling) and the 12 Mile foot march (to be completed on graduation day).

"Zero Day":

Students conduct the obstacle course (not to fail any two minor obstacles, or any one major obstacle), followed by a two mile run.

The Obstacle course is conducted IAW FM 21-20 and consists of the following obstacles:
- ◆ Confidence Climb;
- ◆ High Stepover;
- ◆ Six Vaults;
- ◆ The Tough One;
- ◆ The Weaver;
- ◆ Inclined Wall;
- ◆ Swing, Stop, Jump;
- ◆ Low Belly Over;
- ◆ Low Crawl.

Phase 1: Combat Air Assault Operations:

Students are tested with written and practical exams. The written examination covers:
- ◆ US Army Aircraft Familiarization;
- ◆ Aircraft Safety;
- ◆ Aeromedical Operations;
- ◆ Reverse Planning (of Combat Air Assault Pathfinder Operations);
- ◆ Selection Factors (for a Helicopter Landing Site);
- ◆ Helicopter Landing Site Marking;
- ◆ Pathfinder Operations.

The practical examination will cover aircraft hand and arm signals.

Students also conduct daily PT, including formation runs and a four mile road march. A combat air assault operation will be conducted to conclude Phase One.

Phase 2: Slingload Operations:

The highest percentage of Air Assault School attrition occurs during Slingloading. Students are tested on practical rigging and inspection of slingloads for utility and cargo helicopters. The written examination covers:

♦ Fundamentals of Slingload Operations;

♦ Aircraft Load Limitations;

♦ Equipment Characteristics;

♦ Load Description, Necessary Equipment, Preparation, Rigging and Inspection of:

    1. Bag, Aerial Delivery, Type A-22 (with major components);

    2. M101 Cargo Trailer;

    3. M149 - Series Water Trailer;

    4. M119/105mm Howitzer (in the forward firing position);

    5. Cargo Net;

♦ M998 HMMWV - Shotgun Configuration;

♦ Ground Personnel Responsibilities for Slingload Operation.

The practical examination consists of student inspection of four slingloads. Students are required to find a minimum of three out of four deficiencies in two minutes or less.

Students continue to conduct daily PT, to include formation runs and another forced foot march.

A live slingload operation is conducted to conclude Phase Two.

Phase 3: Rappelling:

During this phase Students learn:

♦ The "Swiss Seat" - the conventional hip rappel seat (90 seconds is the standard for student examination);

♦ Rappel Hook Up Procedures;

♦ Rappel Commands;

♦ Proper Body Position for Rappelling;

♦ Tower and Aircraft Rappelling;

♦ Rappel Grading System.

There is no written examination during this phase; however, students conduct a practical examination - graded on three rappels from a rappel tower.

Students continue to conduct daily PT, to include formation runs and another forced foot march.

Students conduct at least one Combat Air Assault rappel from an aircraft to conclude Phase Three.

12 Mile Foot March:

Students must complete a 12 mile tactical road march, with LBE and "Rubber Duck," carrying a 45 pound ruck with required items. The standard to complete the road march is 3 hours or less.

PT Training:

A minimum of 6 hours of physical fitness training will be conducted during the course. Air Assault cadre will formally lead PT. All runs conducted during the Air Assault course will be run at a pace of 9 minute miles (plus or minus 15 seconds).

Add on Training:

Add on training may be incorporated anywhere in the Air Assault Course as long as it does not interfere with the normal flow of training. Any add on training cannot be used to determine passing/failing of the Air Assault Course.

PREREQUISITES:

To attend Air Assault School, individuals will meet the following prerequisites:

♦ Be a member of the Active Army/ Army Reserve component;

♦ Be a Cadet, a foreign student or other military service personnel;

♦ Must score a minimum of 60 points per event on the Army Physical Fitness Test (APFT) within 30 days of attending the Air Assault course. Soldiers must meet the height/weight standards outlined in AR 600-9 and AR 350-15;

♦ Students of 40 years of age must have a current physical (within 12 months) and be medically cleared by doctor to participate in the course. Unit commanders will verify this requirement.

EVALUATIONS:

Students are evaluated throughout each phase with examinations based on class lecture and practical training. Students must score a minimum of 70% on each examination. Examinations are not cumulative. Retraining and retests are given to students who do not pass initial examinations

Spot Reports are used as a positive reinforcement tool; however, students that accumulate 40 minus points will be dismissed from the course. Students receive spot reports for outstanding and/or unsatisfactory performance.

Specific instances in which spot reports will be written will include, but are not limited to:
- Finishing 12 mile foot march in under 2 hours (+10);
- Achieving a 100% on any phase exam (+10);
- Outstanding motivation/appearance (+5);
- Late for formation (first time) (-10);
- Minor unsafe act (-10);
- Equipment deficiencies during inspections (-5);
- Failing standards on PT runs or forced foot marches (-10);
- Poor motivation (-5);
- Failure to follow instructions (-10);
- Poor personal appearance (-10);
- Major safety violation (-40).

Any spot reports given by cadre on instances not outlined above will be plus or minus 5 points. Positive spot reports will cancel out negative spot reports.

PERSONAL CONDUCT & APPEARANCE STANDARDS:

Student Elimination from Course:

Students will be considered for disenrollment for motivational, disciplinary or academic reasons. Individuals who miss more than one hour of training will be dropped from the course; school commandant may waiver this on a case by case basis.

PREPARATIONS:

Clothing & Equipment Requirements:

Table Air Assault-A lists items to be worn by students attending the Air Assault School, Table Air Assault-B lists items to be carried in students' ruck sacks for the duration of the course. No exceptions are authorized.

Additionally, students must carry a flashlight (which will be attached to LCE suspenders to the top left with clear lens attached) during the 12 mile foot march on day 10.

Since Air Assault School is a division run school, each division has its own standards (while staying within the Air Assault Course Management Plan put out by the US Army Infantry School) therefore, students must get information pertaining to the specific course which they will attend from that division (i.e., TA-50).

REPORTING INFORMATION:

Students are to report to listed locations corresponding with the division running the Air Assault Course they will attend:

101st Infantry Division (ABN):
TAAS 101st ABN DIV (AASLT)
Ft. Campbell, KY 42223;
DSN: 635-3834.

25th Infantry Division (Light):
HHC 25 ID (LITC)
Schofield Barracks, HI 96786;
DSN: 621-5321/5439.

1-10th Aviation Regiment:
D Co. 1-10th AVN Rgt.
The Air Assault School
Ft. Rucker, AL 36362;
DSN: 558-1118/8790.

Table: Air Assault-A	
Items Worn For Training	
ITEM	REMARKS
Note Book and Pen	For classroom instructions; memo pads are not notebooks and are not allowed
Military Identification Card	
Identification tags	One long and one short chain interlaced, with one ID tag per chain; one key, any medical alert badge and barracks pass (if issued) are allowed to be suspended from the chain
Military Issue Eye Glasses	As required; due to fragility of civilian eyeglasses, it is suggested they not be worn during Air Assault training; AR 40-5, Preventive Medicine and AR 40-63, Opthamolic Services do not authorize contact lenses for wear in field (dirty or dusty) environments; because Air Assault students are trained in a field environment, contact lenses cannot be worn during Air Assault training
Cap	BDU
BDU	With appropriate rank, insignia, name tapes, and branch tapes; will be serviceable, clean and up to standard IAW AR 670-1
Web belt	Black
Buckle	Subdued
Undershirts	Brown or other service authorized undershirts, for wear with BDUs
Kevlar Helmet	Serviceable, with chin strap, without cover
Boots	Standard issue combat or jungle; Jump Boots are unauthorized
Cushion Soled Socks	OD/Black, for wear with boots
LCE	Worn **IAW Division SOP**, to include the following: (1) pistol belt, (1 set) suspenders, (2) ammo cases, (2) 1 quart canteens with covers and ear plugs with case, (1) first aid pouch with dressing, (1) canteen cup

Table: Air Assault-B		
Items to be Carried in Students' Rucksacks for Course Duration		
ITEM	QTY	REMARKS
Cap	1 each	BDU
BDU	1 set	With appropriate rank, insignia, name tapes, and branch tapes; will be serviceable, clean and up to standard IAW AR 670-1
Undershirts	2 each	Brown or other service authorized undershirts, for wear with BDUs
Boots	1 pair	Standard issue combat or jungle; Jump Boots are unauthorized
Cushion soled socks	2 pair	OD/Black, for wear with boots
Civilian running shoes	1 pair	
Water proof bag	1 each	
Wet weather Parka	1 each	Soldiers may use Gortex jackets in lieu of wet weather parka
Poncho	1 each	
Poncho Liner	1 each	
Camouflage stick	1 each	

10th Mountain Division:
Ft. Drum AAS 10th Mountain Div.
Ft. Drum, NY 13602-5000;
DSN: 341-4081.

BILLETING:

Adequate billeting facilities to house on and off post students attending the Air Assault school are required. The neatness, cleanliness and security of the building and wall lockers are items of inspection during accreditation visits.

Dining Facilities:

Provisions must be made to ensure that the soldiers attending the course are provided with full dining facility privileges IAW all applicable Army regulations and local policy.

CONTACT INFORMATION:

Commandant
US Army Infantry School
ATTN: ATSH-OTT-C
Ft. Benning, GA 31905-3951;
DSN: 835-3951;
FAX: 835-7838.

REFERENCE:

1. Air Assault Course Management Plan. US Army Infantry School. 31 July 1994.
2. Air Assault School Handbook. 25th Infantry Division (light). December 1997.
3. "Air Assault & Rappel Master Course," Online. Internet. 10 May 2000. Available: http://www.drum.army.mil/lightfitr/AAS1.htm.

NOTES

AIRBORNE

REGULATION:

Course No: 2E-SI5P/SQI7/011-SQIP
Title: Airborne
Length: 3 Weeks
Location: U.S. Army Infantry School - SC: 071
Enl SQI: P
WO SQI: 7
Off SC: 5P
Scope: Course effective: 1 Oct 88
Don and adjust the main and reserve parachutes and individual parachutist equipment; respond to jump commands inside an aircraft; control the body after jumping from an aircraft until parachute opening shock; control the parachute during descent; execute a parachute landing fall; control parachute on landing; make five parachute jumps.
Prerequisite: Commissioned officers, warrant officers, and enlisted personnel: Must volunteer for the course and be less than 36 years of age on the date of application. General officers, field grade officers, warrant officers in grade of W-3 and W-4, and enlisted personnel in pay grade of E5 and above may be considered for a waiver of age when the examining medical officer recommends that such a waiver be granted. Must meet the physical qualifications for parachute duty established in AR 40-501. Male/ Female: Must pass the Army Physical Fitness Test (FM 21-20 w/changes) with a score of 180 points (60 points in each event using the 17 to 21 year age group scale). Test must have been administered not more than 30 days prior to date of application. Enlisted personnel must not have more than 30 days time lost under Section l972, Title 10, United States Code (Page 6-2, AR 614-200). During current enlistment, must have completed basic combat and advanced individual or equivalent training.
Special Information: Commanders selecting personnel to attend this course will refer to AR 614-110 and AR 614-200 for additional information regarding selection and processing of volunteers for airborne training. Soldiers reporting for airborne training must have a copy of an approved physical examination (standard Form 88) prior to inprocessing for airborne training. The physical examination to indicate an applicant's fitness for attendance in airborne training must be administered not more than 12 months prior to date of enrollment. Results of the examination must accompany the application. Standard Form 88 will have a statement to the effect that applicant is or is not qualified to attend airborne school. Each individual must have the following in his possession upon arrival at Fort Benning: A minimum of 10 copies of orders assigning or attaching service member to the 507th Parachute Infantry Regiment for airborne training; Field 201 file; medical records to include current (within 1 year) airborne physical examination that must indicate the purpose (block 5) and acceptability (block 77) for airborne training. If over 35 years of age, individual must have an EKG and a medical age waiver, and DA Form 705. Special clothing and equipment requirements: personnel (to include personnel of other services) reporting for airborne training must have in their possession: two pairs of combat or jump boots; minimum of three sets of work and field uniforms with cloth name tags and insignia; current armed services identification card; current identification tags; one class 'A' or comparable service dress uniform appropriate for season, and sufficient funds to defray personal appearance expenses.
Security Clearance: None

HISTORY OF THE 507:

Perhaps no military development has been so revolutionary as the employment of paratroopers. Certainly none has been so spectacular!

Shortly after World War I General Billy Mitchell proposed that parachuting troops from aircraft into combat could be effective. During the demonstration of his concept at Kelly Field at San Antonio, Texas six soldiers parachuted from a Martin Bomber, landed safely and in less than three minutes after exiting the aircraft had their weapons assembled and were ready for action.

Although the U.S. observers dismissed the concept, not all of the observers arrived at the same conclusion. The Soviets and Germans were impressed with the demonstration. In the USSR static line parachuting was introduced as a national sport and the population was encouraged to join the Russian Airborne Corps. The German observers eagerly grasped the idea and planners worked quickly to develop an effective military parachute organization.

For the first time in August 1930 at Veronezh, Russia Soviet paratroopers participated in military maneuvers. Their actions were so effective that a repeat performance was given in Moscow one month later.

The Germans effectively developed their airborne forces and at the start of World War II used parachute troops in their spearhead assaults.

Spurred by the successful employment of airborne troops by the Germans in their invasion of the Low Countries U.S. military branches began an all-out effort to develop this new form of warfare.

In April 1940 the War Department approved plans for the formation of a test platoon of Airborne Infantry to form, equip and train under the direction and control of the Army's Infantry Board. In June the Commandant of the Infantry School was directed to organize a test platoon of volunteers from Fort Benning's 29th Infantry Regiment. Later that year, the 2nd Infantry Division was directed to conduct the necessary tests to develop reference data and operational procedures for air-transported troops.

In July 1940 the task of organizing the platoon began. First Lieutenant William T. Ryder from the 29th Infantry Regiment volunteered and was designated the test platoon's Platoon Leader and Lieutenant James A. Bassett was designated Assistant Platoon Leader. Based on high standards of health and rugged physical characteristics forty-eight enlisted men were selected from a pool of 200 volunteers. Quickly thereafter the platoon moved into tents near Lawson Field and an abandoned hanger was obtained for use as a training hall and for parachute packing.

Lieutenant Colonel William C. Lee, a staff officer for the Chief of Infantry, was intensely interested in the test platoon. He recommended that the men be moved to the Safe Parachute Company at Hightstown, NJ for training on the parachute drop towers used during the New York World's Fair. Eighteen days after organization the

platoon was moved to New Jersey and trained for one week on the 250 foot free towers.

The training was particularly effective. When a drop from the tower was compared to a drop from an airplane, it was found that the added realism was otherwise impossible to duplicate. The drop also proved to the troopers that their parachutes would function safely. The Army was so impressed with the tower drops that two were purchased and erected at Fort Benning on what is now Eubanks Field. Two more were later added. Three of the original four towers are still in use training paratroopers at Fort Benning. PLF training was often conducted by the volunteers jumping from PT platforms and from the back of moving 2 1/2 ton trucks to allow the trainees to experience the shock of landing.

Less than forty-five days after organization the first jump from an aircraft in flight by members of the test platoon was made from a Douglas B-18 over Lawson Field on 16 August, 1940. Before the drop the test platoon held a lottery to determine who would follow Lieutenant Ryder out of the airplane and Private William N. "Red" King became the first enlisted man to make an official jump as a paratrooper in the United States Army. On 29 August at Lawson Field the platoon made the first platoon mass jump held in the United States.

The first parachute combat unit to be organized was the 501st Parachute Battalion. It was commanded by Major William M. Miley, later a Major General and Commander of the 17th Airborne Division, and the original test platoon members formed the battalion cadre. The Civilian Conservation Corps cleared new jump areas and three new training buildings were erected. Several B-18 and C-39 aircraft were provided for training. The traditional paratrooper cry "GERONIMO" was originated in the 501st by Private Aubrey Eberhart to prove to a friend that he had full control of his faculties when he jumped. That cry was adopted by the 501st and has been often used by paratroopers since then.

The 502nd Parachute Infantry Battalion, commanded by Lieutenant Colonel William C. Lee with men from the 501st as cadre was activated on 1 July, 1941. The 502nd was far below strength and 172 prospective troopers from the 9th Infantry Division at Fort Bragg, NC were needed. The response to Lieutenant Colonel Lee's call for volunteers was startling: more than 400 men volunteered, including many noncommissioned officers who were willing to take a reduction in rank ("take a bust") to transfer to the new battalion.

Airborne experimentation of another type was initiated on 10 October, 1941 when the Army's first Glider Infantry battalion was activated. This unit was officially designated as the 88th Glider Infantry Battalion and was commanded by Lieutenant Colonel Elbridge G. Chapman, Jr. Lieutenant Colonel Chapman later became a Major General and commanded the 13th Airborne Division.

As more airborne units were activated it became apparent that a centralized training facility should be established. Consequently, the facility was organized at Fort Benning on 15 May, 1942. Since then the U.S. Army Parachute School has been known by a variety of names: The Airborne School (1 January, 1946); Airborne Army Aviation Section, The Infantry School (1 November, 1946); Airborne Department, The Infantry School (February, 1955); Airborne-Air Mobility Department (February, 1956); Airborne Department (August 1964); Airborne-Air Mobility Department (October, 1974); Airborne Department (October, 1976); 4th Airborne Training Battalion, The School Brigade (January, 1982); 1st Battalion (Abn), 507th Parachute Infantry, The School Brigade (October, 1985); and the 1st Battalion (Abn), 507TH Infantry, 11th Infantry Regiment (July, 1991).

Although several types of headgear insignia have been worn by parachute and glider organizations since 1942, an insignia peculiar to the Airborne was not authorized until 1949 and did not appear in Army Regulations until 1956. The authorization was first mentioned in AR 670-5 (dated 20 September, 1956), which stated, "Airborne insignia may be worn when prescribed by commander. The insignia consists of a white parachute and glider on blue disk with a red border approximately 2 1/4 inches in diameter overall."

In December, 1943, the all black "555th Parachute Infantry Company (Colored)", later redesignated Company A, 555th Parachute Infantry Battalion (and remembered by many as the "Triple Nickel") arrived at Fort Benning for airborne training. This training event marked a significant milestone for black Americans in the combat arms. The first troops in the unit were volunteers from the all black 92nd Infantry Division stationed at Fort Huachuca, Arizona. After proving their skills the battalion was not sent overseas, but was deployed to the western United States for "Operation Firefly," dropping in to fight forest fires set by Japanese incendiary balloons in the Pacific Northwest. During this mission, the 555th earned the nickname the "Smoke Jumpers." In 1948, after full integration of the Armed Forces was finally effected, black Americans were finally given their full rights as American combat paratroopers and made their first combat jump while attached to the 187th Regimental Combat Team during the Korean War.

On 14 December, 1973 another milestone in Airborne history was established when Privates Joyce Kutsch and Rita Johnson became the first women to graduate from the Basic Airborne Course. Following graduation from a modified, but rigorous, airborne course the two women successfully completed the U.S. Army Quartermaster School Parachute Rigger Course and were assigned to Aerial Delivery Companies at Fort Bragg, NC. Since then, women do not attend a modified airborne course, but complete the full course and meet the same standards as their male counterparts.

Airborne unit combat records tell stories of extreme valor. From the first combat jump during World War II in North Africa, paratroopers have fought with a spirit, determination and tenacity that captured the respect of the world. Future events will continue to find the American paratrooper in the forefront of hostilities.

AIRBORNE CREED:

I am an Airborne trooper!

A PARATROOPER!

I jump by parachute from any plane in flight.

I volunteered to do it, knowing well the hazards of my choice.

I serve in a mighty Airborne Force - famed for deeds in war - renowned for readiness in peace. It is my pledge to uphold its honor and prestige in all I am - in all I do.

I am an elite trooper - a sky trooper - a shock trooper - a spearhead trooper. I blaze the way to far-flung goals - behind, before, above the foe's front line.

I know that I may have to fight without support for days on end. Therefore, I keep mind and body always fit to do my part in any Airborne task. I am self-reliant and unafraid. I shoot true, and march fast and far. I fight hard and excel in every art and artifice of war.

I never fail a fellow trooper. I cherish as a sacred trust the lives of men with whom I serve. Leaders have my fullest loyalty, and those I lead never find me lacking.

I have pride in the Airborne! I never let it down!

In peace, I do not shrink the dullest of duty not protest the toughest training. My weapons and equipment are always combat ready. I am neat of dress - military in courtesy - proper in conduct and behavior.

In battle, I fear no foe's ability, nor underestimate his prowess, power and guile. I fight him with all my might and skills - ever alert to evade capture or escape a trap. I never surrender, though I be the last.

My goal in peace or war is to succeed in any mission of the day - or die, if needs be, in the try.

I belong to a proud and glorious team - the Airborne, the Army, my Country. I am its chosen pride to fight where others may not go - to serve them well until the final victory.

I am the trooper of the sky! I am my Nation's best! In peace and war I never fail. Anywhere, anytime, in anything-

I AM AIRBORNE!

PURPOSE:

The purpose of this course is to qualify the BAC student in the use of the parachute as a means of combat deployment. This qualification is accomplished by:

- ♦ Developing the student's confidence through repetitious training to overcome the student's natural fear of jumping from an aircraft while in flight;
- ♦ Maintaining the level of physical fitness required of a military parachutist through daily physical training;
- ♦ Qualifying the student as a parachutist by performing five satisfactory parachute jumps from an aircraft in flight.

The course develops a sense of leadership, self-confidence, and an aggressive spirit through mental and physical conditioning.

OVERVIEW:

The BAC is divided into three training weeks. Ground Training Week, Tower Training Week and Jump Training Week. The training starts at the individual level and progresses to a team effort.

Ground Training Week (Week 1):

During Ground Week you begin an intensive program of instruction to: build individual airborne skills, prepare you to make a parachute jump and land safely. You will train on the mock door, the 34 foot tower and the lateral drift apparatus (LDA). To go forward to Tower Training Week you must individually qualify on the 34 foot tower, the LDA and pass all PT requirements.

Tower Training Week (Week 2):

The individual skills learned during Ground Week are refined during Tower Week and a team effort or "mass exit" concept is added to the training. The apparatuses used this week are the 34 foot towers, the swing landing trainer (SLT), the mock door for mass exit training and the suspended harness. Tower Week completes your individual skill training and builds team effort skills. To go forward to Jump Training Week you must qualify on the SLT, master the mass exit

Example Training Schedule
Ground Week

MONDAY	
0515-0700	APFT
0915-1215	CMD Briefs/ Mock Door Class/PE
1345-1600	Mock Door PE
1600-1715	MTIE Class

TUESDAY	
0515-0700	PT Mandatory Run (3.2 Mile)
0900-1215	MTIE PE
1345-1600	MTIE PE
1600-1715	PLF Class

WEDNESDAY	
0515-0700	PT Run (3.2Mile)
0900-1215	PLF Grass Drills
1345-1715	LDA

THURSDAY	
0515-0700	PT Run (3.2Mile)
0900-1215	LDA
1345-1715	LDA

FRIDAY	
0545-0700	PT Run (3.2Mile)
0900-1200	MOR
1300-1630	Parachute Maintenance Class/PE
1630-1715	Clear Training Area

Example Training Schedule
Tower Week

	MONDAY	
	0545-0715	PT run (4Mile)
1ST PLT	0915-1145	SH1 Class/PE
	1315-1645	SLT Class/PE
	0545-0715	PT run (4Mile)
2ND PLT	0915-1145	MDME Class/PE
	1315-1645	MTME Class/PE

	TUESDAY	
	0545-0715	PT run (4Mile)
	0915-1145	SLT Class/PE
1ST PLT	1315-1500	SLT PE
	1500-1715	250 Foot Tower Class
	0545-0715	PT run (4Mile)
	0915-1145	SH1 Class/PE
2ND PLT	1315-1500	SLT Class/PE
	1500-1715	250 Foot Tower Class

Example Training Schedule
Tower Week (Continued)

	WEDNESDAY	
1ST PLT	0730-1645	*250 Foot Tower PE
	0545-0715	PT run (4Mile)
2ND PLT	0915-1115	SLT PE
	1315-1645	SLT PE

	THURSDAY	
	0545-0715	PT run (4Mile)
1ST PLT	0915-1115	MDME Class/PE
	1315-1645	MTME Class/PE
2ND PLT	0730-1645	*250 Foot Tower PE

	FRIDAY	
	0545-0715	PT Mandatory run (5Mile)
	0915-1145	SH2 Class/PE
ALL	1315-1500	SH2 PE/ Clear Training Area
	1500-1600	Malfunctions
	1600-1645	Clear Training Area

Example Training Schedule
Jump Week

MONDAY	
0500-0545	First Call
0545-0800	Pre-Jump Training
0800-0900	AJ104
0900-1200	Mock Door
1200-UTC	Load Aircraft / Airborne Ops

TUESDAY	
0430-0515	First Call
0515-0700	Pre-Jump Training
0700-1000	Mock Door
1000-1500	Load Aircraft / Airborne Ops
1500-UTC	Load Aircraft / Airborne Ops

WEDNESDAY	
0800-0845	First Call / Roll Call
0845-1030	Pre-Jump Training
1030-1300	Mock Door
1300-UTC	Load Aircraft / Airborne Ops
1900-UTC	Load Aircraft / Airborne Ops

THURSDAY	
Clearing / Weather Day	

FRIDAY	
1100	Graduation

NOTE: * Indicates training event is optional to Basic Airborne course students.

procedures from the 34 foot tower and pass all PT requirements.

Jump Training Week (Week 3):

Successful completion of the previous weeks of training prepares you for Jump Week. Graduation is normally conducted at 1100 on Friday of Jump Week at the south end of Eubanks Field on the Airborne Walk. However if weather, or some other reason delays the scheduled jumps, graduation may be conducted on Fryar Drop Zone (DZ) after the last jump. Guests and family members are welcome to observe all of the jumps at the DZ, attend the graduation ceremony and participate in awarding the wings. Fryar DZ is located in Alabama on the Fort Benning Military Reservation. Following graduation you are allowed to depart for leave or your next duty assignment.

PHYSICAL TRAINING (PT):

You must be physically fit before you start the BAC. The physically weak are more likely to either not complete the course because of an injury, or fail the course due to an inability to qualify on the training apparatuses. You will have PT the first period each day, followed by seven hours of demanding, rigorous training.

You must qualify during daily PT by completing the exercises and distance run. Of the 4 weekly runs, any student who fails to complete two runs in a week will be eliminated from training.

A typical daily PT session includes 10 chinups, stretching/warm up exercises, calisthenics/maintenance exercises and a 3.2 to 4 mile formation run. Males and females run in the same formation during PT and the average pace is 9 minutes per mile. This policy treats all BAC students as equals and meets current XVIII (82nd) Airborne Corps standards.

PREREQUISITES:

Commissioned Officer, Warrant Officer, Noncommissioned Officer, Enlisted personnel and qualified cadets must:

♦ Volunteer for the course;

♦ Be less than 36 years of age on the date of application;

♦ Physically qualify for parachute duty IAW AR 40-501;

♦ Pass the APFT with a score of 180 points (60 points per event) using the 17 to 21 year age group scale as the standard. APFT must have been administered not more than 30 days prior to date of application. Applicants must be able to complete a 4 mile run within 36 minutes (9 minutes per mile).

Prior to attending the BAC, volunteers must be able to meet certain essential military training prerequisites. The basic military education requirements are:

♦ USMA cadets must complete Cadet Basic Training;

♦ ROTC cadets must complete their second year of military science (MS2) or either the Basic or the Advanced Camp.;

♦ Enlisted personnel must complete basic combat and advanced individual training, OSUT, or other service equivalent training.

Commanders selecting personnel to attend the BAC will refer to AR 614-10 and AR 512-200 for information on airborne volunteer selection and processing.

UNIFORMS:

BDU shirt and trousers, cold weather jackets, black gloves with inserts and brown undershirts will be clean and serviceable IAW AR 670-1. No corporate advertisements, logograms or printing are authorized on undershirts. Uniforms will not be starched.

Belts will be clean, serviceable and worn IAW the student's branches of service.

Boots will be shined to a high luster, free of all dirt or sawdust and laced prior to the first work formation.

Military identification card and identification tags will be worn by all BAC students at all times. One long and one short chain interlaced, with one ID tag per chain. One key, any medical alert badge and barracks pass (if issued) are allowed to be suspended from the chain.

> NOTES:
> No jewelry will be worn in the training area. One designated student per class will wear or carry a watch.
> Male students' hair will be tapered at the back of the neck.
> Female students will ensure their hair does not extend below the bottom edge of the BDU shirt collar. Student head gear in the training area is a serviceable parachutist's helmet.

INSPECTIONS:

Morning Inspections:

Inspections are conducted the morning of each training day to ensure there are no deficiencies in the following areas:

Hair will be cut to the standards contained in AR 670-1.

Male students will have a clean shave unless a valid medical shaving profile has been issued. Students will not wear make up in the training area.

Helmets will be inspected by the company trainers to ensure that the helmets are properly rigged and serviceable.

Military Appearance & Inspection Standards:
There will be a roll call inspection on Friday of the report week to familiarize you with roll call, inspection standards and procedures. Personnel from Reserve Components, National Guard and other services or countries will wear Standard Issue BDU or fatigue (utility) type uniforms for training. Jungle boots, boots with toe and heel caps (e.g., "jump boots") and boots without heels (e.g.; boots with flat, waffled, or rippled soles) are not authorized for wear by BAC students during jump week. All students will comply with U.S. Army Regulations concerning grooming.

PERSONAL CONDUCT & APPEARANCE STANDARDS:

Personal Conduct:

Students attending the BAC are expected to conduct themselves in an appropriate and disciplined manner, on and off duty. BAC students are not authorized to consume alcoholic beverages within 24 hours prior to a training day and are not authorized to possess alcoholic beverages in the billets. Students who violate provisions of the Uniform Code of Military Justice (UCMJ) will be quickly disciplined and may be permanently dropped from airborne training with subsequent assignment as a non-graduate.

Civilian Clothing & Appearance Standards:

Wall locker storage space for personal clothing in the billets is limited; however, a reasonable amount of appropriate civilian clothing may be brought to the BAC. Soldiers at Fort Benning are expected to wear appropriate civilian clothing and present a neat, clean, military appearance during off duty time. Students must be aware that Fort Benning Regulation 600-5 which addresses the wear of civilian clothing on Fort Benning is strictly enforced in on post facilities. Examples of clothing prohibited for wear in on-post facilities are:

- Clothing which presents a provocative appearance;
- Dirty clothing;
- "Underclothing worn as an outer garment;
- Mesh T-shirts;
- "Muscle shirts";
- Tube tops, tank tops;
- Bikini swim suit tops;
- Any shirt which has had the sleeves cut off;
- Clothing that presents a ragged or torn appearance;
- Modified items of military clothing (cut-off BDU trousers, BDU jackets with the sleeves cut-off or shortened);
- Combinations of civilian clothing and the Army PT uniform;
- Clothing with profanity written or printed on it;
- Shorts which do not present a proper or tasteful appearance;
- Shower shoes.

Soldiers are expected to comply with all changes to AR 670-1 that impact personal appearance standards while in civilian clothing.

PREPARATIONS:

Clothing & Equipment Requirements:

Refer to Table Airborne-A on the following page for BAC packing list information.

REPORTING INFORMATION:

When you report wear your BDUs and meet the grooming standards outlined in AR 670-1.

Students must arrive NLT 1200 on their designated report date. Personnel who arrive after 1200 will either roster and train in the next scheduled class or will be returned to their duty station.

Students will report to Building 2748, student accountability will be held NLT 1200 on the class report date. Arrive with the following documents:

Orders:

Students are to bring ten (10) copies of their orders, or DA Form 1610 with fund cite, which assigns or attaches them to the 507th Infantry for airborne training. BAC volunteers may not attend the course in a leave, permissive TDY or permissive jump status.

Physical Examination:

A physical examination dated not more than 12 months before class start date (18 months for cadets) that indicates you are qualified for Airborne Training IAW AR 40-501. SF 88, Block 5, Purpose of Exam should read "Airborne Training" and the qualified box in Block 77 must be checked and "Airborne" entered. Volunteers over 35 years of age must have an EKG and an approved medical age waiver accompanying the physical exam.

> NOTE:
> Volunteers over 35 years of age (General Officers, Field Grade Officers, Warrant Officers (W3-5) and Enlisted personnel in pay grade E5 and above) may attend the BAC when granted an age waiver. When the examining medical officer determines the volunteer is physically capable of completing the BAC, the student's Unit Commander must submit a memorandum stating the volunteer is physically fit for airborne training.

DA form 705, Army Physical Fitness Test (APFT) Score Card:

The APFT must have been administered not more than 6 months prior to the reporting date. (USN and USMC volunteers are given the APFT by the USMC liaison prior to reporting to the BAC. USAF volunteers must present a memorandum that validates the volunteer's physical fitness test score.)

Health & Dental Records, Finance Records, Field 201 File:

Volunteers reporting to the BAC in a PCS or TDY en route status must have these records in their possession.

Inprocessing:

Promptly at 1200 on the reporting date the designated fill company will conduct inprocessing. The inprocessing sequence of events includes Adjutant General, finance, transportation, room assignment, equipment issue and platoon/squad assignment. Inprocessing students should not expect to be released earlier than 1800 hours.

LEAVE & PASS POLICIES:

Leave:

Leave during the course are only granted for valid emergencies; the Company Commander approves emergency leaves. After graduation if the student has a follow on assignment within the continental U.S. he/she will normally be granted 10 days leave. Students being assigned to units outside the continental U.S. may be granted up to 30 days leave.

Passes:

During off duty hours students are normally free to travel within a 50 mile radius of Fort Benning, GA without a valid leave form. Travel outside a 50 mile radius requires an authorization from the Company Commander. You must return well rested and on time for company designated formations and training.

BILLETING:

Housing will be provided in the training company area barracks for all enlisted personnel in the pay grades E1-7. Soldiers are required to clean their living areas daily and to perform additional duties as directed.

Table: Airborne-A		
Required Items Inventory		
ITEM	**QTY**	**REMARKS**
Military Identification Card	1	
Identification Tags	1 set	One long and one short chain interlaced, with one ID tag per chain; one key, any medical alert badge and barracks pass (if issued) are allowed to be suspended from the chain
Military Issue Eye Glasses	2 pair	As required; due to fragility of civilian eyeglasses, it is suggested they not be worn during BAC training; AR 40-5, Preventive Medicine and AR 40-63, Opthamolic Services do not authorize contact lenses for wear in field (dirty or dusty) environments; because BAC students are trained in a field environment, contact lenses cannot be worn during BAC training
Cap	1	BDU
BDUs	3 sets (minimum)	With appropriate rank, insignia, name tapes, and branch tapes
Web belt	2	
Buckle	1	Subdued
Undershirt	5	Brown, or other service authorized undershirts; worn with BDUs
Underwear	5	
Boots	2 pair	Standard Issuec, combat; BAC students are not authorized to wear jungle boots, boots with toe and heel caps (e.g. "jump boots"), or boots without heels (e.g. hoots with flat, waffled, or rippled soles), boots should be broken in and must be highly shined; spit shine is not required
PT Uniform (PFU)	2 sets	Army, gray, or sister service equivalent
Socks	5 pair	Cushion sole, for wear with boots
Shoes	1 pair	Civilian, running
Socks	5 pair	Civilian, white, athletic, no stripes or commercial product markings, crew length; athletic socks which only extend to the ankle are not authorized for wear
Boot Shining Gear	1 set	
Towels	3	
Washcloths	3	
Toiletries		
Padlocks	2	Heavy duty

NOTES:
   1. During the winter season (October -March) personnel must provide their own military issue gloves with liners, black watch cap, and authorized cold weather jacket (i.e., field jacket with liner or Gortex-lied water proof parka).
   2. The Airborne school issues all items of organizational equipment (TA-50) required for Airborne training (i.e., helmet, poncho, canteen).

BOQs for TDY status Commissioned or Warrant Officers and BEQs for NCOs (E8 and E9) are available on a limited basis. Contact the Fort Benning Billeting Office for booking BOQ/BEQ space.

Post Guest House lodging is available to PCS status personnel. Contact the Fort Benning Billeting Office for booking.

Family Members Visiting Fort Benning for BAC Graduation. Post Guest House (The Gavin House) lodging is available to the student's family members who are at Fort Benning for a short time to view Jump Week jumps and attend the BAC graduation ceremonies. Contact the Fort Benning Billeting Office for booking.

> Fort Benning Billeting Office:
> (706) 689-0067.

Dining Facilities:

Student officer and enlisted personnel may eat in the battalion dining facilities (DFAC). During Jump Week, Officer students are required to eat DFAC provided meals.

Money:

While each student must bring sufficient money for personal expenses, the student should not bring more than $50.00 in cash. Additional funds should be in traveler's checks or money orders. Money orders should be made out in the student's name before arrival.

Mail:

The S1, 1/507TH Infantry maintains a roster of all personnel in training. Before your arrival at Fort Benning have your mail addressed to:

> (Student's Name), (Student's SSN)
> Headquarters, 1st Bn (ABN), 507th Inf
> Fort Benning, GA 31905.

Upon arrival and assignment substitute your assigned company to expedite mail delivery. Do not have mail sent to you during the third week of training; you will soon graduate and redirecting of mail will result in mail delivery delay.

POV:

There is a parking lot provided for Basic Airborne Course students to park their POVs for the duration of the course. Vehicles may be used during off duty hours. Students will receive further information regarding POVs during inprocessing.

CONTACT INFORMATION:

Point of contact for the Basic Airborne Course is the US Army Airborne School Accountability NCOIC:

> DSN: 835-4874;
> COMM: (706) 545-4874.

> FAX:
> DSN: 835-3243;
> COMM: (706) 545-4923.

REFERENCE:

1. US Army Formal Schools Catalog. US Army Publishing Agency. DA PAM 351-4, page 46, Table 3-6. 31 October 1995.
2. "The U.S. Army Airborne Schools – Hunters From The Sky." Online. Internet. 10 April 2000. Available: http://www-benning.army.mil/fbhome/11th/airborne/index.htm.
3. "History of the 507th." Online. Internet. 15 May 2000. Available: http://192.153.150.25/airborne/history.html.
4. "The U.S. Army Airborne School." Online. Internet. 10 April 2000. Available: http://www-benning.army.mil/fbhome/11th/airborne/index.htm.

DELTA FORCE

1ST SPECIAL FORCES OPERATIONAL DETACHMENT – DELTA

HISTORY:

Delta Force was created by U.S. Army Colonel Charles Beckwith in 1977 in direct response to numerous, well-publicized terrorist incidents that occurred in the 1970s. Created under the Carter Administration, Delta Force was activated after an impressive simulated attack on a mock terrorist base. From its beginnings, Delta has been heavily influenced by the British SAS, a philosophical result of Col. Beckwith's year long (1962-1963) exchange tour with that unit.

As a counterterrorist group, Delta's main function is in hostage rescue. During Operation *Just Cause* Delta got their chance to do just that. Kurt Muse, an American businessman operating an underground radio station, had been jailed in the city of Modelo. A 160th SOAR (Special Operations Aviation Regiment) MH-6 transported a team of troopers to the rooftop of the jail. The team fought its way down to the second floor and blew the door to Muse' cell, freeing him without injury. As the team and Muse made their way to the roof and the waiting MH-6, Kurt Muse counted at least five bodies. Not all had been killed; one terrified guard had been handcuffed to a staircase railing. Lifting off, the small helicopter was hit by small arms fire and fell to the street below. The pilot slid the aircraft along the ground to a parking lot and attempted to take off again. The aircraft was hit by ground fire again and hit the ground, this time permanently. A passing UH-60 spotted the infrared spotlight held up by a Delta trooper, and soldiers from the 6th Infantry Regiment came to their rescue. Four Delta operators were wounded, but Delta had "officially" validated their existence and saved Kurt Muse' life.

Delta also saw action in Desert Storm, although the full extent of what they did there has not been revealed. Delta Troopers provided security for General Norman Schwartzkopf and also took part in some missions into Iraq to locate Scud missile launchers for destruction. Delta received some unwanted publicity in the disastrous UN Campaign to stabilize the country of Somalia. During their mission in Mogadishu, Somalia, they assaulted different safe houses containing high-ranking members of warring clans and took them prisoner. Unfortunately, during their last mission two of the support helicopters from the 160th SOAR were shot down. Two Delta operators were killed defending the survivors of the second crash, and at least one was killed in an on-foot extraction through a city populated with locals riled up against the Americans. In the early 1990's they were sent in to hunt down rebellious leaders in Somalia and finally in 1991, Delta Force was sent to destroy SCUD missiles.

FORWARD:

The 1st SFOD-Delta (Delta force) is one the Federal Government's CT (Counter-terrorist) Groups. Also known as CAG (*Combat Applications Group*) the Pentagon manages to tightly control what is known about this Unit. Delta Force is controlled by JSOC at Pope Air Force Base in North Carolina; however, its troops train all over the country and even train with the FBI's Hostage Rescue Team (HRT). Their soldiers are recruited from the U.S. Army, mainly from the Special Forces Green Berets and Rangers.

Their main compound is in a remote area of Fort Bragg and it is rumored that up to 2,500 personnel are present at this facility.

Reports of the Delta compound indicate that no expense has been spared, including numerous shooting facilities (both for close quarters battle and longer range sniping), an Olympic size swimming pool, dive tank and a three story climbing wall. Yet, as lavish as these accouterments may seem, they all serve vital roles in training counterterrorists.

Delta is a U.S. Army special operations unit organized to conduct selected missions worldwide, which require the application of a unique variety of special operations skills. The unit is tailored to conduct a full range of special operations across the entire spectrum of conflict. Delta is organized for the conduct of missions requiring rapid response with surgical applications of a wide variety of unique skills, while maintaining the lowest possible profile of U.S. involvement. Accordingly, all soldiers assigned to the unit are carefully selected and specially trained.

Delta is organized into three operating squadrons, all of which (A, B and C) are subdivided into small groups known as troops. It is rumored that each troop, as the case with the SAS, specializes in HALO, SCUBA or other skill groups. These troops can each be further divided into smaller units as needed to fit mission requirements. Delta also maintains support units, which handle selection, training, logistics, finance and the unit's medical requirements. Within this grouping is a little known, but vital technical unit, which is responsible for covert eavesdropping equipment for use in hostage rescues and similar situations.

Skills are enhanced by the unit's participation in an ongoing exchange and training programs with foreign counter-terrorist units, such as (as might be expected) Britain's 22 SAS, France's GIGN, Germany's GSG-9, Israel's Sayeret Matkal/Unit 269 and Australia's own Special Air Service Regiment. Such close cooperation with other groups provides innumerable benefits, including exchanges of new tactics and equipment as well as enhancing relations that might prove useful in later real world operations. Delta troopers are also equipped with the most advanced weaponry and equipment available in the U.S. special operations arsenal.

OVERVIEW:

Delta Training involves runs through CQB (Close Quarters Battle) killing houses - designed to teach teams and individuals how to assault buildings that have been captured by terrorists. Selective firing (whether or not to shoot a target) as well as the double tap (shooting the target twice to make sure that the target does not get up again) are instilled in the counter-terrorism specialists.

During the first 6 months of assignment to Delta, officers and noncommissioned officers are placed in a training program referred to as the Operator Training Course (OTC). OTC is a comprehensive training program designed to provide the future operator with all the skills necessary for successful assignment as a Delta Force Operator. The program of instruction taught during OTC progresses from the basic to the advanced level; training includes training in the following areas: weapons and marksmanship, combat skills, explosives, close quarter battle (CQB), vehicle driving techniques, first aid, infiltration/exfiltration, parachuting techniques (both static-line and free fall) and communications. Upon completion of OTC, operators are assigned to operational elements within Delta.

ASSESSMENT AND SELECTION COURSE (ASC):

FORWARD:

An operational assignment to Delta is contingent upon the successful completion of the unit's Assessment and Selection Course (ASC). The Assessment and Selection Course is conducted two times every year - once in the Spring and once in the Fall. Candidates attend the course in a temporary duty status. The Spring course is conducted in the March-April time frame and the fall course is conducted in the September-October time frame. Individuals who successfully complete the course are then assigned to Delta for follow-on training and subsequent assignment to an operational element within the unit.

This assignment opportunity is available to all soldiers meeting the unit's prerequisites regardless of Military Occupational Specialty (MOS) or Officer Branch. All Officers and Noncommissioned Officers meeting the prerequisites are encouraged to apply.

PURPOSE:

The purpose of the Assessment and Selection Course is to identify those volunteers who are suitable for training and operational duty with Delta. The assessment program gives the unit a unique characteristic; it evaluates individual performance, stamina, determination, self-discipline, and above all, the ability to function effectively under physical and psychological stress.

OVERVIEW:

The Assessment and Selection Course is approximately 30 days in length and is divided into three phases. During the administrative phase, candidates are administered the Army Physical Fitness Test and conduct an 18 mile road march carrying a 40-45 pound ruck sack and weapon. The march must be completed in 4 1/2 hours or less.

The second phase of the course is the instructional phase and consists of a 10 day advanced land navigation course. Its purpose is to bring all applicants to an even level of proficiency prior to the third phase. Candidates who successfully complete the second phase will receive a certificate of completion which can be posted to their official military records, as this phase is a U.S. Army accredited land navigation course.

The third phase of the course is the stress phase. In order to successfully complete this phase, individuals must be able to use a map and compass, accurately navigate across hilly terrain with moderate vegetation, while carrying a 40-

45 pound ruck sack, in addition to rations and water. The distance moved each day varies from 7-40 miles. All course objectives must be accomplished by each volunteer without assistance.

Upon successful completion of the three phases, candidates undergo thorough psychological testing and evaluation, including an in-depth interview by the unit's psychologist. The final determination of a candidate's acceptance to the unit is made by the Commander, 1st SFOD-D upon completion of the personal interview during the Commander's Board. Candidates accepted for assignment will return to their unit and can expect to PCS to Fort Bragg within 60 days.

PREREQUISITES:

General prerequisites for all operational applicants are:

- Male;
- Volunteer;
- United States Citizen;
- MOS/Branch Immaterial;
- Minimum of 22 years of age;
- Possess at least an interim SECRET level security clearance;
- Pass the Army Physical Fitness Test (APFT) IAW FM 21-20;

NOTE: Minimum raw score in each category is 55 pushups in 2 minutes, 62 situps in 2 minutes, and 2 mile run in 15:06 or faster, wearing unit PT uniform (running shoes, shorts, and t-shirt).

- No limiting physical profile;
- Pass a modified Class II Flight Medical Examination;

NOTE: Visual acuity requirement is no worse than 20/200 in both eyes, correctable to 20/20 in both eyes.

- Airborne qualified or volunteer for airborne training/duty;
- Minimum 2 year service obligation remaining upon assignment;
- Army Active, Reserve, IRR, or National Guard.

Additional prerequisites specific to Noncommissioned Officer Operational Applications:

- Rank of SGT, SSG, or SFC with a minimum of four years time in service;

NOTE: Delta will accept applications from E4s in a promotable status, however, all candidates must be promoted to SGT/E5 before attendance to ASC.

- GT Score of 110 or higher;

NOTE: Individuals may retest.

Additional Prerequisites Specific to Officer Operational Applicants:

- ◆ Rank of Captain or Major;
- ◆ Graduate of an Officer Advanced Course (Any Branch);
- ◆ At least 12 months successful Company, Battery, Troop, SFODA or Aviation Platoon command time;
- ◆ College graduate (BA or BS degree).

Reserve component officers should contact the Special Missions Recruiting team and ask to speak with the Recruiting OIC.

Noncommissioned Officers currently in the reserve components need to be pre-qualified by Delta recruiters for active duty accession in the rank of at least Sergeant E5. Commissioned Officers currently in the reserve components need to be pre-qualified to enter the Active Army in the rank of Captain or Major.

PREPARATIONS:

Recommended physical train-up program focuses on conditioning on two areas: the APFT and ruck marching/cross country orienteering. A copy of the program will be included with your application packet.

During your recruiter's processing visit at your installation, you will be administered the Army Physical Fitness Test and a series of written tests, which will take approximately 3 hours to complete. The recruiter will also secure your completed application (with all enclosures) and answer any questions you may have before departing your installation.

If approved, Reserve Component soldiers will attend the Assessment and Selection Course in a temporary duty status while still assigned to their reserve component unit. If selected during the Commander's Board for assignment to the unit, they will then be accessed into the Active Army.

Application:

Soldiers interested in attending the Delta ASC should contact the Special Missions Recruiting Team to request an application packet and schedule a processing trip at their installation.

Phone: 1-800-606-1370;

E-mail: sf-sof-ops@usarec.army.mil.

Recruiters will work with reserve component soldiers to ensure all additional documents are submitted as necessary. This adds additional processing time; therefore, Reserve Component Noncommissioned Officers are especially encouraged to contact the Delta recruiter as early as possible. Reserve Component Officers considering applying for the Assessment and Selection Course should contact the Special Missions Recruiting Team and ask to speak directly to the Recruiting Team OIC for further details.

REFERENCE:

1. "Delta Force." Online. Internet. 29 March 2000. Available: http://specialoperations.com/Army/Delta-Force/default.html,
2. "1st SFOD-Delta." Online. Internet. 29 March 2000. Available: http://www.blarg.net/~whitet/delta.htm,
3. "Special Forces of the World – Teams: "Delta Force (United States)." Online. Internet. 29 March 2000. Available: http://home3.inet.tele.dk/jdj/spec-ops/cont/us-delta.htm.
4. "Delta Force." Online. Internet. 24 May 2000. Available: http://area51phx.freeservers.com/deltaforce.html.
5. "1st SFOD-Delta." Online. Internet. 23 May 2000. Available: http://www.specwarnet.com/americas/delta.htm.

DRILL SERGEANT

REGULATION:

Course No: 012–SQIX
Title: Drill Sergeant
Length: 9 Weeks
Location 1: Drill Sergeant School, Fort Jackson – SC: 615
Location 2: NCO Academy (Infantry) – SC: 698
Location 3: NCO Academy (Engineer) – SC: 652
Enl SQI: X
Scope: Course effective: 1 Oct 85
The course will be designed to provide the candidate information and training techniques for subjects drill sergeants are required to teach in IET to include drill and ceremonies, physical fitness, and weapons training. The candidate will be provided instruction on leadership and counseling applicable to the IET environment. The major emphasis of the instruction will be on how to train initial entry soldiers to become highly motivated, skilled, and physically fit.
Prerequisite: Must meet prerequisites as outlined in AR 614–200.
Security Clearance: None

HISTORY OF THE DRILL SERGEANT:

In the late 1962 the Secretary of the U.S. Army directed Stephen Ailes - the Assistant Secretary - to conduct a survey of recruit training in the Army. This survey was conducted over a long period of time and included a wide variety of experienced personnel. To insure his report would be valid, Secretary Ailes made a comprehensive survey, comparing the training techniques of the Marines, Army, Navy and Air Force.

The final report, as submitted to the Department of the Army, contained five principle findings, with appropriate recommendations and suggestions for eliminating the problems encountered. The comparisons of the Training Centers of the three services with those of the Army demonstrated the attitude of the Noncommissioned Officers within the Army

Training Centers was very poor. Contributing reasons included: long working hours, difficulty of the demanding nature of the work and lack of free time for family concerns. Much of this was caused by inadequate staffing in the training centers.

In addition, it was determined that the caliber of Noncommissioned Officers being assigned to the Army Training Centers was far below the standards required by the other services.

The negative attitude of the trainer was another problem that required attention; the negative attitude had a demoralizing affect on the trainee and resulted in a mental block between the recruit and the trainer, thus causing a negative impact on the qualified trainer and the quality of training presented.

During the period April – June 1963, Pilot Trainer Courses were conducted at Fort Jackson, South Carolina, for selected Officers and Noncommissioned Officers to participate in testing the revised concept of recruit training.

Immediately following, in July and August, this new training concept was tested with a Training Battalion at Fort Jackson and a Training Company at Ft Gordon, Georgia. Fort Leonard Wood, MO Drill Sergeant School began training Noncommissioned Officers for Drill Sergeant duties in September 1964. The success of these tests resulted in the adoption of the new concept, to include the formation of the Drill Sergeant School throughout the Army. This was the beginning of the Drill Sergeant and was the first instance of Drill Sergeants being used to train recruits in the history of Recruit Training Programs throughout the Army.

HISTORY OF THE DRILL SERGEANT CREST:

The crest is the symbol of the Army Training Center. Before 1958, it was the regimental crest with a maroon background. In 1958, it was adopted as the training center's crest and the background was changed to green. The Heraldic Division of the Quartermasters General's Office designed the crest. The thirteen stars represent the thirteen original Colonies. The snake is a symbol of preparedness, as grasps the scroll on one end with his mouth and the other end with his tail. On the scroll is printed the motto, "THIS WE'LL DEFEND," one of the many mottos used in colonial days such as "DON'T TREAD ON ME," "LIBERTY" and many others which were carried on flags and banners. The Armored breastplate is a symbol of strength and the green background is a vestment worn under the Armored Breastplate. The Armored Breastplate is called a Jupon, which represents the Army. The torch is a symbol of liberty that shines over all.

DRILL SERGEANT CREED:

I am a Drill Sergeant.

I will assist each individual in their efforts to become a highly motivated, well-disciplined, physically and mentally fit soldier, capable of defeating any enemy on today's modern battlefield.

I will instill pride in all I train. Pride in self, in the Army, and in Country.

I will insist that each soldier meets and maintains the Army standards of military bearing and courtesy, consistent with the highest traditions of the U.S. Army.

I will lead by example, never requiring a soldier to attempt any task I would not do myself.

But first, last, and always, I am an American Soldier. Sworn to defend the Constitution of the United States against all enemies, both foreign and domestic.

I am a Drill Sergeant.

FORWARD:

Soldiers may volunteer or be involuntarily selected for Drill Sergeant (DS) duty. Since the DS is the primary representative of the Army during the formative weeks of an enlistee's training, only the most professionally qualified soldiers will be assigned to DS duty. Drill Sergeants are authorized only for the specific purpose of training:

♦ Receptees in the reception stations;
♦ Soldiers undergoing initial entry training;
♦ DS Candidates at DS Schools;
♦ Soldiers undergoing English as a second language training at the Defense Language Institute English Language Center (DLIELC), Lackland AFB, TX;
♦ Soldiers undergoing physical readiness training at authorized fitness training units.

AA and USAR soldiers from all career fields will be considered for selection and assignment into the program.

On declaration of general war or full mobilization, provisions of this section remain unchanged.

Drill Sergeant candidates are AA and USAR soldiers who:

♦ Expend Government funds in compliance with AA and USAR DS School/assignment orders;
♦ Have reported to DS School, but were already assigned to the DS School installation when selected for the DS Program.

Upon successful completion of DS School, soldiers will:

♦ Be awarded SQI "X";
♦ Be eligible for SDAP.

Active Army Drill Sergeants will be stabilized for 24 months with an option to extend, on a one time basis, for an additional 6-12 months. (The stabilized tour will begin the month the soldier reports to the DS position and will terminate the last calendar day of the same month 2 years later.) The DS tour will not exceed 36 months. Active Army soldiers will serve only one tour as a DS.

The following reassignments after a tour of DS duty are prohibited:

♦ Assignment outside of the soldier's PMOS/CPMOS;

♦ Assignment to a short tour (dependent restricted) OCONUS area, unless soldier volunteers for such assignment.

Soldiers who extend their tour to 36 months will be reassigned to the OCONUS location of their choice, provided a valid requirement exists. (Actual reassignment date is subject to PCS constraints.)

Drill Sergeant Assignment Preference Program:

Drill Sergeants who successfully complete the 24 month requirement are eligible to assist in their follow-on assignment. Drill Sergeants will complete a DA Form 4187 requesting three different duty stations. The following are the requirements for submission of a request:

♦ Submit request at 13 months prior to your termination date;

♦ You must request three different duty stations (e.g., Fort Bragg, Fort Stewart, Germany, Hawaii and Alaska are considered overseas commands), request must also meet the professional development of your career field (i.e., requesting to go back and lead soldiers in a line unit);

♦ Your termination date;

♦ The DSN number where you can be reached.

Your request must go through the installation's chain of command to the post Drill Sergeant Manager. When your request is received by your assignment manager, he/she will attempt to assign you to one of the three installations requested. If there is not a valid requirement at the requested installation, the assignment manager will contact you and inform you of the assignments that are available. If you come to an agreement on a negotiated assignment, then your Drill Sergeant

preference has been met. The other option an assignment manager has is to leave you at your current duty station and defer your request until your next PCS.

Point of Contact for the Drill Sergeant Assignment Preference Program is:

DSN: 221-3179;
COMM: 703-325-3179.

Active Army Drill Sergeants who are selected for promotion to MSG will continue to serve in authorized DS positions until the last day of the month prior to the promotion. AA DS Candidates who have already started or graduated from DS School when selected for promotion to MSG will continue to comply with DS AIs. (They also will remain a DS until the last day of the month prior to promotion to MSG.)

PREREQUISITES:

Drill Sergeant candidates must meet the following prerequisites:

♦ Be physically fit (minimum profile guide is 111221), meet Army height/weight requirements outhlined in AR 600-9 and be able to pass the APFT (no substitution of events) upon arrival at DS School;

♦ Be 36 years old or less. Volunteers may be 37 years or older provided they have the appropriate medical clearance (AR 40-501) at time of the request. Medical clearance should state that soldier is medically cleared for DS duty;

♦ Have no record of emotional instability as determined by screening of health records and clinical evaluation by competent medical officer;

♦ Have no speech impediment;

♦ Be a high school graduate or possess the GED equivalent;

♦ Display good military bearing;

♦ Have demonstrated leadership ability during previous tours of duty and have demonstrated capability to perform in positions of increasing responsibilities as Senior NCO in the Army, as reflected on the NCOERs;

♦ Have had no court-martial convictions;

♦ Have no record of disciplinary action or time lost under 10 USC 972 or letter of reprimand filed in OMPF during current enlistment or in last 3 years, whichever is longer. Does not include Article 15 directed for filing in the restricted portion of the OMPF;

♦ Active Army soldiers may not have received EB or SRB for current service obligation if PMOS is not among those authorized for DS positions;

♦ Have a minimum GT score of 100;

♦ Be SSG through SFC (not applicable to USAR soldiers);

♦ Have a minimum of 4 years continuous active Federal service;

♦ Have a thorough background screening conducted by PERSCOM;

♦ Have a commander's evaluation by a commander in the rank of LTC or higher.

Commander will personally interview the soldier (this may not be delegated) and ensure soldier meet prerequisites. Commanders will consider the "whole soldier" when making their recommendation. Input should include, but is not limited to, demonstrated leadership ability and potential, physical fitness, character/integrity, the soldier's ability to perform in stressful situations any incidents of abuse which the chain of command is aware of. All negative evaluations must include a full explanation.

U.S. Army Reserve soldiers may have the following waived:

♦ Noncommissioned Education System requirement;

♦ Time in service requirement reduced to 3 years;

♦ Rank requirement reduced to CPL. (To attend AA DS School soldiers must be Prior Service Training Candidate appointed as an acting SGT IAW AR 140-158).

Drill Sergeant School graduates in the grade of CPL, assigned to USAR units, will be considered Drill Corporals until attaining the grade of SGT.

They will not be authorized to wear the DS distinguishing accessories (hat or badge) or to perform as DS until promoted to SGT. (The Drill Corporal will follow the Drill Corporal Program per TRADOC Regulation 350-16.)

Soldiers stationed OCONUS may submit application no earlier than 14 months and no later than 10 months prior to their DEROS.

A curtailment of OCONUS tour for the sole purpose of entry in the DS Program will not be granted.

Soldiers selected, and in receipt of AI, for the DS Program will not be extended OCONUS.

Soldiers based OCONUS must complete at least 36 months at their current installation prior to submitting an application. However, as an exception, soldiers may submit an application earlier when they are assigned to an installation where DS positions are authorized.

Soldiers based CONUS who are located at installations without a DS School will attend school in a TDY and return status.

Soldiers located at installations where a DS School is located will be attached to the school for training.

Soldiers returning from OCONUS will be assigned to the installation where they will be a DS. Soldiers will attend school in a TDY and return status, unless a DS School exists at the installation.

Soldiers must successfully complete DS School prior to performing DS duties.

Since August 1997, PERSCOM has implemented for potential DS Candidates (DA selects and volunteers) the requirement for a commander's recommendation (LTC or higher), which includes a mental health evaluation to determine the emotional stability of the soldier to perform this duty. Also, PERSCOM is screening the soldier's official military personnel file (OMPF) to include restricted file and Military Police/Criminal Investigation Division's records.

Effective 1 April 1998 PERSCOM has implemented the policy to coordinate/screen the following records for all potential DS Candidates.

♦ Department of the Army Inspector's General (DAIG) Records;

♦ Personnel security and criminal records indexed in the Defense Clearance Investigation Index (DCII) as present in the Army Investigative Records Repository (AIRR), Army Crime Records Center (ACRC), Defense Security Service (DSS) and other Federal Agencies and Military Departments;

♦ Official Military Personnel Files (to include the restricted file);

♦ Community and Family Support Center (Family Advocacy) Records.

Soldiers with TYPE I Reports of unfavorable information disqualifiers will be excluded from DS duty permanently. Soldiers with TYPE II Reports of unfavorable information disqualifiers will be excluded for consideration for DS duty for 5 years from the date of the incident. Listed below are the TYPE I and TYPE II reports of unfavorable information disqualifiers:

Automatic Rejection - any records of unfavorable information during the soldier's career involving moral turpitude of the following nature:

♦ Sexual harassment, assault of a subordinate/spouse/child, rape, indecent acts with minors;

♦ Incest, bestiality, homosexual activities, adultery, sexual activity with subordinate soldiers or fraternization;

♦ Conduct in violation of the Army's policy on participation in extremist organizations or activities;

♦ Any court-martial conviction in the soldier's career, provided it has not been reversed by a higher court or other appropriate authority;

♦ Any repeat offenders (or combination) of TYPE II offenses any time during their careers.

TYPE II Reports of unfavorable information disqualifiers - time related - any records of unfavorable information listed below committed within 5 years of Drill Sergeant consideration:

♦ Driving under the influence (DUI);

♦ Assault (other than of a subordinate, spouse or child);

♦ Any drug offense;

♦ Larceny/theft;

♦ Traffic violation with 6 points or more assessed;

♦ Any record of unfavorable information other than the above in the past 5 years.

Soldiers may submit request for information regarding non-election for Drill Sergeant duty to CDR, PERSCOM (TAPC-EPC-S). Points of contact are:

♦ Policy:
TAPC-EPC-O, DSN: 221-6099;

♦ Background screening process:
TAPC-EPC-S, DSN: 221-4802.

PERSONAL CONDUCT & APPEARANCE STANDARDS:

Soldiers may be removed from the DS Program (candidate status or in DS position, as appropriate) for the following reasons:

♦ Arriving unqualified soldiers that do not meet the course prerequisites, to include body composition requirements in AR 600-9;

♦ Failure to pass the APFT (AR 350-41);

♦ Academic failure;

♦ Temporary medical reasons that will prevent soldiers from completing the course in the specified time (TRADOC Reg 350-16);

♦ Administrative (emergency leave and so forth);

♦ Failure to maintain high standards of military appearance, military courtesy, bearing, conduct and/or professionalism. Includes soldiers who don't comply with body composition requirements in AR 600-9 and who test positive for drugs;

♦ Infractions of training policies or violations of the UCMJ;

♦ Lack of proper motivation, provided individual counseling has been unsuccessful. Includes failure to enter or complete DS School due to deficiencies in motivation;

♦ Medical reasons when condition prevents soldiers from performing DS duties, to include pregnancy;

♦ Hardship or family problems that prevent soldiers from performing DS duties.

When a serious incident occurs that requires an investigation, the DS will be suspended from assigned duties and have SDAP suspended, pending completion of the investigation. Mere occurrence of an incident or the conduct of an investigation is not intended to be a basis for removal from the program. Decisions on removal must be based on the circumstances or the completed investigation. Reports of removal are not required if soldiers are cleared and returned to DS duty. (Soldiers who are pending removal or who are temporarily suspended from duties pending completion of investigation will be counted in total (assigned) DS Strength.) When AA soldiers are removed from the DS Program, they will:

♦ Be removed from the school or unit;
♦ Be assigned other duties at the installation (if possible);
♦ Have their SDAP terminated;
♦ Have SQI "X" removed, except if removed for pregnancy.

DA Form 1059 (Service School Academic Evaluation Report) will be completed for soldiers, excluding those who were unqualified upon arrival, removed from DS School. The names of soldiers who were unqualified upon arrival at DS School will be reported, in writing, to PERSCOM (TAPC-EPK-ID).

Soldiers removed for:

♦ Academic failure may reapply for DS School after meeting the training objectives outlined in DA Form 1059;
♦ Temporary medical reasons that will prevent soldiers from completing the course in the specified time (TRADOC Reg 350-16) or Administrative reasons will normally be rescheduled for a later DS School class.

Soldiers removed from the DS Program for pregnancy will receive AIs to report back to DS duties or school, as applicable (normally 6 months after anticipated delivery) unless soldier had completed 12 months or more of DS status when removed.

Removal packets are required when soldiers are removed from the DS Program for failure to pass the APFT (AR 350-41); failure to maintain high standards of military appearance, military courtesy, bearing, conduct and/or profes-sionalism; infractions of training policies or violations of the UCMJ; lack of proper motivation; medical reasons; hardship or family problems. As a minimum include:

♦ Letter of intent to remove;
♦ Soldier's acknowledgment statement required by AR 600-37, or a statement by removal authority stating why it's not included;
♦ Soldier's rebuttal statement, if provided;
♦ All chain of command correspondence/endorsements;
♦ Approval endorsement must be signed by approval, authority and cite removal paragraph and reason;
♦ Justification - copies of formal counseling, Article 15, Court Martial orders, permanent physical profiles (when pregnancy is reason include expected delivery date), as applicable;
♦ Copy of orders revoking SQI "X" (when applicable).

Soldiers removed from the DS Program for: failure to maintain high standards of military appearance, military courtesy, bearing, conduct and/or professionalism; infractions of training policies or violations of the UCMJ; lack of proper motivation or medical reasons when condition prevents soldiers from performing DS duties and when medical profile is permanent, are not eligible for reentry in the program. When a soldier is removed from the DS Program for reasons in AR 380-67, the DA Form 5248-R will be forwarded to U.S. Army Central Personnel Security Clearance Facility.

PREPARATIONS:

DS Candidates will be administered a urinalysis test within 3 days of reporting to DS School.

DS School graduates incur a 24 month obligation for DS duty. Soldiers must take appropriate action to meet the length of service requirement prior to attending school (AR 601-280).

Application:

A volunteer packet includes the following forms.

- ♦ DA Form 4187 - Personnel Action;
- ♦ 2A & 2-1, Personnel Qualification Record Part I & II;
- ♦ Commanders Check List (Sample Memorandum can be found at the end of this chapter);
- ♦ DA Form 3822-R - Mental Evaluation (Signed by a Medical Officer, not an NCO);
- ♦ DA Form 705 - PT Card;
- ♦ Weapons Qualification;
- ♦ Physical Exam, if 36 years of age or older.

Mail your packet to:
PERSCOM
ATTN: TAPC-EPK-ID
2461 Eisenhower Ave.
Alexandria, VA 22331.

REFERENCE:

1. US Army Formal Schools Catalog. US Army Publishing Agency. DA PAM 351-4, page 166, Table 3-35. 31 October 1995.
2. Enlisted Assignments and Utilization Management. US Army Publishing Agency. AR 614-200, 8.12-8.16. 31 October 1997. Online. IBM Book Manager Book Server. Internet. 11 May 2000. Available: http://books.usapa.beloir.army.mil/cgi-bin/bookmgr/BOOKS/R614_200/toc.
3. "Commander's Drill Sergeant Candidate Checklist." Online. Internet. 11 May 2000. Available: http://www-perscom.army.mil/epinf/dsdrlist.htm.
4. "Drill Sergeant Assignment Preference Program," Drill Sergeant Assignment Team. Online. Internet. 11 May 2000. Available: http://www-perscom.army.mil/epinf/dsassignpref.htm.
5. "Frequently Asked Questions," Drill Sergeant Assignment Team. Online. Internet. 11 May 2000. Available: http://www-perscom.army.mil/epinf/dsteam.htm.
6. MILPER Message NR 98_102. Online. Internet. 1 April 1998. Available: http://www-perscom.army.mil/tagd/msg/98-102.htm.

Sample Memoradum
COMMANDER'S DRILL SERGEANT CANDIDATE CHECKLIST

MEMORANDUM FOR Commander, PERSCOM, ATTN: TAPC-EPK-ID, 2461 Eisenhower Avenue, Alexandria, VA 22331

FROM Commander,

Subject: Drill Sergeant Candidate Check List

SECTION I - Identification Data

Name:_____ SSN:_____ RANK:_____

SECTION II - Eligibility Criteria (Determined by Bn Level Cdr or Cdr at 05 level or above)

Does soldier possess the following:	Yes	No
1. Rank of SSG or SFC	_____	_____
2. Minimum GT score of 100 (no waivers)	_____	_____
3. Minimum physical profile 111221	_____	_____
4. High school graduate/GED equivalency	_____	_____
5. BNCOC graduate	_____	_____
6. Qualified with the M16A2 in the last 6 months	_____	_____
7. Minimum of 4 years continuous active service	_____	_____
8. Meets the ht/wt criteria of AR 600-9. (See note 2)	_____	_____
9. Be able to pass the APFT (no substitution of event) (See note 3)	_____	_____
10. Displays good military bearing, has demonstrated capability to perform in positions of increased responsibility	_____	_____
11. Have at least 24 months remaining in service (as a drill sergeant) from report date to gaining installation (See note 4)	_____	_____
12. Record of emotional instability thru a) Screen of health records b) Mental Status Evaluation/Interview (must be attached)	_____	_____
13. Documented speech impediment	_____	_____
14. Record of Misconduct:		
a) Article 15's or other disciplinary action during last five years	_____	_____
b) Any record of court martial conviction in the soldier's career, provided it has not been reversed by a higher court	_____	_____
c) Record of conduct in violation of the Army's policy on participation in extremist organization or activities	_____	_____
d) Record of assault on a subordinate, spouse or child	_____	_____
e) Record of misconduct during the soldier's career involving moral turpitude (See note 1)	_____	_____
f) Record of misconduct in the previous five years involving the following offenses:		
1. DUI	_____	_____
2. Assault (other than subordinate, spouse or child which is permanent disqualification)	_____	_____
3. Any drug offense	_____	_____

    4. Larceny/theft   _____ _____

    5. Traffic violations with six or more points accessed   _____ _____

15. Observed negative reaction to stress   _____ _____

* A response of "yes" to questions 12, 13, 14, or 15 will eliminate a soldier from consideration for the Drill Sergeant Program (include supporting documentation).

NOTES:

1. Morale turpitude involves misconduct of the following nature: incest, bestiality; homosexual activities; adultery; sexual activity with subordinate soldiers; fraternization; sexual harassment; indecent acts with minors; or rape.

2. If the soldier is overweight, action must be taken to ensure he/she is within compliance with AR 600-9, prior to class start date. If soldier is separated from active duty or barred from reenlistment for overweight status please notify this headquarters immediately. If this requirement is the basis for determining that a soldier does not meet the selection criteria for the Drill Sergeant Program, a copy of the appropriate personnel action (Flag or Bar to reenlistment) must accompany this packet.

3. If the soldier is having difficulty passing the APFT, action must be taken to ensure he/she can pass the APFT prior to class start date. If this requirement is the basis for determining that a soldier does not meet the selection criteria for the Drill Sergeant Program, a copy of the appropriate personnel action (Flag or Bar reenlistment) must accompany this packet.

4. Soldier must take appropriate action to meet the length of service requirement prior to attending Drill Sergeant school.

***************************Commander verification*********************

1. IAW AR 614-200, Chapter 8, the above soldier (circle appropriate response)

        a. Does meet selection criteria

        b. Does not meet selection criteria

        Supporting documentation is attached if applicable.

2. Additional Remarks:

Commander comments should include (but are not limited to), leadership abilities; motivation to be a drill sergeant; character/integrity; financial problems; physical fitness; temporary medical profiles; observed reaction to stress; and incidents of spouse, soldier or child abuse. Consider the "whole soldier" in your recommendation. Attach additional sheet if required.

_____   _____   _____

Cdr's DSN#   Cdr's Signature   Date

(LTC or above)

NOTES

GOLDEN KNIGHTS

HISTORY:

The Golden Knights' history begins in 1959, when Brig. Gen. Joseph Stillwell, then Chief of Staff of XVIII Airborne Corps and Fort Bragg, formed the Strategic Army Corps Parachute Team. On June 1, 1961 the Army officially recognized, redesigned and activated the team as the United States Army Parachute Team.

One year later, the Team officially adopted the nickname "Golden Knights" because of their winning record of gold medals and conquest of the skies.

Just as incredible as the demonstration teams are the two parachute competition teams: The Formation Skydiving Team and the Style and Accuracy Team. The teams tour the world competing in parachuting competitions and amazing the parachuting world with their record of 408 national champions, 65 world champions, and 14 national and six world team titles in formation skydiving.

In addition to those accomplishments, they also claim the only six-time world champion parachutist in formation skydiving and the only three consecutive time national champion parachutist in style and accuracy parachuting. These impressive feats have made them not only the most-winning U.S. Department of Defense sports team, but also the most winning parachute team in the world.

Helping support these incredible demonstrators and competitors are the Team's aviation and headquarters sections. The aviation section consists of six fixed wing aircraft and a team of highly experienced pilots and crew members that make sure the parachutist make it into the air safely and quickly. The headquarters section also has a highly skilled team of soldiers and civilians working on the administration, budget, media relations, operations, parachute maintenance and supply concerns of the Team.

During the 40 years since its inception, the Team's mission has remained the same:

♦ To perform live aerial demonstrations for the public and in promotion of the Army's public relations and recruitment efforts;

♦ To compete in national and international parachuting competitions;

♦ To test and evaluate new parachuting equipment and techniques for improved operation and safety.

The exceptional soldiers carrying out this mission are divided into six groups: The Black and Gold Demonstration Teams, the Formation Skydiving Team, the Style and Accuracy Team, an aviation section and a headquarters section.

The Black and Gold Demonstration Teams spend more than 230 days a year entertaining more than 12 million people at air shows and special events around the country and the world. The teams have performed more than 8,500 live aerial demonstrations in all 50 states and 47 countries, earning them the title of the "Army's Goodwill Ambassadors to the World."

Before earning the chance to jump with the Team, each member had to make a different kind of jump by deciding to join the Army. Each Team member is a soldier first and is trained in one of the 200 occupations the Army offers. Some wanted to serve their country or maybe see the world, while others wanted to take advantage of the financial bonuses the Army offered to them, such as up to $50,000 for college, up to $65,000 to repay college loans or up to $20,000 for enlisting in selected military occupations.

For 40 years the Team's superior performances, winning record and exemplary conduct have helped rekindle and sustain a feeling of pride in the hearts of many Americans. The Team's faces may have changed, but every "Golden Knight's" dedication to the Army and the American public has and will continue to remain steadfast well into the 21st century.

FORWARD:

Performing precision aerial maneuvers while falling to earth at speeds reaching 120 miles per hour and landing dead center on target is the trademark of the United States Army Parachute Team, the "Golden Knights."

Now in their 40th year of entertaining both young and old with their amazing aerial skills, the men and women that make up the "Golden Knights" continue to show audiences around the world why they are considered the world's best parachute team.

Stationed at the "Home of the Airborne," Fort Bragg, North Carolina, the 90 soldiers that make up the "Golden Knights" come from many diverse backgrounds and have been trained in various military occupational specialties.

PREREQUISITES:

Soldiers who desire to become members of the USAPT must meet the following prerequisites:
- ◆ Be a volunteer;
- ◆ Be a qualified military parachutist (or agree to attend jump school upon assignment to the team);
- ◆ Hold a valid class "C" international parachuting license or equivalent (waiverable by the Commander of the USAPT);
- ◆ Must be on active duty; soldiers selected for the team must have 3 years of service remaining upon assignment to the team;
- ◆ Have no bar to reenlistment, including ineligibility to reenlist under AR 600-200, chapter 4;
- ◆ Include statement that he or she understands and will comply with the Army's policy concerning drug use.

APPLICATION:

Soldiers meeting the above prerequisites, wishing to apply for consideration for the Golden Knights must submit an application with other required items to:

U.S. Army Parachute Team
ATTN: Admin Section
P.O. Box 70126
Ft. Bragg, NC 28307-0126.

Applications must be submitted no later than the 30th of June during the year you wish to attend tryouts. The sooner you get your application in, the better.

TRYOUT INFORMATION:

Each year, during the fall, the USAPT conducts a tryout period for selected, qualified personnel desiring assignment to the team. The tryout period will normally take 4-6 weeks and will culminate with team selections.

A sample tryout application form can be viewed on the following pages.

CONTACT INFORMATION:

If you need any more information, call:
(910) 396-4800.

REFERENCE:

1. "Team History." Online. Internet. 22 May 2000. Available: http://www.usarec.army.mil/hq/goldenknights/TeamHistory/history.htm.
2. "Tryout Information." Online. Internet. 23 May 2000. Available: http://www.usarec.army.mil/hq/goldemknights/GoldenOpportunities/tryout_information.htm.

UNITED STATES ARMY PARACHUTE TEAM
"GOLDEN KNIGHTS"
TRYOUT APPLICATION FORM

\TRYOUT YEAR: *year you will attend*
RETURN BY: *June 30*   CURRENT DATE: *insert date*

LAST NAME, FIRST MIDDLE	SSN	RANK	DATE OF RANK		
last, first middle	*ssn*	*rank*	*date of rank*		

DATE OF BIRTH	PLACE OF BIRTH	BPED	ETS	LAST PCS
date of birth	*place of birth*	*bped*	*ets*	*ets*

NOTE: UP AR 614-5, personnel assigned to the U.S Army Parachute Team will be stabilized for 36 months. Minimum acceptable time remaining in service from date of assignment to the USAPT is 3 years. If you have less, you WILL be required to reenlist or extend to meet the service requirement.

PMOS *pmos*   SMOS *smos*   AMOS *amos*   DMOS *dmos*
APFT SCORE *000*   APFT DATE *00 month 00*   HEIGHT *00"*   WEIGHT *000lbs*
MARITAL STATUS *status*   NUMBER OF FAMILY MEMBERS *0*
EDUCATION LEVEL: MILITARY *any*   CIVILIAN *any*
PRESENT MILITARY ADDRESS: *full mailing*   PHONE (DSN)*000-0000*
                continue mailing or delete   PHONE (COMM)*(000) 000-0000*
PRESENT HOME ADDRESS: *full mailing*   PHONE *(000) 000-0000*
                continue mailing or delete
AIRBORNE QUALIFIED: YES *X*   NO *X*   (If non-airborne, you must volunteer to attend Airborne School before you can be selected to the USAPT; by submitting this application you are agreeing to fulfill that requirement should you make the Team.)
ARE YOU CURRENTLY ON JUMP STATUS: YES *X* NO *X*
USPA MEMBERSHIP #: *insert no.*   NUMBER OF FREEFALL JUMPS: *insert no.*
NUMBER OF FREEFALL JUMPS IN THE PAST YEAR: *insert no.*
DATE OF FIRST FREEFALL JUMP: *00 Month 00*

Tryouts are held annually to fill vacant positions on the US Army Parachute Team. These positions are usually on one of the demonstration teams; competitors are usually selected from within the Team.

ASSIGNMENTS FOR THE LAST THREE YEARS:

UNIT	FROM TO	SUPERVISORS NAME/PHONE NUMBER
unit	*dates*	*supervisor and contact info*
unit	*dates*	*supervisor and contact info*

PARACHUTING EXPERIENCE: Briefly relate prior parachuting experience and areas of interest, i.e. Demonstrations, Competitions, etc.
insert text here

LIST INDIVIDUAL PARACHUTING REFERENCES AND PHONE NUMBERS:
1.*insert text*
2.*insert text*
3.*insert text*

LIST INDIVIDUAL MILITARY REFERENCES AND PHONE NUMBERS:
1.*insert text*
2.*insert text*
3.*insert text*

Applicants are responsible for keeping the USAPT informed of current military and civilian addresses and telephone numbers. Call in changes to: Commercial (910) 396-4800/4828. The Commander, USAPT will notify applicants that have been accepted for the tryout session by Genser message. A correct message plain language address (PLAD) is essential for this notification. If your unit does not have a separate message PLAD, provide the one for your higher headquarters, with routing (pass to) instructions. Applicants that are not accepted will be notified by letter.

MESSAGE PLAD: *insert as shown below*   (very important)
EXAMPLE OF MESSAGE PLAD: CDRUSAPT FT BRAGG NC//AFPT-CO//

PERSONAL INFORMATION	YES		NO
1.Have you ever defaulted on a loan?	X	N/A	X
2.Have you ever had property repossessed?	X		X
3.Have you had any traffic violations?	X		X
4.Have you ever been cited for DUI?	X		X
5.Have you ever tested positive on a urinalysis for drugs?	X		X
6.Have you ever received punishment under the UCMJ?	X		X
7.Have you ever been arrested?	X		X
8.Have you ever been denied or lost a security clearance?	X		X
9.Do you have a valid civilian or military license?	X	CIV	X
	X	MIL	X

NOTE: If you answered YES to any of the above, except question #9, provide an explanation. If more space is required, attach a continuation sheet.
insert your text or delete

The demonstration teams spend over 250 days per year TDY. It is important that you and your family know this! You must discuss this with your family to ensure there will not be any problems with your continued deployments.

10.**Are you a single parent?** Yes _X_ No _X_ If you answered YES, number of children and ages:
insert text or delete

Forward the completed application, along with a copy of your DA Form 2A, DA Form 2-1, a current DA Photo, and a memorandum signed by your commander (see example on Page 5), to the below listed address. Additionally, enclose a photocopy of your logbook showing your jumps over the last 12 months.

SEND THIS APPLICATION TO: **Commander**
U.S. Army Parachute Team
Attn: Admin NCO
P.O. Box 70126
Ft. Bragg, NC 28307-0126

REMARKS: (Why do you want to be a Golden Knight? Why should you be considered? Is there anything about yourself that we should know, but haven't asked?)
insert text or delete

"I certify that the information contained in this application is true and correct to the best of my knowledge."

_____
SIGNATURE

MEMORANDUM FOR: Commander, United States Army Parachute Team,
Fort Bragg, North Carolina 28307-5000

SUBJECT: Application to the U.S. Army Parachute Team Tryout Program.
1. I am aware that (rank and name of soldier), a member of my command, is applying for a position in the U.S. Army Parachute Team Tryout Program.

2. I understand that if (rank and name of soldier) is accepted to the program, he/she will be TDY (SD if at Ft. Bragg) for the duration of the program.

3. I further understand that should (rank and name of soldier) be selected to become a member of the Golden Knights, the Parachute Team will generate a request to TAPA for immediate reassignment of the soldier.

Your commander's sig. block.
Company level commander w/endorsement from
Battalion Commander.

HALO

MILITARY FREE FALL PARACHUTIST (MFFPC)

REGULATION:

Course No: 2E–SI4X/ASI4X/011–ASIW8
Title: Military Free Fall Parachutist
Length: 5 Weeks, 2 Days
Location: U.S. Army John F. Kennedy Spec Warfare Center – SC: 331
Enl ASI: W8
WO ASI: 4X
Off SC: 4X
Scope: Course effective: 1 Jan 92
Military free fall parachute ground training; physiological training, body stabilization (vertical wind tunnel), basic aircraft procedures, combat equipment (ruck sack and weapon), advanced aircraft procedures to include individual exits with combat equipment, mass exits, grouping exercises, night airborne operations, and life support equipment; and procedures with high altitude airborne operations. Upon completion of the course, the student will be able to perform both night and day combat equipment high altitude military free fall operations.
Prerequisite: Special Operations Forces active or Reserve component commissioned officers, warrant officers, or enlisted personnel who are assigned to, or who are on orders for assignment to, a military free fall coded position; or selected DOD personnel or allied personnel who are qualified military parachutists. Must have passed the high altitude, low opening (HALO) physical examination IAW AR 40–501, chapter 5, paragraph 5–5, within one year prior to class date and must report with complete medical records, including original HALO examination, on day of inprocessing. Must have nine months remaining in service upon graduation.
Special Information: Instructions in AR 40–501, chapter 8, paragraph 8–26c, should be initiated NLT 45 days prior to reporting date. Prerequisite, readmission, or medical waivers from Commander, 1st Special Warfare Training Group Airborne), must be in hand at inprocessing.
Security Clearance: None

FORWARD:

Military Parachutists use the square ram-air canopies for free fall jumping. Although the chute is not normally for used for static line jumping, the MC-5 can be rigged for a static line jump. With a round chute parachutists can jump with a little more equipment, but the landing is harder and the chute is not nearly as maneuverable. The ram-air chute performs more like a wing; providing steer capability and allowing the parachutist more flexibility. However, a ram-air chute doesn't allow for the parachutist to jump with quite as much weight. Parachutists manually deploy the parachute by rip cord on the free fall jumps, usually around 3500 feet, rather than it being extracted by a static-line. Except for water jumps, all jumpers are equipped with automatic opening devices designed to deploy the chute should the jumper be incapacitated, or otherwise unable to deploy his own canopy.

The maximum a jumper can weigh when exiting the aircraft is 360 pounds. Items that might be worn by the parachutist include weapon, oxygen bottles, LBE, GPS, Compass board and/or one or more ruck sacks (Military Free Fall Parachutists are able to rear mount an extra ruck.

PURPOSE:

The purpose of the Military Free Fall Course is to train personnel to be qualified military free fall parachutists. The Military Free Fall Course offers training in military free fall techniques; students learn to maneuver their parachutes with pinpoint accuracy, making as many as 35 individually graded jumps. A number of these jumps are made from altitudes high enough to require oxygen equipment.

OVERVIEW:

This is a 4 week course consisting of military free fall parachute ground training - to include physiological training, body stabilization (vertical wind tunnel), basic aircraft procedures, combat equipment (ruck sack and weapon) procedures, as well as advanced aircraft procedures - to include individual exits with combat equipment, mass exits, grouping exercises, night airborne operations, life-support equipment (oxygen mask and bottles) and procedures with high altitude airborne operations. Students make at least 14 free fall jumps at HALO School.

Training includes:

♦ Military Free Fall Skills;

♦ HALO/HAHO Operations (Day/Night).

General Training Outline:
Week One:

Week one begins with inprocessing, weigh-in, equipment issue, etc.

♦ Students are assigned one instructor and a jump buddy (about your same height and weight so you fall at about the same rate); students have one instructor throughout the duration of the course.

♦ Students will learn about the ram air parachute, emergency procedures, rigging procedures, repack procedures, etc.

♦ Students perform table drills to learn how to fall properly and remain stable.

♦ Students train in the hanging harness to practice emergency procedures (malfunctions, cutaways, entanglements, etc.).

♦ Students also cover jump commands and the oxygen system.

After completing these tasks, students train in the wind tunnel. This consists of a fan that blows at speeds up to 150 miles per hour; it is designed to lift and support the student in the air to simulate free fall. Students use this to perfect body position.

Weeks Two - Four:

Training is primarily focused on students jumping.

♦ Students begin by exiting at 10,000 feet with no extra equipment.

♦ Students work towards exiting at 25,000 feet with full equipment and oxygen.

♦ Students must remain stable, pull at the designated altitude (+/- 200 feet) and land within 25 meters of the group leader.

♦ Weather permitting, students will perform many jumps (including HAHO).

For High Altitude High Opening jumps, parachutists exit at approximately 13,000 feet and deploy the chute within approximately 5 seconds; students then glide 5-10 kilometers (or more depending on exit altitude and winds) to the target.

Graduation consists of equipment turn in, diplomas and paperwork and the requisite class party.

PREREQUISITES:

♦ Special Operations Forces Commissioned Officers, Warrant Officers or Enlisted personnel of the Active or Reserve Components who are assigned to, or who are on orders for assignment to a military free fall coded position or selected DOD personnel or allied personnel who are qualified military parachutists;

♦ Must have passed the high altitude, low opening (HALO) physical examination IAW AR 40-501, chapter 5, paragraph 8, and must report with complete medical records, including original HALO examination, on day of inprocessing. School must be completed within two years of the date on the physical;

♦ Must have nine months remaining in service upon graduation;

♦ Soldiers requesting waivers for disqualifying conditions will submit their physical examinations along with a memorandum requesting the waiver (not later than 30 days prior to the class start date) through the USASOC Medical Training Division for delivery to USAJFKSWCS (where waivers are considered).

Waivers must be approved in writing prior to start date.

The address for the USASOC Medical Training Division is:
    Commander, USASOC
    ATTN: AOMD-MT
    Ft Bragg, NC 28307-5217.

PREPARATIONS:

Instructions in AR 40-501, chapter 8, paragraph 8-26C, should be initiated NLT 45 days prior to reporting date.

Prior to reporting to the MFFPC, students must ensure that all dental, medical, administrative and personnel actions are completed or rescheduled for a future date (after graduation). Company B will not release students during the conduct of the course except for an emergency.

Clothing & Equipment Requirements:

Students will bring all of the uniforms and equipment listed in Table Military Free Fall-A.

Orders:

Orders must state the temporary duty (TDY) itinerary is "Fort Bragg, North Carolina, to Yuma Proving Ground, Arizona and return to home stations or next duty assignment." This facilitates funding the individuals return tickets, especially those individuals on TDY en route to their next duty assignment.

Effective 1 October 1995, Army students reporting to Military Free Fall training must have a memorandum confirming assignment to a military free fall coded position at inprocessing. Personnel reporting without the required memorandum will not be entered into training.

Physicals:

Organization/unit surgeons will base their determination of a soldier's medical qualification/disqualification on AR 40-501, Standards of Medical Fitness (1 May 1989), Interim Change No. 101 to AR 40-501 (1 October 1991), and the USAJFKSWCS Memorandum, "Requirements for Completing Physical Examinations for USAJFKSWCS Schools," 1 March 1995.

Graduation:

Company B will extend class dates to achieve course graduation standards in the event academic requirements are not met because of adverse weather conditions or air scheduling conflicts. Students will remain in the course until the rescheduled graduation dates or return to their parent units without qualification. Students will not make return travel arrangements until the actual graduation dates have been established.

Students will not be allowed to graduate early because of unit deployment, follow-on TDY/

Table: Military Free Fall-A		
Required Items Inventory		
ITEM	QTY	REMARKS
BDU	2 sets	
Cap	1	BDU, with rank and insignia
Undershirt	5	Brown, no logos
Shorts	5 pairs	Running, nylon, black
Socks	5 pairs	Cushion sole, OD or Black
PT Uniform (PFU)	2 sets	Army, gray or sister service equivalent (summer)
PT Uniform (PFU)	2 sets	Army, gray or sSister service equivalent (winter)
Military Gloves	1 pair	Flight gloves or black issue, recommended for use during cold months (gloves have good insulation without sacrificing dexterity)
Notebook	1	Pen and pencil
Flashlight	1	Mini-mag recommended
Boots	2 pairs	Combat or Jungle (Lace through eyelet type), black - boots with open-hook eyelets are unacceptable for wear

temporary additional duty or travel arrangements locked in prior to the graduation date.

REPORTING INFORMATION:

During the first week of training, the headquarters contingent for Company B is in Building D-1209 (Vertical Wind Tunnel [VWT]) at Fort Bragg, North Carolina, at the intersection of Gruber and Mosby Street
    DSN: 239-5661;
    COMM: (910) 432-5661.

Students must report with a Physiological Training Record, High Altitude Parachutist Initial (HAP INT). Students must report to the VWT not later than 1700 on the report date listed in the Army Training Requirements and Resources System (ATRRS).

Officers and enlisted personnel arriving prior to the class start date will report to the Moon Hall billeting office for room assignments or to obtain a statement of non-availability. Reservations for Moon Hall may be made by calling:
    COMM: (910) 436-1669.

Students reporting for inprocessing must have their medical records (with the original "approved" HALO physical which must be current within 2 years from graduation date), a current PANOREX dental X-ray, a copy of DA Form 2A/2-1 or DA Form 2B/2-1 and five hard copies of orders attaching them to Company B, 2nd Battalion, 1st SWTG (A), for the purpose of attending the MFFPC. Students who report without their medical records and orders will not enter training.

BILLETING:

During airborne operations (weeks two through four), students will be billeted at YPG, Arizona. No reservations are necessary, and room assignments are made prior to arrival at YPG. Yuma Proving Ground will not issue statements of non-availability.

Orders to the MFFPC must state that government quarters are available at Fort Bragg for $16 per day and at YPG for $8 per day.

Dining Facilities:

Government mess facilities are not always available because of the training schedule. The use of government mess facilities adversely affects the performance of the mission. Government mess is not available at YPG, Arizona. There are eating establishments on YPG within 1/4 mile from billeting. The nearest town is Yuma, which is 25 miles away. Students on separate rations or per diem will provide for their own meals during training. Company B, 2nd Battalion, 1st SWTG (A) will not issue meal cards.

Students with meal cards must arrange for separate rations or per diem prior to departure from their parent unit.

Transportation:

All students are responsible for providing their own transportation (taxi) from YPG to Yuma airport after graduation. Transportation for all training will be provided by Company B.

CONTACT INFORMATION:

Company B Headquarters is in Building 305 at Yuma Proving Ground (YPG), Arizona.
    DSN: 899-3636/3661;
    COMM: (520) 328-3636/3661.

REFERENCE:

1. US Army Formal Schools Catalog. US Army Publishing Agency. DA PAM 351-4, page 120-121, Table 3-19. 31 October 1995.   2. Thede, James J., TSgt. "HALO School." Online. Internet. 16 May 2000. Available: http://members.tripod.com/~thede/halo.html.
3. "U.S. Army Special Forces: JFK SWCS Advanced Skills Department." Online. Internet. 15 April 2000. Available: http://users.aol.com/armysof1/specialty.html.

MILITARY FREE FALL JUMPMASTER (MFFJMC)

REGULATION:

Course No: 2E–F56/011–F15
Title: Military Free Fall Jumpmaster
Length: 3 Weeks, 2 Days
Location: U.S. Army John F. Kennedy Spec Warfare Center – SC: 331
Scope: Course effective: 1 Oct 93

Military free fall jumpmaster duties and responsibilities altimeters, automatic rip cord release devices, canopy control, emergency procedures, oxygen review and procedures, wind drift calculations, techniques of spotting, packing, rigging and supervision of rigging of individual main parachutes. Jumpmaster practical exercises will be conducted both day and night.

Prerequisite: Special Operations Forces Active or Reserve Component commissioned officers, warrant officers, NCOs, or selected DOD personnel assigned to, or will be assigned to, a military free fall position. Must have completed a recognized static line jumpmaster course and military free fall parachutist course. Must have served as a military free fall parachutist for a minimum of one year and completed a minimum of 35 military free fall jumps. Must pass the HALO physical examination IAW AR 40–501, chapter 5, paragraph 5–5, within 3 years of the class date (2 years for personnel aged 45 and above) and an interim examination within 1 year of class date. Must report with medical records on day of inprocessing and possess a current physiological training (altitude chamber) card.

Special Information: The instructions in AR 40–501, chapter 8, paragraph 8–26c, should be initiated NLT 45 days prior to reporting for USAJFKSWCS courses.

Security Clearance: None

PURPOSE:

The purpose of Military Free Fall Jumpmaster School is to train selected SOF, DOD & Foreign Personnel as Military Free Fall Jumpmasters.

OVERVIEW:

This course covers the areas of Military Free Fall Jumpmaster duties and responsibilities, altimeters, automatic rip cord release devices, canopy control, emergency procedures, oxygen review and procedures, wind drift calculations, techniques of spotting, rigging equipment and supervision of rigging of individual main parachutes and equipment.

Training includes:

◆ Military Free Fall Jumpmaster Technical Skills;

◆ HALO/HAHO Jumpmaster Practical Exercises - (Day & Night).

PREREQUISITES:

◆ Special Operations Forces Active or Reserve Component Commissioned Officers, Warrant Officers Noncommissioned Officers or selected DOD personnel who are assigned to, or who are on order to be assigned to, a military free fall position;

◆ Must have completed a recognized static-line Jumpmaster Course and a Military Free Fall Parachutist course;

◆ Must have served as a military free fall parachutist for a minimum of one year and completed a minimum of 50 military free fall jumps;

◆ Requires current military free fall physical (valid for 3 years, if the soldier is less than 45 years old; must be completed yearly from 45 on) if the soldier is presently on military free fall status/orders. Otherwise, a physical is required within two years through the course completion date.

Soldiers requesting waivers for disqualifying conditions will submit their physical examinations along with a memorandum requesting the waiver (not later than 30 days prior to the class start date) through the USASOC Medical Training Division for delivery to USAJFKSWCS (where waivers are considered). The address for the USASOC Medical Training Division is:

Commander, USASOC
ATTN: AOMD-MT
Ft Bragg, NC 28307-5217.

Waivers must be approved in writing prior to start date.

PREPARATIONS:

The instructions in AR 40-501, chapter 8, paragraph 8-26c, should be initiated NLT 45 days prior to reporting for USAJFKSWCS courses.

Prior to reporting to the MFFJMC, students must ensure that all dental, medical, administrative and personnel actions are completed or rescheduled for a future date (after graduation). Company B, 2nd Battalion, 1st SWTG (A) will not release students during the conduct of the course prior to the end of the course except for an emergency.

Clothing & Equipment Requirements:

Students will bring all uniforms and equipment listed in Table Military Free Fall Jumpmaster-A.

Physicals:

Organization/unit surgeons will base their determination of a soldier's medical qualification/disqualification on AR 40-501, Standards of Medical Fitness (1 May 1989), Interim Change No. 101 to AR 40-501 (1 October 1991) and the USAJFKSWCS Memorandum, "Requirements for Completing Physical Examinations for USAJFKSWCS Schools," 1 March 1995.

Graduation:

Company B will extend class dates to achieve course graduation standards if academic requirements are not met because of adverse weather conditions or air scheduling conflicts. Students must stay until the rescheduled graduation dates or return to their parent units without qualification. Students will not make return travel arrangements until actual graduation dates have been established and the class proctor instructs students to make travel arrangements.

Students will not graduate early because of unit deployment, follow-on temporary duty/temporary additional duty or travel arrangements locked in prior to the graduation date.

REPORTING INFORMATION:

Students should arrive in Yuma, Arizona, no later than 24 hours prior to the start date of their class. All students who are traveling to YPG via POV or any other method other than commercial air must call:

DSN: 899-3617,

COMM: (520) 328-3617

for additional instructions 24 hours prior to arriving at YPG. All other students using commercial air must call the above stated numbers before departing the Yuma airport. Students should call Company B operations prior to their arrival to confirm their inprocessing schedule and to receive any additional special instructions. Students must report to Company B, Building 219 at the MFF Jumpmaster Detachment training facility no later than 0600 on the start date of the course listed in the Army Training Requirements and Resources System (ATRRS).

Students reporting for inprocessing must have their complete medical records (with original HALO physical), a current PANOREX dental X-ray and five copies of orders attaching them to Company B, 2nd Battalion, 1st SWTG (A), for

Table: Military Free Fall Jumpmaster-A		
Required Items Inventory		
ITEM	QTY	REMARKS
BDU	2 sets	Complete, with utilities
Cap	1 each	BDU
Undershirt	5 pair	Brown or OD, no logos
Shorts	5 pair	Running, nylon, black
Shoes	1 pair	Civilian, running, low top
PT Uniform (PFU)	2 pair	Army, gray or sister service equivalent (summer)
PT Uniform (PFU)	2 pair	Army, gray or sister service equivalent (winter)
Military Gloves	1 pair	Flight or black issue, recommend for use during cold weather months (gloves have good insulation without sacrificing dexterity)
Notebook	1 each	Pen, paper, calculator
Flashlight	1 each	Mini-mag recommended
Boots	2 pair	Combat or Jungle (Lace through eyelet type), black - boots with open-hook eyelets are unacceptable for wear
Sunglasses	1 pair	Black framed, non-mirror lenses may be worn IAW AR 670-1
STUDENTS MUST ALSO BRING THE FOLLOWING ITEMS		
Service dictated jump record (i.e., DA 1307, USASOC 1099, AF 922) with proof of free fall jumps.		
Static-line Jumpmaster Course diploma or service equivalent. Military Free Fall Parachutist Course Diploma.		
Medical records with the current physical and physiological training records.		

the purpose of attending the MFFJMC. Students who report without their medical records and orders will not enter training.

Inprocessing:
Prerequisite, readmission or medical waivers from Commander, 1st Special Warfare Training Group (Airborne), must be in hand at inprocessing. Students must also report with medical records on day of inprocessing and possess a current physiological training (altitude chamber) card.

BILLETING:
All students who are attending the course with an ATRRS reserved seat will contact the above numbers for information regarding room assignments. All students must arrive at YPG prior to 1800 hours or billeting will be closed. Company B will only provide rooms for those who possess a reserve seat; all others must obtain a hotel room in downtown Yuma until after inprocessing at 0600 on the course start date. All students that are inprocessed into the course will have rooms assigned at YPG. No reservations are necessary. Company B will not issue statements of non-availability. Orders to the MFFJMC must state that government quarters are available at YPG for a minimum cost of $8 per day. Students will be assigned to a room with two students in each room, with a cost of $4 per day when possible; all others will be assigned a room at a cost of $8 per day. If one student departs the course early, the remaining student in the room is charged $8 per day for the remainder of his stay.

Dining Facilities:
Government mess facilities are not available. There are eating establishments on YPG within 1/4 mile from billeting. Students must be on separate rations or per diem and will provide for their own meals during training. Company B, 2nd Battalion, 1st SWTG (A) will not issue meal cards. Students with meal cards must arrange for separate rations or per diem prior to departing from their parent unit.

Transportation:
All students are responsible for providing their own transportation to and from the Yuma airport via POV, rental car or taxi. Transportation during training will be provided by Company B.

CONTACT INFORMATION:
Company B Headquarters is in Building 305, Yuma Proving Ground (YPG), Arizona.
   DSN: 899-3636/3661;
   COMM: (520) 328-3636/3661.

REFERENCE:
1. US Army Formal Schools Catalog. US Army Publishing Agency. DA PAM 351-4, page 120-121, Table 3-19. 31 October 1995.
2. Thede, James J., TSgt., "Military Free Fall Jumpmaster School." Online. Internet. 16 May 2000. Available: http://members.tripod.com/~thede/mffjm.html.

ADVANCED MILITARY FREE FALL PARACHUTIST (AMFFPC)
REGULATION:
Course No: 2E–F178/011–F66
Title: Advanced Military Free Fall Parachutist
Length: 10 Weeks
Location: U.S. Army John F. Kennedy Spec Warfare Center – SC: 331
Scope: Course effective: 1 Oct 95
Military free fall evaluation jumps using a standard parachute system (e.g. MC–4, MT1–XX, etc), free fall simulator (FFS) training and evaluation, air skills evaluation using nonstandard parachute equipment, and an on the job (OJT) training phase. Upon successful completion of this course the student will be considered an advanced military free fall parachutist.
Prerequisite: Special Operations forces officers, warrant officers, or noncommissioned officers of the Active or Reserve Component military services or selected DOD personnel who are qualified military free fall jumpmasters assigned to a military free fall coded position. Must possess a current high altitude, low opening (HALO) physical examination IAW AR 40–501, chapter 5, paragraph 5–5, within 3 years prior to class date. Must possess a current physiological training card (chamber card AF Form 1274). Must report with complete medical records and chamber card on day of inprocessing.
Special Information: Instructions in AR 40–501, chapter 8, paragraph 8–26c, should be initiated NLT 45 days prior to reporting date. Prerequisite, readmission, or medical waivers from Commander, 1st Special Warfare Training Group (Airborne), must be in hand at inprocessing.
Security Clearance: None

PURPOSE:

The purpose of the Advanced Military Free Fall Parachutist is to train Noncommissioned officers assigned as military free fall parachute instructors to the United States Army John F. Kennedy Special Warfare Center and School, selected SOF, DOD and Foreign Personnel who are qualified in military free fall as Advanced Military Free Fall Parachutists. Personnel from SF Operational units attending the course will return to their units more skilled and competent MFF Jumpers and Jumpmasters.

OVERVIEW:

The primary focus of the course is evaluated jumps using a standard parachute system (e.g., MC-4, MT1-XX, etc.), free fall simulator training and evaluation, air skills evaluation using nonstandard parachute equipment and an on the job training phase.

The course also covers:
- ◆ Advanced Free Fall Skills;
- ◆ Use of Non-Standard Parachute Equipment;
- ◆ Potential New Training (Tandem, MC-5, Etc.).

This is not an MFF Instructor producing course. Upon completion, soldiers are classed as an Instructor Candidate and must complete 3 months of evaluated (OJT) with actual students.

PREREQUISITES:

- ◆ Special Operations Forces Noncommissioned Officers of the Active Component US Army, assigned to the United States Army John F. Kennedy Special Warfare Center and School or assigned to a military free fall coded position who are qualified and current Military Free Fall Jumpmasters;
- ◆ Must be a senior E6 or junior E7 with no more than 12 years of military service;
- ◆ Must posses a current high altitude, low opening (HALO) physical examination IAW AR 40-501, chapter 5, paragraph 5-5, within three years prior to class date;
- ◆ Must possess a current physiological training card (Chamber Card, AF Form 1274). Must report with complete medical records and chamber card on day of inprocessing.

PREPARATIONS:

Instructions in AR 40-501, chapter 8, paragraph 8-26C, should be initiated NLT 45 days prior to reporting date.

Prior to reporting to the AMFFPC, students must ensure that all dental, medical administrative and personnel actions are completed or rescheduled for a future date (after graduation). Company B, 2nd Battalion, 1st SWTG (A) will not release students during the conduct of the course except for an emergency.

Clothing & Equipment Requirements:

Students will bring all uniforms and equipment listed in Advanced Military Free Fall-A During winter classes, students will also bring items listed in Advanced Military Free Fall-B.

Physicals:

Organization/unit surgeons will base their determination of a soldier's medical qualification/disqualification on AR 40-501, Standards of Medical Fitness (1 May 1989), Interim Change No. 101 to AR 40-501 (1 October 1991) and the USAJFKSWCS Memorandum, "Requirements for Completing Physical Examinations for USAJFKSWCS Schools," 1 March 1995.

Graduation:

Company B will extend class dates to achieve course graduation standards if academic requirements are not met because of adverse weather conditions or air scheduling conflicts. Students must stay until the rescheduled graduation dates or return to their parent units without qualification. Students will not make return travel arrangements until actual graduation dates have been set. Students will not graduate early because of unit deployment, follow-on temporary duty/temporary additional duty or travel arrangements locked in prior to the graduation date.

REPORTING INSTRUCTIONS:

Students must report for inprocessing to Company B, Building 305 (conference room) not later than 0645 on the actual class start day. However, students may report two days prior to the class start date if desired. Personnel arriving prior to the class start date will report to the Company B operations office for room assignments. Students should call Company B operations prior to their arrival to confirm their inprocessing schedule and to receive any special instructions.

Students reporting for inprocessing must have their complete medical records (with original HALO physical), a current PANOREX dental X-ray and five copies of orders attaching them to Company B, 2nd Battalion, 1st SWTG (A) for the purpose of attending the AMFFPC. Students who report without their medical records and orders will not enter training. Students will also report with service dictated jump records (i.e. DA 1307, USASOC 1099, AF 922, proof of currency and jumps). U.S. Army students must also bring a copy of DA Form 2A/2-1 or DA Form 2B/2-1.

Inprocessing:
Priority of attendance is USAJFKSWCS military free fall instructors, with slots available

Table: Advanced Military Free Fall-A		
Required Items Inventory		
ITEM	QTY	REMARKS
UDT Shorts	5 pairs	Black PT shorts will accommodate this requirement
Undershirt	5 pairs	Brown
Helmet	1	With goggles and communications (Gentex, Bunny, or motorcycle)
Jump suit	1	Black or flight suit
Gloves	1 pair	Flight or leather
Gloves	1 pair	Gates, If available
Boots	1 pair	Assault - Jungle or Danner
Ruck sack Harness	1	HALO, With attaching straps and lowering line
Knee pads	1 pair	Optional
Ruck sack	1	With Frame
BDU	2 pairs	With appropriate rank, patches and insignia
Cap	1	BDU and beret
Sunglasses	1 pair	
ID Card	1	
ID Tags	1 set	With emergency tag
Chamber Card	1	Current
Oxygen Mask	1	Complete
Emergency Signal Kit	1 set	Shotgun pouch with signal mirror, whistle, 1/4 VS-17 panel, strobe light and compass
STUDENTS MUST ALSO ARRIVE WITH THE FOLLOWING ITEMS		
Current HALO physical (within last two years). Current copy of certified jump record.		

Table: Advanced Military Free Fall-B		
Required Items Inventory Winter		
ITEM	QTY	REMARKS
Undergarments	1 set	Polypropylene, medium and/or lightweight
Sweat suit	1 set	Military issue only, black preferred
Jumpsuit liner	1 set	For HAHO training

to USASFC operational NCOs if course is not filled.

Prerequisite, readmission, or medical waivers from Commander, 1st Special Warfare Training Group (Airborne), must be in hand at inprocessing.

BILLETING:

Company B will assign rooms as students arrive at YPG. No reservations are necessary. Company B will not issue statements of non-availability. Orders to the AMFFPC must state that government quarters are available at YPG for $8 per day.

Dining Facilities:

Government mess facilities are not available. There are commercial eating establishments on YPG within 1/4 mile from billeting. The nearest town is Yuma, which is 25 miles away. Students on separate rations or per diem and will provide for their own meals during training. Company B, 2nd Battalion, 1st SWTG (A) will not issue meal cards. Students with meal cards must arrange for separate rations or per diem prior to departing from their parent unit.

CONTACT INFORMATION:

Company B Headquarters is in Building 305 at Yuma Proving Ground (YPG), Arizona.
   DSN: 899-3636/3661;
   COMM: (520) 328-3636/3661.

REFERENCE:

1. US Army Formal Schools Catalog. US Army Publishing Agency. DA PAM 351-4, page 120-121, Table 3-19. 31 October 1995.
2. Thede, James J., TSgt., "Advanced Military Free Fall School." Online. Internet. 23 May 2000. Available: http://members.tripod.com/~thede/advmff.html.

JUMPMASTER

REGULATION:

Course No: 2E-F60/011-F16
Title: Jumpmaster
Length: 2 Weeks
Location: U.S. Army Infantry School - SC: 071
Scope: Course effective: 1 Jun 88
Jumpmaster a day/night combat equipment jump; demonstrate the proper attaching, jumping, and releasing procedures with an individual weapons and equipment container while participating in an actual jump, attain a passing score on the final written examination at the conclusion of the course; and demonstrate proficiency in the jumpmaster personnel inspection by successfully inspecting two rigged jumpers and one combat-equipped jumper in a 4 minute, 30 second period. (Student must score 70 or higher and miss no major discrepancies.)
Prerequisite: Active Army and Reserve Component officer and enlisted. Must be in grade of sergeant or above. All students must be qualified as a parachutist and have a minimum of 12 static line parachute jumps from USAF aircraft and have been on jump status for 12 months. Must be recommended by battalion commander or officer in the grade of lieutenant colonel.
Special Information: Marine Corps enlisted personnel, sergeant and above, may attend. Corporals may also attend if they are volunteer-qualified military parachutists who have completed at least 15 static line jumps.
Security Clearance: None

PURPOSE:

The Jumpmaster Training Course is the standard US Army course of instruction designed to qualify individuals as jumpmasters for conventional static line parachuting. It is the standard for all airborne unit activities.

OVERVIEW:

The U.S. Army Jumpmaster School trains personnel in the skills necessary to Jumpmaster a combat-equipped jump, the proper attaching, jumping and releasing for combat/individual equipment while participating in an actual jump. Jumpmaster students must demonstrate a high degree of proficiency in the Jumpmaster Personnel Inspection by successfully inspecting three rigged jumpers within 5 minutes (with a score of 70 or higher, missing no major discrepancies). The course is approximately 2 weeks long and contains 97 hours of instruction. Table: Jumpmaster-A outlines the course overview.

PREREQUISITES:

♦ Active Army and Reserve Component Officers and Noncommissioned Officer personnel;
♦ Must be in the grade of SGT, or above;
♦ All students must be qualified and current (jumped within six months or attended jump refresher) paratroopers, have a minimum of 12 static line parachute jumps from USAF high-performance aircraft and have been on jump status for 12 months;
♦ Must be recommended by his Battalion Commander, or Officer in the rank of Lieutenant Colonel;
♦ Officer and enlisted personnel must have a current valid physical examination less than 12 months old;
♦ Applicants must have passed the APFT within 6 months of entry with a minimum score of 180 points (60 points in each event using applicant's age group);
♦ Students must meet the Army height/weight standards;

Table: Jumpmaster- A		
Example Training Overview		
SUBJECT	SCOPE	HOURS
Inprocessing	Administrative in-process of class.	1.5
Orientation and Administration	Orientation on the course requirements that the student must meet to include student handouts, questionnaires, the entire training schedule, and the grading system used to evaluate students.	1
Duties and Responsibilities of the Jumpmaster and Safety	Discussion of the duties and responsibilities of the jumpmaster and safety personnel from the time of notification until completion of the airborne operation.	1
Individual Equipment Containers	Discussion of the characteristics and nomenclature of individual equipment containers to include a demonstration on the correct rigging, attachment, and lowering procedures for the ALICE pack, M1950 weapons case, CWIE, AT4JP, and DMJP.	2.5
Army Aircraft Orientation	Familiarization with the preparation, inspection, and jump procedures for the UH-1H, UH-60A, and CH-47 helicopters.	1.5
Jumpmaster Personnel Inspection	Demonstration of the correct method of inspecting a parachutist and attached combat equipment. Remaining hours are spent on practical exercise using two-man buddy teams, where the student is required to conduct a personnel inspection and find and report major and minor rigging deficiencies that have been placed in parachute assembly and attached equipment. Students are changed over often to ensure all receive the same amount of inspection time.	37
Pre-jump Training	Discussion of the five points of performance and methods of activating the reserve, towed parachutist procedures, collisions, entanglements, and the three types of emergency landings.	1
A-Series Containers	Discussion of the characteristics, capabilities, and methods of packing, rigging, and inspecting the A-series containers, and how to attach and inspect the cargo parachute.	2
Duties and Responsibilities of the DZSO / DZSTL	Discussion of the prerequisites to perform duties as the drop zone support team leader (DZSTL), drop zone safety officer (DZSO), assistant drop zone safety officer (ADZSO). Discussion of tactical DZ assessment and composition of the team for different airdrop scenarios. Scoring procedures using MAC Form 168 are included.	1
Jump Commands, Door Procedures, and Door Bundle Ejection Procedures	Demonstration and practical exercise of the proper sequence of jump commands and time warnings with proper hand-and-arm signals; the door procedures used by a jumpmaster; and door bundle ejection procedures using aircraft mock-ups. Remaining time is spent for practical exercise in the mock-ups (or actual aircraft).	8.5
CARP Drop Zones	Additional discussion includes drop zone surveys (MAC Form 339). Discussion of the methods of marking drop zones for computed air release point (CARP). Discussion of drop zone selection factors. Practical exercise on determining the mean effective wind and use of authorized anemometers. Familiarization with drop zone marking requirements for day and night airborne operations. Discussion of ADEPT options (1,2 and mass exits).	2
Nomenclature Examination	Written nomenclature examination.	0.5
Review and Critique	Brief review of the previous week's instruction to ensure all questions and tasks are clear.	1
Nomenclature Examination Retest	Personnel who failed the initial test are retested.	0.5
Written Examination	Written comprehensive examination which covers all instruction that has been presented.	1

Table: Jumpmaster-A Continued		
Example Training Overview		
SUBJECT	SCOPE	HOURS
Jumpmaster Personnel Inspection Examination	Each student inspects three parachutists-two with no combat equipment and one combat-equipped parachutist (5-minute time limit).	3
Jumpmaster Personnel Inspection Retest	Personnel who failed the initial test are retested.	2
Prejump Training Examination	Oral presentation by each student to determine his ability to effectively conduct prejump training.	6
Jumpmaster Briefing	A briefing on all airborne operations and grading procedures.	1
Aircraft Inspection Class	Practical exercise on aircraft inspection procedures using the C-130 or C-141.	1
Written Examination Retest	Personnel who fail the initial test are retested.	1
Day Practical Work in Aircraft Examination	Graded practical exercise jumpmastering personnel with attached equipment. One-half of students are graded while other one-half act as a jumper. A second lift is required to test the second one-half of class.	14
Maintenance of Air Items	Inspection, maintenance, and turn-in of all air items used during the airborne operations.	1
Out-processing	Administrative out-processing the class.	2
Graduation		1

♦ USMC enlisted personnel (CPL and above) may volunteer to attend this course if they are qualified military paratroopers who have completed at least 15 static line jumps from high-performance aircraft (USAF or USMC).

Waivers:

The submission of requests for waiver is discouraged; course prerequisites have specific rationale and are well established. However service members may request the waiver of a specific course prerequisite. Those waiver requests will be submitted in memorandum format through the member's Battalion Commander (or, first O5 in the chain of command), through:

Commander
11th Infantry Regiment, USAIS
Fort Benning, GA 31905;

to

Commander
1st Battalion (Airborne), 507th Infantry
11th Infantry Regiment
Fort Benning, GA 31905.

All requests for waiver will address a specific prerequisite and contain a complete justification and persuasive argument for granting the waiver. Waiver request submission does not ensure favorable consideration.

REPORTING INFORMATION:

All commanders must ensure applicants report to and sign in at Building 2748 (Student Accountability) on the report date (Sunday).

Students must report with the following items:
♦ Medical examination (Standard Form 88);
♦ DA Form 705 (APFT Scorecard);
♦ Individual DA Form 1307 (Jump Record), must be closed out by their unit;
♦ Identification tags;
♦ Identification cards;
♦ 10 copies of orders;
♦ Individual 2-1.

Inprocessing:

Student inprocessing begins at 0600 Monday morning.

CONTACT INFORMATION:

For more information, contact the US Army Jumpmaster School NCOIC:

HHC 1/507
ATTN: Jumpmaster Branch
Ft. Benning, GA 31905;
DSN: 835-3885;
COMM: (706) 545-4923.

REFERENCE:

1. US Army Formal Schools Catalog. US Army Publishing Agency. DA PAM 351-4, page 45, Table 3-6. 31 October 1995.

2. Static Line Parachuting Techniques and Training. US Army Publishing Agency. FM 57-220, Appendix B. 19 August 1996. Online. General Dennis J. Reimer Training and Doctrine Digital Library. Internet. 29 May 2000. Available: http://155.217.58.58/cgi-bin/atdl.dll/fm/57-220/Appb.htm.

3. "1st BN (Airborne), 507th Infantry." Online. Internet. 29 May 2000. Available: http://www-benning.army.mil/airborne/Jumpmaster/Main.html.

4. "Jumpmaster Admin." Online. Internet. 29 May 2000. Available: http://www-benning.army.mil/airborne/Jumpmaster/Admin.html.

LRSLC

LONG RANGE SURVEILLANCE LEADERS COURSE

REGULATION:

Course No: 2E–F173/011–F67
Title: Long Range Surveillance Leader
Length: 4 Weeks, 5 Days
Location: U.S. Army Infantry School – SC: 071
Scope: Course effective: 1 Oct 95
Command and control, reconnaissance and surveillance operations, field training exercises, threat subjects, land navigation; physical training; communication/electronics, airborne/airmobile operations.
Prerequisite: Active Army male, volunteer, officer or enlisted personnel in CMF's 11B, 96B, 31U, 19D, and all 18 series MOS in grade E–3 through E–7 assigned to or on orders for assignment to a Long–Range Surveillance Company or Detachment in the position of Company or Detachment Commander, Operations Officer, Executive Officer, Surveillance Platoon Leader, First Sergeant or Detachment Sergeant, Platoon Sergeant, Surveillance Team Leader, or Assistant Team Leader, Intelligence FNCO, and other Army personnel involved in Intelligence, Special Forces selected personnel, or must be selected communications Commissioned or Noncommissioned Officer assigned to the Communications Platoon or Section. Must be Airborne qualified. PULHES 111111. Must have 9 month's retainability upon completion of the Long–Range Surveillance Leader Course. Must have a complete physical within 18 months of attendance. Personnel over 40 will be cleared for physical training prior to attending. Record of physical must be brought by the individual when he reports for training. Individual must bring his health and dental records. Dental records must include a full mouth X–Ray (PANOREX). If unit is unable to provide dental records with PANOREX, the unit must provide a letter signed by the Commander verifying that a PANOREX exists at home station and can be made available by sending unit if required. Must have a good performance record with no history of drug or alcohol abuse. Must be Ranger or Special Forces (SF) qualified. SF qualification means those personnel who have received SF training but may not have worked in or been awarded MOS 18. Applicant not SF or Ranger qualified must submit a waiver to the applicant's First Commander (LTC) in his chain of command. This waiver will accompany the student when reporting for training. During inprocessing, all applicants must: a. Pass the Army Physical Fitness Test (APFT) in accordance with FM 21–20; b. Pass land navigation written examination and practical exercise; c. Pass the Combat Water Survival Test (CWST) consisting of three stations: (1) The 15 meter swim—swim 15 meters with rifle, wearing fatigues, boots, and LCE equipment (pistol belt, suspenders, two ammunition pouches, and two full canteens), without the loss of rifle or equipment and without showing unusual signs of fear or panic. (2) Equipment removal—enter from poolside, submerge to a depth of 3 meters, discard weapon and LCE equipment (as above), surface, and swim to poolside without showing unusual signs of fear or panic. (3) The 3 meter drop—walk blindfolded off a 3 meter diving board with weapon and LCE equipment. After entering water, remove blindfold and swim to poolside without loss of equipment or weapon and without showing unusual signs of fear or panic.
Special Information: Applies to those personnel attending the course in support of the Long–Range Surveillance Unit Operations/Training. Must be assigned to or operating in direct support of a Long–Range Surveillance Company/Detachment in a position of Communications Officer, G2 representative, Intelligence Officer, or Communications Base Station Operator. Other Prerequisites as outlined above apply. All students are provided Government rations and quarters during all training. All TDY orders are to reflect that Per Diem or separate rations are not authorized while attending LRSLC. Prior to soldier's attending in a TDY and return status, the parent unit commander will prepare and submit a DA Form 4187 (Personnel Action) stopping the soldier's basic allowance for subsistence (BAS). Soldier will be issued a temporary meal card in accordance with AR 600–38, Paragraphs 3–7, 4–3, and 4–4. Upon completion of the course, the parent unit commander will ensure that the soldier's BAS is reinstated and the meal card is turned in. Students attending in TDY enroute will have their BAS stopped on the effective date of their class and will be issued a temporary meal card by the Ranger Training Brigade. Failing to meet the prerequisites may result in non–enrollment.
Security Clearance: None

FORWARD:

Unit and individual Ranger/LRRP actions have contributed many courageous and daring exploits to the pages of American history. The story is a recurring one, depicting outstanding leadership coupled with the highest applications of the skills used in the art of combat, reconnaissance, surveillance, and communications.

Throughout the 20th century, LRRP units have been formed when needed and have accomplished their purpose with great credit. The American Long Range Surveillance Leaders Course (LRSLC) member will build on the tradition and experience of Rangers and Special Forces of the past and present.

The LRSLC is taught using the most current doctrine. Additionally, emphasis is placed on developing military skills in the planning and conduct of dismounted patrolling, airborne, air assault, and special insertion/extraction operations.

The LRSLC affords the leader the opportunity, by practical application, to develop and improve himself in a rugged course of instruction. It is stress oriented and develops within the LRSLC student the ability to lead and command under heavy mental and physical pressure. The emphasis is on practical, realistic, and strenuous field exercises using the 6 man team as the training vehicle to accomplish this development. The LRSLC is not a mini Ranger Course, but is dedicated to the specific needs of the LRSU leader.

PURPOSE:

The LRSLC develops the technical, tactical, and leadership skills of selected officer and enlisted personnel assigned to LRS, SF and heavy/light division scout and reconnaissance platoons by requiring them to perform specific hands-on tasks to standard, as well as several written examinations to test comprehension. The LRSLC student performs as a team member in a realistic tactical environment under mental and physical stress, approaching that found in combat. It provides the student the opportunity to refine his leadership and tactical skills to a high degree

of proficiency so that he may return to his unit and train his team members.

OVERVIEW:

The active component LRSLC is 33 days in length with an average of 16 hours of training each day, 7 days a week. It is divided into major instructional blocks consisting of communications, intelligence, vehicle identification, survival, and operational techniques (planning, E & R, hide/surveillance, photo imagery, airborne, air assault and special insertion/extraction operations).

The class is referred to as a detachment, consisting of up to 6 teams. The Surveillance Team is the basic unit for instruction.

The instruction is prepared by LRSLC instructors from company D, 4th Ranger Training Battalion. The emphasis is placed on developing the ability of each student to train his soldiers in reconnaissance and surveillance skills and to meet the rigid performance standards of Long Range Surveillance Units.

During the first 21 days, heavy emphasis is placed on the "bread and butter" of the mission: physical training, intelligence, HF communications, planning, patrolling, operational techniques and SERE. During the next 11 days the students are instructed and evaluated on a student-led, non-graded field training exercise and a graded field training exercise.

The Reserve/National Guard LRSLC is accomplished in two phases. Phase I consists of the LRSLC Correspondence Course which can be executed in 6 drill periods conducted at home station. It consists of blocks of training in command and control, intelligence, planning, HF communications, infiltration and exfiltration, SERE, advanced land navigation and a comprehensive examination. Reserve Component students should complete adequate preparatory training in day and night land navigation. Phase II consists of the 15 day resident course. Proof of completion of the LRSLC Correspondence Course is required upon inprocessing.

Example Training Outline - LRSLC	
	DAY 1
	Inprocessing
	APFT / CWST
	Land Navigation (Written)
	Land Navigation (PE)
H	**DAY 2**
F	Intro to LRS OPS
	Land Navigation (Written) Retest
C	**DAY 3**
O	PT (3 Mile Standard Run)
M	**DAY 4**
M	PT (4 Mile Standard Run)
O	**DAY 5**
	Commo Exam
	Airborne Operations - UH-60, TOT: 1600
T	**DAY 6**
H	Commo retest
R	Vehicle ID
E	Land Navigation (PE) Retest
A	**DAY 7**
T	No Training Scheduled
	DAY 8
V	PT (Ruck C/C)
E	**DAY 9**
H	PT (5 Mile Standard Run)
I	**DAY 10**
C	PT (Circuit)
L	Threat Vehicle Exam
E	G2 / OOTW / TACIEW
	DAY 11
	PT (4 Mile Stretcher Run)
I	OPFOR Heavy
N	ERO / IPB
T	Mission Packet
E	**DAY 12**
L	INTEL Exam
	Threat Vehicle Retest
	COMMEX
	DAY 13
	Photo / Recon Sketching

Example Training Outline - LRSLC Continued	
	DAY 14
O	R&S / Hide
P	Classroom, PE, Tactical PE
E	**DAY 15**
R	PT (3 Mile LMU)
A	FRIES / SPIES
T	E&R / DARS
I	Track / Counter
O	**DAY 16**
N	PT (Ruck C/C)
A	JRTC, Lessons Learned
L TECHNIQUES	Battle Drills (PE)
	DAY 17
	PT (LRS Olympics)
	Planning
	Infiltration / Exfiltration
	Warning Order
F	**DAY 18**
T	Planning
X	**DAY 19**
	Planning
N	**DAY 20**
O	Planning
N	FRIES Insertion
	DAY 21
G	Surveillance
R	E&R
A	**DAY 22**
D	E&R
E	Survival
D	Exfiltration / Debrief
	DAY 23
	CACHE Class
	DAY 24
	Survival Techniques
	Warning Order

Example Training Outline - LRSC Continued	
	DAY 25
	Planning
	DAY 26
	Planning
	DAY 27
F	Insertion - C-130, Elizabeth DZ
T	Move to NAI
X	**DAY 28**
	Surveillance on NAI
G	**DAY 29**
R	Surveillance on NAI
A	Move to TAI
D	**DAY 30**
E	Target Acquisition
D	BDA
	Move to DAR
	DAY 31
	E&R
	CACHE Recovery
	DAY 32
	Exfiltration / Debrief
	Redeploy - C-130
	DAY 33
	Outprocess & Critiques
	Graduation (1300)

PREREQUISITES:

♦ Enlisted applicants must be E5 or above. This is waiverable by the unit by the first O5 in the unit chain of command. Approved waivers must accompany application for quotas to LRSLC;

♦ Individuals assigned to or on orders to a LRS unit, a SF A or B Team, or a heavy/light division scout or reconnaissance platoon;

♦ All individuals to include Reserve/National Guard Component must possess a routine medical examination dated within 12 months of their reporting date. Physical examinations must be signed by a medical doctor (not a PA). Medical records must accompany the student and be complete with all results from lab work that pertain to the physical to include a current HIV test and a sickle cell test. Medical Records must include a document stating that a current PANOREX is on file. Physical category must be PULHES 111111. Exception will be granted for a 2 in eyesight. Personnel with profiles prohibiting them from any Physical training or parachute operations will not be enrolled in the course. Personnel over 40 years of age will be cleared for unit physical training by medical personnel (over 40 physical) before attendance;

♦ Applicants must take the Army Physical Fitness Test (APFT) and Combat Water Survival Test (CWST) within 30 days of application. The APFT and CWST are administered the first day of the LRSLC. Failure to pass either test will result in the soldier being dropped from the course. The CWST is tested on a PASS/FAIL basis. Strong, weak, or non-swimmer categories are not recognized. Students must also possess a strong knowledge of land navigation; both day and night;

♦ Students must be airborne qualified. This is waiverable by the first O5 in the soldier's chain of command, and must be presented at enrollment;

♦ Students must be Ranger or Special Forces qualified (active duty only). This is waiverable by the first O5 in the soldier's chain of command, and must be presented at enrollment;

♦ A soldier must pass a basic map reading examination and a land navigation practical exercise on day 1 of the LRSLC. The course does not teach land navigation;

♦ A soldier must have 9 months retainability upon graduation from LRSLC;

♦ Reserve/National Guard personnel are required to complete the LRSLC Correspondence Course (Paragraph 2-142, DA PAM 351-20) and provide certification of completion prior to attending the resident phase;

♦ The soldier must have a record of good duty performance with no history of alcohol or drug abuse;

♦ Must have at least an interim SECRET security clearance.

UNIFORM:

Uniform for physical training is Army issued gray, t-shirt, trunks, all white socks and running shoes. USMC, Navy personnel will wear their service issued physical training uniform. Army issued sweats will be worn during the winter months.

EVALUATIONS:

Task, Conditions and Standards are covered prior to each graded exercise. Combat Critical Tasks are those tasks that the student must pass prior to graduation. Students will receive a brief during inprocessing.

Students must successfully complete the following to standard:

♦ Pass the Physical Fitness Test;

♦ Pass the Combat Water Survival Test;

♦ Pass Land Navigation (written and PE);

♦ Achieve 70% on each examination;

♦ Cannot miss more than 72 hours (Active Component) or 24 hours "Reserve Component" of training due to injury or illness;

♦ Pass 50% of all graded patrols.

Spot reports are an integral part of the LRSLC. They are used as a management tool similar to the Ranger course. Major and minor (plus and minus) spot reports are used. Three major minus spot reports and a student is dropped from the course.

PERSONAL CONDUCT & APPEARANCE STANDARDS:

The honor code is in effect in the LRSLC. Students neither lie, cheat, or steal, nor do they tolerate those who do. Any student who violates the honor code will be given a Special Observation Report (SOR) and be released from the course. This includes comparing notes/answer sheets during the land navigation PE or any other test.

Distinguished Honor Graduate:

The officer or enlisted soldier who distinguishes himself by attaining 90% or above on all graded exercises, receives a first time "GO" on all requirements and passes 50% of his graded patrols. In the event of a tie, the student whose performance is better on patrols as well as his performance on quizzes given periodically will be the distinguished honor graduate.

A Ranger Training Battalion Certificate of Achievement will also he given to the student who scores the highest on the APFT. Additionally, a land navigation award is given to the student who scores the highest on all 3 land navigation events: the written examination, day/ night land navigation PE.

PREPARATIONS:

All applicants planning to attend the LRSLC should be briefed by an NCO or officer who has recently attended the LRSLC prior to making an application.

All commanders must ensure that applicants are in top physical condition when reporting to the LRSLC. Applicants should work on improving upper body strength, foot marching in properly fitted boots with a full ruck sack (50 lb.) for distances up to 15 miles, run 5 miles in 40 minutes, and swimming. Height and weight must be IAW AR 600-9.

The APFT is conducted IAW FM 21-20. U.S. Army APFT Standard will be enforced for each event (pushups, situps, 2 mile run). Students must meet these standards for attendance to the LRSLC. 6 pullups will be administered after the 2 mile run to determine upper body strength before fast-rope operations. Note: pullups are not a graded event. (Uniform for the APFT will be BDUs with running shoes).

The CWST consists of 3 events:

♦ 15 Meter Swim: Swim 15 meters with rifle, wearing fatigues, boots, and LCE (pistol belt, suspenders, 2 ammunition pouches, 2 full canteens), without loss of rifle or equipment and without showing unusual signs of panic or fear;

♦ Equipment Removal: Enter the water from the poolside. Submerge and remain underwater while discarding the rifle and LCE, surface and swim to poolside without loss of equipment or showing unusual signs of fear or panic;

♦ 3 Meter Drop: Walk blindfolded off a 3 meter diving board with rifle and LCE; after entering the water, remove blindfold and swim to the poolside without loss of equipment or showing unusual signs of fear or panic.

Clothing & Equipment Requirements:
Table LRS-A lists the required items inventory for the LRSLC.

Applications:
Officer and noncommissioned officers may apply by submitting a DA Form 4187 through their units. LRSLC allocations are managed at Department of the Army through the Army Training Requirements Resource System (ATRRS).

REPORTING INFORMATION:
All incoming students must report to the LRSLC classroom, Rabel Hall, Building 5008B, Camp Rogers, in the Harmony Church area of Ft. Benning.

Inprocessing:
Inprocessing begins at 0600 hours on day one of the course. Incoming personnel will have in their possession at the time of inprocessing: health records with physical and dental records with current dental panorex or a memorandum for record (MFR) signed by unit CDR/1SG stating that individual has a current dental panorex on file (MFR preferred). 10 copies of their orders. TDY orders will specify the student's hazardous duty authorization.

BILLETING:
Quarters:
Students will be billeted in Building 5016A. Students are encouraged to arrive at Ft. Benning on the day prior (Sunday) to the start of the course. Personnel stationed at Ft. Benning may reside in their local quarters, however, this is discouraged. Once enrolled, all students are required to maintain a room in the LRSLC barracks.

Students on TDY at Ft. Benning to attend only the LRSLC are encouraged not to bring family members.

Because of the limited off duty time available, students are cautioned to bring only a minimum amount of civilian clothing.

LRSLC student billets are arranged in a uniform manner; cleanliness and security, of government and personal property are primary concerns. The student chain of command is responsible for ensuring the billets are ready for inspection at all times.

Dinning Facilities:
All students eat in the Ranger Training Battalion dining facility while in garrison. During field training a Hot-A or MRE is Provided.

While attending the LRSLC, a 4th Ranger Training Battalion meal card will be issued to you. This meal card will be used in the 4th RTBn Dining Facility.

Mail:
The following is the correct mailing address for the LRSLC:
    Rank/Name
    Co D, 4th RTBn (LRSLC)
    Class_____
    Fort Benning, GA 31905.

Laundry Facilities:
A limited number of washers, dryers and hand washing facilities are available in Building 5016A (Student Barracks). Commercial laundries may also be used during off duty time.

Table: LRS-A		
Required Items Inventory		
ITEM	QTY	REMARKS
Uniform	1	Class A
PT Uniform (PFU)	2 pairs	Army, gray (summer)
PT Uniform (PFU)	2 pairs	Army, gray (winter)
Socks	4 pairs	White, athletic, crew length
BDUs	4-6 sets	Must have all authorized patches and no sterile uniforms will be worn; 4 sets of BDUs minimum, 6 sets recommended
Boots	2 pairs	Combat or Jungle boots will be broken in prior attending LRSLC; insulated boots are authorized for wear during the winter season(1October -30 April); waffle sole boots are unauthorized; students must have 1-pair of boots w/Panama sole for fast roping
Socks	6 pairs	Cushion sole
Undershirt	6	Brown
Undershirt	2 pairs	Wool or polypropylene (winter season)
Cap	2	BDU, with "cat eyes" sewn on the rear and subdued rank insignia (officers included)
Belt	2	Black, with buckle
Glove	1 pair	Black, leather, shell (subdued gortex gloves are authorized for wear during the winter season)
Glove	2 pairs	Inserts
Field Jacket	1	Gortex Parka (winter and summer)
Notebooks	1 or more	Pocket size; it is recommended that students bring a small hard covered notebook to use in taking notes throughout the course
Pens/Pencils		Both will be necessary
Weapons cleaning kit	1	Has to include: CLP, 4 cleaning rods, bore brush, patches, and Q-tips, etc.
550 cord	1	100 feet
Bag	1	Duffel, with lock
Locks	2	Combination
Eyeglasses	2 pairs	Military issue, contact lenses are not authorized
Cap	1	Watch, black (winter only)
Wristwatch	1	
Knife	1	Hunting or pocket, folding (blade can not exceed 4 inch)
Sharpening stone	1	
Waterproof bags	5	Plastic (1 gallon Ziploc)
Map case	1	
Sewing kit	1	
Tape	1 roll	OD, Duct or 100 mph
Protractor	2	Plastic
Flashlight	1	Extra batteries with red lens filter
Survival equipment	1	Example: fish hooks, line, candles, fire starting items, small magnifying glass, etc.
Markers	1	Alcohol, with assorted colors
Terrain model kit	1	
Calculator	1	For communications training
LCE	1	Complete: with pistol belt, suspenders, 2 ammo pouches, 2 one quart canteens with covers, 1 canteen cup, first aid pouch with dressing, compass with pouch; butt pack is optional
Entrenching tool	1	E-tool, with cover
Canteen	2	2 quart, with cover and GP strap
USMC / NAVY personnel will wear their service issued physical training uniform.		

Table: LRS-A (Continued)		
Rain parka / trousers	1 set	Gortex authorized
Alice Pack	1	Large, with frame
Sleeping bag	1	1 Oct- 30 Apr
Insulated pad	1	Optional (air mattress)
Bag	1	Waterproof
Bag	1	Duffel
Kevlar helment	1	Airborne configuration, with name on cammo band
Bag	1	Barracks
Gloves	1 pair	Work
Shirt	1	Sleeping
Camouflage stick	1	
Insect Repellent	1	
Magazine	7	30 round
Blank adapter	1	For M4 carbine
Sling rope	1	12 feet, with snaplink
Ghilley suite	1	Recommended
Air Items	1	Single point release
Construction material	1	Hide and Surveillance (i.e., folding saw, pruning shears, etc. are optional)
USMC / NAVY personnel will wear their service issued physical training uniform.		

Pressed BDUs are not worn during the LRSLC, therefore there is no need for commercial washing and pressing. BDUs are generally washed and dried with the rest of the student's laundry.

Telephone Service:

Pay telephones are available at the 4th Ranger Training Battalion area. Telephone service is available through Company D (LRSLC) for emergency use only.

The emergency telephone number during duty, hours is:

DSN: 784-6047/6831;
COMM: (706) 544-6047/6831.

During non-duty hours the Brigade SDNCO number is:

DSN: 784-6768/6781;
COMM: (706) 544-6768/6781.

Pay:

The student's parent unit finance office administers all financial matters to include monthly, travel and per diem pay. Only emergencies will be handled by Ft. Benning.

Money:

Students should bring sufficient funds to defray initial expenses for food, laundry and incidentals.

The purchase of travelers checks prior to arrival at Ft. Benning is recommended. Personal check cashing is available at Ft. Benning but is limited.

Normal expenditures for officer students drawing per diem is approximately $200.00 for the course, $125.00 for officers not on per diem and $40.00 for enlisted.

Company D does not provide a safe for valuables.

Cash collection of statement of charges is used to pay for any government equipment lost or damaged by students prior to graduation.

POV:

There is a parking lot with lights in the 4th Ranger Training Battalion area where students may park their POV for the duration of the course. Vehicles may be used during off duty hours. Students will receive further instructions regarding POVs during inprocessing.

CONTACT INFORMATION:
Questions concerning the LRSLC should be directed to:

Commander
Co D, 4th RTBn
ATTN: LRSLC
Fort Benning, GA 31905;

COMM: (706) 544 6831/6216;
DSN: 784-6831/6216;
FAX: 784-6082.

REFERENCE:

1. US Army Formal Schools Catalog. US Army Publishing Agency. DA PAM 351-4, page 44-45, Table 3-6. 31 October 1995.
2. Long Range Surveillance Leaders Course. SH 21-75-6. September 1998. Online. Internet. 18 May 2000. Available: http://www-benning.army.mil/RTB/LRRS/SHPT1.htm.
3. Rose, Charlie. "Our Heritage," The History Channel. Online. Internet. 18 May 2000. Available: http://www.lrrp.com/history.htm.
4. "Long Range Surveillance Leaders Course (LRSLC) Home Page." Online. Internet. 18 May 2000. Available: http://www-benning.army.mil/RTB/RTBWEB/LRSLC.htm.
5. "Ranger Training Brigade Phone Roster." Online. Internet. 18 May 2000. Available: http://www-benning.army.mil/rtb/PHONE.htm.

NOTES

O.C.S.

OFFICER CANDIDATE SCHOOL

REGULATION:

Course No: 2-7-F1
Title: Officer Candidate School
Length: 14 Weeks
Location: U.S. Army Infantry School - SC: 071
Scope: Course effective: 1 Oct 91
Combined arms tactics (tactical doctrine, airborne/airmobile operations, artillery operations, engineer operations, NBC operations, Air Force operations, field training exercises, and patrolling); staff subjects (personnel, intelligence, operations, logistics, and training management); general subjects (military leadership, effective writing, land navigation, legal subjects, medical subjects, physical training, drill and command, military history, and special presentations); communications/electronics; weapons.
Prerequisite: Army officer candidate must meet the requirements specified in AR 351-5. National Guard officer candidate must meet requirements specified in appropriate State National Guard regulations. Army Reserve officer candidate must meet requirements specified in AR 140-50.
Security Clearance: SECRET

HISTORY:

The idea for the modern Officer Candidate School for Infantry was conceived in June 1938, when a plan for an officer-training program was submitted to the Chief of Infantry by Brigadier General L. Singleton, Commandant of the Infantry School, Fort Benning, Georgia. No action was taken until July 1940, when Brigadier General Courtney Hodges, Assistant Commandant of the Infantry School, submitted a revised plan. The new program went into effect in July 1941, as the Infantry, Field Artillery, and Coastal Artillery Officer Candidate Schools. Other branches later followed with their own Officers Candidate Schools. On September 27, 1941, the first Infantry OCS class graduated 171 second lieutenants out of the 204 men who started the 17 week course.

The man credited with establishing the format, discipline, and code of honor still used in OCS today was General Omar Bradley, then Commandant of the Infantry School. As the Commandant of the Infantry School, General Bradley emphasized rigorous training, strict discipline and efficient organization. These tenets remain the base values of today's Officer Candidate School.

Between July 1941 and May 1947, over 100,000 candidates were enrolled in 448 Infantry OCS classes, of these approximately 67 percent were commissioned. After World War II, Infantry OCS was transferred to Fort Riley, Kansas, as part of the Ground General School. All other Officer Candidate Schools were discontinued.

On November 1, 1947, the Infantry OCS program was discontinued. The final class graduated only 52 second lieutenants.

A shortage of officers during the Korean conflict caused Infantry OCS to reopen at Fort Benning on February 18, 1951. At this time, the course was lengthened from 17 to 22 weeks. The name was changed from The Infantry Officer Candidate School to the First Officer Candidate Battalion, Second Student Regiment. The strength of OCS increased rapidly. As one of eight branch programs, Infantry OCS included as many as 29 companies with a class graduating every week. During the Korean War, approximately 7,000 infantry officers graduated from OCS at Fort Benning.

On August 4, 1953, OCS was reduced from eight to three programs: Infantry, Artillery, and Engineer.

Shortly before the onset of the Vietnam Conflict OCS had been reduced to two programs, Infantry and Field Artillery. During the height of the Vietnam Conflict, Infantry OCS was one of five programs and produced 7,000 officers annually from five battalions at Fort Benning. Towards the end of the conflict OCS reduced to two programs, Infantry and Female OCS. Infantry OCS was reduced to two battalions and presently maintains one battalion.

In April 1973, a Branch Immaterial Officer Candidate School was created to replace the branch specific courses and the length of the course was reduced to 14 weeks. OCS for female officer candidates remained at Fort McClellan, Alabama until December 1976, when it merged with the branch immaterial OCS program at Fort Benning, Georgia.

Today's officer candidates enter the school from throughout the force. OCS continues to provide commissioned officers to the total force for all sixteen basic branches of the Army.

On June 12, 1998 to further integrate the Army, the Army National Guard OCS Phase III candidates began training alongside their active duty counterparts at Fort Benning. Officer Candidates from the National Guard and Army Reserve conduct the final phase of training before commissioning during their 2 week annual training period. Over 650 future officers were trained for the Army in the first year, with similar numbers being trained in subsequent years.

The mission of OCS remains to train selected personnel in the fundamentals of leadership and basic military skills, instill professional ethics, evaluate leadership potential and commission those who qualify as second lieutenants in all sixteen basic branches of the Army.

PURPOSE:

The purpose of the school is to evaluate a soldier's leadership potential and determine if he/she has the qualities, traits and attributes to be a quality officer in the U.S. Army.

The focus of Officer Candidate School is to keep the OCS graduate competitive through company grade.

Objectives of OCS:

The objectives of the OCS program are to:

♦ Develop the leadership ability and professional skills of candidates to prepare them for appointment as second lieutenants in the USAR, and for effective service as commissioned officers in the Active Army;

♦ Serve as a basis for expansion of officer candidate training if mobilization occurs.

OVERVIEW:

Instruction:

Each candidate receives his/her "basic soldiering" instruction from the United States Army Infantry School through classroom instruction and practical application. The basic soldiering topics include leadership, tactics, squad drill, intelligence, land navigation, maintenance and communications. Each candidate must maintain an academic average of 70% or higher. Failure to maintain academic proficiency can result in separation from the class.

Leadership Development:

Leadership development takes place in a rigorous and demanding atmosphere. Each officer candidate learns how to be an officer through the fundamentals of leadership, practical leadership applications and performance evaluations. TACs assess and evaluate how candidates apply Troop Leading Procedures in their leadership positions. Some highlighted leadership opportunities are:

♦ Student chain of command positions in the field and garrison environments;

♦ Road march/obstacle course leader positions;

♦ The Leadership Reaction Course (LRC);

♦ Instruction of physical training, drill and ceremonies and other subjects;

♦ Additional administrative duties such as student company supply officer;

♦ Dining Facility leaders;

♦ Project Officers for Dining In, Graduation Formal and Senior Status Review.

The TACs evaluate and counsel each candidate on his/her performance in a leadership position based on close, daily observation. TACs conduct counseling sessions, address the candidates proficiencies/deficiencies and make recommendations for improvement. In addition, each candidate evaluates his/her peers throughout the course and submits those evaluations to the TACs. Four separate peer evaluations take place during OCS.

Course Overview:
The following is only an outline and may not exactly reflect the training events in sequence.
- BOC = Basic Officer Candidate;
- IOC = Intermediate Officer Candidate;
- SOC = Senior Officer Candidate.

Week One:
BOC Phase:
- Total control - LOCK DOWN. This will remain in effect for four weeks;
- Inprocessing;
- Issue of company items; linen, map case, road guard vest, flashlight, etc.;
- CIF Issue - TA-50;
- Initial APFT;
- Strenuous physical conditioning;
- Initial OCS related protocol and procedural class.

Week Two:
BOC Phase:
- Total control - LOCK DOWN;
- Strenuous PT - ability groups for running are determined from initial APFT run times;
- Candidates begin to lead morning PT;
- Groups are marched to Clothing and Sales to purchase any last required items;
- Initial OCS related protocol and procedural class;
- Obstacle and Confidence courses;
- LRC Leader's Reaction Course;
- Road March #1 (5 mile) - 20 minutes per mile pace or faster;
- Classroom instruction for a week from the Ft. Benning Land Navigation committee;
- Work on room displays and execute company details.

The Three Phases of Officer Candidate School		
Basic Phase Weeks 1-4	Intermediate Phase Weeks Weeks 5-10	Senior Phase Weeks Weeks 11-14
Professional Ethics Soldier Team Development Technical Proficiency Communications Supervision	Soldier Team Development Planning Supervision Communications Tactical Proficiency Use of available systems	Decision Making Professional Teaching/Counseling Planning Supervision Communications
Training Focuses on basic military skills IAW STP 21-1-OFS (MQS) (precommissioning) and is conducted within a tactical and technical training with leadership development designed to produce a candidate ready for intermediate phase.	During this phase candidates are given the opportunity to perfect the skills learned in the basic phase and concentrate on subjects dealing with tactics, patrolling, NBC, and weapons, while further attempting to develop their individual leadership skills.	Candidates contiune to receive academic instruction in areas such as ethics, military justice, logistics and personnel administration. They are expected to show consistent improvement in their leadership skills. Passage to senior phase does not guarantee commissioning. In the last phase, candidates should conduct themselves as officers and receive the same courtesies as officers from basic and intermediate candidates. Senior candidates who are selected will act as mentors to the basic candidates.

Week Three:
BOC Phase:
- ◆ Total control - LOCK DOWN;
- ◆ Strenuous PT - ability groups runs, PU/SU improvement;
- ◆ Candidates lead morning PT;
- ◆ Pre Land Navigation instruction and bivouac is continued by OCS cadre at Kilbourne Range;
- ◆ Road March #2 (5 mile) - 18 minutes per mile pace or faster;
- ◆ Maintain room displays to standard and execute company details.

Week Four:
BOC Phase:
- ◆ Total control - LOCK DOWN;
- ◆ Field PT - conditional stretching, PU/SU improvement;
- ◆ Candidates lead morning PT;
- ◆ FLX 1 (LAND NAV) Yankee Land Navigation Site, Day & Night Land Navigation;
- ◆ Bivouac site established for six days:
- ◆ Field instruction all week from the Ft. Benning Land Navigation committee;
- ◆ Company Commander's inspection upon return from land navigation to enter IOC phase.

Week Five:
IOC Phase:
- ◆ Total control is relaxed and weekend passes are granted on occasion;
- ◆ Strenuous PT - ability groups runs, PU/SU improvement;
- ◆ Candidates lead morning PT;
- ◆ Intense classroom instruction 0830-1700 for entire IOC phase;
- ◆ Maintain room displays IAW OCSSOP standards and execute company details.

Week Six:
IOC Phase:
- ◆ Total control is relaxed and weekend passes are granted on occasion;

- ◆ Strenuous PT - ability groups runs, PU/SU improvement;
- ◆ Candidates lead morning PT;
- ◆ Intense classroom instruction 0830-1700 for entire IOC phase;
- ◆ Road March #3 (5 mile) - 16 minutes per mile pace or faster;
- ◆ Maintain room displays IAW OCSSOP standards and execute company details.

Week Seven:
IOC Phase:
- ◆ Total control is relaxed and weekend passes are granted on occasion;
- ◆ Strenuous PT - ability groups runs, PU/SU improvement;
- ◆ Candidates lead morning PT;
- ◆ Intense classroom instruction 0830-1700 for entire IOC phase;
- ◆ Maintain room displays IAW OCSSOP standards and execute company details.

Week Eight:
IOC Phase:
- ◆ Total control is relaxed and weekend passes are granted on occasion;
- ◆ Strenuous PT - ability groups runs, PU/SU improvement;
- ◆ Candidates lead morning PT;
- ◆ Intense classroom instruction 0830-1700 for entire IOC phase;
- ◆ Road March #4 (7 mile) - 15 minutes per mile pace or faster;
- ◆ Maintain room displays IAW OCSSOP standards and execute company details.

Week Nine:
IOC Phase
- ◆ Total control is relaxed and weekend passes are granted on occasion;
- ◆ Strenuous PT - ability groups runs, PU/SU improvement;
- ◆ Candidates lead morning PT, mid-cycle APFT;
- ◆ Intense classroom instruction 0830-1700 for entire IOC phase;

♦ Road March #5 (10 mile) - 18 minutes per mile pace or faster;

♦ Maintain room displays IAW OCSSOP standards and execute company details.

Week Ten:
IOC Phase:

♦ Total control is relaxed and weekend passes are granted on occasion;

♦ Light PT - conditional stretching, PU/SU improvement;

♦ Candidates lead morning PT;

♦ FLX 2 (STRAC) Squad Tactical Reaction Assessment Course at Garnsey Range;

♦ Road March #6 (12 mile) - 18 minutes per mile pace or faster;

♦ Maintain room displays IAW OCSSOP standards and execute company details.

Week Eleven:
SOC Phase:

♦ Total control is removed, nightly passes issued;

♦ Light PT- conditional stretching, PU / SU improvement;

♦ Candidates lead morning PT;

♦ FLX 3 (CAPSTONE) vic. Detrow - Selby - Rockwell Hills;

♦ Battalion Commander's inspection to enter SOC phase.

Week Twelve:
SOC Phase:

♦ Total control is removed, nightly passes issued;

♦ Strenuous PT - ability groups runs, PU/SU improvement;

♦ Candidates lead morning PT;

♦ Candidates prepare for Dining In and graduation related issues;

♦ Candidates complete outprocessing tasks;

♦ Rooms are to be neat but do not have to meet OCSSOP standards.

Week Thirteen:
SOC Phase:

♦ Total control is remove,.nightly passes issued;

♦ Strenuous PT - ability groups runs, PU/SU improvement;

♦ Candidates lead morning PT;

♦ Candidates prepare for graduation related issues;

♦ Candidates complete outprocessing tasks;

♦ Rooms are to be neat but do not have to meet OCSSOP standards.

Week Fourteen:
SOC Phase:

♦ Total control is removed, nightly passes issued;

♦ Strenuous PT - ability groups runs, PU/SU improvement;

♦ Candidates lead morning PT;

♦ Candidates prepare for graduation related issues;

♦ Candidates complete outprocessing tasks;

♦ Rooms are to be neat but do not have to meet OCSSOP standards.

PT Training:
Physical Training Program Candidates must successfully pass all APFT administered during the course. Candidates failing to score at least 60 points per event on the initial APFT will be sent back to their unit. Candidates not scoring at least 60 points per event on the final APFT at the 17-21 year old standards given during week 12 will not graduate.

The physical training program at OCS is a tough, highly intensive program. Candidates are expected to show up for class in shape and ultimately attain the following goals:

♦ Instruct at least one PT session successfully;

♦ Run five miles in 45 minutes or less;

♦ Complete the conditioning Obstacle Course and Confidence Obstacle Course during week 1;

♦ Complete all road marches (three 5, one 7, one 10, and one 12 mile) - for reference, the 7 mile road march must be completed in 1 hour, 45 minutes;

♦ Score 290 or above (the class average) on the final APFT.

PREREQUISITES:

Eligibility Requirements:

The following personnel may apply for OCS:

♦ Active Army Warrant Officers or Enlisted members who have completed advanced individual training (AIT) may apply. Persons assigned to overseas commands may apply at any time, but will not normally be permitted to return to the continental United States (CONUS) for OCS attendance before completing five-sixths of the prescribed overseas tour (AR 614-30). Persons assigned to Cohesion, Operational Readiness, and Training (COHORT) units may apply at any time, but may not attend OCS until the end of the COHORT unit life cycle;

♦ Former commissioned officers may apply if their only commissioned service was performed in one of the Armed Forces early commissioning programs for students in the health professions;

♦ Warrant OFficers and Enlisted personnel of the USAR not on active duty may apply. These persons will follow guidance in AR 140-50;

♦ Civilians under the OCS Enlistment Option may apply (see AR 601- 210, table 9-5);

♦ Warrant officers and enlisted personnel of the Army National Guard (ARNG) may apply as prescribed by the Chief, National Guard Bureau. Guidance in NGR 351-5 will be followed.

Individuals may not apply if:

♦ They are presently conscientious objectors;

♦ Their selection would clearly not be in the interests of national security (AR 604-5);

♦ They have been separated from any of the Armed Forces under conditions of a nonwaivable disqualification for enlistment (AR 601-210, table 4-2);

♦ They are, or have been, commissioned officers in any component of the Armed Forces;

♦ They have been alerted or are on orders for overseas movement, unless the application was submitted to the unit commander before alert, or receipt of assignment instructions at the installation;

♦ They would have more than 10 years of active Federal service when appointed as a Commissioned Officer;

♦ They are under suspension of favorable personnel actions for military personnel (AR 600-31);

♦ They are attending, alerted for, or on orders to the Defense Language Institute Foreign Language Center (DLIFLC) as a student. Graduates of DLIFLC must complete a minimum 1 year language utilization assignment before they are eligible to attend OCS;

♦ They are warrant officer flight training candidates or Warrant Officers attending a rotary wing aviator course. They are not eligible to attend OCS until they have completed a 1 year utilization tour;

♦ They are Physician Assistant (PA) Warrant Officers attending Phase II, PA training. They are not eligible to attend OCS until they have completed 2 years of utilization;

♦ They are enrolled in AIT and are alerted for or on orders to a COHORT unit.

Eligibility Criteria:

All applicants must:

♦ Be citizens of the United States;

♦ Achieve a GT score of 110 or higher if tested on or before 31 December 1975 or on or after 1 October 1980. Due to the scoring formula used, applicants tested from 1 January 1976 through 30 September 1980, who have not taken a retest, must achieve a GT score of 115 or higher (see AR 611-5, paragraph 3-9, for retesting policy on the Armed Services Vocational Aptitude Battery (ASVAB)). All applicants must also score 90 or higher on the Officer Selection Battery (OSB), Subtest 2;

♦ Pass the Army Physical Readiness Test and meet height/weight standards in AR 600-9;

♦ Have a favorable National Agency Check (NAC) or Entrance NAC (ENTNAC);

♦ Have completed at least 90 semester hours of college study, except for a Medal of Honor or Distinguished Service Cross recipient;

♦ Achieve a score of 80 or higher on the English Comprehension Level Test (ECLT) if the applicant's primary language is other than English;

♦ Be of good moral character;

♦ Have no convictions by civil or military courts. (This does not apply to minor traffic violations with a fine or forfeiture of $100 or less.) An applicant must not have been judged to be a juvenile offender. This applies even if the court sentence, or any part of it, was suspended or withheld, or such conviction was in any way removed from court records by satisfactory completion of a period of probation. This also applies to adverse juvenile adjudications;

♦ Have not been previously disenrolled from officer candidate training;

♦ Be at least 18 and less than 30 years of age at the time of enrollment;

♦ Have completed AIT (Enlisted personnel);

♦ Have had a type "A" medical examination within 6 months before the date of application. Applicants must meet procurement medical fitness standards (except height and weight) prescribed in AR 40-501, chapter 2 and paragraph 7-19, and possess a physical profile serial of at least 222221 (height and weight standards stated above apply).

For information pertaining to waivers, please refer to DA Form 4187, under Application Checklist.

PERSONAL CONDUCT & APPEARANCE STANDARDS:

A key to success is doing the right thing in the absence of orders, guidance, and supervision. Choose the harder right over the easier wrong. The honor system is strictly adhered to and is simply nonnegotiable. Exceed the requirements! Do not come here to meet the requirements of the course. Push yourself and reach for higher heights. Demonstrate your capabilities.

Relief & Disposition of Candidates Not Commissioned:

Candidates who clearly show a lack of aptitude or qualification for commissioned status (see below), as determined under procedures established by the school commandant, will be relieved from OCS. Procedures to determine if the candidate lacks aptitude or qualification for commissioning will be consistent with requirements in AR 351-1, paragraph 3-13b. These procedures will include notice of the deficiency and an opportunity to respond before a decision is made on relief from OCS.

The school commandant, or a named representative, may relieve a candidate whenever a lack of aptitude or qualification for commissioning has been determined. The decision may be due to:

♦ Disciplinary reasons;
♦ Academic deficiencies;
♦ Disqualifying physical conditions;
♦ Deficiencies in leadership;
♦ Security reasons;
♦ Lack of motivation;
♦ Falsification or omission of facts on application;
♦ Honor code violations;
♦ Misconduct.

In addition, the commandant may approve the resignation of a candidate for personal reasons. Candidates may not resign until they have been enrolled in a class and completed at least 4 weeks of training. The only exception will be for the convenience of the Government when personal reasons or physical or mental deficiencies, unforeseen before enrollment, surface. If the commandant approves the resignation of a candidate, the person's name will be reported promptly to HQDA (DAPC-OPP-P). The individual will then be reassigned where needed by the Service.

Warrant officers who do not graduate are immediately available for reassignment. A request for reassignment instructions will be sent, by message, to CDR MILPERCEN ALEX VA// DAPC-OPW//.

The request will include the:
- Person's name, grade, SSN and PMOS;
- Number of days of delay en route desired, if any.

Enlisted persons who do not graduate must complete the time remaining in their current term of enlistment or reenlistment, except as otherwise provided by law or regulation. They are immediately available for reassignment and will be reported as prescribed in AR 614-200.

The application packet will be returned to candidates who fail to graduate from OCS.

Retention of Candidates:
The school commandant may hold over for a later class persons who:
- Fail to complete a course through no fault of their own;
- Fail for other reasons, but whose records show that they may reasonably be expected to overcome their deficiencies by joining a later class.

Candidates described above may be:
- Turned back to the beginning of the next class;
- Required to complete only those portions of the class considered necessary by the commandant.

Persons who miss or cannot actively participate in a significant amount of training for 14 or more days of instruction due to medical reasons may be relieved or turned back to a later class. At the discretion of the commandant, these persons may be assigned to a later class after meeting the medical standards.

AWARDS & HONORS:
Distinguished Graduates:
The commandant may designate as distinguished graduates persons who show outstanding leadership ability and personal traits needed to be successful Regular Army (RA) commissioned officers. To qualify for such designation, a graduate must be in the upper third of the final class standing. After graduation from an OBC, a distinguished graduate may apply for an RA appointment, if otherwise eligible (see AR 601-100, paragraph 2-4c). These graduates will be honored formally at graduation ceremonies:
- Distinguished Honor Graduate. The top graduate of an OCS class will be offered an RA appointment by HQDA (DAPC-OPP-P), if otherwise eligible. The person must accept this offer no later than 1 year from the OCS graduation date to qualify for appointment under this program (see AR 601-100, paragraph 2-4b);
- Distinguished Leadership Graduate;
- Distinguished Academic Graduate.

Robert P. Patterson Memorial Award:
The Commandant, USAIS, will select from each graduating class an officer rated as the most outstanding infantry officer graduate. This person must have distinguished himself by outstanding leadership, academic excellence, aptitude, and character. Before the end of each fiscal year (1 October to 30 September), the commandant will review the records of each person selected from classes during the year. Three of these candidates will be nominated for the Robert P. Patterson Memorial Award.

The CG, USAIC, will forward records of the three selected candidates, with a statement of factors on which the selection was based and the recommended order of nomination, to the Distribution Committee of Community Funds, Inc., 415 Madison Avenue, New York, NY 10017.

The award of a suitably engraved trophy, a scroll or certificate, and a modest cash award (dependent on available funds) will be presented at a ceremony at Fort Benning on 12 February of each year (Mr. Patterson's birthday).

The CG, USAIC, will manage this program and arrange transportation, at Government expense, for appropriate guests and official Army representatives. The CG, TRADOC, will budget for and fund transportation for the recipient.

PREPARATIONS:

Take care of all personal matters before you report in. Bring your medical, dental records, and all other items required for the course. Do not buy new uniforms if your old ones are serviceable. You must arrive fully prepared both mentally and physically. Distractions will hinder your ability to perform at your best.

Get yourself in top-notch physical condition prior to attending this course. Merely meeting the basic APFT standards for your age group will not be sufficient preparation for the physical challenges you are about to encounter. You will be expected to arrive capable of running 4 miles at a 9 minute mile pace.

Of critical note, you will take the APFT at 0430 hours the first Monday of OCS. Failure to meet the minimum standard (60%) in any event will result in disenrollment. Class APFT averages for the initial test are generally in the 260 and above range.

Clothing & Equipment Requirements:

The items listed in Tables OCS-B, OCS-C, and OCS-D are part of your initial basic training issue. It is not required for these items to be new; however, they must be serviceable (free of holes and presentable). Remember all Patches, Rank, Tabs etc must be removed from all uniforms and headgear. Only the "Follow Me" patch should be sewn on the uniforms. Please see the notes section below for other pointers.

Table OCS-B refers to clothing and equipment requirements for summer OCS classes (conducted between May and September. Table OCS-C refers to additional clothing and equipment requirements for winter OCS classes (conducted between October and April). Refer to Table OCS-D for additional required items, Purchase these items at the Fort Benning Clothing Sales store to ensure uniformity.

Additionally:

♦ Bring 25 matching wire hangers (no plastic coating);

♦ Bring laundry soap;

♦ Bring toiletry articles, 1 roll of toilet paper, 1 box of tissues, boot shining equipment (large can of Kiwi polish, edge dressing, leather dye, polish applicator, brush, and rags only. Floor wax, leather luster, etc. are not authorized for shining boots). Do not bring these items in glass containers, glass bottles are prohibited;

♦ If you wear eye glasses, bring 2 pair of military issue glasses of current prescription and a set of protective inserts. Contact lenses are not authorized until Senior Phase. Brown military issued glasses are required;

♦ You may not iron your uniforms, only dry cleaning is authorized;

♦ Remove all patches, tabs, badges, rank, and all other items (not including piping on Class A uniforms for Warrant Officers) from all uniforms.

Application for OCS:

All applicants for OCS will complete a DA Form 61 (Application for Appointment). Applications will be unclassified. Information classified CONFIDENTIAL or higher will be submitted separately with a reference to the application.

Submission by Applicant:

For your local board you will need a total of 4 copies of your OCS packet. That is 1 packet containing all original documents, and 3 photocopies of the original packet. The local

ITEM DESCRIPTION	QTY	REMARKS
Laundry bag	1	Barracks
Duffel bag	1	Nylon
BDU	6	Summer sets with "Follow Me" patch; need not be new, serviceable without holes is acceptable (summer sets are recommended)
Belt buckle	1	STA-Brite
Web belt	2	Black, 1"
Belt buckle	2	Subdued, 1"
Blousing rubbers	1	Green, with hooks
Boots	3 pairs	At least 2 pair must be standard issue and 1 pair Hot Weather Boots (black type) are allowed
Cap	2	BDU
Cap	1	Garrison
Gloves	1 pair	Dress, black
Handkerchief	3	Brown
Handkerchief	3	White
Wire hangers	1	Set of 24 plus 1
ID tags and chain	1 set	1 long and 1 short chain
U.S. insignia	2	Officer, STA-Brite
Jacket	1	Class A with "Follow Me" Patch
Shoe Polish	1	Can Kiwi
Boot Shining Kit	1	With brush and applicator
Toiletry kit	1	Personal hygiene items
Laundry Detergent	1 Box	
Lock	2	Combination, key locks are not allowed
Name Plate	2	Class A / B, plastic
Necktie / Necktab	1	Necktie for men, Necktab for women
HW Shorts	4	PFU, 2 issued
HW Top	4	PFU, 2 issued
Shirt	1	Class A, long sleeve
Shirt	1	Class B, short sleeve
Shirt	1	Dress, white, military
Shoes	1 pair	Dress - Bates "Clorafram" Low Quarters, Male and Female
Shoes	2 pair	Civilian, running
Shoes	1 pair	Shower, no leather or designs allowed
Socks	8 pairs	White, cotton, athletic, crew length
Socks	3 pairs	Dress, black
Socks	15 pairs	Wool, green or black
Bow Tie	1	Black (males only)
Towels	4	Brown, cotton
Face Cloths	4	Brown, cotton
Trousers	2	Class A, dress
Undershirt	10	Brown, cotton, for wear under BDU top
Undershirt	2	White, cotton (males only)
Underwear	10	Brown, cotton (males only)
Road Guard Vest	1	Light weight (orange with yellow trim) - Bike-A-Lite or Veri-Lite

Table: OCS-B — Required Items Inventory - Summer Classes

Table OCS-C		
Additional Required Items for Winter Classes		
ITEM	QTY	REMARKS
Field Jacket	2	BDU, With "Follow Me" patches
Cap	1	Garrison
Cap	1	Pile
Overcoat	1	Class A, dress
CW Bottom	2	Army PFU, gray
CW Top	2	Army PFU, gray
CW Gloves	1 pair	Leather, shell
CW Gloves	1 pair	Wool, inserts
Cap	1	Knitted, wool, black

Table OCS-D		
Additional Required Items Inventory		
ITEM DESCRIPTION	QTY	REMARKS
Notebook	1	8.5" x 11", spiral
Paper	1	Lined
Bag	1	Toiletry, green
Eraser	1	
Index cards	3	3 x 5 packets
Pen	2	Ball point, black
Pencil sharpener	1	
Pencil	2	#2 lead
Pencil	1	Mechanical, .5mm
Rubber Bands	1 Package	
Ruler	1	12 Inch, wooden
OCS Stationary	1 Box	
Stapler kit	1	TOT 50, mini
Book End Set	2	Metal
Army Officer's Guide	1	Book
Dictionary	1	Webster's, pocket
Marker	2	Laundry, black
Marker	2	Permanent, black
Pencil	2	Grease
Brasso	1	
Emblem Refresher	2	M-NU, black
Sewing Kit	1	
Tape	2	Cloth, white, 1" - TM
Tape	1	Electrical, black
Bags	1 Box	Ziploc, gallon size
Boot Laces	1	72", black
Unit Crests	2	11th INF Regt.
OCS Rank	3	STA-Brite
OCS Rank	9	Subdued
Helmet Headband	2	Leather
Soap Dish	1	
Wrist Watch	1	
Shaving Cream	1	Required for male and female soldiers

review board will review your original plus two photocopies leaving one copy for your records. Documents will be placed into your packet in the order listed below the OCS requirements. Once you are DA selected you only need to keep a copy of your packet for your own records.

Application Enclosures:

Enclose a copy of your Enlisted Record Brief (ERB). The ERB must reflect the GT score and must be current. A minimum GT score of 110 is required to apply for OCS. GT score requirements cannot be waived. Also acceptable is the DA Form 2A and DA Form 2-1. For Warrant Officers, submit a copy of the Officer Record Brief.

Enclose your DA Form 2A (this is a print out from PAC showing your status in the Army, check it for accuracy), and your DA Form 2-1 (make sure it has your SAT test score on it as well as your weapons qualifications and specialty schools).

Enclose your DA Form 61, completed under applicable instructions below, to their unit commander. The date the application is submitted to the unit commander will be considered the submission date of the application. If in question, the unit commander will verify the date of receipt. The following documents will be attached to the application:

♦ Documentary evidence of birth or statement of citizenship. An individual who is not a citizen of the United States by birth will submit the proper statement shown in AR 135-100, figure 2-1. Facsimiles or copies of naturalization certificates or certificates of citizenship will not be made. The reproduction of these certificates or any part of them without proper authority is a felony;

♦ Transcript of college credits, or certification of 90 semester hours of college credit from the installation education advisor when college credits are from several sources. If applicable, a statement will be submitted that the applicant has received the Medal of Honor or the Distinguished Service Cross.

1) Soldiers without a baccalaureate degree must place the following statement in item 41 (remarks): I understand that in order to be promoted to the grade of captain I must possess a baccalaureate degree;

2) Soldiers who do not have a baccalaureate degree must provide results of the SAT or ACT exam (must not be over 6 years old). Minimum SAT scores is 850; minimum ACT score is 19. Score cannot be waived;

3) The SAT/ACT may be waived if you are a college graduate and submit an official copy of your college transcripts, which show you have completed all your degree requirements. Transcripts must be official copies and must clearly state you graduated and completed your degree requirements to waive the SAT/ACT requirements;

4) Applicants without recent SAT scores must secure copies of the following items and turn them into the brigade S1 OCS representative to schedule a Scholastic Aptitude Test date:

    a. Applicants 2-1 file;

    b. Applicants 2-A file;

    c. DA Form 4187 request for SAT exam;

    d. College transcripts proving 90 hours minimum;

5) Soldiers with 9 ½ or more years of active federal service must enter the following statement in the remarks section: I understand that under current Army policy I may be required to retire after 20 years active federal service and that I will not retire as a commissioned officer if I do not have a minimum of 10 years active federal commissioned service;

♦ Requests for any necessary waiver (listed under DA Form 4187) with affidavit (if applicable);

♦ Affidavit from previous conscientious objector (if applicable). Applicants who previously were conscientious objectors will attach an affidavit to the DA Form 61, stating abandonment of such beliefs and principles. This statement will show that the person is willing to bear arms and give full and unqualified service to the United States. If the person has demonstrated a change of views by later military service, the affidavit should so state (see DA Form 61, item 24);

♦ Letters of recommendation or character reference from current or previous commissioned officer supervisor (not more than 4 and not more than one page each in length, optional);

♦ Completed DA Form 4322-R (Army Officer Candidate Contract and Service Agreement). DA Form 4322-R will be reproduced locally on 8 1/2" x 11" paper. A copy for local reproduction purposes is at the back of this regulation;

♦ Current official photograph as prescribed in AR 640-30;

♦ Completed DA Form 483 (Officer's Assignment Preference Statement). Use a #2 pencil when filling this out. Applicants will indicate, in order of preference, at least four branch preferences, as follows:

1) Male applicants: 2-Combat Arms, 1-Combat Support Arm, and 1-Combat Service Support;

2) Female applicants: 1-Combat Arm (excluding IN and AR), 1-Combat Support Arm, 1-Combat Service Support, and one of their choice;

3) Applicants who list OD, QM, or SC will enter in the specialty column one of the initial specialties (INSPEC) in which they wish to serve (see table 3-1 and DA Pam 600-3);

4) Male applicants who request Aviation will, if selected for Aviation, attend AD, AR, FA, IN, MI, or SC Officer Basic Course (OBC) prior to flight school;

5) Female applicants who request Aviation will, if selected for Aviation, attend AD, FA, MI, or SC OBC before flight school;

6) Warrant officer aviator applicants who have served a 1 year utilization tour after completing Warrant Officer Flight Training or the Rotary Wing Aviator Course will apply for Aviation;

7) Specialties for applicants who request and are approved for branch assignment to the Medical Service Corps (MS) will be determined by The Surgeon General. This decision will be based on the applicant's professional and educational qualifications. Applicants for MS must possess at least a baccalaureate degree (see AR 135-101, paragraph 1-11d).

Enclose a Secret Security Clearance Statement. Go to the S2 section for your unit. DA requires all OCS applicants to have a minimum of a final secret security clearance, type investigation, and date completed prior to submitting their application packet to DA for selection. This security clearance process can take several weeks. It is essential to start the security clearance investigation as soon as the soldier has been identified as an OCS applicant by his unit commander. A copy of the DA Form 873 may be enclosed in lieu of this statement.

Enclose a copy of your SF 88 & SF 93 (OCS, Airborne, Ranger Physical examination) Report of medical examination indicating soldier is qualified for appointment IAW AR 40-501, chapter 2.

♦ If applying for Aviation branch, the physical must also contain the approval stamp of the Army Aeromedical Center at Ft Rucker. DA Form 6256 (AFAST) and Class 1 Physical are required for Aviation branch applicants;

♦ Make sure your exam is stamped approved for OCS, Airborne, Ranger (Line 42);

♦ Completed DA Form 5339-R (Evaluation Sheet), height and weight of soldier should be placed on this form. Your unit commander will originally fill this out by hand. Then you type this for him to sign. It should Have all "Outstanding" checked.

Enclose a Bodyfat Statement, if necessary (DA Form 5500-R).

Enclose a DA Form 705, PT Card. This requires two valid scores and must be verified by Unit Commander.

Enclose copies of PLDC, BNCOC, or ANCOC Evaluations (optional).

Use a DA Form 4187 requesting a waiver of any civil or military offense. The request should indicate the offense, date, and place occurred and punishment imposed. It must be signed by the applicant and his/her commander. Request for waiver will be submitted, as required, for:

♦ All convictions by civil or military courts, or a person who has been judged a juvenile offender. (This excludes minor traffic violations with a fine or forfeiture of $100 or less.) The request for waiver must include:

1) An affidavit from the applicant that states circumstances of the offense;

2) A copy of all court actions and the final disposition of the case, if available, or correspondence with the court on reasons for lack of records or proceedings;

♦ Disenrollment from a prior officer candidate-type training program;

♦ Curtailment of overseas tour when compliance with completion of five-sixths of the prescribed tour would cause the person to become ineligible because of age or service, or when other circumstances exist that warrant consideration of a waiver;

♦ Age, if applicant would be 30 years of age or older at the time of enrollment. The waiver may be favorably considered only when the person can complete 20 years of Active Federal Commissioned Service prior to his or her 55th birthday;

♦ Enrollment in AIT but not alerted or on orders to a COHORT unit. The request for waiver must state that the applicant has signed and understands the provisions of DA Form 4322-R;

♦ All waiver requests may be consolidated on DA Form 4187.

Do not submit documentation not requested, such as training certificates or recommendations for awards or promotions.

Provide an E-mail address for Personnel Offices to be contacted regarding OCS applications to assist in informing the applicant of any OCS changes.

Mail address for applications is:
HQDA (TAPC-OPD-CP)
200 Stovall St
Alexandria, VA 22332-0413.

Additional Guidance:
DA Pam 600-8, procedure 4-10, has additional detailed guidance for preparing and processing OCS applications.

Installation OCS Structured Interview:
The objective of the Structured Interview is to identify the degree to which the applicant has developed attributes that show potential for a successful career as a professional Army Commissioned Officer. The applicant's past behavior in a variety of situations is evaluated to predict future performance. The interview will be conducted by a panel of three interviewers.

Immediately before the Structured Interview, the panel members will require the applicant to submit a handwritten narrative stating " Why I Want to be an Army Officer." The purpose of this narrative is to give the interviewers a chance to evaluate the applicant's writing and ability to express a desire to serve as a commissioned officer.

The applicant will be allowed a maximum of 1 hour to complete the narrative, it narrative will not exceed one page, and no assistance except an explanation of the question and use of a dictionary will be permitted. The narrative will be attached to DA Forms 6285.

DA Pam 611-5, DA Form 6283, and DA Form 6285 are test materials that will be requisitioned by the activity test control officer according to procedures in AR 611-5.

Withdrawal:
If an applicant desires to withdraw from the program during the selection process, the unit

commander will interview the person to determine the reason. If the applicant persists after counseling, the following actions are required:

♦ The applicant must sign a Withdrawal Agreement stating the specific reasons for withdrawal. (A sample format is at the end of the chapter). The statement will be authenticated by the applicant's unit commander and filed in the person's MPRJ for 1 year, then destroyed;

♦ The person's name, SSN, and reason for withdrawal will be reported promptly by electrically transmitted message to CDR MILPERCEN ALEX VA//DAPC-OPP-P//. An information copy will be furnished to the appropriate MACOM;

♦ All reassignment restrictions will be deleted from the person's DA Form 2-1.

The individual may reapply for OCS training 1 year after the date of withdrawal. The same procedures for submitting the first application will apply.

Retesting:

Applicants who fail to score 90 or higher on the OSB Subtest 2 may be retested. The person's immediate commander may approve the retest per AR 611-5, paragraph 3-9. An alternate version of the test will be used, if possible. A retest will not be given until at least 6 months after the first testing. Requests for additional retesting or retesting as an exception to policy will be sent to USASSC-NCR (ATZI-NCR-MS-D), Alexandria, VA 22332-0400.

Assignment Restrictions:

If selected for OCS training, the applicant will be reassigned to the scheduled OCS class based on assignment instructions from MILPERCEN or the US Army Medical Department Personnel Support Agency (AMEDDPERSA).

An applicant assigned overseas, who is approved for OCS, will remain at his or her current station until five-sixths of the normal overseas tour is completed, unless otherwise directed by MILPERCEN.

Predeparture Interview:

Within 2 weeks before departure for training, the selectee will be interviewed again by the unit commander. This in-depth interview is to verify that the selectee is still qualified and motivated to attend OCS. It insures that no disqualifying factors (e.g., physical, financial, personal or motivational) have surfaced since the selectee appeared before the Structured Interview Board. If problems could adversely affect the person's ability to complete OCS successfully, they should be investigated. Prompt action should be taken to correct the problem or withdraw the selectee from OCS.

Enlisted Service Commitment:

Enlisted Active Army members without enough time remaining in the service to complete OCS training must extend their enlistment before enrollment. (See AR 601-280, chapter 3.) The extension will be processed following selection but before departure from current station.

If discharge is required for immediate reenlistment (see AR 601-280, paragraph 3-1b), the discharge certificate will not be given to the person until after reenlistment has been completed (AR 635-200, paragraph 16-3). DD Form 214 (Certificate of Release or Discharge from Active Duty) will be prepared per AR 635-5, citing the Separation Program Designator in AR 635-5-1.

ENROLLMENT:
Orders:

Candidates will attend OCS in a TDY en route status. However, candidates designated INSPEC 11 will be assigned PCS to Fort Benning. Also, candidates selected for ranger training following completion of OCS may be assigned PCS to Fort Benning. Except as stated above, PCS orders issued for OCS will assign the candidate to ultimate duty station with TDY enroute at OCS and the appropriate OBC. Orders will also include other training for which the person has been selected.

Grade Authorization:

Upon enrollment in a class, candidates will be promoted to pay grade E5 if they then hold a lower grade (AR 600-200, chapter 7). Candidates with a higher grade will retain that grade. Individuals who are promoted on the basis of their attending OCS, who fail to complete the course successfully, may be reduced to the grade held before entering OCS, or to a grade deemed suitable (AR 600-200, chapter 8).

Status of Candidates:

All candidates will be considered equals as students. All insignia of grade and badges (e.g., Ranger Tab, parachutist badge) will be removed from the candidate's uniform during the school term. The officer candidate insignia authorized by AR 670-1 will be worn.

APPOINTMENT & ASSIGNMENT:
Separation from Prior Service:

On the day before appointment, the records of graduates will be closed and discharge certificates will be prepared. A discharge certificate will not be given to a graduate until the oath of office to commissioned status has been taken.

Medical Examination:

Graduates normally will not be required to take a medical examination upon change from enlisted or warrant officer status to commissioned officer status. A proper medical examination taken within the preceding year will serve for appointment purposes. Only graduates who had a serious illness or injury since the last medical examination must be reexamined under the provisions of AR 40-501.

Appointment Procedures:

The DA Form 61 prepared when the person applied for OCS will be used as the application for appointment as a Reserve commissioned officer of the Army. An OCS graduate tendered an appointment becomes a commissioned officer upon taking the oath of office and executing DA Form 71 (Oath of Office--Military Personnel). This act serves as acceptance of the appointment (10 USC 591).

The school commandant is authorized, by direction of the President, to tender to successful graduates appointment as Reserves of the Army in the grade of second lieutenant. Upon receipt of properly executed oaths of office, the commandant will issue commissions (DD Form 1A) for such appointments. The following notation will be typed below the body of the oath on the left side of DA Form 71:

"DD Form 1A (Officer Commission Certificate) issued . . . (Date) . . . "

Branch Assignments:

Officers appointed will be assigned to a branch of the Army Reserve based on the INSPEC for which the graduate was chosen by MILPERCEN.

Each OCS selection board is given a list of specialty quotas based on the Army's needs for newly commissioned officers in various specialties. A large proportion of these needs are in combat arms. In recommending INSPECs, the board considers:

♦ Army and specialty strength requirements;
♦ Personal preferences stated on the DA Form 61;
♦ Educational background;
♦ Prior military training and experience;
♦ Physical qualifications.

Designation of INSPEC and branch is made by MILPERCEN incident to the selection process. The factors listed above are evaluated in making the decision. Branch and specialty assignment may not be changed unless unusual qualifications surface which, through no fault of the individual, were not available to MILPERCEN at the time of designation. If such information is discovered, the candidate may request redesignation through the OCS Battalion Commander to HQDA (DAPC-OPP-P), Alexandria, VA 22332-0400.

Commissioned Service Obligation:

All Active Army OCS graduates will serve at least 3 years in a commissioned officer status on active duty.

REPORTING INFORMATION:

It is strongly advised that new candidates plan on arriving to OCS four days prior to the NLT arrival date on their orders. Typically the companies begin a cycle on a Sunday at 1200 hours.

LEAVE & PASS POLICY:

Leave credit will be carried forward into commissioned officer service (AR 630-5). The school commandant may grant up to 30 days delay en route, chargeable against accrued leave. This delay will not extend beyond the officer's reporting date at the branch service school.

BILLETING:

BAH, BAS, is available for married students, take marriage license and spouses SS# to BN S1.

Off Post Housing:

Families of students attending OCS in a TDY status are not authorized family housing, and must be prepared to live off post. Married candidates attending IOBC following OCS, and are in a PCS status are authorized on post housing if their family will be moving to Columbus. Students not on PCS orders to Ft. Benning and not attending IOBC will not receive payment for the relocation of family members/household goods to Ft. Benning. Therefore, soldiers should carefully consider this option.

Mail:

To contact an Officer Candidate send mail to:
    OC First Name Last Name
    ___ Plt, ___ Company, 3-11 IN (OCS)
    Ft. Benning, GA 31905-5570

Money:

Candidates should prepare for miscellaneous expenses while attending OCS. These expenses usually include such items as laundry/uniform cleaning, contributions to social events, class dues (usually from $25-$50 per month), and the purchase of the OCS packet ($70). These costs average $800-$1000 per candidate during the class. Other potential costs include ensuring your uniform is complete and serviceable. Uniform costs are usually incurred prior to arrival at OCS, as candidates are required to report with a complete, serviceable uniform issue.

POV:

All vehicles owned by soldiers assigned to Ft. Benning must be registered with the Provost Marshall in Soldiers Plaza, Building 2637. The following items are required:
- ◆ Valid Drivers License;
- ◆ Proof of Insurance;
- ◆ Vehicle Registration.

POW:

It is strongly advised that you do not bring POW's if you can store them elsewhere; however, if you must bring them (i.e. conditions of a move) the following applies:
- ◆ Ft. Benning requires all POW's be registered at the Military Police Activity and stored in the unit arms room if you reside in military troop housing (barracks);
- ◆ Upon your arrival at Fort Benning, you are required to turn in your weapon. You will receive three cards (TRADOC/FORSCOM Form 563-R) to complete on your weapon. The cards will be signed by the unit commander and then taken to the Military Police Activity by the unit commander for registration, then stored in your unit's arms room;
- ◆ The weapon cannot be stored in your POV or in your barracks room. Those facilities do not provide the level of security outlined in AR 190-11.

Failure to comply with the firearms policy is a violation of UCMJ.

Though Ft. Benning has outstanding private weapons firing facilities and programs, students will not be allowed to use their weapon prior to senior phase (last four weeks), and then only with coordination/approval of the unit commander and supply sergeant.

CONTACT INFORMATION:

3/11 Infantry Regiment (OCS)
Bldg. 2757
Fort Benning, GA 31905-5570;
COMM: (706) 545-4510/9162;
(706) 545-8377 (FAX);

A Company:
(706) 545-4334 (CQ) Building 2762 B;
B Company:
(706) 545-9174 (CQ) Builindg 2762 A;
Fort Benning Post Directory:
(706) 545-2011.

STUDY GUIDE:

Required knowledge is information that you will need to now and recall on a daily basis. The following is the list of required knowledge and the day of class that each candidate will be expected to recite it verbatim. Since, candidates have little time to learn this information while attending the course, this study guide will help prospective candidates become familiar with the information before they arrive at OCS.

Table: OCS-E	
DAY	REQUIRED KNOWLEDGE
3	General Orders and the Daily Operation Order, Thought for the day, Reminder, Safety Reminder, Battalion SDO, Company Duty TAC, Paraphrase Company Mission
5	Chain of command, OCS Alma Mater and The Army Song
7	OCS Honor Code, The 7 Army Values, 8 Steps of the Troop Leading Procedures
9	Required Attributes
11	Required Skills, 5 Paragraph operation order
13	Influencing Actions, The Untruthful Officer
15	Operating Actions, Officer's Code of Honor
17	Improving Actions, Estimate of the Situation
19	Duty, Honor, Country; Rules of Thumb for Living Honorably
21	The 11th Infantry Crest
25	History of the 11th Infantry regiment (paraphrase)

Some information not given in further detail will be information that candidates will not receive until they arrive. Also, some information (like the daily operations order) changes day to day.

General Orders:

1) I will guard everything within the limits of my post and quit my post only when properly relieved.

2) I will obey my special orders and perform all my duties in a military manner.

3) I will report violations of my special orders, emergencies and anything not covered in my instructions to the Commander of the Relief.

OCS Alma Mater:

Whenever recited, all Officer Candidates who hear must come to the position of attention and recite/sing in unison.

Far across the Chattahoochee, to the Upatoi. OCS our Alma Mater, Benning's pride and joy. Forward ever, backward never, faithfully we strive. To the ports of embarkation, follow me with pride. When it's time and we are called to guard our country's might, We'll be there, with heads held high in peacetime and in fight. Yearning ever, failing never, to guard the memory, The call is clear, we must meet the task for FREEDOMS NEVER FREE!

Army Values:

Principles or qualities intrinsically desirable.

1) **Loyalty** - Bear true faith and allegiance to the U.S. Constitution, the Army, and other soldiers.

2) **Duty** - Fulfill your obligations.

3) **Respect** - Treat people as they should be treated.

4) **Selfless Service** - Put the welfare of the Nation, the Army, and your subordinates before your own.

5) **Honor** - Live up to all the Army values.

6) **Integrity** - Do what's right legally and morally.

7) **Personal Courage** - Face fear, danger, or adversity (physical/moral).

The U.S. ARMY Song:
(Stanza 1)

March along, sing our song with the Army of the free. Count the brave, count the true who have fought the victory. We're the Army and proudly proclaim: First to fight for the right and to guard our nation's might, and the Army goes rolling along. Proud of all we have done, fighting till the battle's won, and the Army goes rolling along.

(Chorus)

Then it's Hi! Hi! Hey!, the Army's on it's way. Count off the cadence loud and strong! For where we go, You will always know that the Army goes rolling along.

(Stanza 2)

Valley Forge, Custer's ranks, San Juan Hill and Patton's tanks, and the Army goes rolling along. Minutemen from the start, always fighting from the heart, and the Army goes rolling along.

(Chorus)

Then it's Hi! Hi! Hey!, the Army's on it's way. Count off the cadence loud and strong! For where we go, You will always know that the Army goes rolling along.

(Stanza 3)

Men in rags, men who froze, still that Army met its foes, and we'll fight with all our might as the Army goes rolling along.

(Chorus)

Then it's Hi! Hi! Hey!, the Army's on it's way. Count off the cadence loud and strong! For where we go, You will always know that the Army goes rolling along. Keep it rolling! And the Army goes rolling along, along.

The Troop Leading Procedures:

1) Receive the mission;
2) Issue the warning order;
3) Make a tentative plan;
4) Initiate necessary movement;
5) Conduct reconnaissance;
6) Complete the plan;
7) Issue an operation order (OPORDER) or fragmentary order (FRAGO);
8) Supervise and refine.

OCS Honor Code:

An Officer Candidate will not lie, cheat, or steal, nor tolerate those who do.

Required Attributes:
Fundamental qualities and characteristics:

1) **Mental** - Possesses desire, will, initiative, judgment, confidence, intelligence, cultural sensitivity, and self-discipline.

2) **Physical** - Maintains appropriate level of health, physical fitness, and military and professional bearing.

3) **Emotional** - Displays self-control, balance, stability and calm under pressure.

The Five Paragraph Operation Order:
Task Organization
1. Situation
   A. Enemy Forces
   B. Friendly Forces
   C. Attachments/Detachments
2. Mission
3. Execution
   A. Concept of Operations
   a. Maneuver
   b. Fires
   c. Counter Air Operations
   d. Intelligence
   e. Electronic Warfare
   f. Engineering
   g. Include additional subparagraphs as required
   B. Tasks to Maneuver Units
   C. Tasks to Combat Support Units
   D. Coordinating Instructions
4. Service Support
5. Command and Signal

Required Skills:
Competence; skill development is part of self-development:

1) **Conceptual** - Demonstrates sound judgment, critical/creative thinking, and moral reasoning (skill with ideas).

2) **Interpersonal** - Shows skill with people; coaching, teaching, counseling, motivating, and empowering.

3) **Technical** - Possesses the necessary expertise to accomplish all tasks and functions (Skill with things).

4) **Tactical** - Demonstrates proficiency in required professional knowledge, judgment, and warfighting. Combination of other skills, applied to train for and win wars.

Influencing Actions:
Method of reaching goals while operating/improving:

1) **Communicate** - Displays good oral, written, and listening skills for individual/groups.

2) **Make Decisions** - Reach logical conclusions based on analysis. Commit people and units to take action. Employ sound judgment and logical reasoning.

3) **Motivate People**- Inspires, motivates, and guides others toward mission accomplishment. Understand and use the needs of individuals to influence their thinking and performance.

The Untruthful Officer:
"The untruthful officer trifles with the lives of his countrymen and the honor and safety of his country." -*General Douglas MacArthur*

Operating Actions:
Short-term mission accomplishment:

1) **Plan & Organize** - Develops detailed, executable plans that are feasible, acceptable, and suitable. Establish a course of action, set goals and priorities, delegate, and allocate resources.

2) **Execute Actions** - Shows tactical proficiency, meets mission standards, and takes care of people/resources. Put plans into action, supervise, and accomplish missions.

3) **Assess Progress/Results** - Uses in-progress, after action and evaluation tools to facilitate consistent improvement and identify lessons.

Officer's Code of Honor:
Every officer holds a special position of moral trust and responsibility. No officer will ever violate that trust or avoid his responsibility for any of his actions regardless of the personal cost. An officer is first and foremost a leader of men. He must lead his men by example and personal actions. He cannot manage his command to effectiveness ... they must be led; and an officer must therefore set the standard for personal bravery and leadership. All officers are responsible for the actions of all their brother officers. The dishonorable acts of one officer diminishes the corps; the actions of the officer must always be above reproach.

Improving Actions:
Long-term improvement in the Army, its people and organization:

1) **Develop People**- Invests adequate time and effort to develop individual subordinates as leaders. Enhances the competence and self-confidence of subordinates.

2) **Build Teams**- Spends time and resources improving teams, groups, and units. Fosters ethical climate. Enhances corporateness and effectiveness of the unit.

3) **Learn from Experience**- Seeks self-improvement and organizational growth; envisioning, adapting, and leading change. Challenges people to design new ways. Applies lessons learned. Turn lessons into better knowledge.

Duty, Honor, Country:
Those three hallowed words reverently dictate what you ought to be, what you can be, what you will be. They are your rallying points:

♦ To build courage when courage seems to fail;

♦ To regain faith when there appears to be little cause for faith;

♦ To create hope when hope becomes forlorn.

Estimate of the Situation:
 Step 1) Detailed mission analysis.
 Step 2) Situation and courses of action.
 Step 3) Analyze courses of action wargame.
 Step 4) Compare courses of action.
 Step 5) Decision.

Rules of Thumb for Living Honorably:
 1) Does this action attempt to deceive anyone or allow anyone to be deceived?
 2) Does this action gain or allow the gain of a privilege or advantage to which I or someone else would not otherwise be entitled?
 3) Would I be satisfied by the out come if I were on the receiving end of this action?

The 11th Infantry Regiment Crest:
 The shield is blue, the Infantry color and carries the castle from the War with Spain in 1898 and Santana's arrow for the regiment's campaign against the Comanches, Cheyenne's and Kiowas in 1874. The crossed kampilan and bolo represent engagements against the Moros of Mindanao and the Filipinos of the Visayas during the War with Spain in 1898. The cross of the ancient Lords of Dun commemorates the crossing of the Meuse River near Dun during WWI and the embattled partition represents the siege of Chattanooga in 1863.

The 11th Infantry Regiment:
 President Abraham Lincoln constituted the 11th Infantry on 3 May 1861. It fought in such battles as Shiloh, Chickamaugua, Murfreesboro, the Battle of Atlanta and the march through Georgia. Between 1898 and 1920, "The Wandering 11th" made 29 changes of station, including seven years of foreign service. From 1904 to 1913, the regiment was stationed in the west, serving in the nearly destroyed city of San Francisco following the earthquake of 1906 and guarding the border in the southwest during the trouble with Pancho Villa and his outlaw army.
 In April 1918, the regiment sailed for France and later joined the 5th Division. The regiment took part in the Vosges Mountains, St. Mihiel and Meuse-Argonne offensives, orchestrating a brilliant crossing of the Meuse River. The 11th Infantry returned to Europe, landing at Normandy in July 1944 and fighting it's way across France as part of Patton's famed Third Army. During the Battle of the Bulge, the Regiment conducted a night river assault across the Rhine River, giving General Patton a division bridgehead over the Rhine two days ahead of Marshall Montgomery's famous crossing.
 The Regiment returned to the United States and underwent several changes from 1950 until 1962 when it was redesigned as the First Battalion, 11th Infantry, serving at Fort Benning, Georgia, as part of the 5th Infantry Division at Fort Carson, Colorado. In July 1968, the 11th Infantry deployed for action in Vietnam and operated in Cam Lo, Dong Ha, Quang Tri Khe Sahn.
 The Regiment returned to Fort Carson in August 1972 as part of the 4th Infantry Division, where it stayed until January 1984 when it was deactivated. On 14 August 1987, student battalions of the School Brigade at Fort Benning were redesigned as 1st, 2nd and 3rd Battalions, 11th Infantry. On 8 February 1991, the School Brigade was redesigned as the 11th Infantry Regiment.

REFERENCE:
1. US Army Formal Schools Catalog. US Army Publishing Agency. DA PAM 351-4, page 44, Table 3-6. 31 October 1995.
2. US Army Officer Candidate School. US Army Publishing Agency. AR 351-1. 14 September 1985.
3. "Welcome to the Officer Candidate School!" Online. Internet. 11 May 2000. Available: http://www-benning.army.mil/ocs/index2.htm.

Interview Guidance and Checklist Format

The interview with an applicant who has been accepted for the US Army Officer Candidate School (OCS) is one of the most important parts of the screening and selection procedure. It is not too late to preclude any person from attending if this interview uncovers problems that make the applicant no longer qualified. Some major problems for candidates at the school are listed below and should be discussed with the applicant. These questions will assist the interviewer and can be expanded if necessary:

1. Have you incurred any physical injuries since your last medical examination? If so, have they been evaluated by a military physician?

2. (For female applicants only) Are you pregnant? If so, under AR 40-501, you are medically disqualified for OCS training.

3. Are you aware that OCS training places strenuous requirements on your physical, psychological, and mental resources?

4. Does your immediate family have any health problems that may interfere with your performance at OCS?

5. Have you discussed the strenuous requirements you will be under while attending OCS with your immediate family members? Have you told them that you will have little time for them while in training?

6. Do you have any personal, legal, or financial problems that could arise during training to interfere with your performance?

7. Are you prepared to accept all aspects of your training, including those which you may not like or understand?

8. Do you consider yourself physically fit for OCS?

9. Do you know any cause that would make you ineligible for OCS training now?

Narrative Summary of Predeparture Format

(To be accomplished within 14 days immediately before selected applicant's release from installation control.)

1. On ... (Date) ..., ... (Name, Grade, and SSN) ..., was interviewed by the undersigned to determine whether any disqualifying personal reasons or physical or mental problems have surfaced since applicant's selection for OCS.

2. Applicant (is still) (is not) qualified to attend OCS. (If disqualified, explain reasons for disqualification in detail.)

3. Applicant (should attend OCS as scheduled) (should not attend OCS as scheduled). Appropriate action should be taken to remove individual from further consideration for OCS at this time.

Signature of Applicant's Unit Commander)

(Date)

Withdrawal Agreement Format

(Date)

1. I, ..., hereby withdraw from the OCS program for the following reason(s):

(Explain reasons for withdrawal in detail)

2. I have been counseled by my unit commander concerning my decision to withdraw, and I persist in this decision. I understand that upon withdrawal I will not be allowed to reapply for OCS training for at least 1 year from the date of this withdrawal and that I will be required to serve the remainder of my enlistment obligation.

3. I further understand that if I waived my enlistment commitment in order to attend OCS, it will not be reinstated.

(Applicant's Signature)

(Signature of Applicant's Unit Commander)

OLD GUARD

3RD UNITED STATES INFANTRY

HISTORY:

The 3rd U.S. Infantry (The Old Guard) is the oldest infantry unit in the Army, predating the Constitution of the United States of 1784. Since 1948, The Old Guard has been stationed in the Washington, D.C. area at Fort Myer and Fort McNair.

As a unit of The U.S. Army Military District of Columbia (MDW), the 3rd U.S. Infantry is charged with the unique mission of providing security for the nation's capital, acting as the U.S. Army's official ceremonial unit and performing tactical infantry missions.

The unit received its name from General Winfield Scott at the victory parade in Mexico City in 1848 following the Mexican War. As the 3rd Infantry approached, Scott removed his hat and said, "Gentlemen, take off your hats to The Old Guard of the Army."

The 50 well earned battle streamers, a valorous unit award and a meritorious unit citation attached to the regimental colors attest to the unit's heroic past from the earliest Indian Campaigns to Vietnam. In 1987 and 1993, the unit was presented with Superior Unit Award, which is the Army's highest peacetime award.

The distinctive dress blue uniforms are familiar sight to many Americans - since the 3rd U.S. Infantry participates in ceremonies at the White House, the Pentagon, national memorials and elsewhere throughout the area. Additionally, elements of the unit are regularly on the road, bringing the unit's brilliant military pageantry to audiences throughout the nation.

Soldiers of the 3rd U.S. Infantry also maintain a faithful 24 hour vigil at the Tomb of the Unknowns, provide casket teams, firing parties and marching platoons for funerals in Arlington National Cemetery, as well as participate in parades and festivals throughout the United States.

FORWARD:

The Old Guard maintains a constant readiness for its security role and the possible deployment of its soldiers by conducting a year round tactical training program culminating with intensive training at various combat training centers.

The 3rd U.S. Infantry is a fully structured MTOE unit, made up of eight companies. Company A, stationed at Fort McNair, is the Commander-in-Chief's Guard, representing one of the most historically famous units in the Army. Companies B, C and D are line companies that share in the ceremonial and field training responsibilities. Each of these companies is comprised of a marching platoon, a firing-party platoon, a casket-team platoon and a headquarters or support section. Company E (Honor Guard) also has additional platoons made up of the Continental Colors, the U.S. Army Drill Team and a special detachment of tomb guards for the Tomb of the Unknowns.

The Presidential Salute Guns Battery, Caisson Platoon, Scout Platoon and the 289th Military Police Company (Minus) all fall under Company H. The Fife and Drum Corps is a separate company. Headquarters Company, the eighth company, is responsible for battalion support for The Old Guard.

As the Army's official representative in the National Capital Region, The Old Guard brings to mind the thousands who have given their lives for the nation and those who stand ready to defend it.

The Old Guard is nationally and internationally acclaimed as the standard bearer for ceremonial excellence. This is a prestigious unit with a unique mission; comprised of fit, disciplined and motivated soldiers who are proud of what they do; recognized as one of the Army's most challenging, rewarding and sought after assignments; capable and prepared to execute specified contingency operations; whose soldiers are prepared for seamless integration into the deployable Army.

MISSION:

"The Old Guard" conducts Joint Service and Army ceremonies, memorial affairs and special events which exemplify the excellence of the U.S. Military to the nation and the world, as well as maintains individual, squad and platoon level proficiency to attract and develop tactically and technically competent soldiers and leaders.

OVERVIEW:

"The Old Guard" is one of a kind unit that offers unique experiences to qualified soldiers. The majority of the soldiers are infantrymen, including MOS 11C who man the Presidential Salute Gun Battery; however, positions are available for male and female soldiers in the Military Police Corps and various support MOS fields. Every soldier within "The Old Guard" is fully qualified to conduct military ceremonies regardless of MOS.

SPECIALTY UNITS:

Once assigned to "The Old Guard", soldiers looking to challenge themselves even further may want to try out for one of our specialty units.

- The U.S. Army Drill Team;
- The Continental Color Guard;
- The Old Guard Caisson Platoon;
- The Guards of Honor at the Tomb of the Unknowns.

Each of these highly motivated groups of soldiers has a specialized, dedicated role that

supports the mission of "The Old Guard" and represents our Army.

The Fife and Drum Corps:

The Old Guard Fife and Drum Corps is the only unit of its kind in the armed forces. The unit is designed to resemble the Revolutionary Fife and Drum Corps and parades in the uniforms of General George Washington's Army, complete with tri-corn hats, white wigs, vests, overalls, waistcoats and red great coats. The drum major wears a large fur and leather helmet, which was the British Light Infantry cap.

The corps, comprised of 70 men and women, uses 11 hole wood fifes, one-valve bugles and handmade rope-tensioned drums - replicas of the instruments used during the War for Independence. The unit's music reflects our American heritage.

In addition to marching at normal Army cadence of 120 steps per minute, the Corps also marches at the old cadence of 90 steps per minute and at a slow, stately "troop" of 60 steps per minute when saluting reviewing parties.

MP Company (Minus):

Military police became part of the 3rd U.S. Infantry on November 1st, 1994, when the 1st platoon, 289th Military Police Company was reactivated. The attachment of an MP Platoon to The Old Guard serves two purposes: it provides expanded opportunities for women soldiers in the regiment and it will help fulfill the contingency mission of the 3rd U.S. Infantry. The contingency plan for the MDW area has always called for a military police platoon to assist the 3rd U.S. Infantry in carrying out its mission.

In addition to contingency and tactical duties, members of the MP platoon participate in ceremonial functions and funerals. Women MPs and all members of the platoon have the same opportunity as other Old Guard soldiers to participate in specialty units such as the U.S. Army Drill Team after one year of service in the regiment.

Caisson Platoon:

The cadence of a funeral procession in Arlington National Cemetery is tapped out by the rhythmic "clip-clop" of seven handsome horses. Astride four of the horses, soldiers sit ramrod straight. The men and horses are members of the Caisson Platoon of the 3rd U.S. Infantry.

During a procession, six horses of the same color, paired into three teams, make up the team that pulls the flag-draped casket on a black artillery caisson. Although all six animals are saddled, only those on the left have mounted riders. This is a tradition that began in the early horse-drawn artillery days when one horse of each team was mounted while the other carried provisions and feed.

The riders are dressed in the Army blue uniform with riding breeches and boots with spurs. To the left front of the team, on a separate mount, rides the section chief who commands the caisson unit.

One of the older traditions in a full honor funeral is the caparisoned (riderless) horse. The horse is led behind the caisson wearing an empty saddle with rider's boots reversed in stirrups. This indicates the warrior will never ride again. Tradition allows a caparisoned horse to follow the casket of a soldier or Marine in the rank of Colonel or above. Presidents of the nation, as Commander-in-Chief, are given the same honor.

Tomb Guards:

The Tomb of the Unknowns in Arlington National Cemetery is guarded year round, 24 hours a day, by sentinels of The Old Guard. The guard is changed in an impressive ceremony at the tomb every half hour April 1st through September 30th. During the winter months, the guard is changed hourly.

At his post, the tomb sentinel crosses the 63 foot walkway in a special measured cadence of exactly 21 steps. The sentinel faces the tomb for 21 seconds before retracing his steps. The number 21 is symbolic of the highest salute accorded dignitaries in military and state ceremonies. As a gesture against intrusion on his post, the weapon is always shouldered on the side farthest from the tomb.

Only under exceptional circumstances may the tomb guard speak or alter his silent measured tour of duty.

Commander-In-Chief's Guard:

In 1776, General George Washington, Commander-in-Chief of the Continental Army, issued an order to select exemplary men to guard himself. This unit became the Commander-in-Chief's Guard.

Company A of The Old Guard organized a replica of the Commander-in-Chief's Guard to honor this historically famous unit.

The guard is organized as prescribed by Revolutionary War General Baron Friedrich Von Steuben. The group has 58 privates, three corporals, three sergeants, a lieutenant and captain. A color team of one ensign and five corporals completes the group. The color team bears a duplicate of the flag Washington's headquarters carried throughout the Revolutionary War.

The Salute Guns Platoon:

The Presidential Salute Guns Battery, also known as The Salute Guns Platoon, renders honors to foreign dignitaries and heads of state visiting the White House, the Pentagon and other places in the area. It also fires the final salute during many funerals at Arlington National Cemetery. Not only does this platoon provide ceremony support, but the mortar men provide 81mm mortar direct fire support during the tactical training of 3rd Infantry units.

During ceremonies the platoon fires six 3 inch antitank guns mounted on 105mm howitzer chassis. Three man crews, consisting of a watchman (time keeper), loader and gunner, fire at intervals from three to eight seconds, depending on the type of ceremony.

Every summer the Salute Guns Platoon joins The U.S. Army Band, "Pershing's Own," in performing Tchaikovsky's "1812 Overture" at the Washington Monument.

Drill Team:

The U.S Army Drill Team has been thrilling Americans for more than 25 years by silently tossing into the air and catching bayonet-tipped rifles.

Its intricate maneuvers, including such breathtaking routines as the "Front-to-Rear Overhead Rifle Toss," are the result of superb discipline, training and constant practice. Dangerous drills are preformed without vocal cadence, command or musical cues.

This team supports MDW's ceremonial commitments and Army recruiting from its home at Fort Myer. The Old Guard is the only Army unit authorized to parade with fixed bayonets.

Competition is intense for a place on this elite team and a vacancy is filled only after months of drill practice. The strength and dexterity to handle the 1903 Springfield rifle and trim military bearing, are essential.

PREREQUISITES:

Do you have what it takes?

Are you a well-disciplined soldier? Do you have high levels of military bearing and pride in serving your country? Are you up to the challenge of representing the Army and the United States to the nation and the world? If you answer YES to these questions, then the 3rd United States Infantry, more commonly known as "The Old Guard," may be the place for you.

As a highly visible unit, "The Old Guard" has standards and requirements that must be met by soldiers interested in joining the ranks. In accordance with AR 614-200, and "Old Guard" recruiting policy, soldiers must:

◆ Be a member of the Regular Army;
◆ Be a volunteer;
◆ Have a GT Score of 110 or higher;
◆ Meet the height requirement:
Males - 5 ft 10 in to 6 ft 4 inches tall;
Females - 5 ft 8 in to 6 ft 4 inches tall;
◆ Have no physical profile (no shaving profile or facial hair allowed);
◆ Have no civil convictions;

◆ Be able to apply for, and receive, the appropriate security clearance which is needed for duty with The Old Guard;
◆ Be able to perform ceremonial functions without glasses or with contact lenses;
◆ Have minimum retainability upon reporting to The Old Guard of 30 months for PFC and 36 months for SPC/CPL and above.

All UCMJ violations are evaluated on a case by case basis. There must be a valid position available in The Old Guard (MOS and pay grade); refer to Table Old Guard-A for a list of MOSs and corresponding ranks available for an Old Guard assignment.

Officer Assignment Summary:

The Old Guard is constantly looking for the best and brightest officers to represent our Army and Nation to the world. The requirements listed below refer to CMF 11 series jobs. The Old Guard also has opportunities for Signal, Chemical, Military Intelligence, Medical Service, Quartermaster (WO), Chaplain, and Ordinance (WO) Officers who want a challenge. Contact the Adjutant for details.

Officers wishing to be assigned to the Old Guard must:

◆ Be 70" or taller (males);
◆ Have superior military appearance and bearing;
◆ Be physically fit with no limiting profiles;
◆ Be eligible for TOP SECRET presidential support duty security clearance.

Officers should also:

◆ Be right handed or able to use right hand for saber manual;
◆ Have good vision or be able to wear contact lenses;
◆ Have no mustaches.

Captains serve as Company Commanders and Staff Officers. Lieutenants serve as rifle platoon leaders, specialty platoon leaders and staff officers.

MOS	MOS DESCRIPTION	RANK
	**Table: Old Guard-A**	
11B	Infantry	PVT-MSG
11C	Indirect Fire Infantryman	PVT-SFC
11Z	Infantry Senior Sergeant	MSG
25M	Vulcan System Mechanic	PVT-SGT
25V	Combat Documentation/Production Specialist	PVT-SPC
31U	Signal Support Systems Specialist	PVT-SFC
43M	Fabric Repair Specialist	PVT-SGT
44B	Metal Worker	PVT
46Q	Journalist	PVT-SSG
46R	Broadcast Journalist	PVT-SGT
51B	Carpentry and Masonry Specialist	PVT-SGT
52D	Power Generation Equipment repair	PVT
54B	Chemical Operations Specialist	SGT-SSG
55B	Ammunitions Specialist	SGT
63B	Light Wheel Vehicle Mechanic	PVT-SFC
63Z	Mechanical Maintenance Supervisor	MSG
71D	Legal Specialist	SPC
71L	Administrative Specialist	PVT-SSG
71M	Chaplain Assistant	PVT
73C	Finance specialist	PVT
75B	Personnel Administration Specialist	SPC
75H	Personnel Services Specialist	SSG-SFC
77F	Petrole Supply Specialist	PVT-SFC
88M	Motor Transport Operator	PVT-SFC
88N	Transportation Management Coordinator	SSG
91B	Medical Specialist	PVT-SFC
91C	Practical Nurse	SGT
91T	Animal Care Specialist	SSG
92A	Automated Logistical Specialist	PVT-SGT
92G/94B	Food Service Specialist	PVT-MSG
92Y	Unit Supply Specialist	PVT-MSG
95B	Military Police	PVT-SFC

Duties and leadership responsibilities include all those normally associated with positions in a combat arms brigade.

APPLICATION:

If you meet the prerequisites and are interested in volunteering for The Old Guard, you will need to submit the following "The Old Guard" Recruiting Team:

♦ A copy of your DA Forms 2A and 2-1;

♦ Two letters of recommendation;

♦ A copy of your current APFT card;

♦ A height and weight statement from your local Physician's Assistant (PA);

♦ NCOs need to submit copies of their last three NCOERs.

INPROCESSING:

Start Right:

All incoming soldiers to the Fort Myer Military Community attend the two-day "Start Right" program that brings together all inprocessing services, such as personnel and finance, to save soldiers time and frustration. The program ends with a bus tour of MDW and the Washington, D.C., area. Family members and new civilian employees are also invited to attend the tour. To "Start Right," newcomers to the Fort Myer Military Community should call (703) 696-3510 and arrange attendance at one of the sessions, which are run as often as twice a week.

Items that newcomers should bring to the program include 12 copies of their orders and all amendments thereto, their Leave Form (DA-31) and their Rations Form (DA-4187).

CONTACT INFORMATION:

If you are "up to the challenge," contact "The Old Guard" Recruiting Team:

http://www.mdw.army.mil/oldguard/recruit.htm;

DSN: 426-3149/3150;

COMM: (703) 696-3149/3150.

REFERENCE:

1. 1999 U.S. Army Military District of Washington. US Army Publishing Agency. 1999. "Duty Honor Pride," 3rd United States Infantry (The Old Guard) Pamphlet. 1999.

2. "3rd United States Infantry (The Old Guard)." Online. Internet. 23 May 2000. Available: http://www.mdw.army.mil/MDWINST.HTM.

3. "Volunteers Needed." Online. Internet. 23 May 2000. Available: http://www.perscom.army.mil/epinf/TOGVOL.HTM.

PATHFINDER

REGULATION:

Course No: 2E-SI5Q/011-ASIF7
Title: Pathfinder
Length: 3 Weeks
Location: U.S. Army Infantry School - SC: 071
Enl ASI: F7
Off SC: 5Q
Scope: Course effective: 1 Jan 88 Navigate cross country on foot; establish and operate a day/night helicopter landing zone; establish and operate a day/night parachute drop zone; conduct sling load operations; aircraft rappelling; provide air traffic control and navigational assistance to aircraft within an operational site control zone.
Prerequisite: Active Army and Reserve Component commissioned officers, 2LT-CPT, whose actual or anticipated duty assignment requires performance or knowledge of pathfinder duties; enlisted personnel who have a minimum of 1 year active service and are PFC-SFC. Actual or anticipated duty assignment requires performance or knowledge of pathfinder duties in MOS 11B, 11C, 11H, 11M, 19D, 76Y or 88M. Officer and enlisted personnel must have a current valid physical examination less than 12 months old. Applicants must possess a minimum physical profile serial of 111121 and have no speech impediment.
Special Information: Marine Corps personnel, company grade officers and corporals through gunnery sergeant, may attend.
Security Clearance: None

HISTORY:

US Army Pathfinders trace their origins to the massive airborne operations of World War II. After a series of mishaps involving airborne troops, it was decided that a force of trained men was needed to help guide transport aircraft and gliders to their intended destinations. A concept originally developed by the British was used as a model.

The original group of volunteers was selected from members of the 82nd Abn Division's 505th Parachute Infantry Regiment. The men were trained to parachute in and mark parachute Drop Zones (DZs) and glider Landing Zones (LZs). The Pathfinders would use colored lights, flares, panels, and smoke to mark the DZ/LZ's. They also provided radio check points to aid in aircraft navigation.

The experimental Pathfinder group was first used during the Allied invasion of Sicily in 1943. Pathfinder teams jumped in ahead of the main assault force. The teams marked drop zones and set up radar homing devices to guide aircraft to their targets.

The next large scale use of Pathfinders teams occurred during the D-Day operations. Pathfinder teams from the 82nd and 101st Airborne Divisions were dropped in a few hours before the main assault was to begin. German antiaircraft fire caused many of the aircraft transporting the Pathfinders to veer off course. Because of the disorganized nature of the drop, Pathfinder teams were scattered all over the French countryside. Many men found themselves operating alone or in areas they knew nothing about. Many teams were unable to reach their objectives and their missions met with various levels of success. Not long after the Pathfinders landed, the main assault force began landing. The Pathfinders linked up with whatever units they could, and eventually they were able to make their way back to their parent units. Pathfinders went on to participate in every major airborne operation of the war.

With the end of hostilities in 1945 the US began a massive draw down of its military and most of the Pathfinder units were disbanded. After the Air Force became a separate service in 1947 the Air Force claimed that only qualified Air Force personnel should guide Air Force aircraft. The remaining Pathfinder units were disbanded and their tasks were assigned to the Air Force's new Air Resupply and Communications Service, the predecessor to the Combat Control Teams.

With the Army's increased use of helicopters during the 1950's, a need was once again felt for the renewed services of Pathfinders. The first group to form a new pathfinder unit was the 11 Air Assault Division (TEST), the first Army unit to actively utilize the helicopter's mobility. As the US became more deeply involved in Vietnam, the Army began to deploy large numbers of combat troops. As these units began to arrive in Vietnam, many began to establish provisional pathfinder units. Pathfinder's were usually assigned to their parent organization's aviation unit. Operating as four man teams they secured, marked, cleared, and established DZ/LZ's; they provided initial aircraft guidance at remote locations and provided some limited air traffic control capabilities.

Unfortunately some unit commanders felt that any unit that "drained" away some of their best trained men, was a luxury that they could not afford. As a result some of the men who volunteered were not qualified. Some teams were misused or deployed for missions outside of their scope. Many of the men assigned as pathfinders had no formal training, instead learning their skills on the job. However most units found the pathfinders services helpful, in their day to day combat operations.

Originally established in England during WWII, the US Army Pathfinder School is located at FT. Benning's Lillyman Hall. Potential pathfinders spend approximately three weeks learning and practicing their new skills. When the US Air Force assumed the combat air traffic control duties in 1951, the school was closed. In 1955, the school was reopened under the Airborne-Air Assault branch of the Infantry School. It continues to operate to this day.

Today's Pathfinders are trained in airborne, small boat, vehicle, foot, and sometimes free fall infiltration techniques. These small four man teams may be parachuted in up to 72 hours in advance of the main assault force. They provide DZ/LZ surveys; site security; initial aircraft guidance, and mark and clear drop zones for follow-on forces. They are capable of engaging in demolition operations to clear DZ/LZ's of obstacles. If equipped with laser targeting devices (LTD) they may also designate targets of opportunity for air strikes. Pathfinders may be expected to coordinate aircraft movement, control parachute drops of personnel and equipment, conduct slingload operations and provide initial weather information to commanders.

Currently the US Army only maintains three pathfinder units:

- 101 Avn. Regiment Pathfinder Co.;
- 101 Abn. Division (Air Assault);
- 17 Avn. Bde Pathfinder Section;
- C/509 Inf. (Pathfinder).

Some of the most recent Pathfinder operations were conducted during Operation Desert Storm. Pathfinder teams assigned to the 101 Abn. Div. (AA), deployed in support of the 101's air assault into Iraq. The Pathfinder teams were flown into Iraq by division aviation assets. Once there, the ground the teams deployed radio homing beacons and helped establish Forward Arming and Refueling Points (FARPs) for the division's aviation units. The Pathfinders also acted as the Aviation Brigade's Quick Reaction Force. On one occasion the platoon rushed out to retrieve EPWs (Enemy Prisoners of War) for interrogation by Army intelligence staff. One three man Pathfinder team was compromised by Iraqi troops operating in the area. The teams commander immediately called for an emergency extraction. Because of an emergency situation elsewhere, the team was ordered to remain in place. With no choice left the teams commander ordered an attack on the Iraqi's position. The Pathfinders successfully attacked and captured an Iraqi bunker; in the process they captured a number of EPWs and classified documents. All three men later received Bronze stars for their actions.

Pathfinder teams have also deployed to support US domestic law enforcement agencies, during counter drug operations. The Pathfinder teams provided tactical ground intelligence to law enforcement aviation assets, during aerial drug sweeps.

FORWARD:

Army Pathfinders primarily provide navigational assistance and advisory services to military aircraft in areas designated by supported unit commanders. Their secondary missions include providing advice and limited assistance to units planning air assault/airdrop operations. Appropriately equipped and trained Pathfinders can fulfill the following responsibilities:

♦ Reconnoiter areas selected by supported unit commanders and select LZs and DZs;

♦ Infiltrate areas of operation by foot, vehicles,watercraft, rappel or parachute from aircraft;

♦ Prepare LZs and DZs to include establishing and operating visual and electronic navigational aids and removing minor obstacles;

♦ Employ GTA radio communications to provide pilots with guidance and air traffic advisories within an area of operations;

♦ Advise pilots concerning friendly mortar and artillery fires through direct coordination with fire support units;

♦ Provide technical assistance for the assembly of supplies, equipment, and troops before aircraft loading for deployment to LZs and DZs;

♦ Advise and provide limited physical assistance in preparing and positioning supplies, equipment, and troops for air movement;

♦ Conduct limited NBC monitoring and surveying of designated areas;

♦ Provide limited weather observations, to include wind velocity and direction, cloud cover, visibility, and approximate cloud ceiling;

♦ Operate, by agreement with the USAF, DZs and airfields for USAF aircraft in the absence of CCT;

♦ Survey DZs for use by USAF and Army aircraft (in this situation, it maybe necessary to provide Pathfinders with radios [UHF or VHF] that are compatible with USAF radio equipment. Aviators and pathfinders must coordinate to ensure they understand ground markings and radio procedures to be used).

Working in teams of three to five men, Pathfinders are inserted up to 72 hours before a flight operation to establish and maintain security on and around the LZ. They determine if the ground can handle an aircraft, assess how many aircraft can land at one site, and gauge if the slope of the ground will hinder a landing.

The Pathfinders feed intelligence on enemy activity to the incoming aviators and other concerned elements. Pathfinders also give search and rescue support in the event an aircraft is downed and, if necessary, can destroy the aircraft. They also manage and inspect slingload operations.

Pathfinders accomplish their missions through infiltration by foot, parachute, rappelling, vehicle or watercraft.

To perform their missions Pathfinders must carry with them at all times their ruck, a radio, NVDs, an infrared strobe for signaling aviators and all individual equipment a pathfinder will need to survive for three days.

Pathfinders are inserted at night, some distance away from the LZ. If obstacles are encountered on the LZ, the soldiers must determine if they should reduce, remove or mark them.

Contact with the enemy or unexpected problems with the landing zone can force the Pathfinders to move many kilometers to an alternate LZ. If the soldiers don't get extracted after completing their mission, they may have to walk out.

Because they are on their own, each Pathfinder is combat-lifesaver qualified. These skills are also necessary for their other duties: searching for downed aircraft and rescuing their crews.

At the LZ, Pathfinders use mathematical formulas to determine if a landing will be hampered by variables such as wind condition and ground slope. They often do this at night, number crunching with a pocket calculator.

PURPOSE:

The purpose of the Pathfinder Course is to train personnel to serve as Pathfinders in support of airmobile operations. Emphasis is placed on development of individual proficiency in air traffic control procedure and a thorough understanding of supported aviation unit SOP.

OVERVIEW:

Pathfinder School is a 3 week course in which the student:
+ Navigates dismounted;
+ Establishes and operates a day/night helicopter landing zone;
+ Establishes and operates a day/night CARP, GMRS, and Army VIRS parachute DZ;
+ Conducts sling load operations;
+ Provides air traffic control and navigational assistance to RW and FW airborne operations.

Students participates in a 3 day FTX as a member of a Pathfinder Team (Team Leader and Assistant Team Leader are graded positions).

PREREQUISITES:
+ Active Army, Reserve, National Guard Officers (2LT to CPT) or Enlisted personnel (PFC to SFC) whose actual or anticipated duty assignment requires performance of Pathfinder duties in CMFs 11, 12, 13, or 18 and MOSs 11B, 11C, 11H, 11M, 19D, 92Y, 88M, 93C;
+ Warrant Officers (WO1 to WO3) with MOSs 131A, 180A, or 921A may attend;
+ Enlisted applicants must have a GT score of 100, or above;
+ All applicants must have passed a valid Pathfinder physical within one-year, have a minimum profile serial of 111121 and have no speech impediment;

Example Training Schedule	
Pathfinder	
Day 1	
0700-0800	Inprocessing
0800-0830	Pathfinder Orientation
0830-1230	Slingload 1 & 2
1230-1300	Lunch
1300-Comp	Slingload Hands On (*4)
Day 2	
0800-1200	Slingload Hands On (*4)
1200-1300	Lunch
1300-Comp	Slingload Hands On (*4)
Day 3	
0800-0830	Slingload Written Exam / Review
0830-1130	Slingload Hands On Test (*4)
1130-1300	Lunch
1300-1500	ATC 1 & 2
1500-1600	Aero-Medevac
1600-UTC	Map Marking / Section Time
Day 4	
0700-0800	Slingload Written Retest
0800-Comp	Slingload Hands On Retest (*4)
0800-1100	Transmission Practice
1100-1200	ATC / Med Exam & Review
1200-1300	Lunch
1300-Comp	HLZ 1-4
Day 5	
0001-2400	No Training
Day 6	
0001-2400	No Training
Day 7	
0700-080	ATC / Med Retest
0800-1200	PZ 1-4
1200-1300	Lunch
1300-1500	Review HLZ / PZ Issue Homework
1500-Comp	Troop Leading Procedures
Day 8	
0700-1100	HLZ Cadre Led (*2)
1100-1200	HLZ / PZ Exam & Review
1200-1300	Lunch
1300-Comp	DZ 1, 2, 3
Day 9	
0800-0830	HLZ / PZ Retest
0830-1200	DZ 4, 5, 6
1200-1300	Lunch
1300-1430	Review DZ Class / Issue Homework
1430-1530	Troop Leading Procedures
1530-Comp	Basic Airborne Refresher

Example Training Schedule	
Pathfinder Continued	
Day 10	
0700-1500	Cadre led CARP / GMRS / Door Bundles - 1X C-130, TOT: 1300 Hrs, Arkman DZ (*2)
1500-1630	DZ Exam & Review
1630-Comp	Pre-Jump
Day 11	
0700-Comp	VIRS Jump - 2X UH-60, TOT: 1100, Pathfinder DZ (*2)
1530-Comp	DZ Retest
1500-Comp	FTX Prep & Rig Rucks
Day 12	
1100-2400	No Training
Day 13	
0001-2400	No Training
Day 14	
0001-2400	No Training
Day 15	
0500-0600	Manifest Call / MACO / Pre-Jump
0600-0700	FRAGO (Planning)
0700-0730	Movement to LAAF
0730-0830	Draw & Don Parachutes
0830-0900	Load Aircraft - TOT: 0900, Fryar DZ
0900-2400	FTX (*1,2,3)
Day 16	
0001-2400	FTX (*1,2,3)
Day 17	
0800-1000	Final Exam
1000-1130	Outprocessing
1130-1300	Lunch
1300-Comp	Recovery / Graduation Rehearsal
1400-Comp	AAR
Day 18	
0700-0900	Final Exam Retest
1000-Comp	Graduation

NOTES:
*1. Each student will be graded in a Leadership position (day or night, TL or ATL).
*2. Students must provide their own meal.
*3. Each section will do Night Sling Load.
*4. The following items of equipment will be rigged: HMMWV, Water Buffalo, A-22 Bag, Cargo Net & Water Bilvet.

♦ Physicals for Airborne qualified personnel must indicate "Cleared to participate in airborne operations";

♦ Upon completion of the course, service member must have a minimum of one year remaining in the service. Active and Reserve Marine Corps Officers (2LT to CPT) and Enlisted personnel (PFC to SFC) in logistics and combat arms may attend;

♦ Active and Reserve Air Force enlisted personnel serving as combat control team/forward air controllers (SGT to MSGT) may attend.).

MOS skills: 55B, 68J, 77F, and 31 series assigned to the 160th SOAR (A) will be accepted by an exception to policy.

The submission of requests for waiver is discouraged; course prerequisites have specific rationale and are well established. However service members may request the waiver of a specific course prerequisite. Those waiver requests will be submitted in memorandum format through the member's Battalion Commander (or first O5 in the chain of command), through:

Commander
11th Infantry Regiment, USAIS
Fort Benning, GA 31905;

to:

Commander
1st Battalion (Airborne), 507th Infantry
11th Infantry Regiment
Fort Benning, GA 31905.

All requests for waiver will address a specific prerequisite and contain a complete justification and persuasive argument for granting the waiver. Waiver request submission does not ensure favorable consideration.

PREPARATIONS:

Clothing & Equipment Requirements:

All students must have the items listed in Table Pathfinder-A for the course. If you are not issued these items, they will be provided. Table Pathfinder-B lists optional equipment students may also choose to bring to the course.

REPORTING INFORMATION:

All commanders must ensure applicants report to and sign in at Building 2748 for student accountability on the report date.

Sign in at Building 2748, no later than 2400 (Sunday) the day before the class starts. You may report to Building 2748 in civilian clothes to sign in. You will then report to Building 2593 at 0700. Your duty uniform will be BDU's (no rigger belts, A7A straps or shirts with organizational print on them) with soft cap, no berets. Bring notebook, pen, highlighter and water container (during summer months i.e., water bottle). Ensure you bring 10 copies of your orders, your physical examination (Airborne, Ranger, HALO, Scuba or class three exam). There will be absolutely no exceptions for missing either orders or your physical.

Inprocessing:

Student inprocessing begins at 0645 Monday morning. All service members report with a current physical (Physical must be taken within one year of the ATRRS report date to the course), identification tags, identification cards, 10 copies of orders and 2-1.

BILLETING:

Course attendees will be on full per diem and will pay mess/billeting. Non-availability statements are not authorized. Pathfinder School has no billeting or mess facilities and students are not issued meal cards.

Quarters:

Students need to make reservations with Ft. Benning Guest Housing:

Olsen Hall, COMM: (706) 689-0067.

Table: Pathfinder-A		
Required Items Inventory		
ITEM	QTY	REMARKS
Pack	1	ALICE, Complete, with Frame
Bag	1	Sleeping
LCE	1	Complete
Canteen	1	With cover
Belt	1	Web
Poncho	1	Gortex jacket acceptable (Gortex jacket will not be issued)
Helmet	1	Ballistic
Air items	1 set	

Table: Pathfinder-B		
Optional Equipment Inventory		
ITEM	QTY	REMARKS
Calculator	1	
Pens	1 set	Alcohol, with eraser
Compass	1	Draftsman, for drawing circles
Compass	1	Lensatic
Highlighters	2	
Earplugs	1 set	With case
Note taking materials	1 set	Pens, paper, pencils, erasers

NOTES: Bring appropriate seasonal gear (military issue). It is strongly recommended that students bring the items listed in the Optional Items Inventory.

Dining Facilities:

Though there are dining facilities available, the Pathfinder training schedule and POI does not allow for normal mess hours to be adhered to. Any student attending Pathfinder School not on full per diem/TDY will encore the cost of meals at their own expense.

Pay:

Any personnel attending Pathfinder School needs to be on order for full per diem/TDY.

Transportation:

Pathfinder students need to furnish or arrange for transportation while attending the course. The transportation provided by the Pathfinder School is for movement to and from training areas in a field environment.

CONTACT INFORMATION:

Points of contact for the US Army Pathfinder School are:

NCOIC:
DSN: 835-3218;
COMM: (706) 545-3218.

FAX:
DSN: 835-4923;
COMM: (706) 545-4923.

HHC 1/507
ATTN: Pathfinder Branch
Ft. Benning, GA 31905.

REFERENCE:

1. US Army Formal Schools Catalog. US Army Publishing Agency. DA PAM 351-4, Page 46, Table 3-6. 31 October 1995.
2. Pathfinder Operations. US Army Publishing Agency. FM 57-38. October 1968.
3. "The U. S. Army Pathfinder School." Online. Internet. 11 May 2000. Available: http://192.153.150.25/airborne/pathfinder/admin.html.
4. "Pathfinder." Online. Internet. 23 May 2000. Available: http://www.specialoperations.com/Specialties/pathfinder.html.
5. SFC Larry Lane. "Going in First." Originally printed in Soldiers Magazine. Online. Internet. 23 May 2000. Available: http://www.specwarnet.com/americas/pathfinder_article.htm.
6. Dominique Sumner. "US Army Pathfinder Units." Online. Internet. 23 May 2000. Available: http://www.specwarnet.com/americas/army_pathfinders.htm.

75TH RANGER REGIMENT

HISTORY:

"Rangers Lead the Way!" - The motto of the United States Army Ranger, a special breed of soldier who has done just that since the 17th Century Colonial America. From the start, the Ranger has been a soldier who combines daring with great skill at warfare to accomplish his mission. This proud tradition still exists as an integral part of the Ranger Regiment.

The Rangers trace their origin back to the frontiersmen of the New World. The settlers there encountered stiff resistance from some of the native Indian tribes who practiced a form of warfare alien to the settlers. Using concealment, long range scouting and swift savage raids, the Indians inflicted a heavy toll on colonists and their property.

The Americans responded by adopting these tactics, applying them effectively against the marauding parties of the East Coast tribes. Bands of men would often leave their settlements to search for approaching Indian raiding parties; upon completing their mission, they would report that they had "ranged" or patrolled a certain distance from their homes. The use of "ranged" led to naming these scouts "rangers."

The first organized Ranger unit was activated in 1670 to combat a hostile tribe under the leadership of Metocomet, also called King Phillip. The Rangers, commanded by Captain Benjamin Church, crushed the attacks and ended King Phillip's War in 1675.

The French and Indian War:

The French and Indian War saw the return of the Rangers. Major Robert Rogers from New Hampshire organized nine companies to fight for the British from 1756 to 1763. He published a list of 28 common-sense rules and a set of 19 standing orders stressing operational readiness, security and tactics. He established a training program in which he personally supervised the application of his rules. In June 1758, Rogers was conducting live fire training exercises.

Rogers' operations were characterized by solid preparation and bold movements. His Rangers' most famous action was a raid against the Abenaki Indians, renowned for their ferocity. 200 men traveled by foot and boat and covered 400 miles in roughly 60 days. Reaching the native camp undetected on September 29, 1759, the Rangers destroyed the camp and killed several hundred Indians. The once fearsome Abenaki tribe never posed a threat again.

The Rangers broke new ground in waging war in another way; while other units bivouacked for the winter, they took the fight to the Indians and French on skis, snowshoes, and even ice skates. The Rangers distinguished themselves as scouts and lethal adversaries.

The Revolutionary War:

Little more than a decade later, the Continental Congress called for ten companies of "expert riflemen" from Pennsylvania, Maryland and Virginia. Called the "Corps of Rangers" by General George Washington, this group of 500 men would also be known as "Morgan's Riflemen" for their commanding officer, Colonel Daniel Morgan. The Rangers caused great losses to British troops at the battles of Freeman's Farm in September 1777 and Cowpens in January 1781.

English General John Burgoyne stated that Morgan's Riflemen were "the most famous corps of the Continental Army, all crack shots."

Also active during the Revolutionary War were Thomas Knowlton's Connecticut Rangers. This force of less than 150 handpicked men was used primarily for reconnaissance. Knowlton was killed leading his men in action at Harlem Heights.

Another Ranger unit of the Revolutionary War operated from the swamps of South Carolina. Here Colonel Francis C. Marion raised a group called Marion's Partisans. The Partisans were all volunteers with little or no military training but were experts in handling horses and rifles. They ranged in number from a handful to several hundred at one time. Normally working separately from the Continental Army, the Partisans carried out frequent attacks against the British camps and outposts, severely disrupting lines of communication and supply. Marion's men would often capture or kill colonists sympathetic to Great Britain; this deprived the King's Army of an efficient intelligence network in the Carolinas.

While the Partisans chiefly fought a guerrilla war from their island base deep in the marshes, they also took part in the capture of three forts and fought on the first line in the Battle of Eutaw Springs, a crucial engagement of the war. In many of their actions, these men referred to Rogers' standing orders for their standards.

The fighters from South Carolina finally established themselves as such a threat to British plans for conquest that a detachment led by Lieutenant Colonel Banastre Tarleton was assigned to wipe them out, but failed. Tarleton once chased Marion's band through 25 miles of swamp and brush; upon reaching a section that seemed impossible to navigate, Tarelton cursed Marion, crying, "the damned swamp fox, the devil himself could not catch him." Marion was called the "Swamp Fox" from then on.

Ranger tactics weren't used only by Americans during the War for Independence. John Simcoe's Queen's Rangers, Patrick Ferguson's Rangers and Thomas Browne's King's Carolina Rangers all applied their scouting and weapons skills in support of the crown.

The War of 1812:

In the time period between the Revolutionary War and the Civil War, American Ranger units saw more action against the British in the War of 1812. According to the Army Register for December 28, 1813, at least 12 companies were active during this time. Rangers would also continue their familiar role of patrolling in search of Indian parties in several states. The Texas Congress mobilized a ranging company in the mid 1830s; these volunteers, issued only ammunition by the state, would soon become the celebrated Texas Rangers.

The American Civil War:

When war broke out between the union and the secessionist states, it was the Confederacy that employed Ranger tactics more widely and with greater success. The prominent rebel Rangers were groups led by Colonel John Singleton Mosby, General John Hunt Morgan, and Colonel Turner Ashby.

Colonel John S. Mosby organized his Rangers in north central Virginia in January 1863. From a three man scout unit in 1862, Mosby's force grew to an operation of eight companies of Rangers by 1865. Heavily influenced by Francis Marion, Mosby adopted a similar style of hit and run operations that plagued Union officers and left them bewildered and wondering where he would strike next. This confusion led wary Federal units to reinforce too many points, draining needed soldiers away from the front lines. Mosby's force would then select a weaker target and deal another strong blow to their enemies.

Mosby's Rangers were proficient riflemen and horsemen who knew the stretch of Virginia in detail. They were so confident of their mastery of the terrain that they would even carry out night operations, a first at that time.

Mosby's most well known mission didn't result in a firefight or a single Ranger casualty. A Union colonel named Percy Wyndham once insulted

Mosby and his group by calling them criminals. Mosby resolved to make Wyndham pay for his words by kidnapping him. Wyndham was located at Fairfax Courthouse, Virginia (a Union Army post deep behind the lines). Mosby moved out at night with 29 men. They first cut the telegraph wires running between Centerville and Fairfax. They moved past light sentry patrols and arrived at what was supposed to be Wyndham's house. Their information was wrong, Mosby learned from one of his prisoners that Colonel Wyndham had recently left the camp. He also discovered that a General Edwin H. Stoughton was in Fairfax; Mosby set out to capture the Union commander instead. Posing as Federal messengers, Mosby and his men gained entry to the general's home, grabbed him and returned to a Confederate camp. That night the Rangers succeeded in seizing a Union general, several other officers and enlisted men and numerous horses while in enemy territory and had sustained no injuries.

Mosby's unit contributed greatly to the Southern cause. Their deeds would win their Virginia home the name "Mosby's Confederacy." General Sheridan considered him the South's most annoying guerrilla. General Ulysses S. Grant once ordered that family members of Mosby's Rangers be captured and even called for a summary execution of known Rangers without benefit of trial.

Confederate General John Hunt Morgan and his cavalry unit began their work in December 1861. Their greatest effort started in July 1863. Morgan and his Rangers attacked at Green River Bridge, Kentucky. Forced to withdraw, they passed through Lebanon, Kentucky, where they captured the town's garrison. Morgan's men then stole two streamer ships, crossed the Ohio River, moved to Corydon, Indiana and seized the town. Union troops and gunboats were scrambled to stop them. While Federal soldiers pursued them and civilians panicked, Morgan's Rangers kept moving. They came within a days ride of Lake Erie - this was the deepest Rebel penetration northward in the Civil War. The group was finally forced to surrender near East Liverpool, Ohio near the close of July, after causing widespread hysteria

and diverting Federal soldiers from the approaching Battle of Chickamauga.

Colonel Ashby's Rangers also played their part in fighting for an independent South, using the same methods as Mosby and Morgan.

The Union's only notable employment of Rangers was the capture of General Longstreet's ammunition train by Mean's Rangers. Mean's band never accomplished their original mission: the elimination of Mosby's Rangers.

After the close of the Civil War, recognized Army Ranger units would disappear for more than 70 years.

The Second World War:

The time - June 19, 1942, the place - Carrickfergus, Northern Ireland: 2,000 handpicked volunteers led by Major William O. Darby endured rigorous training at the hands of British Commandos. By the end of the program, 500 men were left. They became the 1st Ranger Battalion. 50 of these Rangers took part in the raid on Dieppe on France's northern coast along with Canadian and British commandos.

The 1st Ranger Battalion participated in the initial landing at Arzeu, Algeria. They carried out crucial night operations in Tunisia and took part in the Battle of El Guettar. Their valor was recognized with a Presidential Unit Citation, the equivalent of awarding each man in the battalion the Distinguished Service Cross.

Two more battalions, the 3rd and 4th, were created by Major Darby towards the end of the campaign in Tunisia. These battalions, along with the 1st, would be called "Darby's Rangers" or the Ranger Force. They would spearhead the invasion of Sicily at Gela and Licata and play a part in the conquest of Messina. At Salerno they would fight off eight Nazi counterattacks for 18 days to hold the Chunzi Pass. The Rangers experienced fierce winter and mountain combat in clearing the entrance to the narrow pass leading to Cassino. At Anzio they would defeat the beach defenses and secure the town.

Darby's Rangers suffered a severe setback on January 30, 1944, when the three groups were discovered infiltrating near Cisterna and were virtually wiped out by German armor and infantry. Of the 767 men in the Ranger Force, 761 were killed or captured. The survivors were sent back to the United States and transferred to the Special Service Force, a joint Canadian-American special operations unit.

Colonel James Rudder formed the 2nd Ranger Battalion at Camp Forrest, Tennessee on April 1, 1943. The men of 2nd Battalion, along with those from 5th Battalion - activated at Camp Forrest in September 1943 - participated in the June 6, 1944 D-Day invasion at Omaha Beach, Normandy. D, E and F Companies of the 2nd Battalion were assigned to neutralize a German artillery battery located on Pointe Du Hoc. 220 men scaled the sheer face of the cliff through a storm of weapons fire and mortar and grenade explosions. Though only 90 were able to fight when they reached the top of the Point, the gun emplacements were silenced.

During the initial assault on Omaha Beach, Brigadier General Norman D. Cota, assistant division commander of the 29th infantry Division, realized that the invasion force must push on past the beach or suffer intolerable losses. He chose the Rangers of the 5th Battalion, led by Lieutenant Colonel Max Schneider, to make a way through the murderous fire with the command "Rangers, lead the way off this beach!" General Cota's order has become the familiar motto, "Rangers lead the way."

The 6th Battalion was formed in September 1944 in the Pacific theater. The commanding officer was Lieutenant Colonel Henry Mace. The 6th was unique among the Ranger Battalions - it was the only one to conduct special operations. The soldiers of the 6th were among the first American units to return to the Philippines. All of their missions were usually a task force, company or platoon size element that operated behind enemy lines and involved long range reconnaissance and hard hitting long range combat patrols.

A reinforced company would later make a daring rescue mission in January 1945. The Rangers made a 29 mile forced march past enemy lines in search of the Japanese prison camp at Cabanatuan, Philippines where American and Allied prisoners of war were held. After finding the camp, they crawled almost a mile over flat, exposed terrain and attacked Japanese positions. Over 200 enemy soldiers were slain. Two Rangers were killed and ten others wounded. More than 500 prisoners of war were liberated, all within 20 minutes of the start of the siege.

The 6th would later prepare the way for the 14th Airborne to make a jump onto Camalugian Airfield and bring an end to the fighting in the Philippines. All the Japanese prisoners of war taken during this operation were captured by one platoon from the battalion.

Though not called Rangers, the servicemen in the 5307th Composite Unit (Provisional) carried out Ranger type missions in northern Burma from February to August 1944.

Activated on October 3, 1943, the 5307th drew from seasoned combat veterans throughout the Southwest Pacific. Two battalions headed by Colonel Charles Hunter sailed from San Francisco on the Lurline to Noumea, New Caledonia, then to Brisbane, Australia; a short stop at Perth and finally connected with a third battalion in Bombay, India on October 31, 1943. Each battalion was composed of two combat teams. Each team was identified by a different color for airdrop/resupply purposes (red, white, blue, orange, green, khaki).

Trained to perform long range patrols and function in the enemy's rear area, the 5307th disrupted Japanese supplies and communication. Their mission was to pave the way for the construction of the Ledo Road, a connection between the Indian railway and the old Burma Road to China, and possess Myitkyina Airfield, the only all weather landing strip in north Burma.

The 2,997 man force, then under the command of Brigadier General Frank D. Merrill, would endure Burma's harsh climate, dense terrain, along with fatigue and the diseases native to the tropics; still they soundly defeated veteran Japanese soldiers in 35 engagements. To the American public, the 5307th became "Merrill's Marauders" for their stamina and profess-ionalism deep in enemy territory.

The Marauders would end their successful campaign at Myitkyina Airfield. Suffering heavy losses from exhaustion and illness, they nevertheless overcame the Japanese and seized the strip. The 5307th would be redesignated the 475th "Mars Task Force" after this action.

The Korean War:

When World War II ended, the Rangers were disbanded, just as they had been after other conflicts in America's past. In 1950, the Army Chief of Staff selected Colonel John Gibson Van Houton to create a Ranger training program at Ft. Benning, Georgia. The goal of the training was to create a headquarters company and four Ranger Infantry Companies (Airborne).

As many as 5,000 soldiers from the 82nd Airborne Division alone volunteered for the 6 week course. Teaching amphibious and airborne infiltration, sabotage, demolition's and familiarization with U.S. and foreign weapons, the program was intended to create highly skilled soldiers capable of moving "40-50 miles, cross country, in 12 to 18 hours, depending on the terrain."

The graduates of the school were organized into eight companies, each of which was attached to a conventional infantry division. The 1st, 2nd, and 4th Ranger Companies finished the first cycle on November 13, 1950. 3rd Company remained at Ft. Benning to train the remaining 5th, 6th, 7th, and 8th Companies. The 2nd Ranger Company was made up entirely of black volunteers who were experienced troopers from the 555th (Triple Nickel) Infantry Regiment (Airborne).

Throughout the winter of 1950 and the spring of 1951, the Rangers went into battle. They were nomadic warriors - attached first to one regiment, then to another. They performed "out front" work: scouting, patrols, raids, ambushes, spearheading assaults and counterattacking to restore lost positions.

The 1st Ranger Infantry Company (Airborne) once went nine miles behind enemy lines and destroyed the headquarters of the 12th North Korean Division. Two North Korean Regiments fled from the area as a result.

The 2nd and 4th Ranger Companies made a combat jump at Munsanni and were seen moving north of the 38th parallel by reporters for Life magazine. The Rangers of the 4th Company executed a daring over water raid at Hwachon Dam. The 3rd Ranger Company had the motto; "die, bastard, die."

The 5th Ranger Company performed brilliantly during the Chinese "5th Phase Offensive." The Ranger Company commander held the line with Ranger sergeants commanding other line infantry units.

The 8th Ranger Company (known as the "Devils") would kill 70 Chinese soldiers in an encounter with two Chinese Reconnaissance Companies.

The 6th Ranger Infantry Company (Airborne) would later be moved to Europe because of growing concern over Communist Block interest in expanding to the west. Those Rangers would be the first Army unit to conduct a mass, tactical, free fall jump.

On October 22, 1951 the Chief of Army Field Forces would change the emphasis of Fort Benning's Ranger program from training airborne companies to teaching individuals. The last of the Ranger Companies were deactivated less than a month later.

Vietnam:

In Vietnam the LRRPs (Long Range Reconnaissance Patrols) would inherit the Ranger lineage. Thirteen companies (charlie - papa, minus juliet) were assigned to brigades, divisions, and field units to act as eyes and ears inside land claimed by the Viet Cong and the North Vietnamese Army. They would work in small groups and rely on stealth to evade enemy observation. LRRP teams would also attack the enemy using hit and run raids and ambushes. The LRRPs would be redesignated the 75th Infantry Regiment (Ranger) on June 1, 1969. One Ranger, Staff Sergeant James A. Champion of Lima Company, is still missing in action today. The

LRRP/Rangers were disbanded at the end of the Vietnam War. Many of them transferred to the 82nd Airborne Division.

The frustrating pattern of activating then deactivating Ranger units after the current crisis had come to a halt in 1973. Army Chief of Staff General Abrams called for the establishment of a permanent Ranger presence in the Army - the 1st Ranger Battalion was activated on February 8, 1974 at Fort Stewart, Georgia after originally forming at Fort Benning. The 2nd Ranger Battalion would be formed on October 1, 1974. The 1st Battalion would establish headquarters at Hunter Army Airfield, Georgia, while 2nd Battalion would settle at Fort Lewis, Washington.

The Iranian Crisis:

The ill fated attempt to rescue the American Embassy personnel held hostage in Teheran, Iran (code named Desert One) was primarily a Special Forces Operation. It is not generally known that Rangers were also to take part. While 1st Special Forces Operational Detachment Delta was to perform the actual rescue, Company C, 1st Battalion, 75th Infantry Regiment (Ranger) was to provide security for the men and equipment.

The rescue force assembled in Egypt on 21 April 1980. Three days later, a fleet of C-141s carried the 120 man force to Masirah Island, off the coast of Oman, where they transferred to three MC-130s accompanied by three fuel bearing EC-130s. They landed 200 miles southeast of Teheran at 2200 hours and waited for the arrival of eight RH-53D Sea Stallion helicopters from the aircraft carrier Nimitz. A twelve man road watch team, composed primarily of Rangers, was along to secure the site while the helicopters refueled. The team would return to Egypt on one of the MC-130s.

Delta was to be flown to a hide site before dawn on 25 April by the RH-53Ds, which would remain at their own hide site until the assault on the compound where the hostages were held. The plan was to use the helicopters to ferry the hostages awaiting transport.

The task of Company C 1/75, was to secure a landing area for the transports. The Rangers were to fly from Egypt to Manazariyeh, Iran and take the airfield there. They would land, if possible, or jump if resistance was offered. Once the airfield (which was thirty five miles south of Teheran) was secure, the Rangers would hold it while the C-141s arrived to airlift the hostages and their rescuers back to Egypt. The Rangers would then "dry up" or remove all signs of their presence, render the field useless and be airlifted out.

Taking and securing a hostile airfield within enemy territory is one of the primary components of the Ranger mission. They were prepared to hold the field as long as necessary if there were not enough transports to take everyone out in one trip. During training, the Rangers worked out all probable scenarios on a mock-up of the type of airfield in Iran.

Desert One was aborted at the first stage when two Sea Stallions crashed into each other on landing, killing the crews. One helicopter had aborted before leaving the carrier. It had been determined that at least six helicopters were necessary for the mission to succeed fewer than six automatically canceled the rescue attempt. Company C 1/75 never left Egypt. The Rangers in the road watch team returned with Delta.

Grenada:

The Rangers had little time to prepare for their role in Urgent Fury, the invasion of Grenada. Within hours of receiving orders to move, Ranger units were marshalling at Hunter Army Airfield, Georgia, prepared to board C-130s and MC-130s for the ride to Grenada. Their first objective was Point Salines Airfield, located on the island's most southwestern point. While securing the airfield, Rangers were to secure the True Blue Campus at Salines, where American medical students were in residence. As quickly as possible, Ranger units were then to take the army camp at Calivigny.

Things started to go wrong as the operation began. A Navy SEAL team was unable to get ashore; they were to have provided intelligence on the airfield at Salines. H-hour, originally scheduled during darkness, was moved several times until morning twilight. In the lead MC-130s there were problems with the inertial navigation equipment. Since there were no hatch mount antennas on the cargo doors of the aircraft, communications to Ranger units were delayed, passing through Air Force communications.

While in the air, the Rangers were notified of photographic intelligence indicating obstructions on the field. Instead of landing, the majority of transport would have to drop all the Rangers at Salines so the runway could be cleared.

In some aircraft the men were told to remove their harness, ruck sack, and main and reserve parachutes. These items were placed in kit bags and moved forward to facilitate off-loading troops and cargo. Before long, the loadmasters were yelling, "Only thirty minutes fuel left. Rangers are fighting. Jump in Twenty minutes."

These Rangers now had to re-rig for the drop, unpacking nonessential equipment and pulling on parachutes. Ruck sacks had to be hooked under the reserve pack and weapons strapped to the left side. Under these conditions it was not possible for the jumpmaster to check each man, so buddy rigging was employed.

Aboard the lead MC-130, navigation equipment failed and the pilot reported he could not guarantee finding the landing zone. Rain squalls made it impossible to employ a lead change, so both lead aircraft pulled away to the south. As the Rangers approached the target, the aircraft were out of assigned order and the planned order of arrival was no longer possible. This meant that the runway clearing team would not be the first on the field. The Rangers then requested a mass parachute assault, a contingency previously planned, so that only the order of exit from the aircraft would be affected, but the Air Force refused to conduct a mass drop.

On October 25, 1983 at 0534, hours the first Rangers began dropping at Salines: a platoon of B Company, 1/75 and the Battalion Tactical Operations Center (TOC), followed almost 25 minutes later by part of A Company, 1/75. Over a half hour later the rest of A Company, 1/75, minus seven men were over Salines. It was now 0634 hours, but the remaining men of 1/75 would not be on the ground until 0705 hours.

Men of 1/75 assembled on the east end of the runway. They were short C Company, 1/75, which had been sent with sixty Special Operations Forces troops to take the Richmond Hill prison. The Ranger Battalions were already operating below strength. One reason for this seems to have been the fact that a limited number of aircraft and aircrews were trained for night operations.

Over one and a half hours elapsed from the first drop of 1/75 until the last unit was on the ground shortly after seven in the morning. These men jumped from 500 feet so they would be in the air between 12 and 15 seconds. Their drop zone was very narrow because there was water on the north and south sides only a few meters from the runway.

At 0707 hours the 2nd Battalion began to drop. For several hours their aircraft had orbited, waiting to unload and refuel. They dropped in a much shorter period, and all but one man was safely on the ground. One Ranger broke his leg and one Ranger's static line became tangled as he exited the aircraft, dragging him against the tail of the plane before he was hauled back aboard. 2/75 assembled on the western end of the runway.

Once on the ground, 1/75 was not under effective fire and thus could begin to clear the runway of blocking trucks and bulldozers. Some of the vehicles had keys in them; others were hot wired and removed. A Cuban bulldozer was used to flatten the stakes that had been driven into the ground with wires between them, and to push aside the drums placed on the runway. For fifteen minutes there was no enemy fire, and the Rangers worked without interruption.

By 1000 hours, 1/75 had its second platoon at the True Blue Campus and its first and third platoons had moved north of the runway. In the center, B Company, 1/75 had moved north and was holding the high ground, not far from the Cuban headquarters. Units of 2/75 had cleared the area west of the airfield as well as the area north of their drop zone to Canoe Bay. The airfield was secure, and the C-130s, which had gone to Barbados to refuel, returned to unload equipment that had not been dropped - which included jeeps, motorcycles and Hughes 500 Defender helicopters.

Eight hours after landing, the commander of B Company, 2/75 was notified that two Rangers were missing near their positions. The company commander decided the missing men must be near a building which lay between B Company and the Cuban positions. A Cuban construction worker was sent forward with an eleven man Ranger squad under a flag of truce. While the Rangers remained outside, the Cuban entered and spoke with those inside, who agreed to a truce if the Rangers would treat the Cuban wounded. Two Rangers and seventeen wounded Cubans were evacuated. Afterward, the Ranger commander called for the Cubans to surrender, 80 to 100 did so. The remainder surrendered later, after a brief fight, to the 82nd Airborne.

At 1530 hours that afternoon a counterattack was launched toward A Company, 1/75, consisting of three BTR-60s, which moved through 2nd platoons firing positions, firing toward the runway. The Rangers countered with rifles, M60s, LAWs, and a recoilless rifle. Two of the BTRs hit each other when the first one halted. Both were disabled. The third began a hasty retreat and was hit in the rear. It was finally destroyed by an AC-130 Spectre gunship.

The last action of the first day took place east of True Blue Campus, where Rangers came under fire from a house on top of a prominent hill 1,000 meters east of the runway. No Spectre gunship was available, so an A-7 attack plane finally destroyed the house, but only after several duds landed alarmingly near the Rangers.

At the end of the first day in Grenada, the Rangers had secured the airfield and True Blue Campus at a cost of five dead and six wounded. Unfortunately, C Company, 1/75 had run into a more difficult situation. When their Black Hawk helicopters arrived at the prison, the local defenses were active. Perched on a high ridge whose sides were almost vertical and covered by dense foliage, the prison was surrounded by walls twenty feet high and topped with barbed wire and watchtowers covering the area. Intelligence had failed to report the presence of two antiaircraft guns on a ridge some 150 feet higher then the prison, which brought the Black Hawks under

fire. It was impossible to use ropes to lower the Rangers. The helicopters had to remain steady during this operation, making the Rangers and crews easy targets. No air support was possible at this time, since all small aircraft were engaged at Salines.

At least two attempts were made to bring the Black Hawks in to unload troops, but antiaircraft fire hit pilots, crew and the attacking troops. Suppressive fire from the Black Hawks was ineffective. Although some Rangers walked away from the crashed Black Hawks, others were badly hurt and were not immediately evacuated. Part of the evacuation problem seems to have been that Army pilots could not land aboard Navy ships because they were not qualified to do so, although this requirement was eventually waived.

Intelligence failed again as the Rangers were not informed until 1030 hours on the morning of the 25 October that there were still students at the second campus on Grand Anse. Students reported guards in the area, but the Rangers thought that they could bring the students out. A heliborne operation with Marine airlift from Guam was planned. Marine helicopter squadron 261 was to provide the helicopters, with supporting fire from ships off the coast and the Marines two remaining Cobra attack helicopters. American suppressive fire would continue until 20 seconds before the Rangers were committed.

The Rangers would fly to the objective in three waves, each composed of three CH-46s. Each wave of three would carry a company of Rangers (about 50 men). A Company, 1/75 would go in first, followed by B Company, 1/75, which was to cordon off the campus to prevent outside intervention. C Company, 1/75 would then arrive, its mission: to locate the students and pack them into four CH-53s waiting offshore.

During lift off, the order of aircraft somehow became confused. Instead of the lead flight having three CH-46s carrying A Company, 1/75, the first load had one from A Company, and two from B Company. Consequently, the second wave had two from A Company, and one from B Company. The first three aircraft missed the designated beach in front of the campus. There was sporadic small arms fire, but the only serious damage came from overhanging trees. One helicopter shut down and was abandoned in the surf, the Rangers scrambled out as water poured in. Later a tree damaged a second machine.

The orbiting Sea Stallions were now brought in to remove the students. The Ch-46s returned and extracted the Rangers, completing the entire operation in 26 minutes. After leaving the beach, they realized that eleven men sent up, as a flank guard had not returned. By radio these men were told to move toward positions held by the 82nd Airborne. The Rangers were not sure they could safely enter those lines, so they decided to use one of the inflatable boats from the disabled helicopter. However, the rafts had been damaged during the air assault. The Rangers soon had to swim alongside their damaged boat. Having battled surf and tides for some time, they were spotted, picked up at 2300 hours, and brought to the USS Caron lying off the coast.

One of the Rangers' initial objectives, Calivigny barracks, had not been secured. Lying about 5 kilometers from the airfield, the barracks reportedly housed and trained troops. On 27 October, under the command of a Brigade Headquarters from the 82nd Airborne Division, a full scale attack was carried out by 2/75 and reinforced by C Company, 1/75.

Four waves of four Black Hawks - each carrying a company to assault the camp - were to fly out to sea before heading to the beach, flying low over the water at about 100 knots. Spectre gunships and Navy A-7s furnished support. At Salines the Army had seventeen 105mm howitzers; at sea, the USS Caron would supply fire support. A Company, 2/75 was to land at the southern end of the compound, C Company, 2/75 was to set down on the left and right. B Company, 2/75 was to land in the southeast, assault suspected antiaircraft guns and rejoin the other companies in the north. In reserve was C Company, 1/75, which would also hold the southern end of the perimeter.

The Black Hawks came in over the waves, climbing sharply to the top of the cliffs. Quickly the pilots slowed down in order to find the exact landing zone inside the perimeter. Each Black Hawk came in rapidly, one behind the other. The first helicopter put down safely near the southern boundary of the camp and was followed by the second. The third Black Hawk suffered some damage, spun forward, smashing into the second machine. In the fourth Black Hawk, the crew saw what was happening and veered hard right; the aircraft landed in a ditch, damaging its tail rotor. Apparently not realizing that the helicopters rotor was damaged, the pilot attempted to move the Black Hawk, which rose sharply, seemed to spin forward, and crashed. In twenty seconds three machines were down. Debris and rotor blades flew through the air, badly wounding four Rangers and killing three, the only deaths in 2/75.

A Company, 2/75 regrouped as C Company, 2/75 landed on large concrete pads on the edge of the compound. B Company, 2/75 also landed safely, and moved onto its objective. C Company, 1/75 also landed without incident. Contrary to expectations, the barracks were deserted; the Rangers found nothing. This was their last action before returning to the United States.

Just Cause – Panama:

On October 3, 1984 the Department of the Army announced the activation of the 3rd Ranger Battalion and on February 3, 1986 the 75th Ranger Regimental Headquarters at Fort Benning. This historic event marked a new era for the Rangers; with over 2000 soldiers, the modern battalions had a number of men unseen since World War II.

The entire Regiment would participate in the invasion of Panama on December 20, 1989. The Rangers were to secure Torrijos-Tocumen International Airport, Rio Hato Military Airfield, and then Noriega's beach house. Rangers who dropped at Torillos later moved into Panama City, where they took the military headquarters of the Panamanian Defense Forces. Conducting simultaneous low level parachute jumps 1/75, C Company, 3/75 and Team Gold from RHQ would capture Torrijos-Tocumen International Airport, while 2/75, Companies A and B 3/75 and Team Black of RHQ would take over Rio Hato Airfield. At Rio Hato heavy antiaircraft fire was encountered and one Ranger was hit in the back of the head while still in the airplane; however, he survived.

The Rangers secured the perimeter of the field before the Panamanians began to test the defenses. At Rio Hato the Rangers were supported by AC-130 Spectre gunships, whose target acquisition cameras found targets in the dark. Two hours after the drop at Rio Hato, the airfield was secure enough for transport aircraft to begin landing with supplies and additional equipment for the Rangers.

Once the airfields were secure, the Rangers then carried out special operations in support of Joint Task Force (South). They moved against the Panamanian Special Forces called the "Mountain Troops." Rangers moved from house to house in the compound and the village where the families of the soldiers lived. Many of the Mountain Troops were caught trying to shave off their distinctive beards. On the fifth day of the operation the Rangers were sent to secure Calle Diez, an area some twenty to twenty five miles from Panama City, held by the "Dignity Battalions."

Rangers took pictures of Panamanian and foreign property, aircraft, shops and houses to show that property was still intact and protected by the U.S. Army. This prevented false claims and probably saved the United States many hundreds of thousands of dollars. Rangers also guarded buildings - such as the Vatican embassy where President Noriega took refuge - to see that no damage was done. Sustaining five killed in action and 42 wounded, the Rangers captured 1014 prisoners of war and over 18000 Panamanian arms. They accomplished the mission given to them for operation Just Cause: the removal of Manuel Noriega and members of the Panamanian Defense Force loyal to him.

Desert Storm:

The Rangers fought again in Operation Desert Storm. 1st Ranger Battalion - B Company and 1st Platoon, with weapons platoon attachments of A Company - deployed from February 12, 1991 to April 6, 1991. They conducted pinpoint raids and quick reaction force missions in cooperation with Allied Forces. The Rangers sustained no casualties. In December 1991, 1/75 and the Regimental Headquarters Company deployed to Kuwait in a routine training exercise as a show of force. The Rangers jumped into Kuwait during daylight hours.

Somalia:

The next deployment of the Rangers occurred in Somalia in 1993. B Company, 3/75 was deployed from August 26, 1993 to October 21, 1993 to assist United Nations Forces in bringing order to a desperately chaotic and starving nation. The Rangers took part in seven missions trying to capture Mohammed Aidid and his top lieutenants in order to end Aidid's guerrilla war against the U.N.'s efforts to feed the Somali people.

On October 3, 1993 (exactly nine years after the reactivation of 3rd Battalion), B Company, and members of Special Force Operational Detachment- Delta set out to capture two of Aidid's officers in the Olympic Hotel, one of the most dangerous parts of the city. After moving to the objective, the team assigned to grab the two followers of Aidid succeeded in their task and called for extraction within twenty minutes of the first assault. The Humvees were dispatched to evacuate the prisoners and the assault force. After being ambushed at the K-4 traffic circle the Humvees would reach the Olympic Hotel and begin extracting. At this point a rocket propelled grenade shot down a UH-60 Black Hawk, and the Rangers would begin a courageous rescue operation that would grow into the most intense firefight since the Vietnam War.

The Rangers moved to and secured the downed UH-60 as another Black Hawk was shot down. Under severe fire from machine guns and hand and rocket propelled grenades, the Rangers grouped together and established a perimeter inside buildings to treat their wounded and wait for extraction. The relief column, composed of cooks and other Rangers received heavy fire enroute to their fellow Rangers. They would be reinforced with elements of the 10th Mountain, Pakistani and Malaysian armored vehicles to help extract the wounded and fallen Rangers.

The Rangers returned to the airfield early in the morning on October 4, having lost 6 men and sustaining numerous wounded. The Somalis fared far worse, the Rangers delivered devastating firepower and killed approximately 300 of their forces, wounding more. A Company, 3/75 would deploy to Somalia from October 5, 1993 to 23 October 1993 in support of other United Nations operations.

The Rangers have led the way in battle from the era of the flintlock to the age of the night vision device and the M16A2. Stealth, speed, bravery and a commitment to duty have been the attributes of the men who have borne the title "Ranger." A look into the Ranger past is no dead history exercise, but a glimpse at what Rangers have always been and remain as to this day.

Motto:

Sua Sponte - of their own accord. The original Marauders, like today's Rangers, were all volunteers.

Ranger Creed:

Recognizing that I volunteered as a Ranger, fully knowing the hazards of my chosen profession, I will always endeavor to uphold the prestige, honor, and high esprit de corps of the Rangers.

Acknowledging the fact that a Ranger is a more elite soldier who arrives at the cutting edge of battle by land, sea, or air, I accept the fact that as a Ranger my country expects me to move further, faster, and fight harder than any other soldier.

Never shall I fail my comrades I will always keep myself mentally alert, physically strong, and morally straight and I will shoulder more than my share of the task whatever it may be, one hundred percent and then some.

Gallantly will I show the world that I am a specially selected and well trained soldier. My courtesy to superior officers, neatness of dress, and care of equipment shall set the example for others to follow.

Energetically will I meet the enemies of my country. I shall defeat them on the field of battle for I am better trained and will fight with all my might. Surrender is not a Ranger word. I will never leave fallen comrade to fall into the hands of the enemy and under no circumstances will I ever embarrass my country.

Readily will I display the intestinal fortitude required to fight on to the Ranger objective and complete the mission, though I be the lone survivor.

Standing Orders of Rogers' Rangers:

Don't forget nothing.

Have your musket clean as a whistle, hatchet scoured, sixty rounds powder and ball, and be ready to march at a minutes warning.

When you're on the march, act the way you would if you was sneaking up on a deer. See the enemy first.

Tell the truth about what you see and what you do. There is an army depending on us for correct information. You can lie all you please when you tell other folks about the Rangers, but don't never lie to a Ranger or officer.

Don't never take a chance you don't have to.

When we're on the march we march single file, far enough apart so one shot can't go through two men.

If we strike swamps, or soft ground, we spread out abreast, so it's hard to track us.

When we march, we keep moving till dark, so as to give the enemy the least possible chance at us.

When we camp, half the party stays awake while the other half sleeps.

If we take prisoners, we keep'em separate till we have had time to examine them, so they can't cook up a story between'em.

Don't ever march home the same way. Take a different route so you won't be ambushed.

No matter whether we travel in big parties or little ones, each party has to keep a scout

20 yards ahead, 20 yards on each flank, and 20 yards in the rear so the main body can't be surprised and wiped out.

Every night you'll be told where to meet if surrounded by a superior force.

Don't sit down to eat without posting sentries.

Don't sleep beyond dawn. Dawn's when the French and Indians attack.

Don't cross a river by a regular ford.

If somebody's trailing you, make a circle, come back onto your own tracks, and ambush the folks that aim to ambush you.

Don't stand up when the enemy's coming against you. Kneel down, lie down, hide behind a tree.

Let the enemy come till he's almost close enough to touch, then let him have it and jump out and finish him up with your hatchet.
- Major Robert Rogers, 1759.

RANGER ATTRIBUTES:

Rangers are guided by the Ranger Creed, General Abrams' original Charter and Major Rogers' Standing Orders in all that they do. By applying the values represented in these, a Ranger is able to select a proper course of action for any situation.

The essence of military courtesy is mutual respect. All Rangers are treated with dignity and consideration. Leaders will maintain a professional approach in training Rangers. Insults, hazing, or other types of maltreatment are unnecessary and unprofessional. A Ranger is a Ranger upon completion of RIP/ROP. The Rangers are one of the very small number of units in the Army with summary release authority; therefore, performance to standard is simple. If a Ranger fails to perform to standard after adequate counseling and training, he will be released.

Rangers allow their performance to speak for themselves. Bragging is neither required nor attractive. Quiet, confident competence is the mode of behavior.

Rangers train 48 weeks of the year. Rangers have about two weeks of leave in the summer and two weeks of leave in the winter.

There are three readiness levels in the Ranger Regiment: Ranger Ready Force One, Ranger Ready Force Two and Ranger Ready Force Three. During RRF1, very stringent personnel accountability procedures are imposed.

All Rangers have a fresh haircut before first formation of the first duty day of each week. The hair will be very close on the sides and not exceed one inch on top. The hair will present a tapered/blended look; no mustaches are worn.

Rangers always lead the way in discipline; except for safety, there is no talking or shouting in the air or on the drop zone. Noise and light discipline are strictly observed.

Rangers are always prepared to take notes.

Rangers execute frequent live fire exercises; safe handling of weapons are instinctive.

Rangers learn faster and retain information longer in a controlled stress environment. That environment is created by the intensity and high standards to which they train; a Ranger trained to standard will produce a highly disciplined, well trained Ranger.

Rangers that attend Ranger School are expected to graduate and receive their tab. Rangers are expected to set the standard and bring credit to the Regiment. Any Ranger who fails to graduate due to "lack of motivation", SOR, or Peers will be released from the Regiment.

MISSION:

The mission of the Ranger Regiment is to plan and conduct special military operations in support of United States policy and objectives. This mission is accomplished by strike, light infantry and special military operations against targets and under conditions which require the unique capabilities of the unit.

Targets for the Ranger Regiment are strategic, of significant tactical value, extremely time sensitive or of a critical nature. Operations conditions require the Ranger Regiment to be highly trained, highly deployable, flexible and totally reliable.

ORGANIZATION:

The 75th Ranger Regiment, composed of three Ranger battalions, is the premier light infantry unit of the United States Army. Headquartered at Fort Benning, Georgia, the three Ranger battalions that comprise the 75th Ranger Regiment are geographically dispersed. Their locations are:

♦ 1st Battalion: 75th Ranger Regiment, Hunter Army Airfield, Georgia;

♦ 2nd Battalion: 75th Ranger Regiment, Fort Lewis, Washington;

♦ 3rd Battalion: 75th Ranger Regiment, Fort Benning, Georgia.

In addition, the Ranger Training Brigade Headquarters, Ranger Training Brigade, is located at Fort Benning, Georgia. Its battalions are dispersed among the following training sites:

♦ 4th Ranger Training Battalion - Fort Benning, Georgia;

♦ 5th Ranger Training Battalion - Dahlonega, Georgia;

♦ 6th Ranger Training Battalion - Eglin Air Force Base, Florida.

CAPABILITIES:

The Army maintains the Regiment at a high level of readiness. Each battalion can deploy anywhere in the world with 11 hours notice. Because of the importance the Army places on the 75th Ranger Regiment, it must possess a number of capabilities. These capabilities include:

♦ Infiltrating and exfiltrating by land, sea and air;

♦ Conducting direct action operations;

♦ Conducting raids;

♦ Recovery of personnel and special equipment;

♦ Conducting conventional or special light infantry operations.

To maintain readiness, Rangers are constantly training. Their training encompasses arctic, jungle, desert and mountain operations, as well as amphibious instruction. The training philosophy of the 75th Ranger Regiment dictates the unit's high state of readiness. The philosophy includes performance oriented training emphasizing tough standards and a focus on realism and live fire exercises, while concentrating on the basics and safety. Training at night, during adverse weather or on difficult terrain multiply the benefits of training events. Throughout training, Rangers are taught to expect the unexpected.

THE BATTALIONS:

Each Ranger battalion has an authorized strength of 580 personnel assigned to three rifle companies and a headquarters company. The rifle companies consist of 152 Rangers each, while the headquarters company has the remaining Rangers assigned. Ranger battalions are light infantry and have only a few vehicles and crew served weapons systems. Standard weapon systems are listed below:

♦ 84mm Ranger Antitank Weapons system (RAWS): 16;

♦ 60mm mortars: 6;

♦ M240G Machine Guns: 27;

♦ Squad Automatic Weapons (SAW): 54.

THE MEN:

All officers and enlisted soldiers in the Regiment are volunteers. Those volunteers selected for the 75th Ranger Regiment must meet tough physical, mental and moral criteria. All commissioned officers and combat arms NCOs must be airborne and Ranger qualified and have demonstrated a proficiency in the duty position for which they are seeking.

Upon assignment to the Regiment, both officer and senior NCOs attend the Ranger Orientation Program (ROP) to integrate them into the Regiment. ROP familiarizes them with Regimental policies, standing operating procedures, the Commander's intent and Ranger standards.

Enlisted soldiers assigned to the Regiment go through the Ranger Indoctrination Program (RIP). RIP assesses incoming Rangers on their physical qualifications and indoctrinates basic

Regimental standards. Failure to pass ROP or RIP is justification to transfer soldiers from the Regiment.

Junior enlisted soldiers who are not Ranger qualified attend the U.S. Army Ranger Course. The chain of command sends the soldier to a pre-Ranger Program, which ensures that he is administratively, physically and mentally prepared for the course. Then he attends Ranger School. The result of this demanding selection and training process is a Ranger who can lead effectively against enormous mental and physical odds.

Please refer to Table 75th-A for a list of enlisted MOSs and ranks eligible for the 75th Ranger Regiment, and Ranger training.

APPLICATION:

Personnel interested in Ranger Training and assignment to the 75th Ranger Regiment should refer to AR 614-200, Chapter 5, Section 1. Soldiers should submit packets (including updated 2-1) to:

Commander, PERSCOM
ATTN: TAPC-EPK-I (RANGER)
2461 Eisenhower Ave
Alexandria, VA 22331-0452.

Soldiers should also fax a courtesy copy of their DA Form 4187 to the Ranger branch through PERSCOM:
DSN: 221-4880;
COMM: (703) 325-4880.

CONTACT INFORMATION:

Soldiers may contact the Ranger Team for information through the above mailing address or:
DSN: 221-7676/5566;
COMM: (703) 325-7676/5566.

MOS	MOS DESCRIPTION	RANK
	Table: 75th-A	
	Enlisted Eligibility for 75th Ranger Regiment	
11B	Infantry	PVT-MSG
11C	Indirect Fire Infantryman	PVT-MSG
13F	Fire Support Specialist	PVT-MSG
31C	Radio Operator-Maintainer	PVT-SSG
31U	Signal Support Systems Specialist	PVT-SFC
31Z	Senior Signal SGT	MSG-SGM
35E	COMSEC Repairer	PVT-SSG
54B	Chemical Operations Specialist	PVT-SFC
55B	Ammunitions Specialist	SSG
63B	Light Wheel Vehicle Mechanic	PVT-SFC
71D	Legal Specialist	PVT-SFC
71L	Administrative Specialist	PVT-SFC
71M	Chaplain Assistant	SPC-SGT
73D	Accounting Specialist	PVT-SGT
74C	Telecommunications Operator	PVT-SFC
75B	Personnel Administration Specialist	PVT-SGT
75H	Personnel Services Specialist	SSG-SFC
88N	Transportation Management Coordinator	SGT
91B	Medical Specialist	PVT-SFC
92A	Automated Logistical Specialist	PVT-SGT
92Y	Unit Supply Specialist	PVT-SFC
96B	Intelligence Analyst	PVT-SFC
92G	Food Service Specialist	PVT-SFC
96D	Imagery Analyst	SGT-SFC
97B	Counterintelligence Agent	PVT-SSG

RANGER INDOCTRINATION PROGRAM (RIP)

FORWARD:

RIP is a training and selection program run by the Ranger Regiment; it is staffed by noncommissioned officers from the Ranger Regiment. Its mission: the training and indoctrination of soldiers newly assigned to the regiment. This training period is normally 3 weeks long and is designed to physically and mentally toughen the newly assigned soldier as well as to teach him the basic skills and techniques needed to function as a member of his Ranger squad. RIP has the responsibility of identifying and eliminating any newly assigned soldier who does not demonstrate the dedication, motivation, physical fitness and emotional stability required of a Ranger.

CREED:

RIP candidates are expected to learn and recite the Ranger Creed.

PURPOSE:

The mission of the Ranger Training Detachent is to select and prepare candidates (skill level 1) for service in the 75th Ranger Regiment. The Ranger Indoctrination Program is an assessment and selection program for grades E1-4.

OVERVIEW:

Students are trained on land navigation, combat lifesaver, basic knots and the history of the Ranger Regiment. Students also conduct an APFT, a CWST, fast rope repelling, defensive driving and training on Ranger SOPs. To help each student determine his strengths and weaknesses, each student is also evaluated by his peers.

The Land navigation course is conducted at Cole Range for three days. Students must find five out of seven points on the day land navigation course, given point grid coordinates, a compass and map and four hours. Students must

Example Training Schedule - RIP	
DAY 0	
THURSDAY	
1300-1500	Inprocessing / Equipment Issue / POV Inspection
DAY 1	
MONDAY	
0500-0530	First Call
0530-0730	APFT
0730-0800	Chow
0800-0830	Hygiene / Room Inspection
0845-0915	RCO / RSM / 1SG Brief
0930-1045	Equipment Issue / DX
1045-1200	Knot Class
1200-1230	Chow
1245-1700	Equipment Tie Down Class
1700-1730	Chow
1730-1800	Camouflage
1800-1900	Ranger Standards
DAY 2	
TUESDAY	
0530-0545	First Call
0545-0630	PLT PT (3 Mile Run, Abdominal Workout)
0630-0715	Hygiene / Chow - MRE
0715-0730	Movement
0730-1100	CWST
1100-1130	Movement
1130-1200	Chow - MRE
1200-1600	Map Reading
1630-UTC	Chow
* Draw Range Equipment	
DAY 3	
WEDNESDAY	
0530-0600	First Call
0600-0700	PT (5 mile Standard Run)
0700-0730	Hygiene / Range Preparations
0700-0830	Establish Range
0730-0800	Chow
0800-0830	Movement
0900-1100	Cadre-led Land Navigation
1100-1300	Dead Reconning Course
1300-1330	Chow - MRE
1330-1630	Land Navigation
1630-1800	Patrol Base class
1800-1830	Chow - MRE
1830-2030	Night Dead Reconning class

Example Training Schedule - RIP	
DAY 4	
THURSDAY	
0530-0600	First Call
0600-0730	PT (6 Mile Road March)
0730-0830	Hygiene / Chow - MRE
0830-0900	TAC Assessment Class
0900-1600	Land Navigation
1600-1800	Combatatives
1800-1830	Chow - MRE
1830-2330	Night Land Navigation
2400-0700	Patrol Base ACT
DAY 5	
FRIDAY	
0700-0730	PT (Abdominal Workout)
0730-0800	Hygiene / Chow - MRE
0800-1300	Land Navigation Test
1300-1330	Range Breakdown
1330-1430	Movement
1430-1630	Equipment Maintenance
1630-1700	Counseling / Safety Brief
1700-1800	Chow
DAY 6	
SATURDAY	
No Training Scheduled	
DAY 7	
SUNDAY	
No Training Scheduled	
DAY 8	
MONDAY	
0530-0600	First Call
0600-0730	PLT PT (3 Mile Run / Upper Body)
0800-0830	Hygiene / Chow - MRE
0830-1200	Med Class / CLS
1200-1300	Chow
1300-1730	Med Class / CLS
1730-1800	Chow
* Lock Down Implement Hydration SOP, Lights Out 2200	
DAY 9	
TUESDAY	
0330-0400	First Call
0400-0730	PT (10 Mile Road March)
0730-0900	Hygiene / Chow - MRE
0900-1230	Med Class / CLS
1230-1330	Chow
1330-1600	Med Class / CLS
1600-1700	Ethics Class
1700-1730	Chow

Example Training Schedule - RIP	
DAY 10	
WEDNESDAY	
0530-0600	First Call
0600-0730	Combatatives
0730-0900	Hygiene / Chow - MRE
0900-1200	Med Class / CLS
1200-1300	Chow
1300-1400	Med Class / CLS
1300-1400	CWST Retest
1400-1630	Pack Ruck / Rig
1630-UTC	Airborne Video
1700-1730	Chow
DAY 11	
THURSDAY	
0530-0600	FIRST CALL
0615-0730	PT (3 Mile Run / Abdominal Workout)
0615-0730	PT (5 Mile Standard Run Retest)
0800-0830	Hygiene / Chow - MRE
0830-0900	Movement
0900-1200	BATT II
1200-1230	Chow
1230-1645	Ranger History
1700-1730	Chow
DAY 12	
FRIDAY	
0500-0530	First Call
0530-0545	IMC
0545-0630	SAT
0630-0700	Movement
0700-0800	Draw Parachutes / Rig
0800-0900	Load Aircraft
0900-UTC	Airborne Ops
DAY 13	
SATURDAY	
No Training Scheduled	
DAY 14	
SUNDAY	
No Training Scheduled	
DAY 15	
MONDAY	
0530-0600	First Call
0600-0800	APFT Retest
0600-0800	CLS Retest
0600-0800	Soccer
0830-0900	Hygiene / Chow - MRE
0900-0915	Movement
0915-1015	Beret Issue

Example Training Schedule - RIP	
DAY 15 - CONT.	
1015-1030	Movement
1030-1230	Critical subjects Review
1230-1300	Chow
1300-1500	Extremist/Sexual Harassment Class
1500-1600	Critical Subjects Test
1500-1600	S2 Inprocess
1600-1615	Movement
1630-1700	Chow
DAY 16	
TUESDAY	
0530-0600	First Call
0600-0730	PLT PT (3 Mile Run / Abdominal Workout)
0730-0800	Chow
0800-0900	Hygiene / Room Inspection / Critical Subjects Retest
0900-1200	Fast Rope / Knot Test
1200-1230	Chow
1230-1630	S2 Inprocess
1630-1700	Chow
DAY 17	
WEDNESDAY	
0530-0600	First Call
0600-0730	Combatatives
0730-0800	Chow
0800-0900	Hygiene / Room Inspection
0900-1000	Counseling
1000-1200	Graduation Rehearsal
1200-1300	Chow
1300-1345	Graduation Preparations
1345-1500	Movement
1500-1600	Graduation
1600-UTC	Movement
DAY 18	
THURSDAY	
0730-0800	Work Call / Linen Turn-in
0800-0830	Chow
0830-0930	Equipment Turn-in
0930-1000	201 File Issue
1000-1030	Medical Records Issue
1030-UTC	Outprocessing
1300	Ship

find three out of seven points on the night land navigation course, also given point grid coordinates, a compass and map and four hours.

Students are trained for three days in a Combat Lifesaver course, at the end of which each student becomes a certified Combat Lifesaver.

Physical training includes an obstacle course, forced foot marches and combatatives.

During the course a BN TAC from each of the three Ranger Battalions is present to observe training and consult with candidates.

During RIP, candidates will participate in the following training events:

- ◆ Daily Physical Training;
- ◆ Ranger History Test;
- ◆ Map Reading;
- ◆ APFT;
- ◆ Airborne Operation;
- ◆ Ranger Standards;
- ◆ Day and Night Land Navigation;
- ◆ 5 Mile Run;
- ◆ Combatives;
- ◆ Knots;
- ◆ Combat Water Survival Test;
- ◆ 6, 8 and 10 mile road marches;
- ◆ Driver Training (DDC Card);
- ◆ Fast Rope Training;
- ◆ Combat Lifesaver Certification.

UNIFORMS:

Students wear the BDU uniform with soft cap, and LBE, they carry the "rubber duck" for the course. Students should keep their boots shined to standard of AR 670-1 (clean and black, not spit shined).

The PT uniform is the standard army gray pt uniform. For combatative pt, students wear the BDU uniform without the soft cap and belt, with white socks and sneakers. Students do not wear dog tags with their pt uniform.

INSPECTIONS:

There will be at least one barracks inspection during the course.

PERSONAL CONDUCT & APPEARANCE STANDARDS:

Students will be recycled for any of the following reasons:

- Missing a block of instruction;
- Lack of motivation.

Students will be dropped from the course for honor code violations (cheating).

PREPARATIONS:

Students should take necessary steps to prepare for ruck marches (especially in taking care of their feet). Ensuring that there are no foot or leg injuries and to break in their boots prior to attending the course.

Students should not bring winter BDUs or have stamped name tapes (basic issue) on their BDUs.

Unauthorized Items:

- Foot Powder;
- Enhancers (ripped fuel, amino acid, creatine, etc.);
- Nonprescription Drugs;
- Spandex;
- Civilian Eyewear.

Additional Optional Equipment:

- Knife (Leatherman, Gerber, etc.);
- Alcohol Pens.

Graduation:

In order to graduate from RIP candidates must meet the following requirements:

- 60% APFT in the 17-21 age group;
- 5 mile run at no slower than 8 minutes per mile;
- Successful completion of CWST (must be able to complete 15 meters in BDUs, boots and LBE);
- Must complete 2 of 3 road marches, one of which must be a 10 mile road march;
- 70% on all exams.

Upon graduation from RIP, soldiers will be awarded the Ranger Scroll - not to be confused with the Ranger Tab, which is awarded upon graduation from Ranger School (see Ranger School) - and assigned to one of the three Ranger Battalions or 75th Regimental Headquarters. Graduates of RIP are also authorized to wear the Black Beret.

LEAVE & PASS POLICY:

There are two weekends during the course students may be locked down for deficiencies or forced hydration periods. Generally, students will have one free weekend, and an additional 12 hours of down time during the course.

BILLETING:

Quarters:

Students will be billeted in barracks with the 75th Ranger Regiment.

Telephone:

Telephone use is only permitted when students are not training. In case of emergency, students can be contacted through the Charge of Quarters (CQ) desk:

COMM: (706) 545-3785.

POV:

Students may bring a POV to the course, but must have it inspected before driving privileges will be instated.

Money:

Student are not to have more that $50 with them while attending RIP.

RANGER ORIENTATION PROGRAM (ROP)

PURPOSE:

The purpose of ROP is to train, assess and select NCOs and Officers for service in the 75th Ranger Regiment.

OVERVIEW:

ROP candidates will participate in the following training events:

- Force Protection/Antiterrorism brief;
- Daily Physical Training;
- APFT (with chinups);
- Regimental Standards;
- Airborne Refresher/Operation;
- Fast Rope Training;
- Special Operations Orientation;
- Fire Support Assets Brief;
- Weapons Familiarization Exam;
- Communications Familiarization;
- CWST;
- Road March;
- 5 Mile Run.

PREPARATIONS:

Graduation:

In order to graduate from ROP candidates must meet the following requirements:

- 80% on APFT by age group for all Officers and combat arms NCOs;
- 70% on APFT by age group for all non-combat arms NCOs;
- 6 chinups;
- 12 mile road march with 45 pound ruck sack within 3 hours, for all officers and combat arms NCOs;
- 10 mile road march with 45 pound ruck sack within 2.5 hours for all non-combat arms NCOs;
- Successful completion of CWST (must be able to swim 15 meters in BDUs, boots & LBE);
- 70% on Ranger History examination;
- 5 mile run less than 40 minutes;
- 70% on self paces SOP examination;

- Psychological assessment by USASOC psychologist;
- Successful recommendation from RASP board interview.

REFERENCE:

1. "Volunteers for the 75th Ranger Regiment." Online. Internet. 16 May 2000. Available: http://www.perscom.army.mil/epinf/75th_rgr.htm.
2. "Volunteers for the 75th Ranger Regiment." Online. Internet. 3 April 2000. Available: http://www.perscom.army.mil/epinf/75th-rgr.htm.
3. "75th Ranger Regiment." U.S. Army Special Operations Command. Online. Internet. 15 April 2000. Available: http://users.aol.com/armysof1/Ranger.html.
4. "The 75th Ranger Regiment." Online. Internet. 4 April 2000. Available: http://www.ohiovet.com/lazydog/bucyrus/75th.htm.
5. "Ranger Indoctrination Program." Online. Internet. 16 May 2000. Available: http://www.goarmy.com/job/branch/sorc/75th/html/rip.htm.
6. "The 75th Ranger Regiment." Online. Internet. 4 April 2000. Available: http://www.ohiovet.com/lazydog/bucyrus/75th.htm.
7. "Ranger Orientation Program." Online. Internet. 16 May 2000. Available: http://www.goarmy.com/job/branch/sorc/75th/html/rop.htm.

RANGER SCHOOL

REGULATION:

Course No: 2E–SI5S–5R/011–SQIV–G
Title: Ranger
Length: 8 Weeks, 5 Days
Location: U.S. Army Infantry School – SC: 071
45 DA PAM 351–4 • 31 October 1995
Enl SQI: V
Off SC: 5S
Scope: Course effective: 1 Oct 95
The course consists of three phases. The first phase is conducted at Fort Benning, Georgia, for 20 days. The second phase (mountains) is conducted near Dahlonega in the mountains of northern Georgia for 20 1/2 days. The third and final phase (swamp/jungle) is conducted at Eglin Air Force Base in the swamps of western Florida for 17 1/2 days. Three
days are used for out–processing and graduation.
Prerequisite: Male volunteer, Active Army or Reserve Component Officer or NCO of any branch. Enlisted applicant below SGT must submit a request for waiver of NCO grade to the applicant's first commander (colonel) in the chain of command. Waiver will include the most recent Army physical fitness test results and time served in leadership positions. Request for waiver is endorsed by the individual's company and battalion commanders. Approved waiver must accompany application for quotas to the Ranger course. Medical examination records must accompany individual and be dated within 18 months of his reporting date stating that the applicant is medically qualified to attend Ranger School and has had a blood chemistry test (containing electrolytes) and liver and kidney function tests as a part of the examination. Individual must bring his health and dental records. Dental records must include a full–mouth X–ray (panorex). If unit is unable to provide panorex, the unit must provide a letter signed by the commander verifying that a panorex exists at home station and is available by sending unit if requested. The first four days of Ranger School will assess individual readiness to participate in Ranger training. Student who successfully completed the first four days of the course will remain in training. (Those who do not successfully complete each event or allowable retest, are offered an opportunity to 'recycle' into the next Ranger class, contingent upon approval from parent unit). Commander will certify that applicant is proficient in the following tasks: Army Physical Fitness Test consisting of 52 push-ups, 62 sit–ups, and a two–mile run in running shoes in 14: 54 minutes or less. In addition, applicant must execute six chin-ups (palms facing toward the face).

Combat water survival test consisting of three stations. The 15–meter swim: swim 15 meters with rifle, wearing BDUs, boots, and load–carrying equipment (pistol belt, suspenders, two ammunition pouches, and two full canteens), without loss of rifle or equipment and without showing unusual fear or panic. The 3–meter drop: walk blindfolded off a 3–meter diving board with rifle and LCE. After entering the water, remove blindfold and swim to poolside without loss of rifle or equipment and without showing signs of fear or panic. Equipment removal: from poolside, enter water and immediately submerge and remain under water. Discard rifle and remove LCE. Surface and swim to poolside without showing unusual signs of fear or panic. Five–mile run (8 minutes/mile pace), 8–mile foot march (15–minute/mile pace) with 35–pound ruck sack. Day and night land navigation. Ranger stakes consisting of 13 tasks. A minimum of 10 tasks will be tested and applicant must receive a 'go' in seven of the 10 tested tasks. (One retest is allowed per task failed). Ranger stakes tasks are as follows: Maintain an M60 MG (STP 7 11BCHM14–SM–TG, PG 3–270, 071–312–3025); load an M60 MG (STP 21–4 SMCT, PG 251, 071–312–3027); prepare a range card for an M60 MG (STP 7–11BCHM14–SM–TG, PG 3–260, 071–312–3007); perform operator maintenance on an M249 MG (STP 7–11BCHM14–SM–TG, PG 3–130, 071–312–4025); operate an M249 MG (STP 7–11BCHM14–SM–TG, PG 3–151, 071–312–4027); employ an M18A1 claymore mine (STP 21–4 SMCT, PG 317, 071–325–4425); send a radio message (STP 21–4 SMCT, PG 47, 113–571–1016), encode and decode messages using KTC 600 tactical operations code (STP 7–11BCHM14–SM–TG, PG 3–454, 113–573–4003); maintain an M16 rifle (STP 21–4 SMCT, PG 110, 071–311–2025); correct malfunctions of an M16 rifle (STP 21–4 SMCT, PG 152, 071–311–2029); perform a functions check on an M16 rifle (STP 21–4 SMCT, PG 135, 071–311–2026); employ hand grenades (STP 21–4 SMCT, PG 304, 071–325–44407); maintain an M203 grenade launcher (STP 7–11BCHM14–SM–TG, PG 3–192, 071–311–2125).
Special Information: Student will report with a commander's statement certifying the applicant is proficient in the following military skills needed for successful completion of the Ranger course: call for and adjust indirect fire (STP 21–24 SMCT, PG 55, 061–283–6003); camouflage yourself and your individual equipment (STP 21–1 SMCT, PG 393, 051–191–1361); use KTC 1400 (STP 7–11BCHM14–SM–TG, PG 3–457, 113–573–4006); navigate from one point on the ground to

another point while dismounted (ISTP 21–24 SMCT; PG 21, 071–329–1006); determine the grid coordinates of a point on a military map (STP 21–1 SMCT, PG 76, 071–329–1002); determine a magnetic azimuth using a lensatic compass (STP 21–1 MCT; PG 90, 071–329–1003); determine the elevation of a point on the ground using a map (STP 21–24 SMCT, PG 36, 071–329–1004); determine a location on the ground by terrain association (STP 21–1 SMCT, PG 87, 071–329–1005); measure distance on a map (STP 21–1 SMCT, PG 105, 071–329–1008); convert azimuths (STP 21–24 SMCT; PG 28, 071–329–1009); determine azimuth using a protractor (STP 21–24 SMCT, PG 45, 071–510–0001); orient a map using a lensatic compass (STP 21–24 SMCT, PG 30, 071–329–1011); orient a map to the ground by map–terrain association (STP 21–1 SMCT, PG 72, 071–329–1012); locate an unknown point on a map and on the ground by intersection (STP 21–24 SMCT, PG 39, 071–329–1014); locate an unknown point on a map and on the ground by resection (STP 21–24 SMCT, PG 42, 071–329–1015); prime explosives non-electrically (STP 7–11BCHM14–SM–TG, PG 3–480, 051–193–1003); clear a misfire (STP 7–11BCHM14–SM–TG, PG 3–488, 051–193–2030); practice preventive medicine (STP 21–1 SMCT, PG 338, 081–831–1043); prepare an M136 launcher for firing (STP 21–1 SMCT, PG 199, 071–054–0001); operate night vision goggles AN/PVS–5 (STP 7–11BCHM14–SM–TG, PG 3–340, 071–315–0030) (AN/PVS–7 to replace AN/PVS–5 as stocks become available in FY92/93). Winter period is 15 Oct – 15 Apr; summer period is 16 Apr – 14 Oct. The following uniform items are required for summer and winter: BDU jacket and trousers – 6 ea; CAP, BDU – 2 ea; belt, waist web – 2; boots, combat, black – 2 pr; boots, jungle – 2 pr (can only be used in Florida phase during winter period); boots, jungle, hot weather (black) (are equivalent to black leather boots and can be worn throughout the course, winter and summer); gloves shell leather – 2 pr (winter); 1 pr (summer); Gore-Tex gloves (Army intermediate cold–wet gloves are authorized or suitable substitute meeting specifications (Gore-Tex Best Defense – Floxor) as tested and approved by Natick Labs are approved for wear); ID card and tags – 1 set; inserts, gloves, wool – 2 pr; socks, wool, cushion sole – 14 pr; socks, heavyweight (white) – 4 pr; socks, black dress or polypropylene – 3 pr; name tape (last name) – 2 ea; running shoes – 1 pr; sweatband Kevlar – 1; undershirt, cotton brown – 7; undershirt, winter (sleeping shirt or field jacket liner) – 1 (winter only); underwear, long – wool or polypropylene – 2 (winter only – optional). Individual can bring and use any wool or polypropylene commercial undergarments during winter season. (If the color is other than OD or brown, the garment will not be visible when worn). The following non–issue items are required for summer and winter: blousing garters – 3 pr; pocket notebook; pencils; combination locks – 3; eyeglasses, military – 2 pr with retaining bands; towels – 2; foot powder – 2 cans (antifungal and antiperspirant – encouraged); toilet articles; 2 large cans of black or silicone shoe polish; pocket knife; sewing kit; wristwatch (inexpensive but durable); black tape, friction or electrical – 2 ea; extra bootlaces – 2 pr; waterproof bags zip-lock) – 12 ea; one set of civilian clothing; approved military flashlight (mini,

mag, or L–shaped, or flashlight code 4 Jr (mini–flashlight) with adequate battery supply). The following optional items may be brought to the Ranger course: Whetstone; map case; map markers; nylon cord (550 type) (50 ft); penlight with batteries; laundry soap (small box); OD wood sweater (Army or USMC type); large trash bag; small waterproof bags (zip-lock); shower shoes; shoe shine brush; drawers, cotton, underwear; knee pads (black or OD in color). Contact lenses are not authorized during the Ranger course. Uniforms will have all insignia removed except name tag and US Army. Boots should be well broken in prior to beginning the course. Jungle boots are not authorized during the winter in the Benning, mountain, or desert phase of training. Boots, jungle (black jungle) hot weather are authorized for wear in summer months and in the Florida phase. High tech or insulated type boots ARE NOT AUTHORIZED in the course. Ripple sole boots are not authorized for climbing in the mountain phase Gore-Tex sock 'booties' are authorized as 'under wear.' However, boots must be appropriately oversized with double insert capability to accommodate foot march requirements. No class A uniform is required during the course. Enlisted applicant must have a standard score or 90 or higher in aptitude area CO or IN. The course is taught on 68 consecutive days. **Security Clearance:** None

FORWARD:

The actions of Ranger Units and individual Rangers have contributed many courageous and daring exploits to the pages of American history. The story is a recurring one, depicting outstanding leadership coupled with the highest application of the skills used in the art of warfare.

Throughout the military history of the United States, Ranger units have been formed when needed and have accomplished their purpose with great distinction. Rangers of the past have provided a firm foundation upon which the Rangers of today have continued to build. The present day Ranger is a man who is a graduate of the most demanding training program in the United States Army today - the U.S. Army Ranger Course.

The Ranger Course instruction develops tough, capable and highly confident combat soldiers. The current approach to the Ranger Course, training individuals rather than units, was initiated in January 1952, when the United States Army Infantry School conducted the first Ranger Course at Fort Benning, Georgia.

The Ranger Course affords soldiers the opportunity, by practical application, to develop and to prove themselves under rugged conditions.

The course is stress oriented and develops within the Ranger student the ability to function under heavy mental and physical stress. Emphasis is placed on realistic, strenuous field exercises. The Infantry rifle squad and rifle platoon conducting patrolling operations is the training vehicle used to accomplish individual development.

The Ranger Course is taught using the most current tactical doctrine. Ranger training develops military skills and knowledge of subjects required to perform as a small unit leader in a combat environment.

High standards are required and maintained despite the stressful environment in Ranger training. The Ranger Course produces a mentally hardened soldier that possesses an enhanced capability to perform combat arms related associated functional skills; he is more confident in his ability to withstand the stresses of combat to overcome all obstacles and accomplish his mission under extremely adverse conditions.

The Ranger proves during the Ranger Course that he can overcome seemingly insurmountable mental and physical challenges. He has demonstrated, while under simulated combat conditions, that he has acquired the professional skills and techniques necessary to plan, organize, coordinate and conduct small unit operations. He has demonstrated that he has mastered basic skills needed to plan and execute dismounted small unit day and night operations, low altitude mountaineering, and infiltration as well as ex-filtration techniques via land, air and sea. As a result of proving that he can successfully accomplish these tasks during the Ranger Course, he is authorized to wear the Ranger Tab. The graduate of the Ranger Course is the epitome of the U.S. Infantryman.

The soldier who has experienced combat knows the value of tough, realistic training in military skills. He knows that he must be able to successfully accomplish any mission which his unit has been organized, equipped and trained to perform in the shortest time possible, with the least expenditure of resources (men and equipment) and with the least confusion, to maintain a combat effective unit. The Ranger Course provides tough, realistic training with a minimum of formal classroom instruction.

The following information is intended to answer typical questions for the prospective Ranger student.

The Ranger Training Brigade trains students from all services of the United States Armed Forces and many allied countries. No insignia of rank is worn by students during the course; all students are addressed as "Ranger".

Throughout the course the "Buddy System" is used to instill a spirit of teamwork and cooperation. Each Ranger student must know his buddy's location and welfare at all times throughout the course. As a rule, new buddy teams are designated at the beginning of each phase.

U.S. Army graduates of the Ranger Course are awarded an Additional Skill Identifier (ASI) or an MOS suffix letter:

♦ Airborne qualified officer graduates are awarded the ASI 5S; airborne qualified enlisted graduates are awarded the MOS letter V;

♦ Non-airborne officer graduates are awarded the ASI 5R; non-airborne enlisted graduates are awarded the MOS suffix letter G.

Airborne qualified international students are awarded US parachute wings after completing the course, assuming successful completion of parachute jumps.

Units sending soldiers TDY and return are authorized to stabilize a soldier for 24 months (no longer than 48 months time on station) upon successful completion of Ranger School.

PURPOSE:

The purpose of the Ranger Course is to teach and develop Combat Arms functional skills relevant to fighting the close combat, direct fire battle. Leadership development is a tertiary benefit to the student – not the course purpose. Selected officer and enlisted personnel will be challenged by being required to perform effectively as small unit leaders in a realistic tactical environment under mental and physical stress approaching that found in combat.

The Ranger Course provides the student with practical experience in the application of the tactics and techniques of Ranger operations in wooded, lowland swamp and mountainous environments. Emphasis is placed on development of fundamental individual skills through the application of the principles of leadership while further developing military skills in the planning and conduct of dismounted infantry, airborne, air assault and amphibious squad and platoon size combat operations.

OVERVIEW:

The Ranger Course is 61 days in length with an average of 19.6 hours of training each day, seven days a week. It is divided into three phases of training, with each phase being conducted at a different geographical location. The first phase (Benning Phase) is 21 days in length and is conducted by the 4th Battalion, Ranger Training Brigade (RTB) at Fort Benning, Georgia. The second phase (Mountain Phase) is 21 days in length and is conducted by the 5th Battalion, Ranger Training Brigade at Camp Frank D. Merrill near Dahlonega, Georgia. The third phase (Florida Phase) is 17 days in length and is conducted by the 6th Battalion, Ranger Training Brigade at Camp James E. Rudder at Eglin AFB, Florida. Two days of the course are consumed by travel, maintenance, in/out processing and graduation.

Rangers are assigned to one of the three Ranger Training Companies of the 4th Battalion upon arrival at Fort Benning and will be trained by that unit's cadre utilizing small group instruction techniques throughout the phase. Upon rotating through the other phases, the same procedures are followed.

The emphasis during the course is on practical, realistic and strenuous field training, where the Ranger student will be taught Ranger related skills based on current tactical doctrine. The student is exposed to conditions and situations, which closely approximate and often exceed those he would encounter in combat. Fatigue, hunger, the necessity for quick, sound decisions and the requirement for demonstrating calm, forceful leadership under conditions of mental and emotional stress are all experienced in the Ranger Course.

The instruction is conducted with units that vary in size from an infantry rifle squad to a rifle platoon, in distance traveled from 2 to 30 kilometers, and in duration from 1 to 12 days. The qualified Ranger student has been trained to effectively function under conditions of simulated combat stress. He is evaluated as a small unit leader in a series of field training exercises, which are conducted primarily at night under all weather conditions. Frequent and unexpected enemy contact, reduced sleep, difficult terrain and the constant pressure of operating within restrictive time limits all contribute to this atmosphere of stress.

The Benning Phase:

The Benning Phase of Ranger training is designed to assess and then to develop the military skills, physical and mental endurance, stamina and confidence a soldier must have to successfully accomplish combat missions. It is also designed to teach the Ranger student to properly sustain himself, his subordinates and to maintain his equipment under difficult field conditions during the subsequent phases of Ranger training. If a student is not in top physical condition when he reports to the Ranger Course, he will have extreme difficulty keeping up with the fast pace of Ranger training, especially during the initial phase.

The Benning Phase is executed in two parts. The first part is the Ranger Assessment Phase (RAP) conducted at Camp Rogers in the Harmony Church area of Fort Benning. This phase consists of an APFT and Combat Water Survival Test (CWST), 5 mile run, 3 mile run with an obstacle course, a 12 mile foot march, night and day land navigation tests, medical considerations class and 10 event Ranger Stakes. Advanced physical training assures physical and mental endurance and the stamina required for enhancing basic Ranger characteristics: commitment, confidence and toughness. Additionally, the student completes the Water Confidence Test at Hurley Hill (Victory Pond) and 7 1/2 hours of combatives vicinity Camp Rogers.

The second part of the Benning Phase is conducted at nearby Camp William O. Darby. The emphasis at Camp Darby is on the instruction in and execution of squad combat operations. The Ranger student receives instruction on airborne/air assault operations, environmental and fieldcraft training, executes the Darby Queen obstacle course and learns the fundamentals of patrolling, the warning order/ operations order format and communications.

The fundamentals of combat operations include battle drills (React to Contact, Break Contact, React to Ambush, Platoon Raid), Demolition's Training, Airborne Operations, Air Assault Operations, Crawl, Walk, Run FTX; these are the principles and techniques that enable the squad to successfully conduct reconnaissance and raid missions.

The Ranger student must then demonstrate his expertise through a series of cadre and student led tactical operations. As a result, the Ranger student gains tactical and technical proficiency, confidence in himself and prepares to move to the next phase of the course - the Mountain Phase. Following the Benning Phase, students are normally provided a short break to launder uniforms, get hair cuts and purchase any sundry items or TA-50 they may have lost, destroyed or exhausted prior to their departure to Camp Frank D. Merrill, Dahlonega, GA.

The Mountain Phase:

During the Mountain Phase, students receive instruction on military mountaineering tasks as well as techniques for employing a platoon for continuous combat operations in a mountainous environment. They further develop their ability to command and control a platoon size element through planning, preparing and executing a variety of combat missions. The Ranger student continues to learn how to sustain himself and his subordinates in the adverse conditions of the mountains. The rugged terrain, severe weather, hunger, mental and physical fatigue and the emotional stress that the student encounters afford him the opportunity to gauge his own capabilities and limitations as well as that of his "Ranger Buddies."

In addition to combat operations, the Ranger student receives five days of training on military mountaineering. During the first three days of mountaineering (Lower) he learns about knots, belays, anchor points, rope management and the basic fundamentals of climbing and rappelling. His mountaineering training culminates with a two day exercise (Upper) at Yonah Mountain applying the skills learned during Lower mountaineering. Each student must make all prescribed climbs at Yonah Mountain to continue in the course. During the FTX, Ranger students perform a mission that requires the use of their mountaineering skills. Combat missions are directed against a conventionally equipped threat force in a Mid-Intensity Conflict scenario. These missions are conducted both day and night over an eight day field training exercise (FTX) and include moving cross country over mountains, conducting vehicle ambushes, raiding communications/mortar sites, and conducting a river crossing or scaling a steep sloped mountain.

The Ranger student reaches his objective in several ways: cross country movement, airborne insertion into small, rugged drop zones, air assaults into even smaller landing zones on the sides of mountains or an 8-10 mile foot march over the Tennessee Valley Divide (TVD). The stamina and commitment of the Ranger student is stressed to the maximum. At any time, he may be selected to lead tired, hungry, physically expended students to accomplish yet another combat mission. At the conclusion of the Mountain Phase, the students move by bus or parachute assault into the Third and final (Florida) Phase of Ranger training, conducted at Camp Rudder, near Eglin AFB, Florida.

The Florida Phase:

The Third or Capstone Phase of Ranger School is conducted at Camp James E. Rudder

(Auxiliary Field #6), Eglin AFB, Florida. Emphasis during this phase is to continue the development of the Ranger student's combat arms functional skills. He must be capable of operating effectively under conditions of extreme mental and physical stress. This is accomplished through practical exercises in extended platoon level operations in a jungle/swamp environment. Training further develops the students' ability to plan for and lead small units on independent and coordinated airborne, air assault, small boat and dismounted combat operations in a Mid-Intensity Combat environment against a well-trained, sophisticated enemy.

The Florida Phase continues the progressive, realistic OPFOR scenario. As the scenario develops, the students receive "in-country" technique training that assists them in accomplishing the tactical missions later in the phase. Technique training includes: small boat operations, expedient stream crossing techniques and skills needed to survive and operate in a jungle/swamp environment.

The Ranger students are updated on the scenario that eventually commits the unit to combat during techniques training. The 12 day FTX is a fast paced, highly stressful, challenging exercise in which the students are further trained, but are also evaluated on their ability to apply small unit tactics/techniques. They apply the tactics/techniques of raids, ambushes and movement to contact to accomplish their missions.

Upon completion of the Florida Phase of training, students move by parachute assault or bus to Fort Benning, Georgia. Ranger students graduate two days later if they have passed all requirements.

PREREQUISITES:

The Ranger Training Brigade has developed a comprehensive program to reduce attrition in Ranger School. This program went into effect with class 9-95. Part of the plan reduces the number reporting to Ranger School to the course load as defined by valid ATRRS slots, and targets training only leaders in the MOSs outlined in the Chief of Staff of the Army's (CSA's) attendance policy dated SEP 94.

Effective 31 July 95 the following changes were implemented as criteria for Ranger School attendance:

♦ The Ranger School will no longer accept walk-ons or extra students. Students will only be accepted if they have a valid ATRRS slot;

♦ E5 and above can attend in MOSs specified below. Grade waiver by the first COL Commander in the chain of command will only be accepted for E4/CPL assigned to leadership positions.

Applicants who fail to meet the attendance policy will be returned to their units.

Commanders are reminded of their responsibility to ensure that applicants are in top physical condition and certify their proficiency. Recent experience indicates that some applicants reporting to the course are unable to pass the APFT (52 pushups, 62 situps, 2 mile run in running shoes in 14:54 or less, and 6 chinups) or the Combat Water Survival Test (15 meter swim with equipment, 3 meter blindfold drop and removal of equipment). Applicants are returned to their units if either of these entry requirements are not met.

Other criteria eligibility will be as per chief of staff attendance policy message dated Sep 94.

♦ For enlisted personnel, Ranger Training is available on a voluntary basis for soldiers who are in the following MOS's:

11B - Infantryman;
11C - Indirect Fire Infantryman;
11H - Heavy Anti-armor Weapons Infantryman;
11M - Fighting Vehicle Infantryman;
12B - Combat Engineer (In companies that directly support Infantry Battalions);
13F - Fire Support Sergeant (Habitually associated in Direct support to Infantry Battalions);
18B - Special Forces Weapons Sergeant;
18C - Special Forces Engineer Sergeant;
19D - Cavalry Scout;
19E - Armor Crewman;

♦ Those enlisted soldiers of any MOS or specialty assigned to Ranger coded positions within the 75th Ranger Regiment or Ranger Training Brigade must attend;

♦ For Commissioned Officer Personnel, Ranger Training is available on a voluntary basis for officers in the following career management fields:

11A - Infantry Officer;

12A - Armor Officers allocated against authorized 12C positions;

12C - Cavalry Officers;

13A - Battalion and Company fire support officers (habitually associated in direct support to Infantry Battalions);

18A - Special Forces Officer;

21B - Combat Engineer (in companies that directly support Infantry Battalions);

♦ Those officers of any branch or specialty assigned to Ranger coded positions within the 75th Ranger Regiment or the Ranger Training Brigade must attend;

♦ Ranger coded positions are limited to the following:

a. Selected Ranger Regiment positions;

b. Selected positions in Infantry Battalions, Companies, Platoons and Long Range Surveillance Units;

c. Selected Instructors at the Infantry School;

d. Selected Observer-Controllers at the Combat Training Centers;

e. Selected Instructor positions at the School of Americas;

f. Selected positions in Cavalry Scout Troops that are assigned to Infantry/ Armor Battalions and Armored Cavalry Regiments;

g. Selected positions in Special Forces Operational Detachment-A Teams;

h. Selected positions in Fire Support Teams habitually associated in Direct support to Infantry Battalions;

i. Selected positions in Engineer Companies that directly support Infantry Battalions;

♦ All personnel must possess a special pre-Ranger (IAW AR 614-200 and DA PAM 351-4) medical examination signed by a medical doctor or flight surgeon dated within 12 months of their reporting date stating the applicant is medically qualified and stamped approved for attendance at Ranger School. If individual is airborne qualified, medical examination will indicate Ranger/Airborne. Individuals must bring their health records with certification of an HIV test within the past 24 months. Health records must accompany the individual, dental records are not brought, but a statement signed by the individual's commander indicating a PANOREX is on file at home station is mandatory. Individuals with previous hot or cold weather injuries are not enrolled during these high risk periods. (Cold weather period includes classes 1 through 5, and hot weather period includes classes 9-11);

♦ Ranger School (Ranger Assessment Phase) assesses individual readiness to participate in Ranger training. Students who successfully complete the first six days of the course will remain in training. Individuals who do not complete each RAP event successfully may be afforded retests. Those failing retests may be offered the opportunity to "Recycle" into the next Ranger class upon approval from their parent unit. Retests and recycles are not automatic. Unit commanders must certify that the Ranger candidate is proficient in the following tasks:

a. Army Physical Fitness Test (APFT) consisting of 52 pushups, 62 situps, and a 2 mile run in running shoes in 14:54 minutes or less. In addition, applicants must execute 6 chinups (palms facing toward the face). The APFT will be conducted IAW FM 21-20 with changes;

b. Combat Water Survival Test (CWST) consisting of three stations:

(1) The 15 Meter Swim: Swim 15 meters with rifle, wearing BDUs, boots, and load carrying equipment (LCE, Pistol belt, suspenders, two ammunition pouches, and two full canteens), without loss of rifle or equipment and without showing fear or panic;

(2) The 3 Meter Drop: Walk blindfolded off a 3 meter diving board with rifle and LCE. After entering water, remove blindfold and swim to poolside without loss of rifle or equipment and without showing fear or panic;

(3) Equipment Removal: Enter water and submerge from poolside, discard rifle, remove LCE ensuring that it is totally free from the body and swim to poolside without showing fear or panic;

c. Five Mile Formation Run, (8 minute/ mile pace in running shoes on a hard surface, over rolling terrain) (no retest);

d. Twelve Mile Tactical Foot March. Students must complete the tactical foot march at a rate of 15 minutes per mile with a 40 pound ruck sack (winter), or a 35 pound ruck sack (summer); course is conducted on unsurfaced roads with rolling hills (no retest);

e. The night and day land navigation test is a combination course. The test is conducted in the early morning hours and concludes in daylight. Students must correctly locate the required number of stakes within the prescribed time period to receive a GO; one retest is afforded each Ranger;

f. Ranger Stakes consists of ten tasks. Ranger stakes are part of the grading criteria in RAP. Ranger stakes allows the Ranger cadre to work with Ranger students before, during and after the hands-on test to ensure the task has been accomplished to standard. Ranger stakes tasks are as follows:

(1) Maintain an M60 MG (STP 7-11BCHM14-SM-TG, pg 3-270, 071-312-3025);

(2) Load an M60 MG (STP 21-1 SMCT, pg 251, 071-312-3027);

(3) Prepare a Range Card for an M60 MG (STP 7-11BCHM14-SM-TG pg 3-260, 071-312-3007);

(4) Perform operator maintenance on an M249 MG (STP 7-11BCHM14-SM-TG, pg 3-130, 071-312-4025);

(5) Operate an M249 MG (STP 7-11BCHM14-SM-TG, pg 3-151, 071-312-4027);

(6) Employ an M18A1 Claymore mine (STP 21-1 SMCT, pg 317, 071-325-4425);

(7) Place a radio into operation (AN/PRC-77 or AN/PRC-119) and troubleshoot. (TM 5820-890-10-1, Section. II-III, and TM 5820-627-12, with changes 1,2 and 3);

(8) Send a radio message (STP 21-1 SMCT, pg 47, 113-571-1016);

(9) Encode and decode messages using KTC 600 Tactical Operations Code (STP 7-11BCHM14-SM-TG, pg 3-454, 113-573-4003);

(10) Use night vision devices (AN/PVS-4, AN/PVS-7 and unaided night vision);

♦ Commanders will ensure that applicants are proficient in each of the below listed military skills which are needed for successful completion of the Ranger Course:

(1) Call for and adjust indirect fire (STP 21-24 SMCT, pg 55, 061-283-6003);

(2) Camouflage yourself and your individual equipment (STP 21-1 SMCT, pg 393, 051-191-1361);

(3) Use KTC 1400 (STP 7-11BCHM14-SM-TG, pg 3-457, 113-573-4006);

(4) Navigate from one point on the ground to another point while dismounted (STP 21-24 SMCT, pg 21, 071-329-1006);

(5) Determine the grid coordinates of a point on a military map (STP 21-1 SMCT, pg 76, 071-329-1002);

(6) Determine a magnetic azimuth using a lensatic compass (STP 21-1 SMCT, pg 90, 071-329-1003);

(7) Determine the elevation of a point on the ground using a map (STP 21-24 SMCT, pg 36, 071-329-1004);

(8) Determine a location on the ground by terrain association (STP 21-1 SMCT, pg 87, 071-329-1005);

(9) Measure distance on a map (STP 21-1 SMCT, pg 105, 071-329-1008);

(10) Convert azimuths (STP 21-24 SMCT, pg 28, 071-329-1009);

(11) Determine azimuth using a protractor (STP 21-24 SMCT, pg 45, 071-510-0001);

(12) Orient a map using a lensatic compass (STP 21-24 SMCT, pg 30, 071-329-1011);

(13) Orient a map to the ground by map-terrain association (STP 21-1 SMCT, pg 72, 071-329-1012);

(14) Locate an unknown point on a map and on the ground by intersection (STP 21-24 SMCT, pg 39, 071-329-1014);

(15) Locate an unknown point on a map and on the ground by resection (STP 21-24 SMCT, pg 42, 071-329-1015);

(16) Prime explosives non-electrically (STP7-11BCHM14-SM-TG, pg 3-480, 051-193-1003);

(17) Clear a misfire (Demolitions) (STP 7-11BCHM14-SM-TG, pg 3-488, 051-193-2030);

(18) Practice preventive medicine (STP 21-1 SMCT, pg 338, 081-831-1043);

(19) Prepare an M136 Launcher for firing (STP 21-1 SMCT, pg 199, 071-054-0001);

(20) Operate night vision goggles AN/PVS-7 (STP 7-11BCHM-SM-TG, pg 3-340, 071-315-0030);

♦ Enlisted applicants must have a standard score of 90 or higher in aptitude area CO and 12 months or more of active duty service remaining after the completion of the course;

♦ No security clearance is required;

♦ No additional obligated service is incurred by active Army commissioned officers for attending the course;

♦ Students are not required to be airborne qualified, but are encouraged to attend airborne training due to the airborne opportunities (6 possible jumps).

RTB Commander has authority to waive any of the above criteria.

INSPECTIONS:

Ranger Instructors (RIs) offer students an amnesty period for contraband items after the accountability formation. RIs will conduct a comprehensive 100% inspection of students after the amnesty period.

EVALUATIONS:

Combat Operations:

Each student is evaluated on his abilities continuously throughout the Ranger Course. Student are evaluated based on how effectively they influence their subordinates and use available resources in accomplishing all assigned tasks and missions.

Each student is evaluated at least once in each phase in combat operations and other combat related functional skills. Of these, at least one combat operation in the Mountain and Florida Phases must be passed. One of these graded combat operations must be in a primary leadership position (i.e. PL, PSG). A student must maintain a 50 percent "GO" rate in all graded evaluations in order to graduate.

Critical Incident Report (CIR) Spot Reports:

These reports are established as an additional means of evaluating student performance primarily in a non-graded position. They reflect both good and bad performance. They are divided into four categories: "Major Satisfactory," "Minor Satisfactory," "Major Unsatisfactory," and "Minor Unsatisfactory." Three minor CIRs are equivalent to one major CIR. Any Major or Minor Satisfactory CIR cancels a Major or Minor Unsatisfactory CIR, respectively. Five Major or equivalent Minor Unsatisfactory cumulative CIRs in any phase warrant an academic review board and could warrant recycle or relief from the course. Spot reports are cumulative from phase to phase.

Special Observation Report (SOR):

An unsatisfactory SOR (normally for lying, cheating or stealing) is grounds for dismissal. A student with an approved SOR is subject to recycle to any phase of training or drop from the course, based upon the seriousness of the offense.

PEER Evaluations:

Students receive a PEER Evaluation at the end of each phase of training. A score of 60 percent on each peer evaluation must be attained in order to receive a "GO". A student's academic record is reviewed if he does not obtain a "GO" on 2 of 4 peer evaluations to determine his disposition (i.e., continue in the course, recycle or drop from the course). Students are encouraged to be very detailed and specific in their narrative peer comments.

Phase Reviews:

At the end of each phase (Benning, Mountains and Florida) of the Ranger Course, the battalion chain of command responsible for the phase reviews academic records to determine eligibility for remaining in the course. The battalion commander makes a decision on relief, recycle or continuation of any record of substandard performance. The Brigade Commander is the reviewing authority. The following guidelines are used in evaluating students after each of the respective phases:

♦ Benning Phase - 4th Battalion, Ranger Training Brigade:
(1) A student must pass all of the following events or be boarded and possibly recycled:
a. Ranger Assessment Phase;
b. APFT;
c. CWST;

d. 5 mile Run;
e. Night/Day Navigation Test;
f. 12 Mile Tactical Foot March;
g. Water Confidence Test (WCT);
h. Darby Queen Obstacle Course;
(2) Any student receiving three Major or equivalent Minor Unsatisfactory CIRs during this phase, or if the student has accumulated five Major or equivalent Minor Unsatisfactory CIRs, his academic file is reviewed by the Battalion Commander to determine the student's suitability for continuing the course;
(3) The student must attend 75 percent of mission technique classes and combatives training;
(4) The student must attend cadre-led combat operations mission;
(5) Each student must successfully pass the end of phase peer evaluation;
♦ Mountain Phase - 5th Battalion, Ranger Training Brigade:
(1) Each student must pass one leadership evaluation in the Mountain Phase;
(2) Any student receiving three Major or equivalent Minor Unsatisfactory CIR's during this phase, or accumulating five Major or equivalent Minor Unsatisfactory CIRs, will be reviewed by the Battalion Commander to determine the student's suitability for continuing the course;
(3) Each student must demonstrate proficiency in mountaineering techniques as well as pass the knot test, belay and practice falls, the two man party climb, the balance climb and direct aid climb;
(4) Each student must successfully pass the end of phase peer evaluation;
♦ Florida Phase - 6th Battalion, Ranger Training Brigade:
(1) Each student must pass one leadership evaluation in the Florida Phase;
(2) Any student receiving three Major or equivalent Minor Unsatisfactory CIR's during this phase or accumulating five Major or equivalent Minor Unsatisfactory CIRs, will be reviewed by the Battalion

Commander to determine if the student is recycled, dropped from the course or graduated;

(3) Each student must successfully pass the end of phase peer evaluation;

♦ After the Mountain and Florida phases of Ranger School, those students down one or more patrols (e.g. two GOs, three NO GOs) are generally recycled rather than forwarded.

NOTE: Students must pass 50 percent of total patrols, one which must have been a primary leadership position (PL, PSG) in order to graduate. An exception being Benning where a patrol deficit may result in a board.

PERSONAL CONDUCT & APPEARANCE STANDARDS:

If a student misses more than 72 hours of training during the entire Ranger Course, he is recycled or dropped.

Students who do not meet enrollment criteria are not enrolled. The following conditions will preclude enrollment:

a. A physical profile;

b. Recall by parent unit;

c. Lack of sufficient remaining service (i.e. 1 year remaining time in service after graduation from Ranger School);

d. Failure to meet height/weight requirements IAW AR 600-9;

e. Outdated medical exam (exam must be dated within 12 months of course start date and stamped approved for "RANGER/AIRBORNE," if the individual is airborne qualified, otherwise the physical must be stamped approved for "RANGER";

f. Failure to produce verification of a PANOREX;

g. Verified emergencies requiring the student's presence at home;

h. Previous hot/cold weather injuries;

i. Previous Lack of Motivation (LOM) drops without a written waiver approved by the RTB Commander;

j. Previous SOR drops who have been barred from course enrollment without a written waiver approved by the RTB Commander.

Misrepresentation of Application (MOA):

Attempts to withhold any of the above information constitutes a misrepresentation of a student's application to enter the course. Any attempt at misrepresentation subjects the student to being dropped from the course, regardless of the time the offense is discovered.

Prior LOM or SOR drops are required to report this information during inprocessing on DAY 1. Failure to report this information is an MOA.

RTB SR TAC conducts a records check for an approved waiver once the student has not-ified them of his prior drop status (LOM/SOR). The student's sending unit chain of command is notified if an approved waiver is not found. The student's chain of command must support the request for a waiver. The request proceeds to the RTB Commander with an endorsement and recommendation from the Brigade SR TAC. Final decision is made by the RTB Commander.

The Brigade SR TAC fully documents all MOA cases.

RANGER COURSE SELECTION CRITERIA & AWARDS:

Awards listed below are designed to recognize outstanding achievement during the Ranger Course. Dependent on class performance all or some of these awards may be presented upon graduation. There is no requirement for every award by category of rank to be issued.

William O. Darby Award:

The criteria used in selecting the William O. Darby Award winner is:

♦ The Darby Award winner is the top Distinguished Honor Graduate, with highest peer rating, most positive spot reports and the best performance in both tactical and administrative leadership positions;

♦ He must have clearly demonstrated himself as being a cut above all other Rangers;

♦ He is recommended by the battalion commanders and brigade SR TAC after review of all academic records. Final approval authority is the RTB Commander.

A Ranger class is not required to have a William O. Darby award recipient. There will be no more than one William O. Darby award recipient per class.

Distinguished Honor Graduates:

There is one Distinguished Honor Graduate. The officer or enlisted honor graduate with the best overall performance; he must be recommended by the battalion commanders and brigade SR TAC. The RTB Commander is the final approving authority for Distinguished Honor Graduate. If students in a category, officer or enlisted, do not meet the honor graduate criteria, the one student in that category with the best overall performance record is designated the honor graduate for that category, and there is no distinguished honor graduate.

Ralph Puckett Award:

Criteria used to select the Ralph Puckett Awardee (Officer) of the Ranger course are:
♦ Meet the course graduation criteria;
♦ Pass all graded leadership positions;
♦ Pass all peer reports;
♦ No major items of equipment lost due to negligence (as evidenced by SPOT reports);
♦ All unsatisfactory SPOT Reports cancelled;
♦ No recycles, other than for compassionate or medical reasons;
♦ No retests on any critical tasks.

Glenn M. Hall Award:

Criteria used to select the Glenn M. Hall Awardee (Enlisted) of the Ranger Course are:
♦ Meet the course graduation criteria;
♦ Pass all graded leadership positions;
♦ Pass all peer reports;
♦ No major items of equipment lost due to negligence (as evidenced by SPOT reports);

♦ All unsatisfactory SPOT Reports cancelled;
♦ No recycles, other than for compassionate or medical reasons;
♦ No retest on any critical tasks.

Merrill's Marauder's Award:

Criteria used in selecting one officer and one enlisted for the Merrill's Marauder Award are:
♦ Must have passed the land navigation course (no retest);
♦ Must have passed all peer evaluations and have the highest cumulative score.
The student who received the highest score in land navigation will be selected.

Benjamin Church Leadership Award:

Criteria used in selecting one officer and one enlisted man, who have demonstrated outstanding leadership throughout the entire course are:
♦ Must be recommended by all Bn Commanders, BN TACs and Bde SR TAC;
♦ May not have been a recycle for any academic reason (i.e., Peers, Spots or Patrols);
♦ Must have a positive spot record;
♦ Must have not been a SOR case at anytime in the course.

Noncommissioned Officer Association Award:

Given to the top enlisted graduate of each class regardless of other awards received and is sponsored by the NCOA of Columbus, GA.

PREPARATIONS:

Ranger qualified officers or NCOs should brief all Ranger School candidates on the course prior to their attendance.

All Commanders must ensure that applicants are in top physical condition when reporting for the Ranger Course. Applicants should concentrate on improving upper body strength and foot marching in properly fitted boots, with a full ruck sack, for distances up to 15 miles.

The Ranger Program Performance Statistics for the fiscal year 1995 indicated the highest rate of attrition occurred during the Ranger Assessment Phase of training. During RAP, all evaluations are objective in nature and examine skill proficiency. In order to better prepare for Ranger School a generic outline of the first five days (the Ranger Assessment Phase) of Ranger School is listed below:

NOTE: This schedule is subject to change.

Day 1:
(1) Event - APFT;
(2) Event - CWST;
(3) Medical Considerations Class;
(4) Average Sleep - 5 Hours or less.

Day 2:
(1) Event - PT (Standard: 5 mile run in 40:00 minutes or less after PT IAW FM 21-20);
(2) Event - Land Navigation Review;
(3) Event - Terrain Association;
(4) Event - Hand to Hand Combat;
(5) Average Sleep - 3 Hours.

Day 3:
(1) Event - Night/Day Land Navigation Test;
(2) Event - Rangers In Action Demonstration;
(3) Event - Water Confidence Test;
(4) Event - Battle Drill/Patrolling Techniques;
(5) Event - Hand to Hand Combat;
(6) Average Sleep - 5 Hours.

Day 4
(1) Event - 3 Mile Ranger Run/Malvesti Field Obstacle Course;
(2) Event - Ranger Stakes;
(3) Event - Day Land Navigation Retest (Night/Day);
(4) Event - Battle Drill/Patrolling Techniques;
(5) Average Sleep - 5 Hours.

Day 5:
(1) Event - 12 Mile Foot March;
(2) Event - Troop Leading Procedures;
(3) Event - Hand to Hand Combat;
(4) Average Sleep - 5 Hours or less.

Clothing & Equipment Requirements:
Please refer to Tables Ranger-A, Ranger-B and Ranger-C for items inventories of required, authorized and unauthorized equipment, respectively. The packing list for Ranger School is the same for summer and winter months. All uniforms must be serviceable with all insignia removed. Name tags and U.S. Army tapes must be sewn on all BDU Shirts. Only unmodified military issue Black Leather Combat boots and on some occasions the Black Hot Weather and Green Jungle boots are authorized. All boots should be broken in prior to arriving. Only standard issue military soles are authorized. Oversize boots and double layer sock systems are not authorized. Only military issue boot inserts are authorized for wear during training (unless prescribed by a physician).

NOTES: All foreign students are authorized to bring their own military issued equivalent equipment.

All other uniforms and equipment are issued by the Ranger Training Companies. It is not necessary for the student to purchase equipment other than the items stated in the items inventories. Any items not listed are unauthorized.

Table Ranger-D refers to items of equipment issued by the Ranger Training Brigade/Central Issue Facility to those students enrolled in the course.

Table Ranger-E refers to equipment issued by the 4th Ranger Training Battalion for the duration of the Ranger course and DXed or reissued in each of the phases as required.

Table Ranger-F refers to equipment which will be issued by 5th Battalion for the Mountain phase of Ranger School and returned prior to the student's departure.

Table: Ranger-A		
Required Items Inventory		
ITEM	QTY	REMARKS
Adaptor	1	Firing, M4 (TOE soldiers only)
Mouthpiece / Mouth guard	1	Athletic
Batteries	4	D cell
Belt	2	Black, web, with buckle
Tape	2 rolls	Black, friction or electrical
Cap	1	Watch, black
Boots	2 pairs	Combat, leather, Army issue (8430-00-141-0796)
Camouflage Stick	2	Military issue
Cap	2	BDU
Coat	6	BDU (Temperate or Hot Weather)
Locks	4	Combination, key locks are unauthorized
Compass	2	Lensatic, military issue
Civilian clothes	1	Shirt, pair of pants, pair of socks, jacket, pair of shoes
Dressing	2	First aid
Bag	1	Duffel
Bootlaces	2 pairs	Extra
Eyeglasses	2 pairs	Military issue with retainer band
Flashlight	1	L-shape, with red lens, military issue
Foot Powder	2	Goldbond, etc.
Gloves	2	Shell, leather, black, military issue (8415-00-268-8350)
ID Card	1	Current
ID Tags	1 set	With one long and one short breakaway chain
Repellent	1	Insect, non-aerosol, military issue
Glove	2	Inserts, wool, green (8415-00-682-6577)
Lip Balm	1	Military Issue
Magazine	7	M16 (TOE soldiers only)
Medical Tags	1	Alert tags or bracelet
Name Tape	2	Last name
Notebook	3	Pocket size
Pens	2	Black ink
Pencils	2	Mechanical, with erasers
Knife	1	Pocket (folding blade 4" or less)
Polypro	1	Sleep shirt or field jacket liner
Protractors	2	
HW Top	1	PFU, gray
HW Bottom	1	PFU, gray
CW Top	1	PFU, gray
CW Bottom	1	PFU, gray
Razor	1	Shaving, non-electric
Razor Blades	12	
Sewing Kit	1	
Shaving Cream	1 can	Minimum 7 oz.
Shoe Polish	2	Black, silicone, large cans
Running Shoes	1 pair	
Brush	1	Shoe shine
Shoes	1	Shower
Soap	2	Bars, minimum 3 oz.

Table: Ranger-A (Continued)		
Required Items Inventory		
ITEM	QTY	REMARKS
Soap Dish	1	
Socks	12 pairs	Wool, cushion sole, OD or black (8440-00-153-6717)
Socks	4 pair	White, athletic, crew length
Mirror	1	Small
Sunscreen	1	Military issue
Sweatband	1	Helmet liner, Kevlar
Trousers	6	BDU (Temperate or Hot Weather)
Undershirt	7	Brown (Army), for wear under BDU tom
Toothbrush	1	
Toothpaste	2	Tubes, minimum 2 oz.
Towels	2	Cotton, large, brown
Washcloths	2	
Waterproof Bags	25	Ziploc, small
Weapons Cleaning Kit	1	Small Arms
Whistle	1	OD, military issue
Wristwatch	1	

Table: Ranger-B		
Optional Items Inventory		
ITEM	QTY	REMARKS
Acetate/Clear shelf paper	1 roll	
Markers/Erasers	1 pack	Alcohol
Boots	2 pairs	Hot weather, black or green (8430-00-141-0796)
Bungee Cord	6	Black or gray
Underwear	7 pairs	Cotton
Cards	1 pack	Index
Lighter	1	
Trash Bags	1 box	Large, black
Laundry Soap	1 box	Powder, small box
Leatherman type tool	1	Leatherman, Gerber, etc.
Letter Writing Material	as needed	Stationary, stamps, etc.
Map Case	1	
Cord	50 feet	Nylon, 550 type
Pace cord	1	
Penlight	1	Mini-mag light, with AA cell batteries
Eyeglasses	1	Protective
Religious Writings	as needed	Bible, Koran, etc.
Status cards	1 pack	
Tape	1 roll	100 mph type
Terrain Model Kit		Small
Matches	1 box	Waterproof
Whetstone	1	
Wrist Compass	1	
Waterproof Bags	1 box	Small, Ziploc

10 cans of dip/snuff or 10 packs cigarettes or 10 packs of chewing tobacco or 10 packs of chewing gum (5-7 ticks per pack), Ranger students can have any combination of the above not to exceed 10 items per phase (e.g. 7 gum, 3 tobacco, etc.)

Table: Ranger-C	
Unauthorized Items Inventory	
ITEM	
Civilian GPS	
Civilian Long Underwear	
Contact Lenses	
Filled in Operations Order, FRAGO or ANNEX Formats	
Non-military or Modified Issue Boot Soles, Insulated or HI-TECH Boots	
Non-military or Modified Issue Boot Inserts	
Knee or Elbow Pads of any kind	
Spandex Athletic Wear or Underwear	
Nomex, Goretex, Polypro Gloves	
Vitamins or Supplements of any kind	
Gortex, Polypro Socks	
Civilian Medications (i.e., Asprin, Tylonel, Vitamins, etc.)	
No personal TA 50	
Cash over $50.00	
Any item not listed in this ANNEX is unauthorized and are Grounds for Immediate Relief	

Table: Ranger-D		
Items Issued at Ranger CIF		
ITEM	QTY	REMARKS
Bag	1	Barracks
Bag	2	Duffel
Bag	2	Clothing, waterproof
Belt	1	Individual Equipment
Canteen	2	Plastic, one quart, with cover
Canteen	2	Plastic, two quart, with cover
Case	1	First Aid
Case	2	Small arms ammo
Cup	1	Canteen
Field Pack	1	ALICE, large, with frame
Strap	1	Shoulder, left
Strap	1	Shoulder, right
Strap	1	Waist, combination
Helmet	1	Kevlar
Chinstrap	1	Helmet, Kevlar
Cover	1	Helmet, camouflage
Suspension	1	Helmet, Kevlar
Pad	1	Paratrooper
Strap	1	Retaining / CRO
Entrenching Tool	1	E-tool, with cover
Liner	1	Poncho, camouflage
Mittens	1 pair	Insert, wool, TF
Mittens	1 pair	Shell, nylon, TF
Overshoes	1 pair	Vinyl, green
Parka	1	Cold Weather (Gortex)
Parka	1	Wet Weather

Table: Ranger-D (Continued)		
Items Issued at Ranger CIF		
ITEM	QTY	REMARKS
Poncho	1	Camouflage, nylon
Bag	1	Sleeping, universal
Strap	2	TD-CARGO-LC-1
Suspenders	1	LCE
Trousers	1 pair	Wet Weather
Scarf	1	Wool
Undershirt	2	Cold Weather, polypro
Drawers	1 pair	Cold Weather, polypro
Gloves	1 pair	Leather, work
Liner	1	Field Jacket

Table: Ranger-E		
Items Issued at 4th RTB		
ITEM	QTY	REMARKS
Adapter	1	Blank Firing
Magazines	7	Ammunition
Compass	1	Lensatic
Dressing	1	First Aid
Air items	1 set	
Camouflage Stick	1	
Sling	1	M16
Handbook	1	Ranger
Map Protractor	1	Plastic
Whistle	1	
Bacalave	1	
Water Purification Tablets	1	Bottle
Foot Powder	1	Bottle
Insect Repellent	1	Bottle
Lip Balm	1	Tube
Sun Screen	1	Bottle

Table: Ranger-F		
Items Issued at 5th RTB		
ITEM	QTY	REMARKS
Boots	1 pair	Vapor Barrier (VB)
Equipment	1 set	Rappelling

Applications:

Application for Ranger training (for 75th Ranger Regiment volunteers) will be submitted through command channels to:

PERSCOM
ATTN: TAPC-EPK-I
2461 Eisenhower Ave.
Alexandria, VA. 22331-0452.

All requests for TDY and return are submitted through command channels to PERSCOM, Specialized Training Management Branch (TAPC-EPT-F). Selection criteria and application procedures are outlined in AR 614-200, Chapter 5, Section 1.

Ranger Graduation:

Relatives and friends of the graduating Ranger students are invited to attend the Ranger graduation ceremony held at Victory Pond (outdoors on a potentially rough surface) at 1100. If the Ranger graduation is during the winter months, it is advisable for the guests to wear warm clothing since the ceremony lasts approximately one hour.

NOTE: RTB Headquarters is the site of the Ranger Hall of Fame. Families may desire to set aside time to view the Hall of Fame and to observe available videos.

Zero Week (An optional program precedeing the official course):

The 4th RTB conducts a Zero Week for each class. The Zero Week program starts one week prior to the class reporting date. Applicants must report on Monday NLT 0600, to HHC, 4th RTBn in the Harmony Church area, Fort Benning, Georgia. Students will report with closely cropped hair cuts. All incoming Ranger students will have in their possession: health records, to include a medical examination signed by a doctor (IAW AR 614-200 and DA PAM 351-4) and dated within 12 months from the reporting date, twenty copies of their orders with amendments and certification by their company commander of Army Physical Fitness Test (APFT), Combat Water Survival Test (CWST), prerequisite skill completion and a memorandum signed by their commander verifying that a PANOREX exists. Incoming Ranger students will bring all required uniforms and equipment IAW SH 21-75.

The Zero Week program performance stat-istics for FY95 indicate a lower rate of attrition during the first five days of Ranger training. It is not designed to train Ranger School candidates to graduate from the Ranger Course. Zero Week is not intended to make a soldier proficient in any single task. Sustainment training is conducted to reinforce present skills and allow partial acclimation. Students receive a 24-48 hour pass at the end of Zero Week.

The Zero Week Mission is to conduct Ranger Zero Week to better prepare students for Ranger School.

The Zero Week Intent is to mentally harden soldiers and acclimate them to the Georgia weather; soldiers are given the opportunity to passed the APFT and CWST. Those who do not successfully complete the APFT/CWST are allowed to retest on day one of the Ranger Course.

Zero Week Events include the APFT and CWST (if passed counts for Ranger School), 5 mile run (same pace as Ranger School, 40 minutes total), Physical Training (daily), basic map reading review, Land Navigation Course (same course as Ranger School), Ranger Stakes, Battle Drills, Troop Leading Procedures, Warning Order, Fragmentary Order, Time Schedule and Duties and Responsibilities of Key Personnel (Squad Leader, A and B Team Leaders).

REPORTING INFORMATION:

Ranger students will report to Building 5024 to sign in with the Brigade Headquarters Detachment NLT 0800. No exceptions are made for any student. A student arriving with orders stating a report time later than 0800 hours may be offered a recycle into the next class. The student's sending unit is notified of this action. Incoming students reporting time is preferably between 0530-0700 on the start date for their class. RTB is located 12 miles from the Main Post area. Directional signs are located on post and on Highway 27 south of Columbus. Students should report with closely cropped hair cuts.

Inprocessing:

The first day of Ranger training consists of course inprocessing, and Day 1 of the Ranger Assessment Phase (RAP). Day 1 arrivals are enrolled in the Ranger Course and will proceed with the following events:

♦ Each student signs in at Building 5024 on a personal data card, ("Green Card");

♦ Students are broken down into groups for APFT and CWST testing immediately after sign in. 4th RTBn cadre conduct the APFT and CWST. The following items should be placed in a plastic trash bag for APFT/CWST and brought with the student at sign in: 1 set of BDU's, 1 pair of boots, 1 pair of socks, 1 BDU cap, 1 brown undershirt, 1 large brown towel and 1 pair of running shoes;

♦ 4th RTBn medical personnel screen each student's medical record for required shots, current physical exam, previous hot/cold weather injuries, insect bite allergies, active profiles and HIV test within past two years;

♦ Students are tested on the APFT and CWST. Failures (after retest) are separated and placed in a holding area;

♦ Students passing the APFT and CWST return to Building 5024 for further Inprocessing. APFT and CWST failures continue inprocessing, but are separated into their own group;

♦ Students fill out mail cards, personnel register cards and S1 folders;

♦ All students move to the RTB classroom for Main Post AG and Finance inprocessing after completing events listed above;

♦ Students are organized for count by unit, grade, sister services and international students;

♦ APFT and CWST failures are taken to the 4th RTBn S3 (Bn TAC NCO) after inprocessing is completed. They remain under Bn TAC NCO control until the Brigade SR TAC finalizes their status;

♦ The Brigade SR TAC briefs the Ranger Class on the RTB Academic Standard Operating Procedures (SOP). Students are asked to sign and mail a formatted letter to their next of kin upon completion of briefing;

♦ A representative of the Brigade SR TAC Office and 4th RTBn S3 coordinates the following tasks:
(1) The Ranger Class is broken down into three training companies (A, B, and C). The Day 1 recycles from previous classes and zero week students are assigned to companies by the 4th RTBn S3 TAC NCO;
(2) Rosters of the incoming class are verified by total count and recycle count.

♦ The Brigade SR TAC finalizes the class roster and submits a copy to the RTB Commander.

LEAVE & PASS POLICY:

No student is removed from an outlying battalion for other than medical reasons without the approval of the battalion commander and notification of the Brigade SR TAC. Battalion commanders should consult the RTB Commander prior to removing a student from training. Students are only authorized leave for a verified emergency requiring the student's presence. The leave period will not exceed ten days. The battalion notifies the Brigade SR TAC office as soon as possible, specifying the student's name, roster number, leave address, leave dates and reason for emergency departure. All emergency situations are verified/confirmed through Red Cross channels.

Battalions sending a student on leave/emergency will receive a control number from RTB S1.

Students returning from leave report to the RTB S1 during duty hours, or the RTB SDNCO during off duty hours.

Students required to go on leave or pass from the Ranger Course are administratively recycled or dropped.

The RTB S1 with the approval of the Brigade Commander can grant students ordinary leave during the block leave period.

Students are placed on an authorized pass at Fort Benning after the first phase and after the Mountain Phase of the Ranger Course, time permitting. Students are placed on an authorized pass at Fort Benning after the Florida Phase is completed and prior to graduation, time permitting.

Passes allow students the opportunity to clean and prepare all individual items of clothing and equipment for the next phase of training. Students get a fresh haircut and take care of financial or personal situations that require attention. The last pass is to furnish each student with time to begin outprocessing from Fort Benning.

A battalion formation is held for accountability purposes after each pass. All students are required to be in duty uniform with their equipment at the designated formation time. Students that return late from pass are dropped from the course. Students are inspected immediately after returning from pass to ensure they do not possess contraband items.

Students are required to perform the following while on break:

(1) Get a fresh Ranger haircut.

(2) Replace or repair any missing TA-50 items or any other mandatory clothing/equipment.

(3) Get clothes washed.

Students are prohibited from doing the following while on break:

(1) Traveling further than 25 miles from Fort Benning.

(2) Wearing sterile or unserviceable BDUs, mixed uniforms or PT uniform off post.

(3) Operating any POV or ride in a vehicle with another Ranger student as the operator.

(4) Consumption of any alcohol or drugs.

(5) Bringing "any food items" to include food supplements back to the RTB area.

Violation of any of the above policies will subject students to UCMJ action and termination from the Ranger Course.

In case of an emergency while on pass or leave, contact the SDNCO at COMM: (706) 544-7212/7430, and give your name, stating the problem and leave a number where you can be reached.

BILLETING:

All students arriving prior to the class starting date are required to provide their own living accommodations. All students, once enrolled, are required to live in the Ranger company barracks.

Students TDY at Fort Benning to attend only the Ranger Course should not bring dependents. Dependent housing may be procured off post in the Columbus area; students should contact the Housing Referral Office for assistance. Government family quarters are not available for students assigned to Fort Benning on TDY.

Because of the limited time available off duty, students are cautioned to bring only a minimum amount of civilian clothing with them. Luggage is not permitted to be stored in the billets.

Ranger student billets are arranged in a uniform manner. Cleanliness and security of government and personal equipment are primary concerns. The student chain of command is responsible for ensuring the billets are ready for inspection at all times.

Dining Facilities:

All Ranger students - enlisted, officer, sister service and allied are issued a DD Form 714 (Meal Card), by the 4th RTBn on Day 1 of the course. All students sign the DA Form 3032 (Signature Headcount Sheet) before each meal in garrison. The existing one line entry method on DA Form 3032 is used for MRE issue. Students report lost meal cards through the chain of com-mand to the S1, 4th RTBn. Students use their ID cards when they lose their meal cards, as no replacement is issued.

Each battalion prepares DD Form 1475 (Basic Allowance for Subsistence Certification) for inclusion in each student's academic record. This form accounts for meals consumed during the phase. As many DD Form 1475 as necessary are prepared to cover the entire period that the student is under control of that battalion. A DD Form 1475 is completed and included in each student's academic record prior to the student leaving that battalion's location for the next phase of training, or for home station.

At the completion of Ranger School all U.S. Army enlisted and sister service enlisted personnel not on BAS or per diem hand carry their DD Form 1475 to their home station Finance and Accounting Officer (FAO) for reimbursement for missed meals.

At the completion of Ranger School all U.S. Army officers have a DA Form 4187 (Personnel Action) completed by the 4th RTBn for a payroll deduction to pay for their meals. The data for the DA Form 4187 originates from the completed DD Form 1475. Student officers do not take their DD Form 1475 with them when they leave. The DD Form 1475 is not sent to an FAO. The DD Form 1475 serves as a record for officer students and is only used within the RTB.

All sister service officers, allied students, and any sister service enlisted personnel on BAS or per diem, pay for meals they consumed at the end of the course using the DD Form 1475 to compute the amount they owe. The DD Form 1475 is not given to the student or sent to an FAO, but used as a record within RTB. A Memorandum for Record is prepared stating the number of meals consumed and the amount paid by the student. The memorandum is prepared by the 6th RTBn during outprocessing and prior to graduation.

Mail:
All mail received for students within the Ranger Training Brigade is issued to them. Mail is delivered to all students expeditiously during FTXs and in garrison. The following procedures are used with the Ranger Training Brigade:
♦ Mail received by unit mail clerks is picked up by company mail handlers and delivered to students;

♦ Ranger students are discouraged from receiving packages while they are in training. All packages received for students are held until the end of the FTX training.
Below are the current mailing addresses for each phase:

Fort Benning Address:
Rank/Name 000-00-0000 (SSN)
 4th Bn, RTBn (SQD) (PLT
ATTN: (Class), (Company)
Fort Benning, GA 31905.

Mountain Address:
Rank/Name 000-00-0000 (SSN)
5th Bn, RTBn (SQD) (PLT)
ATTN: (Class), (Company)
Camp Frank D. Merrill
Dahlonega, GA 30533-9499.

Florida Address:
Rank/Name 000-00-0000 (SSN)
6th Bn, RTBn (SQD) (PLT)
Attn: (Class), (Company)
Camp James E. Rudder
Eglin AFB, FL 32542.

Laundry Facilities:
A limited number of washers, dryers and hand-washing facilities are available at the Ranger Camps. Commercial laundries also may be used during off duty time.

Starched fatigues are not worn during Ranger School; therefore, there is no need for commercial starching and pressing. Fatigues are generally washed and dried with the rest of the student's laundry.

Telephone Service:
Pay telephones are available at all three locations that training is conducted except Camp Darby at Fort Benning, GA. Telephone service is available through the Ranger Training Brigade for emergency use only; the emergency telephone number is:
COMM: (706) 544-0768/6911/6602.

Money:

Ranger students are not authorized to have more than $50.00 in cash in their possession at any time. (Debit cards and checkbooks are authorized but are discouraged).

Students should bring sufficient funds to defray initial expenses for food, laundry and incidentals. Pay may not be available at Fort Benning until one or two weeks after students report.

The purchase of travelers checks ($10 and $20 denominations) prior to arrival at Fort Benning is recommended. Personal check cashing facilities are available at Fort Benning, but limited at the other three camps.

Normal expenditures for officer students drawing per diem is approximately $200 for each phase of the course, $125 for officers not on per diem, and $40 for enlisted students.

HHC, 4th Battalion, RTB provides a company safe for students to secure any excess money.

Pay:

All financial matters to include monthly, travel and per diem pay is administered by the Ranger Battalion to which the student is assigned.

Pay for allied students is administered by the International Student Training Division, USAIS.

To facilitate pay matters, it is strongly recommended that incoming students establish a checking account with a banking facility prior to reporting to Ranger School and make arrangements to have their paycheck sent directly to the bank.

Students are encouraged to replace in kind any government equipment lost during the course. Statements of Charges or Cash collection vouchers are also accepted.

POV:

There is a parking lot at the Camp Rogers RTB area that is lighted, fenced and locked. Students reporting with privately owned vehicles must park them in the lot during inprocessing and leave them there for the duration of the course. Vehicles belonging to individuals who are at Fort Benning to attend the Ranger Course do not have to be registered on post if they are parked in this lot.

Medical Records:

Medical records are collected by the 4th RTBn medics and are kept at 4th RTBn Aid Station. Students going to the hospital for treatment are logged out by the company commander, 1SG or OPNS NCO. Students return to the company to sign in.

Academic and any medical records of any students dropped from the course are returned to the Brigade SR TAC Office.

The 4th RTBn Aid Station returns medical records to students upon release or graduation from the Ranger Course.

Medical personnel in all phases are responsible for returning medical paperwork to Fort Benning prior to class graduation. All medical paperwork is consolidated in the student's original medical record folder.

Religious Services:

Each battalion conducts religious services twice in all phases of the Ranger Course. The conduct of religious services, however, will not take precedence over mission accomplishment. The mission has priority should a conflict between the two occur.

CONTACT INFORMATION:

Senior TAC (POC for Student in/outprocessing) contact information is as follows:

SR TAC NCOIC:
DSN: 784-6613/6604;
COMM: (706) 544-6613/6604;

SR TAC FAX:
COMM: (706) 544-6821.

Questions concerning the Ranger Course should be directed to the SR TAC Office or to:

Commandant
United States Army Infantry School
ATTN: ATSH-R-O
Fort Benning, GA. 31905-5000.

BDE S3:
DSN: 784-7212/6980, EXT 230;
COMM: 706-544-7212/6980.

REFERENCE:

1. US Army Formal Schools Catalog. US Army Publishing Agency. DA PAM 351-4, page 46-47, Table 3-6. 31 October 1995.
2. Ranger Handbook. US Army Infantry School; Ft. Benning, GA. SH 21-76. July 1992.
3. "Student Orientation." Online. Internet. 16 May 2000. Available: http://www-benning.army.mil/RTB/RANGER/EQUIP.HTM.
4. "U.S. Army Rangers: History." Online. Internet. 15 April 2000. Available: http://users.aol.com/armysof1/rgrstory.html.

FOR MORE INFORMATION ON RANGER TRAINING

CHECK OUT

The Interactive Ranger Handbook XXI
by
Timothy P. Dunnigan

YOU CAN FIND IT ON THE WEB

AT

WWW.TYLERENTERPRISES.COM

RANGER HANDBOOK XXI

RANGER TRAINING BRIGADE
UNITED STATES ARMY INFANTRY CENTER, FORT BENNING, GEORGIA

Includes:

Ranger Handbook
FM 7-8, Infantry Rifle Platoon and Squad
Video Instruction
Rangers In Action Demonstration
Ranger Instructor Interviews
Extensive Ranger Photo Library

SCUBA

COMBAT DIVER QUALIFICATION COURSE

REGULATION:

Course No: 2E–SI4W/4Y/011–ASIW7/W9
Title: Special Forces Combat Diver Qualification
Length: 4 Weeks, 2 Days
Location: U.S. Army John F. Kennedy Spec Warfare
Center – SC: 331
Enl ASI: W7
WO ASI: 4Y
Off SC: 4W
Scope: Course effective: 1 Oct 94
Day and night ocean subsurface navigation swims;
deep dives, diving physics, marine hazards, tides and
currents, buoyant ascents; submarine lock–in/lock–out
procedures.
Prerequisite: Active Army or Reserve component or
selected DOD personnel assigned or on orders to a
Special Operations Forces unit. Male commissioned
officer, warrant officer, or enlisted personnel. Must pass
a scuba physical examination IAW 40–501, Chapter 5,
paragraph 5–8 within one year of course completion
date and must report with medical records on day of
inprocessing. Must pass the APFT with a minimum of
70 points in each event and an overall score of 210 or
above (scored on 17–21 year age group IAW FM 21–
20. Must meet the height and weight standards as
outlined in AR 600–9.
Special Information: The original SF 88, SF 93, and
allied documents will be forwarded directly to the
USAJFKSWCS Surgeon IAW AR 40–501, Chapter 8,
paragraph 8–26c. Must pass an entrance examination
at C Company, Key West, Florida, consisting of the
following requirements; Swim 500 meters, nonstop,
(on the surface) using only the breaststroke or
sidestroke; tread water for two minutes continuously,
with both hands out of the water; swim 25 meters
underwater without breaking the surface with any
portion of the body; and retrieve a 20 pound weight
from a depth of 3 meters. Must have completed a pre–
Combat Diver Qualification course (CDQC) program
conducted at parent unit. Must report with
certification of pre–CDQC completion signed by
battalion commander. (Recommend using pre–CDQC
training package exported by SWCS in July 1991 to
prepare for this entrance examination).
Security Clearance: None

PURPOSE:

The purpose of the Combat Diver Underwater
Operations Course is to train personnel as
qualified military combat divers trained in
waterborne operations to include day and night
ocean subsurface navigation swims, deep dives,
diving physics, marine hazards, tides and currents,
submarine lock-in/lock-out procedures and
open-circuit swims.

OVERVIEW:

The Combat Diver Course is a 4 week course
that teaches students the use of open/closed-
circuit SCUBA equipment, underwater search
techniques and long range underwater compass
swims, as well as medical and physical aspects of
underwater diving.

The course covers:
- ◆ Open Circuit Operations;
- ◆ Surface and Subsurface Operations;
- ◆ Deep Dives;
- ◆ Diving Physics/Injuries;
- ◆ Water Infiltration.

*NOTE: The closed circuit training portion of combat diver school has been
discontinued. In its place, the cadre has developed and implemented a Water
Infiltration Course (WIC). This mini WIC consists of zodiac operations and
navigation, numerous surface swims, an end of course FTX, Klepper operations,
waterproofing of gear, planning, etc.*

Table Combat Diver-A outlines the course
overview.

General Training Outline:
Week One:
- ◆ "Boat house boogie" (FAST 2 mile run);
- ◆ Conditioning in pool - laps and flutter kicks;

♦ Instruction on dive equipment and procedures.

Week Two:
  ♦ "Ditching & Donning":
  1. Enter pool;
  2. Swim underwater to depth of 15 feet;
  3. Remove face mask, snorkel, fins, twin tanks and leave on pool bottom, placing weight belts on top;
  4. Take one breath of compressed air;
  5. Surface and breathe;
  6. Return to the bottom of the pool, put on weight belt and other equipment;
  7. Begin using compressed air again;
  ♦ "Harassment Dive":
  1. Enter pool;
  2. Swim around edge at the bottom;
  3. Instructors will pull face masks, remove fins and oxygen tanks, etc, this continues for an hour;
  NOTE: Failing either of these exercises results in discharge from SCUBA school.
  ♦ 500 meter navigation dive evaluation;
  ♦ Classroom instruction.

Week Three:
  ♦ Student dives, day and night;
  ♦ 1500 meter navigation dive evaluation;
  ♦ Classroom instruction.

Week Four:
  ♦ Night dives;
  ♦ Team swim;
  ♦ 3000 meter navigation dive evaluation;
  ♦ End of course test;
  ♦ FTX;
  ♦ Graduation.
  NOTE: Combat Diver classes include, but are not limited to: diving physics, marine hazards, tides and currents, buoyant ascents

Table: Combat Diver-A	
Example Training Overview	
INSTRUCTION	TNG TIME
Course Overview	2 Hours
Dangerous Marine Life	1 Hour
Specialized Physical Conditioning for Combat Diver Qualification	1 Hour
Oxygen Tolerance/ Chamber Pressure Test	7 Hours
500-Meter Team Selection Swim	2 Hours
Physics	3 Hours
Inspection and Maintenance of Individual Swim Equipment	13 Hours
Diving Physiology	1 Hour
Diving Injuries	2 Hours
Anti-Swimmer Systems	1 Hour
Determining Duration of Air Supply	1 Hour
Decompression	4 Hours
Regulator Repair	4 Hours
Tides, Waves, and Currents	2 Hours
CPR	6 Hours
Altitude Diving	2 Hours
Open-Circuit SCUBA Training	
INSTRUCTION	TNG TIME
Use of Fins and Mask	4 Hours
Use of Open-Circuit Equipment and Buddy Breathing	4 Hours
Open-circuit SCUBA Tank Charging	2 Hours
Ditching and Donning Single Hose Open-Circuit Equipment	4 Hours
Specialized Waterwork and Equipment	4 Hours
Open-Circuit Compass Swims	20 Hours
130' Open-Circuit Qualification Dive	4 Hours
Operations	
INSTRUCTION	TNG TIME
Surface Swims	9 Hours
Advanced Open Water Practical Exercise	4 Hours
Team Swims	2 Hours
Introduction to Para-Scuba	1 Hour
Bouyant Ascent	2 Hours
Submarine Lock-in/out Training/Practical	4 Hours
Underwater Searches	5 Hours
Cast and Recovery	4 Hours
Waterproofing and Bundle Rigging	2 Hours
Ship Bottom Search	4 Hours
Infiltration Techniques	2 Hours
Field Training Exercise	22 Hours

PREREQUISITES:

♦ Male Commissioned Officer, Warrant Officer, Enlisted member of the Active Army or Reserve Component or selected DOD personnel assigned or on orders to a special operations forces unit;

♦ Must have passed a Scuba physical examination IAW AR 40-501, Chapter 5, paragraph 5, within two years of course completion date and must report with medical records on day of inprocessing;

♦ Must have successfully completed a pre-Combat Diver Qualification Course (CDQC) program conducted at parent unit;

♦ Must meet the height/weight standards as outlined in AR 600-9. If a waiver is required, the original Standard Form 88, Standard Form 93 and allied documents will be forwarded directly to the USASOC Surgeon IAW AR 40-501, Chapter 8, paragraph 8-26C;

♦ Must pass the APFT with a minimum of 70 points in each event and an overall score of 210 or above (scored on 17-21 year old age group) IAW FM 21-20;

♦ Must pass an entrance examination at C Company, Key West, Florida, consisting of the following requirements:

1. Swim 500 meters, nonstop (on the surface), using only the breaststroke or sidestroke;

2. Tread water for two minutes continuously, with both hands and ears out of the water;

3. Swim 25 meters underwater without breaking the surface with any portion of the body;

4. Retrieve a 20 pound weight from a depth of 3 meters;

It is recommended that students use the pre-CDQC training package exported by SWCS in May 1995 to prepare for this entrance examination.

PREPARATIONS:

It is imperative that all administrative actions or problems be settled with the student's parent unit prior to the student's departure from his home station. The training site at Key West has no administrative assets to handle such actions.

Pre-SCUBA:

The pre-CDQC course is a ten day course that teaches and tests the students on their swimming abilities. In this course students are constantly stressed. The class determines which soldiers, if any, will attend the Combat Diver Qualification Course. The first week of the course is designed to build confidence; the second week develops individual skills. To complete the course, students must develop teamwork and depend on their buddies.

During the first nine days of training, students learn about ditch and don and knot tying; soldiers perform 20 pound weight recovery exercises and 16 pound belt swims. By course end students must swim 3000 meters in BDUs; students must swim 50 meters underwater in one breath; students must have the ability to hold their breath underwater for two minutes. In some courses, students spend one hour daily learning physics, dive tables and physiology. Students may not have to achieve the standards of the course during the first nine days of training; however, they must pass all the tasks on the test day.

Clothing & Equipment Requirements:

As a minimum, each student will bring items of uniform and equipment listed in Table Combat Diver-B:

Note: Students may wear personal wet suit booties, coral booties, or a similar type footgear for the swims. However, Company C will not issue these items to the students.

REPORTING INFORMATION:

Students will report to Building KW 100, United States Naval Air Station, Trumbo Point Annex, Key West, FL during duty hours and to the charge of quarters (CQ), Building KW 700

		Table: Combat Diver-B		
Required Items Inventory				
ITEM	QTY	REMARKS		
Undershirt	8	Brown or olive drab (OD)		
Swim Trucks	2 pair	Underwater Demolition Team (UDT) Army swim trunks or unit issue physical training (PT) shorts, with standard OD name tape sewn on the right front leg, centered 1 inch above the bottom		
BDU	2 sets	Without patches, insignia or reflective tape		
Cap	2 sets	BDU, without patches, insignia or reflective tape; berets will not be worn in Key West, Florida		
Socks	6 pairs	White, athletic, no stripes/logos, crew length		
Shoes	1 pair	Civilaian, athletic - running, lace type		
Bag	1	Duffel or Aviator's bag		
Calculator	1	Hand held		
Notebook	1	Loose-leaf binder		
Watch	1	Waterproof		

after duty hours. Students will report no earlier than two days prior to the reporting date (the dining facility will be closed prior to this time) and no later than 2400 on the reporting date.

Students must be assigned to or on orders for assignment to duty requiring participation in waterborne/underwater operations.

Students must report with certification of pre-CDQC completion signed by the Battalion Commander.

Inprocessing:
APFT will be conducted at 0500 the next day; inprocessing will begin at 1000 in Building KW 100.

BILLETING:
Students will be billeted in the Company C billets. Statements of non-availability will not be issued.

Dining Facilities:
Mess facilities will be provided at no cost to the students. Meal cards will be issued at Key West.

Money Requirements:
Students should bring enough money for personal needs for four weeks (access to government check cashing facilities is limited).

POV:
Travel to Key West will be by commercial air or privately owned vehicle. Students will not use privately owned vehicles while attending the course.

REFERENCE:
1. US Army Formal Schools Catalog. US Army Publishing Agency. DA PAM 351-4, Page 121, Table 3-19. 31 October 1995.
2. Watson, Mark PFC. "Pre-scuba offers grueling test in confidence." The Bayonet. 5 May 2000. Page A-6.
3. U.S. Army Special Forces: "JFK SWCS Advanced Skills Department." Online. Internet. 15 April 2000. Available: http://users.aol.com/armysof1/specialty.html.
4. Thede, James J., TSgt. "US Army Combat Divers Course," Online. Internet. 16 May 2000. Available: http://members.tripod.com/~thede/scuba.html.
5. Biank, Tanya S., "Fighting for Breath." Online. Internet. 24 May 2000. Available: http://www.fayettevillenc.com/foto/news/content/1998/tx98apr/m30scuba.htm.

SERE

SURVIVAL, EVASION, RESISTANCE, AND ESCAPE - HIGH RISK

REGULATION:

Course No: 3A–F38/012–F27
Title: Survival, Evasion, Resistance, and Escape (SERE) High Risk
Length: 3 Weeks, 4 Days
Location: U.S. Army John F. Kennedy Spec Warfare Center – SC: 331
Scope: Course effective: 1 Oct 93
Intensive training in support of the code of conduct; survival field–craft with application to worldwide environments; and techniques of evasion, resistance to interrogation and exploitation, and escape from captivity. Will also participate in a survival FTX and in a resistance training laboratory.
Prerequisite: Active and Reserve Component personnel of the armed forces of the United States specified by DOD Directive 1300.7 and AR 350–30 to receive level C code of conduct/SERE training. Foreign students must meet requirements as stated in SERE Classification Guide. Must possess current Standard Forms 88 and 93 (within 12 months of class reporting date) conforming to mobilization standards of AR 40–501, Chapter 3. In addition, the student must possess a normal EKG and satisfactory urinalysis test within one year of course date, and must report with medical records on day of in–processing. Any abnormalities will have accompanying evaluation by appropriate medical specialist. Must attain a score of 180 points on APFT, with at least 60 points per event (17 to 21 year old age group), passed within 30 days of reporting date to SERE high–risk course and given IAW FM 21–20. Personnel currently on jump status must present a copy of hazardous duty orders.
Security Clearance: SECRET

PURPOSE:

The purpose of SERE is to train selected personnel on code of conduct, survival, evasion, resistance and escape.

The JFK Special Warfare Center & School SERE/Terrorism Antiaction Department teaches the SERE Level-C training course to soldiers who are in a high-risk-of-capture category, which includes Special Forces, Rangers and aviators. The course is designed to give students the skill to survive and evade capture; or - if captured - to resist interrogation/exploitation and plan their escape.

OVERVIEW:

The course includes a classroom phase, a field phase and a resistance training laboratory which simulates the environment of a prisoner-of-war compound.

Personnel are intensively trained in support of:
♦ General Survival Skills;
♦ Evasion Planning;
♦ Code of Conduct;
♦ Resistance to Exploitation & Political Indoctrination;
♦ Escape Planning.

PREREQUISITES:

♦ Active and Reserve component personnel of the armed forces of the United States specified by DOD Directive 1300.7 and AR 350-30 to receive Level C Code of Conduct/SERE training. Level C training is for soldiers whose wartime position, MOS or assignment has a high risk of capture, and whose position, rank or seniority make them vulnerable to greater than average exploitation efforts by a captor. Examples include personnel who operate forward of the FLOT - such as Special Forces, Pathfinders, selected aviators, flying crew members and members of Ranger Battalions. Peacetime level C personnel are those who - due to assignment or mission - have a high risk of being taken hostage by terrorists or being detained by a hostile government in a peacetime environment. Examples include Special Forces, selected military attaches, members of Ranger Battalions and anyone in special support missions near conflict areas. Foreign students must meet requirements as stated in SERE Classification Guide;

♦ Must possess current Standard Forms 88 and 93 conforming to mobilization standards of Chapter 3, AR 40-501. School must be completed within two years of date on physical;

NOTE: When SERE is done in immediate succession with SFQC, the physical that was acceptable for SFAS/SFQC will suffice, providing the physical has not expired.

♦ In addition, the student must possess a normal EKG and a satisfactory urinalysis test within two years of course completion date and must report with medical records on day of inprocessing. Any abnormalities will have accompanying evaluation by appropriate medical specialist;

♦ Must attain a score of 180 points on APFT, with at least 60 points per event, passed within 30 days of reporting date to SERE High-Risk Course and given IAW FM 21-20.

Soldiers requesting waivers for disqualifying conditions will submit their physical examinations along with memorandum requesting the waiver (NLT 30 days prior to class start date) through the USASOC Medical Training Division for delivery to USAJFKSWCS (where waivers are considered). The address for the USASOC Medical Training Division is:

Commander, USASOC
ATTN: AOMD-MT
Ft Bragg, NC 28307-5217.

PREPARATIONS:

Clothing & Equipment Requirements:

Refer to Table SERE-A for a list of required items, Table SERE-B for a list of unit issue items, Table SERE-C for a list of field equipment items, Table SERE -D for a list of optional equipment items and Table SERE-E for unauthorized equipment items list.

If you have any questions about the required clothing or equipment resolve them before you depart your unit.

This Clothing and Equipment List supersedes all previous U.S. Army SERE (Level C) Course Clothing and Equipment List.

NOTES:
1. Bring only enough cash to pay for 23 meals at the Dining Facility. PX can cash checks for $20.
2. No machetes or other knifes with a blade over 12 inches allowed. K-bar, Survival Knifes, Swiss Army Knifes, Gerber tools, etc. are allowed.
3. A small Post Exchange Annex may be available during portions of the SERE Course. Normal hours of operation are Mon, Wed, Fri, 1200-1600hrs.

Physicals:

Organization/unit surgeons will base their determinations of a soldier's medical qualification/disqualification on AR 40-501, Standards of Medical Fitness (1 May 1989), Interim Change No. 101 to AR 50-401 (1 October 1991), and the USAJFKSWCS Memorandum, "Requirements for Completing Physical Examinations for USAJFKSWCS Schools," 1 March 1995.

REPORTING INSTRUCTIONS:

Because some students will be coming from distant stations (TDY students) and other students are already stationed at Fort Bragg (local students), some of the following will not apply equally. Students must have all of their affairs in order prior to inprocessing. No time will be available to return leased vehicles or perform other non-course activities after reporting for inprocessing.

TDY students staying overnight at Moon Hall should be checked out of Moon Hall prior to 0645 Monday morning. Transportation is scheduled to arrive at Moon Hall at 0700 Monday. Students who desire transportation should place their baggage on board the transport and board themselves. Transportation will depart Moon Hall at 0715 and arrive at the Special Operations Academic Facility, Building D-3915, at about 0720.

All students report to Room 275, USAJFKSWCS Special Operations Academic Facility (SOAF), Building D-3915. Building D-3915 is bordered by Zabitowski Road, Ardennes Street, Merrill Street and Bastogne Drive.

Table: SERE-A		
Required Items Inventory		
ITEM	QTY	REMARKS
Bag	2	Duffel, with lock or Aviator's Kit Bag
Bag	1	Barracks
Cap	1	BDU
BDUs	3 sets	
BDU Shirt	1	Sterile for Evasion FTX, name tag and US Army only
BDU Trousers	4	
Belt	1	Black, with buckle, subdued, non-stretch
Undershirt	6	OD or brown
Bra	4	Females only
Underwear	6	
Socks	6 pairs	Boot, cushion sole, OD or black
Boots	2 pairs	Combat, leather, issue only
Boots	2 pairs	Jungle, summer months only
Towel	2	
Gloves	1 pair	Leather, black, standard issue only
Gloves	1 pair	Inserts, wool, standard issue only
Field Jacket	1	With liner
Shirt	1	Sleeping or wool sweater
Underwear	1 set	Long, polypropylene/cotton

Table: SERE-B		
Unit Issue Items		
ITEM	QTY	REMARKS
Compass	1	Lensatic, with case
Flashlight	1	With batteries, issued or mini-mag
PT Uniform (PFU)	1	Sevice issue
Running shoes	1 pair	
Socks	2 pairs	White, athletic, crew ength
Belt	1	Reflective
Cap	1	Watch, black
CW Top	1	Army PFU, issue, gray or other service standard issue
CW Bottm	1	Army PFU, issue, gray or other service standard issue
Scarf	1	Wool
Sewing kit	1	
Toilet articles	various	19-day supply
Knife	1	Pocket and/or survival with sheath, no longer than 4" inch blade
Shower shoes	1 pair	
Note book	assorted	Pocket size, With pens and pencils
Fire starting device	1	Lighter, matches, etc.
Wrist watch	1	
Quarter	1	$0.25
Earplugs	1 pair	For helicopter operations
Glasses	2 pairs	Perscription, military issue, if required, no sunglasses

Table: SERE-C		
Field Equipment		
ITEM	QTY	REMARKS
Field Pack	1	OG1061 Ruck Sack, large
Frame	1	For field pack
Bag	2	Waterproof
Belt	1	Individual equipment (part of LCE)
Suspenders	1	LCE or tactical vests, unit issue
Ammo Pouches	2	
First Aid Pouch	1	
Canteen	2	1 quart, with cover
Cup	1	Canteen
Entrenching tool	1	E-tool, with carrier
Liner	1	Poncho
Poncho	1	
Parka	1	Wet weather or parka, Gortex
Trousers	1	Wet weather or parka, Gortex
Scarf	1	Wool
Sleeping bag	1	
Sleeping mat	1	

Table: SERE-D		
Optional Equipment		
ITEM	QTY	REMARKS
Glasses	1 pair	Safety goggles, clear lenses only
Poncho	1	Second (extra)
Cup	1	Canteen, Second, Extra
Note book	1	8 1/2" x 11"

Table: SERE-E	
Unauthorized Equipment	
ITEM	REMARKS
Reading material	Exceptions: religious materials such as Bible, Koran, etc. or materials related directly to SERE, such as Five Years to Freedom, or Bravo Two Zero
Audio/Visual	Radios, cameras, CD players, walkmans, camcorders, etc.
Contact lenses	
Machetes/Knives	With blades over 12" inches long are not allowed. K-bar, Survival knives, Swiss army knives, Gerber tools, etc. are allowed

All students will report with the following:
- ♦ ID card, ID tags, and meal card;
- ♦ Orders (five copies), TDY students will have DD Form 1610 or Format 400 TDY orders. Local students will have Format 440 attachment orders;
- ♦ Medical records with an appropriate surgeon approved SERE physical examination (original only);
- ♦ DA Form 705 (PT test) or equivalent evaluation;
- ♦ Swim test certification (Marines, Special Forces-qualified soldiers and Rangers are exempt);
- ♦ All required clothing and equipment.

BILLETING:

TDY students arriving at Fort Bragg should register at Moon Hall (Army hotel) NLT Sunday evening, the day before the course start date. Moon Hall is located in Building D-3601; COMM: (910) 436-1669. Moon Hall is for billeting only. Course cadre will not be present at check-in.

Students must provide a copy of orders to the Moon Hall receptionist at check-in. In order to expedite checkout, management suggests paying all expenses the night before checkout to avoid checkout lines. Those students who settle their accounts the night before checkout should inquire at that time about express checkout for course students.

CONTACT INFORMATION:

Operations Sergeant contact number is:
DSN: 239-8415;
COMM: (910) 432-8415.

REFERENCE:

1. US Army Formal Schools Catalog. US Army Publishing Agency. DA PAM 351-4, page 122, Table 3-19. 31 October 1995.
2. "SERE School." Online. Internet. 17 May 2000. Available: http://members.tripod.com/~thede/sere.html.
3. "JFK SWCS SERE/Terrorism Counteraction Department." U.S. Army Special Forces. Online. Internet. 15 April 2000. Available: http://users.aol.com/armysof1/SERE.html.

NOTES

SNIPER

REGULATION:

Course No: 010-ASIB4
Title: Sniper
Length: 5 Weeks
Location: U.S. Army Infantry School - SC: 071
Enl ASI: B4
Scope: Course effective: 1 Oct 95
Sniper tactics; staff subjects (intelligence, mission, training, command and control, and training management); basic sniper skills; marksmanship.
Prerequisite: Must be 11B, 11M, OR CMF 18, PFC-SFC (grade waiverable), active duty or reserve. Must have a good performance record with no history of alcohol or drug abuse, must be a volunteer and be recommended by his commander. Must be in excellent physical condition (70 percent or better in each event of the APFT) with a corrected vision of 2200-20/20. Must not have a record of disciplinary action. Must be knowledgeable of skill level 2 tasks. Must have attained a GT score of 110 or higher. Must have qualified expert with the M16A2 within six months of course attendance. Normal color vision (must be annotated on SF 88, test to be conducted within six months of course conducted under the direction of a qualified psychologist. Upon reporting to the USASS, students are required to have the following: DA Form 2-1, DA Form 2A, medical records, commanders recommendation, DA Form 3822-R, SF 88, and rifle marksmanship score card.
Security Clearance: None

HISTORY:

The term "sniper" originated in the 19th century with the British Army in India where the snipe was a favorite game fowl. The snipe is small and fast, and an extremely difficult target. The successful snipe hunter was an expert shot and proficient in other arts of the hunter; however, the proficiency of the military sniper evolved into an art as advancements in weapons, equipment and techniques were made.

The use of sharpshooters (or snipers) can be traced in US military history from the Revolutionary War. During the American Civil War, General Hiram Berdan was an exponent of the art and helped perfect the techniques used by snipers.

In World War I, the British Army encountered expert German Marksmen equipped with special rifles and telescopic sights. The term "sniper" was applied and popularized. German snipers forced the British Army to employ the same techniques, and under the leadership of Major Hesketh-Pritchard, a sniper course (the first Army School of Sniping, Observing, and Scouting) was organized. By the end of the war, the British were able to beat the Germans at their own game.

FORWARD:

The primary mission of a sniper in combat is to support combat operations by delivering precise long-range fire on selected targets. Snipers therefore create casualties among enemy troops, slow enemy movement, frighten enemy soldiers, lower enemy moral and add confusion to enemy operations. Snipers are also called upon to collect and report battlefield information.

The task of a military sniper is to combat and neutralize highly important, specific pinpoint targets. Snipers are no longer limited to live targets, the sniper's task includes combating of very important technical facilities such as generators, radar directing centers, radio direction-finding stations, electronic installations and other similar objects. They must also collect information for their Intelligence Officer. Snipers have the capability to destroy or disable any enemy targets with their .50 caliber rifles. They wear ghilley suits, which offers excellent concealment and can keep a sniper hidden from hostile forces only a few feet away; however, snipers are normally hundreds of yards away from their targets. They support infantry and assaults with their extremely accurate fire. To aid them, snipers also carry MP5's and/or 9mm hand guns for close quarters combat. However, if they are forced to use these weapons, the mission has failed or their position has been compromised and they are struggling to reach the evacuation point.

PURPOSE:

The purpose of Sniper School is to train selected soldiers to engage point targets with long-range precision fire, to train sniper field craft techniques, to develop Sniper Doctrine and provide subject matter expertise to the force.

PREREQUISITES:

♦ Must be a volunteer and have the commander's recommendation;
♦ Must be in the grade of E3-7 (waiverable);
♦ Must score 70% in each event of the standard APFT for the appropriate age group, which will be conducted on the class start date. All students must achieve the standard;
♦ Students must be CMF 11B, 11M or in the CMF 18 series (non-waiverable);
♦ Students must have a GT score of 110 or higher (non-waiverable);
♦ Students must have 20/20 vision or correctable to 20/20 and have normal color vision;
♦ Must show documentation that the last two (2) weapons qualifications with the M16A1/M16A2 were at the expert level;
♦ Must have a minimum of 1 year of retainability (non-waiverable);
♦ Must have no adverse disciplinary history of any kind. (non-waiverable);
♦ Must be dependable and capable of working alone under adverse conditions for extended periods of time;
♦ Must show documentation of a Psychological Evaluation.

Commanders are responsible for ensuring their soldiers meet all the prerequisites as outlined in DA PAM 351-4. Soldiers not meeting the prerequisites will be returned to their unit.

PERSONAL CONDUCT & APPEARANCE STANDARDS:

Personnel caught with the following while attending the Sniper School will be dismissed immediately:

♦ Females in the Barracks;
♦ Controlled Substances;
♦ Firearms;
♦ Ammunition;
♦ Pyrotechnics;
♦ Switchblades;
♦ Straight Razors.

PREPARATIONS:

Clothing & Equipment Requirements:
Table Sniper-A lists a required items inventory; Table Sniper-B lists an optional items inventory.

REPORTING INFORMATION:

Students will report to the US Army Sniper School Headquarters, Building 4882, Harmony Church, no later than 0800 hours on the reporting day (day prior to the class start date).

Students arriving prior to 0600 hours on the class reporting date will report to the SDNCO, 2nd Battalion, 29th Infantry Regiment, in Building 73 on main post.

Inprocessing:
Inprocessing will begin at 0800 hours on the class reporting date in Building 4882, Harmony Church. Students arriving after 1200 hours on the class start date will not be inprocessed into the course.

Soldiers must bring the following items for inprocessing:

♦ 5 complete copies of all orders (NG/USAR must bring 10 copies);
♦ Valid ID card and 2 sets of metal ID Tags with chains;
♦ Unit issued Meal Card (non-waiverable);

ITEM	QTY	REMARKS
Table: Sniper-A		
Required Items Inventory		
LCE	1	To include, but not limited to: 2 ammo pouches and a first aid pouch
Ruck Sack	1	Large and complete with frame
Canteens	2	1 quart, with covers
Poncho	1	
Liner	1	Poncho
Bag	1	Waterproof
Cammo face paint	1	
Calculator	1	
Padlock	2	Combination or key
Clipboard	1	
BDUs	4 sets	One pair will be unserviceable by the end of training
Caps	2	BDU
Socks	4 pairs	
Undershirt	4 pairs	To be worn under BDUs
Boots	2 pairs	Combat or jungle; one pair will be unserviceable by the end of training
PT Uniform (PFU)	2 sets	Gray, complete sets
Running shoes	1 pair	
Seasonal military attire		Gortex, polypro, etc.
Civilian Clothing		In good taste
Toiletries		
Earplugs	2 sets	With case
Entrenching tool	1	E-tool, with case
Compass	1	Lensatic
Protractors	2	
Pens/pencils	2	Mechanical pencils are strongly recommended
Hat	1	Boonie for ghilley suite

ITEM	QTY	REMARKS
Table: Sniper-B		
Optional Items Inventory		
Saw	1	Small (handsaw)
Knife	1	Blade length will be 4 inches or less
Pruning shears	1	
Binoculars	1	Miniature
Camera	1	With Tripod

◆ Medical Records (with over 40 PT clearance, as applicable);

◆ 2 copies of DA Forms 2-1 and 2A;

◆ Weapons qualification card (current, within the last 6 months);

◆ Must show documentation of a Psychological Evaluation.

Students must meet the height/weight standards of AR 600-9 at the time of inprocessing.

BILLETING:

Quarters:

This is a resident course, whether the student is assigned to Ft. Benning or not. The school barracks is "home" to the students for five weeks. During the students' tenure at the Sniper School, a 2200 hours curfew is in effect. Failure to comply with this curfew may result in dismissal from the course.

Dining Facilities:

Government meals are provided by the US Army Sniper School during the five week period. All students must bring a meal card issued by their unit.

Mail:

Students wishing to receive mail while attending this course must have correspondence sent to the following address:

Student Name, Roster #
US Army Sniper School, Class #
ATTN: Student Operations,
C Co, 2/29th Inf Regt
Ft. Benning, GA 31905.

POV:

Student parking is provided for students that travel to Ft. Benning by POV. All vehicles must be in a safe operating condition with current registration and proof of insurance. Students will only drive their POV after duty hours. All personnel are subject to the laws of the state of Georgia and Fort Benning. Violation of these laws will result in dismissal from the course.

CONTACT INFORMATION:

It is advisable to call the point of contact (POC) approximately 2 weeks prior to the class start date to receive any changes or obtain additional information.

POC/SME for the U. S. Army Sniper School can be contacted at:

DSN: 784-6006/6985;
FAX: 784-6693.

E-mail:

sniperschool@benning-emh2.army.mil

REFERENCE:

1. US Army Formal Schools Catalog. US Army Publishing Agency. DA PAM 351-4, page 43, Table 3-6. 31 October 1995.
2. Sniper – Training and Employment. US Army Publishing Agency. TC 23-14. June 1989.
3. "2nd Battalion, 29th Infantry Regiment." Online. Internet. 11 May 2000. Available: http://192.153.150.25/29thinf/c229.htm.
4. "Sniper Mission and Tactics." Combat Zone. Online. Internet. 11 May 2000. Available: http://members.tripod.com/~combat_arms/tactics.html.

SOTIC

SPECIAL OPERATIONS TARGET INTERDICTION COURSE

REGULATION:

Course No: 2E-F67/011-F19
Title: Special Operations Target Interdiction
Length: 6 Weeks
Location: U.S. Army John F. Kennedy Spec Warfare Center - SC: 331
Enl ASI: W3
Scope: Course effective: 1 Oct 94
Maximum hands-on training in advanced rifle marksmanship, techniques of observation, judging distance, advanced methods of concealment, camouflage, stalking, target selection, interdiction and airborne operations.
Prerequisite: Active Army and Reserve Component personnel assigned to or on orders to a Special Forces detachment or Ranger Company, currently Special Forces or Ranger qualified, and selected DOD personnel. Enlisted grades SPC through SFC. Commissioned Officers 2LT through MAJ and Warrant Officers in MOS 180A. Passing score on the Army Physical Readiness Test within six months, certified in writing by unit commander. Must have scored Expert with current service rifle in accordance with current qualification standards within 12 months, certified in writing by unit commander. No history of drug or alcohol abuse. No courts martial during current enlistment. General technical test score of 110 (nonwaiverable). Must have current periodic physical. Must report with medical records and psychological evaluation (MMPI or CPI) on day of inprocessing. Vision must be correctable to 20/20 in each eye. Must be currently on jump status.
Security Clearance: SECRET

PURPOSE:

The purpose of SOTIC is to train selected personnel in the technical skills and operational procedures necessary to deliver precision rifle fire from concealed positions to selected targets in support of special operations forces. Course emphasis is to provide the force with personnel who can achieve first round hits from a cold barrel on these high value targets. Additionally, personnel will be able to correct for wind and determine the previous round's bullet trace to achieve second round hits if necessary.

OVERVIEW:

SOTIC is a six week course conducted at Fort Bragg, North Carolina. Training includes marksmanship, observation techniques, concealment and camouflage. There are approximately 19 days of field duty with a 36 hour final field training exercise.

Students are encouraged to attend this course with their unit assigned M24 sniper system.

Class Size:
(1) Maximum - 24 students;
(2) Optimum - 24 students;
(3) Minimum - 8 students.

PREREQUISITES:

Students must meet the following prerequisites; students who fail to meet these prerequisites will be returned to their parent unit untrained.

♦ Must be currently assigned to or on orders to a Special Forces Detachment or Ranger Company, currently Ranger or Special Forces qualified, selected DOD personnel may also attend;

♦ Must have a current periodic physical. Vision must be correctable to 20/20 in each eye;

♦ Must have in their possession a memorandum from their Unit Commander certifying that the student has scored expert with the M16A1/M16A2 rifle in accordance with FM 23-9 (M16A1

Rifle and M16A2 Rifle Marksmanship, July 1989) within 12 months of the reporting date;

♦ Must have undergone a psychological evaluation (Minnesota Multi-Phasic Personality Inventory) under the direction of a qualified psychologist within 12 months of the reporting date;

♦ Must have in their possession an original verification of their security clearance (copies unacceptable), dated no earlier than 30 days prior to the course starting date;

♦ Must meet the Army height/weight standards as prescribed in AR 600-9;

♦ Must currently be on jump status and be medically qualified to participate in airborne operations.

Requests for waivers must be addressed to the Commander of the SOTIC course, see contact information.

Waivers must be approved prior to the class starting date. Personnel who report on the class starting date without an approved waiver will be returned to their parent unit untrained.

PERSONAL CONDUCT & APPEARANCE STANDARDS:

The use of alcohol or illegal drugs is strictly forbidden during SOTIC. These items will not be brought to the training site. Any student found under the influence of such items will be removed from training immediately and returned to his parent unit for appropriate actions.

PREPARATIONS:

SOTIC is a high-risk course. Students must be in top physical condition and must not be under any medication that may affect their reflexes or their judgment. Local commanders should screen all attendees to ensure they meet the prerequisites for course attendance.

Students must ensure that all dental, medical, administrative and personnel actions are completed prior to the course starting date. No routine medical appointments will be allowed during the course.

Clothing & Requirements:

Refer to Table SOTIC-A for a list of required uniforms and equipment; Table SOTIC-B lists additional optional equipment.

REPORTING INFORMATION:

Students will report to Company D at Building O-3550 prior to 1700 on the course report date. Students must have their medical records, including a copy of the student's psychological evaluation, with them when they report for inprocessing.

Students arriving after duty hours prior to the starting date should obtain lodging at Moon Hall (bachelor enlisted quarters [BEQ]). Company D maintains a 24 hour guard post located within the compound. Additionally, personnel reporting prior to the course starting date should secure any weapons in the company arms room. Students reporting after the closing of inprocessing will not be permitted to start the course and will be returned to their parent unit.

Students will be attached to Company D, 2nd Battalion, 1st Special Warfare Training Group (Airborne), U.S. Army John F. Kennedy Special Warfare Center and School, Fort Bragg, North Carolina 28307-5200.

BILLETING:

Temporary duty orders should reflect that rations and quarters are not available. As a result, it is recommended that off post parent units provide a rental car for their students attending the course.

On post BEQ reservations may be available if coordinated for at least 45 days prior to the course starting date. If the BEQ is unavailable, statements of non-availability will be issued and students may billet off post. It is the responsibility of the student to file an accurate travel voucher upon his return to his parent unit.

Table: SOTIC-A		
Required Items Inventory		
ITEM	QTY	REMARKS
Ruck Sack	1	
BDU	3 sets	Seasonal
Cap	1	BDU
Boots	2 pairs	Black, jungle are authorized, Gortex boots may be worn only in the field
LCE	1	Complete
Canteen	2	1 quart, with cover
Cup	1	Canteen
First Aid Pouch	1	With field dressing
PT Uniform (PFU)	1 set	Seasonal, parent unit uniform is acceptable
Poncho	1	
Liner	1	Poncho
Bag	1	Waterproof
Paper, pads	2	
Pencils	2	Mechanical pencils are strongly recommended
Entrenching tool	1	E-tool, with case
Compass	1	Lenstatic
Flashlight/Penlight	1	With batteries & lens
Eyeglasses	2 pairs	
Sewing kit	1	
Toilet articles		
Civilian Clothes		
Fatigues	1 pair	Old, sterile
Coveralls	1 set	Preparation for ghilley suit
Padlocks	2	
Gloves	2 pairs	Black, shell
Gloves	2 pairs	Wool, inserts
Field Jacket	1	
Sweat Shirts	2	
Air items: H-harness, Modified 18-inch attaching straps, Hook pile tape lowering line and Jump helmet (Kevlar)		
Identification card & dog tags		

Table: SOTIC-B
Optional Equipment
ITEM
Suspenders
Camp / Survival Saw
Hearing Protection: earplugs or earmuffs
Personal Camouflage sticks/paints: 1 tan, 1 light green, 1 sand, 1 brown
Rain Suit, Complete
Pruning Shears
Sewing Awl

Mail:
Students can be contacted at Fort Bragg by mail:
Full Name, SSN
Class: (Name and Number)
Co D, 2nd Bn 1st SWTG (A)
Fort Bragg, NC 28307-5200.

NOTE: Mail should not be sent to the above address after the fifth training week.

Money:
Students should bring adequate money for incidentals.

POW:
Student loaner systems are available. Privately owned weapons are not authorized on MacRidge Triangle Compound. Any weapons bought while attending the SOTIC will not be stored in the Company D arms room.

CONTACT INFORMATION:
Commander
1st Special Warfare Training Group (Abn)
ATTN: AOJK-GP
Fort Bragg, NC 28307-5200.

REFERENCE:
1. US Army Formal Schools Catalog. US Army Publishing Agency. DA PAM 351-4, page 121, Table 3-19. 31 October 1995.
2. "U.S. Army Special Forces JFKSWCS Advanced Skills Department." Online. Internet. 30 May 2000. Available: http://users.aol.com/armysof1/specialty.html.

SPECIAL FORCES

HISTORY:

Today's U.S. Army Special Forces are the official descendents of World War II's 1st Special Service Force, a combined Canadian and American unit originally trained for sabotage missions in Nazi occupied Norway. However, SF also owes much of its traditions to the wartime Office of Strategic Services (OSS). OSS Operational Groups, OSS Detachment 101 and Jedburgh teams parachuted behind enemy lines to organize resistance fighters; Detachment 101 in Burma and the Operational Groups and Jedburgh teams in Europe. Shortly after the war, the OSS was dissolved and the United States lost the capability to conduct unconventional warfare.

It was not until June 20, 1952 that a military unit - the 10th SF Group - was formed at Fort Bragg to meet the need for a force able to wage guerilla warfare in the event of a Russian invasion of Western Europe. The new unit was placed under the command of Colonel Aaron Banks, a former Jedburgh team member. Banks' new group trained in unconventional warfare, jungle and underwater operations, demolitions, airborne techniques and foreign weapons.

The new SF Group continued to grow. In November 1953 it deployed to Bad Tolz, West Germany, but it left behind a cadre to activate the 77th SF Group. In June of 1957 a cadre from 77th moved to Okinawa to form the 1st SF Group. In June 1960 the 1st SF was formed under the Combat Arms Regimental System to be the parent regiment for all SF Groups. Concurrently, the 77th SF Group was redesignated as the 7th SF Group.

By 1960 SF soldiers from the 1st and 7th Groups were serving temporary duty as advisors in South Vietnam, where the South Vietnamese troops were fighting communist guerillas. In September 1961 the 5th SF Group was formed with its orientation toward the republic of Vietnam.

The next month, the Army authorized the wearing of the Green Beret for SF soldiers. The beret - unofficial headgear for years - was worn officially for the first time during President John F. Kennedy's visit to Fort Bragg on October 12, 1961. President Kennedy said the beret would remain "a mark of distinction in the trying times ahead."

Those times were not far away. The new 5th Group was soon sending increasing numbers of Mobile Training Teams (MTT) to South Vietnam and in October 1964 5th Group Headquarters moved to Nha Trang. SF missions in Vietnam included training South Vietnamese in counterinsurgency and strike operations and conducting civic action programs. They also trained various mountain tribes, collectively termed Montagnards, to fight Viet Cong and North Vietnamese Forces in South Vietnam's central highlands.

During the same period SF units sent a number of MTT to Laos, Liberia and various Latin American countries. To meet the demands of these numerous missions, SF expanded with the activation of the 3rd, 6th, and 8th SF Groups.

Toward the close of the Vietnam War came troop reductions. The 3rd SF Group was deactivated in December 1969, the 6th in March 1971, the 8th in June 1972 and the 1st in June

1974. With cutbacks reaching nearly 70 percent, the remaining SF units found themselves well below their former personnel strengths.

Increasing awareness of the need for SF in the early 1980s resulted in a revitalization and expansion of SF; as a result the 1st SF Group was reactivated in 1984.

U.S. Army SF today are responsible for conducting unconventional warfare, strategic reconnaissance, foreign internal defense, direct action missions and other special operations missions. Worldwide mission requirements in the 1980s have increased the need for SF soldiers to conduct these missions. SF units are active today in the Middle East, Asia and Latin America. MTT have been sent to the Philippines, Lebanon and El Salvador where they have provided training in counterinsurgency, civic action and special operations. The missions have been on the "cutting edge" of United States foreign policy in these critical areas around the world.

SPECIAL FORCES CREED:

I am an American Special Forces soldier. A professional! I will do all that my nation requires of me.

I am a volunteer, knowing well the hazards of my profession. I serve with the memory of those who have gone before me: Roger's Rangers, Francis Marion, Mosby's Rangers, the first Special Service Forces and Ranger Battalions of World War II, the Airborne Ranger Companies of Korea.

I pledge to uphold the honor and integrity of all I am - in all I do. I am a professional soldier. I will teach and fight wherever my nation requires. I will strive always, to excel in every art and artifice of war. I know that I will be called upon to perform tasks in isolation, far from familiar faces and voices, with the help and guidance of my God.

I will keep my mind and body clean, alert and strong, for this is my debt to those who depend upon me. I will not fail those with whom I serve. I will not bring shame upon myself or the forces. I will maintain myself, my arms, and my equipment in an immaculate state as befits a Special Forces soldier.

I will never surrender though I be the last. If I am taken, I pray that I may have the strength to spit upon my enemy. My goal is to succeed in any mission - and live to succeed again.

I am a member of my nation's chosen soldiery. God grant that I may not be found wanting, that I will not fail this sacred trust.

"De Oppresso Liber"

FORWARD:

Special Forces - commonly referred to as Green Berets - are strategic, multipurpose forces capable of rapid response to various contingencies throughout the world. Their mission is to organize, train, equip and direct indigenous forces in unconventional warfare and foreign internal defense. For this reason, they possess foreign language and area orientation skills. Most SF soldiers work on a 12 man Operational Detachment Alpha (SFOD-A) team, sometimes called an "A" Team.

SFODA:
The standard SFODA consists of:
- Commander (CPT);
- Assistant Detachment Commander (WO);
- Operations Sergeant (Team Sergeant) (MSG);
- Assistant Operations & Intelligence Sergeant (SFC);
- Communications Sergeant (SFC);
- Weapons Sergeant (SFC);
- Engineer Sergeant (SFC);
- Medical sergeant (SFC);
- Communications Sergeant (SSG);
- Weapons Sergeant (SSG);
- Engineer Sergeant (SSG);
- Medical Sergeant (SSG).

SF DISTINCTION:
Degree of Expertise & Responsibility:
Each member of an SFODA is a self-sufficient expert in his branch or MOS and is capable of directly applying his skills or instructing others in

his specialty. His specialized training and expertise prepare him for levels of responsibility that are higher than what he would normally experience in the conventional Army. He is expected to exercise more initiative, self-reliance, maturity and resourcefulness than his conventional counterpart.

SF plan, conduct and support special operations in all operational environments. The U.S. Army organizes, trains, equips and provides SF to perform seven primary missions: unconventional warfare, foreign internal defense, direct action, special reconnaissance, counter-proliferation, information warfare/command and control warfare and counter-terrorism (counter-terrorism is a primary mission only for designated and specially organized, trained and equipped units). In addition to the seven primary missions, SF may participate in any of several collateral activities: security assistance, humanitarian assistance, coalition liaison, counter-drug activities, personnel recovery and countermine activities.

Regional Orientation:

Each SF soldier is assigned to one of five SF Groups. Each Group is responsible for several missions in a designated area of the world, or area of operations (AO). The SF soldier closely studies his Group's AO and trains to the unique demands of this area of the world.

Intercultural Communication:

The SF soldier learns a foreign language and works closely with the indigenous people in his Group's AO. Unlike the conventional soldier, the SF soldier is often called upon to interact closely with - and live under the same conditions as - people of a foreign culture. Not only does he perform his job expertly, he also serves as a representative of the United States (U.S.).

Missions & Collateral Activities:

Soldiers in general purpose units train for conventional warfare; in contrast, SF soldiers are called upon to accomplish a wide variety of unconventional missions. The SF soldier serves in the roles of teacher and helper, as well as warrior.

Common Myths About SF:

A common misconception about SF is that the work is glamorous and filled with the adventure and excitement of exotic travel and direct action missions. In reality, the SF soldier spends a great deal of time preparing for missions and training exercises. He studies to maintain his MOS and language skills and analyze his Group's AO. When he does deploy, he may find himself living in conditions that most civilians would consider austere at best. The work is physically and mentally demanding and frequently extends for long periods of time.

SF SOLDIERS:

Characteristics of the Successful SF Soldier:

Although there is prestige in wearing the Green Beret, SF soldiers are not boastful or arrogant. They are most accurately described as "quiet professionals."

Successful SF soldiers tend to be:

- Independent;
- Flexible;
- Goal-Oriented;
- Resourceful;
- Self-Confident;
- Team Players;
- Good Trainers;
- High In Initiative;
- Completely Trustworthy;
- Superior In Technical Skills;
- Skillful In Dealing With People;
- Open To Different Cultures;
- Strongly Committed To SF;
- Service-Oriented.

SF VOLUNTEERS:

Soldiers volunteer for SF for many reasons. Among them are:

Rewards:

Rewards for a job well done are not motivators in SF. SF is strong in terms of intangible rewards: job satisfaction, training opportunities, professionalism, responsibility and feelings of camaraderie and belonging.

Training:
SF soldiers are recognized around the world as a highly skilled professional soldier. Initial specialty training in weapons, engineering, medical or communications develop expert soldier skills.

Job Satisfaction:
SF soldiers report that overall job satisfaction are unmatched by any other job in the Army. On the other hand, some soldiers report that they expected to travel more, train more and conduct more real-world missions than they have thus far.

Education:
SF soldiers are provided outstanding career opportunities in the Noncommissioned Officer Education System. All specialists who graduate from the SFAS Course are schedule for the Primary Leadership Development Course (if not a previous graduate). Noncommissioned Officers in SF receive Noncommissioned Officer Education System development with less time in service than most all other military occupational specialties (MOS).

Money:
SF soldiers receive accelerated rates of promotion when compared with most MOSs. SF soldiers typically receive more monthly pay than soldiers in most MOSs. In addition to the comparable base pay, basic allowance for quarters and basic allowance for subsistence, SF soldiers receive extra monthly pay as an incentive for parachute, diving or demolition duty. SF soldiers who reenlist receive some of the highest bonus payments allowed in the Army. Opportunities to become a Special Operations Warrant Officer with as little as 3 years experience on an SFODA are outstanding when compared with other career management fields (CMF). SF soldiers earn thousands of dollars more than soldiers in other MOSs.

Adventure:
SF soldiers are afforded opportunities not available to soldiers in conventional units. SF soldiers are deployed worldwide.

Sense of Community:
Team members work closely together and rely on each other for long periods of time - both during deployments and in garrison - developing close inter-personalities, team cohesion and esprit de corps. The sense of community and support among soldiers and their families is generally considered higher in SF than in the Army as a whole.

Service to Country:
Unit and individual SF actions have contributed many courageous and daring exploits to the pages of American history. An SF soldier serves with distinction:
- ♦ He wears the Green Beret;
- ♦ He wears the SF Tab;
- ♦ He wears the silver wings of a parachutist.

Pros and Cons (Reported by SF soldiers):
Pros:
- ♦ Professionalism of fellow SF soldiers;
- ♦ Less formal authority exerted by superiors and high mutual respect;
- ♦ High levels of responsibility and self-discipline;
- ♦ Experience with other cultures.

Cons:
- ♦ Time spent away from home and family;
- ♦ Difficulties in training people from other cultures;
- ♦ Low standards of living in some countries where SF teams operate.

MILITARY CAREER:
Missions:
Any SF soldier may be called upon to perform in any of the following seven primary missions:

Unconventional warfare is a broad spectrum of military and paramilitary operations, normally of long duration, predominately conducted by indigenous or surrogate forces who are organized, trained, equipped, supported and directed in varying degrees by an external force. It includes guerilla warfare and other direct offensive and low visibility, covert or clandestine operations, as well as the indirect activities of subversion, sabotage, intelligence collection and evasion.

Foreign internal defense is the participation by civilian and military agencies of a government in any of the action programs taken by another government to free and protect its society from subversion, lawlessness and insurgency. The primary SF mission in this interagency activity is to organize, train, advise and assist host nation military and paramilitary forces.

Direct action operations are short-duration strikes and other small-scale offensive actions by special operations forces to seize, destroy or inflict damage on a specified target; or to destroy, capture or recover designated personnel/material.

Special reconnaissance is reconnaissance and surveillance conducted by SF to obtain or verify, by visual observation or other collection methods, information concerning the capabilities, intentions and activities of an actual or potential enemy. SF may also use hydrographic or geographic characteristics of a particular area. It includes target acquisition, area assessment and post-strike reconnaissance.

Counter-proliferation is action taken to locate, identify, seize, destroy, render safe, transport, capture or recover weapons of mass destruction.

Information warfare/command and control warfare are actions taken to achieve information superiority in support of national military strategy by affecting adversary information or information systems, while leveraging and protecting U.S. information and information systems.

Counter-terrorism includes offensive measures taken by civilian and military agencies of a government to prevent, deter and respond to terrorism. The primary mission of SF in this interagency activity is to apply specialized capabilities to prelude, preempt and resolve terrorist incidents abroad.

Collateral Activities:

In addition to the seven primary missions, SF soldiers perform these collateral activities:

Security assistance is a group of programs authorized by the Foreign Assistance Act, the Arms Export Control Act or other related U.S. statutes. The primary SF role is to provide mobile training teams and other training assistance. Public law prohibits personnel providing security assistance from performing combat duties.

Humanitarian assistance is any military act or operation of a humanitarian nature. These include disaster relief, noncombatant evacuation operations and support to and/or resettlement of displaced civilians.

Coalition liaison and other security activities ensure the physical security of important persons, facilities and events.

Counter-drug activities are measures taken to disrupt, interdict and destroy illicit drug activities.

Personnel recovery includes activities designed to locate, recover and restore to friendly control selected persons or material that are isolated and threatened in sensitive, denied or contested areas.

Counter-mine activities attempt to reduce or eliminate the threat to noncombatants and friendly military forces posed by mines, booby traps and other explosive devises.

Deployments:

No one can tell you with certainty how often you will be deployed; time away from home varies. The length of any one deployment can range from about 1 week to 179 days (6 months), but no longer. The average length of deployment is closer to 1-2 months.

Soldiers usually know well in advance about scheduled deployments. However, sometimes there are unscheduled deployments with little or no advance warning.

Some SF soldiers experience long and frequent separations from their families.

Soldiers sometimes deploy individually, as well as with their team or with larger size units.

The time spent away from home varies greatly from soldier to soldier and from year to year. The amount of deployment time for a given soldier will depend on his:

◆ SF Group, its AO and national priorities regarding that part of the world;

◆ A Team and its specialty - if it has one (i.e., SCUBA);

♦ MOS (shortage MOS may deploy more often);

♦ Individual schooling requirements;

♦ SF Group commander.

In-Garrison Activities:

Work in garrison varies in type and intensity, depending upon the previous and upcoming training assignments and missions. Generally, SF soldiers are either planning or preparing for deployment or are deployed. Although they need to be ready to deploy at a moment's notice, they always have a long-range training plan that they follow. Garrison work often has the following characteristics:

♦ Slower, more flexible pace than when deployed;

♦ Emphasis on quality time with family and taking care of needed family or personal business;

♦ Emphasis on training or preparing for the next deployment or training exercise, performing tasks such as:

-Maintaining equipment;

-Training fellow team members in MOS skills (cross training);

-Preparing and researching lesson plans for teaching missions;

-Physical training;

-Language training;

-Rehearsals to practice team combat skills in accordance with standing operating procedures.

Training:

Expect to participate in training events both in the continental United States and outside the continental United States. The following are characteristics of typical team training:

♦ Time spent in close quarters with other team members;

♦ Much preparation time involving study, research and planning;

♦ Harsh, uncomfortable living conditions, isolated from the world;

♦ Fast paced activities, with little opportunity for sleep or relaxation.

In terms of individual training, the typical SF soldier has considerable opportunities compared to soldiers in other branches. Advanced specialized training is available for specific mission profiles; for example, SCUBA (self-contained underwater breathing apparatus) and HALO (high-altitude low-opening) training.

Promotions:

Promotion rates in SF are among the best in the Army for both officers and NCOs. Moreover, the performance of SF soldiers tends to be relatively high. Therefore, soldiers who get promoted in SF are consistently high performers.

Another career path that some SF soldiers choose is that leading to the drill sergeant, recruiting duty and WO program. SF offers an excellent opportunity for an NCO to become a WO.

Typically, Sergeants are promoted to SSG as soon as they meet minimum time in grade standards, if they perform well. SSGs normally find themselves in a promotable status toward the end of their initial 4 year SF tour. Promotable SSGs will attend ANCOC around their ninth year of Army service. Promotions are generally consistent with the conventional Army, but on occasion there are accelerated promotions.

It is possible for some NCOs to go to the Defense Language Institute or to attend SF medical cross training after serving 2 years in a Group. These soldiers will return to their Groups to employ their new skills on an SFODA after successfully completing training.

After a soldier has acquired about 4 years of experience to round out his SF training, he may be assigned away from an Operational Group to serve as an instructor at the USAJFKSWCS or to serve in a specialized position that draws on his regional experience. During this period, the soldier broadens his knowledge of how the Army works and gains an understanding of the work that goes into developing and sustaining a special operations force.

Soldiers who perform exceptionally well in both the operational and support environment will find themselves returning to an Operational

Group to assume responsibilities as the senior NCO of an SFODA. The next step is selection as Team Sergeant, a critical opportunity in an SF NCO's career, since the Team Sergeant is instrumental in preparing his SFODA to execute missions and is charged with developing his young NCOs into outstanding SF soldiers. After 1-3 years of Team Sergeant time, an NCO may be selected to serve in key special operations positions throughout the world.

Master Sergeants with outstanding files may be selected to attend the Sergeants Major Academy. Graduates from the Academy will be assigned to positions of significant responsibility throughout the world pending selection for promotion to Sergeant Major (SGM). Duty positions for SGMs are designed to shape policy for the future of SF or to enforce the high standards associated with a career in special operations.

HOW YOU QUALIFY:

The road to SF starts with the Special Forces Assessment and Selection (SFAS) Program. If selected, you will receive qualification training in the Special Forces Qualification Course (SFQC). Upon Graduation from the SFQC, if you are not already foreign language qualified, you will receive foreign language training. You then begin your first assignment with an SF Group, usually on an SFODA.

FAMILIES IN SF:

In SF - as elsewhere - families and individuals are unique; however, SF families appear to share certain characteristics. Many families characterize themselves as independent and self-sufficient. Balanced with this is a strong sense of community with other SF families.

Family Satisfaction in SF:

Most wives report that they are proud of their husband and his work. Most also report satisfaction in knowing that their husband experiences a great deal of job satisfaction in SF, more than he would in any other job. The independence that most wives experience out of necessity is often seen as a plus. SF wives report

becoming more self-sufficient. The SF community can also be a source of satisfaction for families, because they feel a true bond with other SF families.

Wives of SF soldiers describe themselves as:
- Independent;
- Self-sufficient;
- Flexible;
- Strong;
- A "jack of all trades";
- Supportive of their husband's work;
- Having outside interests;
- Outgoing.

Common Issue for Families in SF:

The total number of times an SF soldier is away from home in one year may be the same or even less than the number of times he would be away from the home in a conventional combat arms unit; however, most SF families report that the length of time the soldier is away at one time is an issue with which they must contend. The SF soldier may be gone for several weeks or months at a time when he is deployed for training, missions or away at schools. Time away tends to be greater for soldiers who are on an SFODA than for soldiers with other assignments.

Most deployments are planned well in advance and families are given the soldier's location and address; however, there are rare times when the soldier deploys unexpectedly or is not able to disclose his exact location. The family may be unable to call him directly during these situations. The unpredictability of such deployments can cause stress for the family because they are unable to plan for his absence and they are sometimes unable to plan on his exact return date.

The time the soldier is away can be particularly stressful for the families with children. When her husband is away the wife typically must assume all the responsibilities, such as childcare, household finances and household upkeep. Keeping the children's relationship with their father secure and outgoing is another challenge when the father is away for long periods.

The transition time when the soldier is leaving and returning from deployments can also be stressful and emotional for both husband and wife. Many wives settle into new routines when the husband is away and must then readjust these routines when he returns. On the other hand, some husbands and wives report a positive outcome when the husband returns from deployments because they experience a repeated honeymoon period.

Some wives report that they've had to adjust to the realization that their husbands truly love their jobs and are committed to their team and its missions. Some wives find it disconcerting that their husband spends so much time with his team, even when the team is not deployed. On the other hand, many wives spend a great deal of time socializing with other wives on the team, so that the team's closeness is a positive factor for everyone in the family.

Common family stresses in SF are:

- Length of time the soldier is away;
- Number of times the soldier is away, especially when he is on an SFODA;
- Loneliness due to separations;
- Difficulties of communication due to soldier's schedule;
- Difficulties maintaining relationships between father and young children;
- Transition times of leaving and returning and disruptions of routines;
- Inability to plan family vacations or activities when unscheduled deployments arise;
- Difficulties of maintaining household finances.

Family Support Mechanisms:

SF have been in the forefront of the Army with respect to support for families. They were one of the first to develop family support groups that schedule get-togethers for wives and families, both when the husband is away and when he is in garrison. The purpose of the family support group is to help families - especially wives - build support networks.

When the soldier begins the SFQC the company will introduce the wife to the family support group. The meetings - which are open to all - provide opportunities to discuss issues and share information. Each SF Group also has its own family support group. Also, there are many other formal and informal sources of support for SF families. A family member in SF never needs to feel alone.

Sources of support for SF families include:

- Family support groups;
- Close, supportive relationships among team members and their wives (the team is often described as a "second family");
- "Chain of concern" rosters used to pass along information and assistance;
- Chaplain's office and family support centers on post;
- Family information briefings before major deployments;
- Phone "hot lines" that are used when soldiers are deployed unexpectedly to provide information about the soldier's whereabouts and scheduled return.

SF MOSs:

18A DETACHMENT COMMANDER:

MISSION:

The Detachment Commander is an 18A Captain. He commands the detachment and is responsible for everything that the detachment does or fails to do. The Commander may command and/or advise an indigenous battalion combat force.

OVERVIEW OF TRAINING:

- SFAS = 24 days;
- SFQC = 24 weeks;
- Language Training = 17-23 weeks;
- SERE = 3 weeks (if not already attended);
- Infantry Officer Advanced Course (if not already attended).

Upon completion of the SFQC all officers will be re-branched to the SF Branch (18A). The SERE Level C Course must be satisfactorily completed before or immediately after the SFQC. SERE is a requirement for branch qualification (see also the SERE section in this book). Officers will ordinarily complete the Infantry Officer Advanced Course (IOAC) prior to SFQC. If officers have not completed IOAC prior to SFQC, they will proceed to IOAC following SF qualification.

18B WEAPONS SERGEANT:

MISSION:

Weapons Sergeants are familiar with weapons systems found throughout the world. They gain extensive knowledge about every type of small arms and indirect fire weapons (mortars). They learn capabilities and characteristics of U.S. and foreign air defense and antitank systems, as well as how to teach marksmanship and employment of weapons to others. Weapons Sergeants employ conventional and unconventional tactics and techniques as tactical mission leaders. They assist the operations sergeant in the preparation of the operations and training portions of area studies, brief backs and operation plans/orders. They recruit, organize, train, advise and/or command combat indigenous forces up to company size.

OVERVIEW OF TRAINING:
- SFAS = 24 days;
- SFQC = 24 weeks;
- Language Training = 17-23 weeks.

18C ENGINEER SERGEANT:

MISSION:

Engineer Sergeants are experts in the planning and constructing of buildings and bridges, as well as in demolition. Construction requires learning to read blueprints and to construct a theater of operations building and field fortifications. Demolition requires learning about land mine warfare, non-electric and electric firing systems and how to improvise with substitutes for standard ammunition and explosives. Engineer Sergeants plan, supervise, lead, perform and instruct all aspects of combat engineering and light construction engineering. Engineer Sergeants construct and employ improvised munitions, plan and perform sabotage operations and prepare the operation plans/orders. They can

recruit, organize, train, advise and/or command indigenous combat forces up to company size.

OVERVIEW OF TRAINING:
- SFAS = 24 days;
- SFQC 24 weeks;
- Language Training = 17-23 weeks.

18D MEDICAL SERGEANT:

MISSION:

Medical Sergeants are specialists in many different areas of human and animal physiology. Medical Sergeants specialize in trauma management, infectious diseases, cardiac life support and surgical procedures and learn the basics of veterinary medicine. Both general health care and emergency health care are stressed in training. Medical Sergeants provide emergency, routine and long term medical care for detachment members and associated allied members, as well as host nation personnel. They train, advise and direct detachment routine, emergency and preventive medical care. They establish field medical facilities to support detachment operations. They provide veterinary care. They prepare the medical portion of area studies, brief backs and operation plans/orders. They can train, advise or lead indigenous combat forces up to company size.

OVERVIEW OF TRAINING:
- SFAS = 24 days;
- SFQC = 6 weeks (phase 1);
- SOCM = 24 weeks (phase 2 begins);
- SFMS = 20 weeks (phase 2 continued);
- SFQC = 5 weeks (phase 3);
- Language Training = 17-23 weeks.

Soldiers selected to attend the SFMS Course (MOS 18D) attend the course for a period of 44 weeks at Fort Bragg, North Carolina. The medical training is divided into two portions: first, the SOCM Course which is 24 weeks long; second, the SFMS Course which is 20 weeks long. Normally, 18Ds attend Phase 1 (6 weeks) prior to the SOCM course and Phase 3 (5 weeks) after the SFMS course.

The 24 week SOCM Course covers anatomy, physiology, pharmacology and advance trauma training. Along with this training, soldiers will complete the Emergency Medical Technician Paramedic (EMT-P) Course and will take the National Registry Examination for an opportunity to obtain the registry's EMT-P qualification.

The 20 week SFMS Course covers dental, surgical, anesthesia, veterinary, laboratory and X-ray subjects.

18E COMMUNICATIONS SERGEANT:

MISSION:

Communications Sergeants are experts in sending/receiving the critical messages linking the SFODAs with their command and control elements. Training entails extensive use of the Morse code system, cryptographic systems, burst outstation systems and common radios found throughout the Army. They become familiar with antenna theory and radio wave propagation, as well as how to teach it to others. Communications Sergeants install, operate and maintain FM, AM, HF, VHF, UHF and SHF communications in voice, continuous wave and burst radio nets. They advise the detachment commander on communications matters. They train the detachment members and indigenous forces in communications.

They prepare the communications portion of area studies, brief backs and operation plans/orders. They can train, advise or lead indigenous combat forces up to company size.

OVERVIEW OF TRAINING:
- SFAS = 24 days;
- AIMC = 8 weeks;
- SFQC = 24 weeks;
- Language Training = 17-23 weeks.

Morse Code Training:
Soldiers in MOS 18E (Communications Sergeant) complete the 8 week AIMC at Fort Bragg, North Carolina. This training covers radiotelegraph procedures, military block printing and practical exercises sending and receiving Morse code at various speeds.

SFAS:

REGULATION:
Course No: 2E–F129/011–F44
Title: Special Forces Assessment and Selection
Length: 3 Weeks, 3 Days
Location: U.S. Army John F. Kennedy Spec Warfare Center – SC: 331
Scope: Course effective: 1 Oct 87
Special Forces Assessment and Selection measures the candidates' personal attributes to gain a broad assessment of their potential and qualities for selection to a Special Forces MOS or branch qualifying course.
Prerequisite: Active Army and Reserve Component. Male only volunteers, SPC–SSG and 1LT–CPT, and MOS/specialty. Armed Forces Classification Test area score minimums: GT–110; FA–100; and ST–100. High school graduate or GED equivalent. Must be a PLDC graduate and meet requirements for Special Forces training contained in AR 614–200. Must not have been identified for QMP or involuntary separation from the service. Must meet fitness standards in AR 40–501, Chapter 5, paragraph 5–3, within one year of report date and must report with medical records on day of inprocessing. Must pass the APFT with a minimum of 60 points in each event and an overall score of 206 points or above (scored on the 17 to 21 year age IAW FM 21–20. Must pass a 50 meter swim test, unassisted, wearing fatigues and combat boots. Any variation from above standards requires waiver by Commander, USAJFKSWCS.
Special Information: Must be eligible to attain a SECRET security clearance.
Security Clearance: None

NOTE: Security clearance requirement is intended to reduce problems that may occur with candidates selected for SFQC that do not have a security clearance; SFQC requires a minimum SECRET security clearance.

SFAS FORWARD:

Career management field (CMF) 18 includes positions concerned with the employment of highly specialized elements to accomplish specially directed missions in times of peace and war. Many of these missions are conducted at times when employment of conventional military forces is not feasible or is not considered in the best interest of the United States. Training for/ participation in these missions are arduous, somewhat hazardous and are often sensitive in nature. For these reasons every prospective "Green Beret" must successfully complete the 3 week SFAS Course.

The SFAS Course assesses and selects soldiers for attendance at the SFQC. This program allows SF an opportunity to assess each soldier's capabilities by testing his physical, emotional and mental stamina. SFAS also allows each soldier the opportunity to make a meaningful and educated decision about SF and his career plan.

Fewer than 50% of the soldiers who start SFAS program are selected for training. The program is voluntary and soldiers may withdraw at any time after day six.

SFAS PURPOSE:

The purpose of SFAS is to identify soldier's who have potential for SF training. The program has two phases. The first phase assesses physical fitness, motivation and ability to cope with stress. Activities in this phase include psychology tests, physical fitness and swim test, runs, obstacle courses, rucksack marches and military orienteering exercises. An evaluation board meets after the first phase to determine which candidates will be allowed to continue in the program.

The second phase assesses leadership and teamwork skills. Another board meets at the end of the second phase to select those soldiers who may attend the SFQC and the SFDOQC.

SFAS OVERVIEW:

SFAS is a 3 week program run by the U.S. Army John F. Kennedy Special Warfare Center and School (USAJFKSWCS) at Fort Bragg, North Carolina. After completing the application procedures and receiving a date to attend SFAS (usually through the assistance of an SF recruiter), the soldier reports to Fort Bragg on temporary duty (TDY) status.

Training Outline:
Day 1-6:
  Inprocessing, Physical Fitness Test, Physical Training (PT), Swim Test, Ruck Marches, Obstacle Course.
Day 7-11:
  Military Orienteering, Battle March.
Day 12-13:
  Log drill, General Subjects.
Day 14-19:
  Situation and Reaction Stakes, Long-Range Movement.
Day 20-21:
  Selection, Outprocessing.

SFAS PREREQUISITES:

♦ Must be an active duty male soldier;
♦ Must be a U.S. citizen;
♦ Must be Airborne qualified or volunteer for Airborne training;
♦ Must be able to swim 50 meters wearing boots and battle dress uniform (BDU);
♦ Must score a minimum of 206 points on the Army physical fitness test (APFT), with no less than 60 points on any event, using the standards for the 17-21 age group;
♦ Must be able to meet medical fitness standards as outlined in AR 40-501.

Additional Criteria Exclusive to Enlisted Applicants:
♦ Enlisted applicants must be in the pay grade of E4-7;
♦ Must be a high school graduate or have a general educational development certificate;
♦ Must have a general technical score of 110 or higher;
♦ Must not be within 120 days of reporting to a new assignment (permanent change of station [PCS]) or attending a school that will ultimately require a PCS at point of application approval;
♦ Must not have 30 days or more lost under Title 10, United States Code, section 972, within current or preceding enlistment;
♦ Must meet eligibility under Retention Control Points to graduate SFQC.

Additional Criteria Exclusive to E7 Applicants:
♦ No more than 14 years active duty time in service;
♦ No more than 12 months active duty time in grade;
♦ Be a qualified parachutist (SQI: P or V);
♦ Not currently in a restricted MOS;
♦ Meet all requirements in accordance with AR 611-201 and AR 601-210.

Additional Criteria Exclusive to Officer Applicants:

♦ Officer applicants must be in any Officer Personnel Management Division - managed branch (except Aviation) and be in the grade of Captain or First Lieutenant;

♦ Have at least a SECRET security clearance prior to arrival at Fort Bragg and meet eligibility criteria for a TOP SECRET clearance;

♦ Have completed the Officer Basic Course and have been successful in your branch assignments prior to application for SF;

♦ Have a Defense Language Aptitude Battery (DLAB) Score of 85 or higher (or a Defense Language Proficiency Test (DLPT) of a minimum score of R1/L1);

♦ Have a minimum of 2 years remaining service obligation upon completion of Special Forces Detachment Officer Qualification Course (SFDOQC).

All Applicants must not:

♦ Be under suspension of favorable personnel action;

♦ Have been convicted by court-martial during their current term of service;

♦ Have received an Article 15 for drug-related offense;

♦ Have voluntarily terminated Airborne school or SF training;

♦ Exceed weight standards in accordance with AR 600-9;

♦ Be barred to reenlistment.

SFAS PREPARATIONS:

When you report to Fort Bragg, NC you should be at 100 percent physical ability with zero percent stress level. Any of the following might cause you stress while attending SFAS:

♦ Wife not in agreement with you;

♦ Financial problems at home;

♦ Medical problems with yourself or family;

♦ Not sure SF is what you want;

♦ Low self-esteem or lack of motivation;

♦ Not in top physical shape for SFAS;

♦ Just there to escape your present unit or duty assignment.

Physical preparation is crucial. Remember to bring boots that are well broken in - not new.

Clothing & Equipment Requirements:

Refer to Tables Special Forces-A, Special Forces-B and Special Forces-C on the following pages for SFAS clothing and equipment requirements.

Documentation Procedures:

The following lists all documentation necessary to be considered for attendance at SFAS. Reproduced copies must be clear and legible. There is no requirement for DA Form 4187 (Personnel Action) for this application. Provide the documents listed below to your SF recruiter:

♦ Medical records (to include shot record);

♦ Volunteer statement;

♦ DA Form 2A (Personnel Qualification Record, Part 1, Enlisted Peacetime) - may be obtained from your personnel and administration center or personnel staff noncommissioned officer;

♦ DA Form 2-1 (Personnel Qualification Record, Part 2) - may be obtained from your personnel and administration center or personnel staff noncommissioned officer;

♦ DA Form 873 (Certification of Clearance and/or Security Clearance Determination) or statement from S2, if security clearance is not reflected on your DA Form 2A;

♦ DA Form 705 (Army Physical Fitness Test Scorecard);

♦ Swim test statement. Must be certified by a soldier of at least one pay grade higher in rank (statement and affidavit enclosed). Soldiers who cannot be administered the SF 50 meter swim test due to nonavailability of facilities must submit an affidavit attesting to their ability to successfully complete the SF 50 meter

Table: Special Forces-A		
Minimum Required Items Inventory		
ITEM	QTY	REMARKS
Military identification card	1	
Identification tags	1 set	One long and one short chain interlaced, with one ID tag per chain; one key, any medical alert badge and barracks pass (if issued) are allowed to be suspended from the chain
Military issue eye glasses	2 pairs	As required; due to fragility of civilian eyeglasses, it is suggested they not be worn during training; AR 40-5, Preventive Medicine and AR 40-63, Opthamolic Services do not authorize contact lenses for wear in field (dirty or dusty) environments; because students are trained in a field environment, contact lenses cannot be worn during training
Cap	1	BDU
BDUs	4 sets (minimum)	No rank, badges, or unit patches will be worn on the three of the four BDU, only name tape and U.S. Army
Web belt	2	
Buckle	1	Subdued
Undershirt	5	Brown or other service authorized undershirts, worn with BDUs
Underwear	5	
Boots	2 pairs	Standard issue combat
Socks	5 pairs	Cushion soled, for wear with boots
Shoes	1 pair	Civilian, running
Towels	2	
Toiletries		To include a shaving kit and personal hygiene items
Pocket notebook & pencils	1	
HW Bottom	1	Army PFU, gray
Jacket	1	Field, with liners
Gloves	1 pair	With liners
Cap	1	Pile, seasonal
Underwear	1 set	Long, Seasonal
ORB		For all officers
100 mph electrical tape		Optional

Table: Special Forces-B		
Items Issued to SFAS Candidates		
ITEM	QTY	REMARKS
Harness, suspenders	1	
Canteen	2	One quart, with cover
Canteen	1	Two quart, with cover
Canteen cup	1	
Compass	1	With case
Waterproof bags	2	
Sleeping bag	1	
VS-17 panel	1	
Belt	1	Pistol, LCE
Flashlight	1	
Ruck sack	1	With frame
Ponchos	2	
Sleeping pad	1	
Strobe light	1	Field, seasonal
Pants	1 pair	

Table: Special Forces-C
Unauthorized Items Inventory
ITEM
Paints
Chemical lights
Alcoholic beverages
Ammunition & pyrotechnics
Stoves
Firearms
Radios & tape players
Non-issue maps
Non-prescription drugs
Vitamins

swim test. The swim test will be administered to all students upon arrival at Fort Bragg at the start of SFAS, and swim failures will not be allowed to continue the course;

◆ Original SF 88 (Report of Medical Examination) and SF 93 (Report of Medical History) along with all supporting documents.

The SF medical examination must be accomplished in accordance with AR 40-501. The SF medical examination must be completed and approved by an SF surgeon prior to/within 1 year of attendance at SFAS. Volunteers will provide the documentation of their medical examination to their SF recruiter who will forward it for review to the SF surgeon. In order to prevent processing delays on your application you must:

◆ Type or print. The forms must be legible. Send original SF 88 and SF 93. This examination must be accomplished in accordance with AR 40-501, chapters 2 and 5, and paragraph 3, No! (keep a copy for your records.);

◆ SF 88 - annotate block 23, Valsalva, and block 32, Digital Rectal;

◆ SF 88, block 48 - include the EKG report of EKG tracing (if EKG results indicate other than normal reading, you will need a consult from a cardiologist or internal medicine);

◆ SF 88, blocks 45 and 47 - ensure the laboratory findings are completed. HIV results need not be redone with physical but must be updated yearly and must be included and annotated in block 50;

◆ SF 88, block 50 - Sickle Cell results annotated from test or previous physical examination;

◆ Ensure the Chest X-ray results are annotated from test or previous physical examination;

◆ If your blood pressure exceeds 140/90 (SF 88, block 57), you need a 5 day blood pressure check to accompany the SF physical;

◆ The minimum visual acuity standard for SF is uncorrected 20/70 in the better eye and 20/200 in the weaker eye. Distant visual acuity must be correctable to 20/20 in one eye and 20/100 in the other eye within 8 diopters of plus or minus refractive error. If you are in doubt about your eyesight, schedule an Optometrical consult and forward the results and a request for waiver of the vision requirement with your physical;

◆ Ensure the every block on SF 88 that requires an entry is completed (give a copy of the Special Forces Physical Form located at the end of this chapter to clinic conducting your physical.);

◆ The medical report should also state that you meet the height/weight standards per AR 600-9;

◆ Ensure that the physician signs block 79 and the dentist signs block 81 on SF 88;

◆ If you have retained hardware, ensure the physician includes a consult on the retained hardware and if it is removable or not, and if it will affect your SF training;

◆ If you are in doubt, call your SF Officer Recruiter before you mail your application and physical.

Personnel Records:
Ensure your DA Form 2A and DA Form 2-1 reflect the selection criteria in chapter 3. If your records do not reflect the listed selection criteria, then include copy of either the Service School Academic Record or Diploma.

Applications:
Completed applications will be forwarded to the recruiter responsible for servicing your designated area as listed in Table Special Forces-Addresses.

For your reference, SFAS Enlisted and Officer Application Checklists are also included at the end of this chapter.

PHYSICAL PREPARATIONS:

Most candidates find SFAS to be physically demanding. During inprocessing candidates must score a minimum of 206 on the Army Physical Fitness test for the 17-21 year old age group and they must swim 50 meters while dressed in boots and fatigues. All assessment activities require the soldier to be well prepared physically.

Ruck marching and foot care are especially important to any soldier's preparation.

PT Preparations:

A sample SFAS Preparatory PT schedule taken from PT 31-210-SWCS is included at the end of this chapter. It is important for personnel preparing for SFAS to obtain their own copy of the PT 31-210-SWCS from their SF recruiter.

Prior to each workout, 10-15 minutes should be devoted to performing stretching exercises. Additionally, USAJFKSWCS Surgeon recommends a well balanced diet be incorporated with this recommended PT program and that daily fluid (water) intake be increased.

Do not stop the 5 week program. If you have met all the goals then modify program by increasing distance and weight and decreasing times. Be smart, don't injure yourself.

The responsibility to get in shape is yours and yours alone. Work out on your own time if that is all you have. If you go to the field, work on strengthening drills: pushups, situps, pullups and squats (with extra weight) when you can, as often as you can. The mission is to get in shape.

Eat things that are good for you and stay away from junk food and fat foods.

You need to be in very good shape and able to carry a rucksack day after day for the entire time you are at SFAS. This is an assessment of you. You will be challenged.

The Army Research Institute (ARI) has been able to closely correlate performance on the APFT and a 4 mile ruck sack march with success in SFAS. During fiscal year (FY) 89 and FY 90, ARI evaluated the cumulative APFT score (17-21 age group standard) with the percent of candidates who started SFAS and who passed

the course. The results are listed in the APFT Correlation Table.

The higher the APFT score, the greater the percent who passed the course. You need to be in top physical condition and you should do well in SFAS.

Foot March Preparations:

For forced marches select boots that are comfortable and well broken in (not worn out).

APFT Correlation	
APFT SCORE	PERCENT PASSING SFAS COURSE
181	5
187	15
200	26
213	38
226	46
239	56
252	61
265	61
278	60
284	73

Wear lightweight fatigues and thick socks (not newly issued socks). Army issue boots are excellent if fitted properly. Non-padded biker shorts worn under fatigues will prevent chaffing of inner thighs.

Utilize map and compass techniques whenever possible during forced march cross country.

Insoles specifically designed to absorb shock (sorbathane or similar) will reduce injuries.

Wash and dry the feet daily if possible. During the winter spray the feet daily with an aluminum chlorohydrate antiperspirant. Do this two or three times a day for a week and then once a day for the rest of the winter. If fissures or cracks occur in the feet, discontinue spraying until healed and then use less frequently to control sweating. This process will stop approximately 70 percent of the sweating in your feet. Discontinue spraying during the summer months.

Massage the feet daily, especially after marching. Use talc or antifungal powder.

Keep nails trimmed but not too short. Long nails will wear out socks; short nails don't provide proper support for the ends of the toes.

Take care of blisters. Clean with betadine and let dry for 5 minutes. Release fluid from the side of the blister a with clean, sterile needle. Gently press the fluid out leaving the surface intact. Make a doughnut of moleskin to go around the blister and apply it to intact skin. Wrap the entire toe or just over the top of the moleskin with a loose wrap of adhesive tape.

Good socks provide a variety of protection:

♦ They insulate the foot from cold, heat and fire;

♦ They protect the foot from abrasion by the inside of the boot;

♦ They provide cushioning from shock to the soles of the feet;

♦ They aid moisture transfer from the skin to the boot surface;

♦ They allow for swelling and expansion of the foot during heavy marching.

A good sock is dense enough to prevent abrasion of the foot at areas of high compression. The best type are density woven and do not separate under high compression. They should be uniform in thickness over the entire foot. The best issue sock is the tan/ski mountain sock, 75 percent wool, 5 percent nylon; however, polypropylene socks are better. The knap should face out away from the foot. The best commercial socks are those which are density woven with a non-cushioned sole and made of wool.

The old style boot is best waterproofed with oils and waxes. This should be done routinely to reestablish water repellency. Seams and welts are the most important points to cover.

The new speed lace combat boot has silicone treated leather and must be waterproofed only with a silicone material. Siliconized leather retains its water vapor permeability and breathability, while being highly waterproof. Use of oils and waxes will destroy the ability of siliconized boots to remain breathable, waterproofed and will also compromise the ability to siliconize the leather itself. Silicone treated leather does not take a high shine.

There is a boot to fit every size and width foot. Great care must be taken to ensure that boots are fitted properly for the planned use of your feet. The boot you "mill around" in on post is not the best one for road marching. Your foot will lengthen, widen and generally swell during a march from the load you carry and the pounding that occurs.

Correct fitting of boots requires a little time but the benefits are worth the effort. Each foot should be measured; don't assume they are both the same size and shape. A thin inner sock and a thick outer sock should be worn during the fitting and a pack with the appropriate weight to be carried should be on your back. Stand on the shoe sizing device and lean slightly forward, with some weight on the ball of your foot. Measure the length and width of each foot two or three times to ensure that you have the proper size information; your foot will lengthen and widen under load. This sizing process will allow you a large enough boot to accommodate the proper socks and the change in foot size while you march. You compensate for changes in foot volume (swelling) by having two different thickness of insoles for the boots, a sixteenth and an eighth inch. When you start to march, use the thicker insole; midway you will change to dry socks and also switch to a thinner insole if necessary to accommodate your swollen feet. During the beginning of the march be thinking about your feet; if you feel any slight compression or abrasion of your feet, stop and apply tape or moleskin to the area. Don't wait until you have a blister to care for your feet.

This system of foot care works. For years soldiers have had sore blistered feet after a march. All of the fitness training in the world is worthless if your feet are not fit to carry you into battle and back. Corns, bunions and blisters are signs of unfit feet. Taking care of your feet is one of the few things you can do to make your life better in the Army. Proper foot care prevents blisters and sore feet, increases march proficiency, protects against trench foot/frostbite and improves your overall soldiering capability.

Have overshoes available if it is wet or you need a bit more insulation.

Use vapor barrier (VB) boots for short treks, sedentary tasks or guard duty where marching with loads is not necessary; heavy marching with VB boots will produce blisters. The foot becomes damp and the skin softens inside the VB boot. Great care is necessary to prevent blisters while walking in this boot.

The greatest heat loss from the foot occurs through the sole and the toe cap of the boot. You must insulate your foot from the soles of a leather boot with insoles and there must be enough volume in the toe cap to allow for thick socks and air space around the toes. This requires a boot with a larger than normal inside volume.

The foot must be kept down and back in the boot, it should not slide forward or backward with each stride. To prevent this - especially with speed lace boots - the following procedure is helpful:

♦ The boot should be laced very snugly up the foot to the ankle break and tied;

♦ The boot should then be laced looser above the ankle to allow for calf expansion and movement of the Achilles tendon.

Two sets of laces may be necessary to accomplish this. Some boots have a locking hook at the point on the ankle where the lace should be tied to allow for one set of laces. This procedure greatly reduces blister formation and enhances foot comfort during heavy marching.

ARI evaluated the ability of SFAS students to perform a 4 mile rucksack in BDUs, boots, M16, LBE and a 45 pound ruck sack. During FY 89 and FY90 the time required to perform the 4 mile rucksack march was compared with the percent of candidates who passed the course. The results are listed in the Ruck March Correlation Table.

The less time to complete the 4 mile ruck march, the greater the percent who passed the course. The soldiers who prepare for SFAS should succeed at SFAS.

SFAS REPORTING INFORMATION:

All incoming applicants will report to HHC, 1st Battalion (Airborne), Building MT 7413, Corner of F Street & 5th Street, Fort Bragg, North Carolina prior to 2300 on the reporting date.

Ruck March Correlation	
RUCK MARCH TIME (MIUTES)	PERCENT PASSING COURSE
Greater than 62	16
60	32
58	48
56	58
54	63
52	65
50	70
48	74
46	87
45	79

The HHC, 1st Special Warfare Training Battalion (Airborne) area is located near the 1st Corps Support Command area on 5th and F Streets, near Chapel 4.

SFAS LEAVE & PASS POLICY:

Ordinary leave will not be used in conjunction with your TDY period at SFAS unless you graduate from the course. Leave enroute may be taken after SFAS for graduates prior to return to home station.

SFAS BILLETING:

Government rations and quarters will be available during SFAS. Meal cards will be issued during inprocessing.

Mail:
Because your period of TDY at SFAS is so short there will be no incoming mail.

Money:
Do not carry more than $100; more than $40 is prohibited in the training area.

POV:
Travel to Fort Bragg, North Carolina by privately owned vehicle is not authorized.

Emergencies:
In case of a real emergency during your temporary duty (TDY) at Fort Bragg, NC your family members are to contact the 1st Special

Warfare Training Group (Airborne) S1 (the number is listed under Contact Information).

Travel Information:

Civilian clothing is authorized for travel, but will not be worn in the training area. Due to some incidents of lost luggage, it is highly recommended that you carry at least one complete uniform on the plane/bus with you.

CONTACT INFORMATION:

For more information contact the 1st Special Warfare Training Group (Airborne) Headquarters S1 at:

DSN: 236-1839/2356;
COMM: (910) 396-1839/2356.

After duty hours use:
COMM: (910) 396-4801/5885.

BEAR PROGRAM:

Successful completion of SFAS is a prerequisite for BEAR applications. BEAR forms along with a copy of your SFAS certificate must be forwarded through retention offices to the Retention management Branch of the United States Total Army Personnel Command.

SFQC:

18A DETACHMENT COMMANDER
REGULATION:

Course No: 2E–18A
Title: Special Forces Detachment Officer Qualification
Length: 24 Weeks
Location: U.S. Army John F. Kennedy Spec Warfare Center – SC: 331
Off AOC: 18A
Scope: Course effective: 1 Oct 94
General subjects, special operations, Special Forces planning, engineer and weapons training, communications and medical training, special reconnaissance, direct action, unconventional warfare, foreign internal defense, counter-guerrilla operations, SERE level C training, air operations, land navigation, small unit tactics, combat operations, basic marksmanship, an unconventional warfare field exercise, mission planning, and special reconnaissance operations.
Prerequisite: Active and Reserve Components of the armed forces. Must be a male commissioned officer managed by the Officer Personnel Management Directorate. Rank of captain in the fourth through seventh year in service. Have completed basic and advanced resident course in a basic branch. Must have successfully completed the Special Forces Assessment and Selection program. Have a DLAB score of 85 or higher or be able to validate a language proficiency rating of 1/1 or higher. Must pass the Special Forces physical exam IAW AR 40–501, Chapter 5, paragraph 5–3, within one year of class date and must report with medical records on day of inprocessing. The exam must not expire for the duration of the course. Be eligible for TOP SECRET clearance in accordance with AR 380–67. Must be airborne qualified and be a volunteer for Special Forces training in accordance with AR 614–162. Applicants should volunteer in their third year of service.
Special Information: The SERE course is taught within this course. Upon completion of this course, students will enter into a special operations forces basic military language course of instruction. The Commanding General may waive the language requisite for those who meet the minimum requirement.
Security Clearance: SECRET

18B WEAPONS SERGEANT
REGULATION:

Course No: 011–18B30
Title: Special Forces Weapons Sergeant
Length: 24 Weeks
Location: U.S. Army John F. Kennedy Spec Warfare Center – SC: 331
Enl MOS: 18B3
Scope: Course effective: 1 Oct 94
Common leader training, indirect fire weapons, small arms, antitank weapons, air defense systems, operations, Special Forces basic skills training in air operations, general subjects, land navigation, small unit tactics, combat operations, special operations, permission training, basic rifle marksmanship, and a field training exercise.
Prerequisite: Active and Reserve Component of the armed forces. A male volunteer in the rank of SGT, SSG, or SFC by exception. Possess any MOS in the Army inventory. Meet requirements for Special Forces Training contained in AR 614–200. Minimum GT score of 110. Be tested in the TABE (Level D) no later than six months before entry into this course and have the TABE results with him at that time. Be PLDC qualified and airborne qualified. Pass the APRT with a minimum of 60 points in each event and overall score of 206 or above (scored on 17 to 21 year age group IAW FM 21–20. Must have successfully completed the Special Forces Assessment and Selection program. Must pass the Special Forces physical exam IAW AR 40–501, Chapter 5, paragraph 5–3, within one year of class date and must report with medical records on day of inprocessing.
Special Information: Phase 1, MOS qualification and common leader training, and Phase 2, Branch Training (to be taught in the A–Detachment concept) are presented in a 24 week period. Upon completion of the 24 week Special Forces qualification course, students will enter into a special operations forces basic military language course of instruction. The Commanding General may waive the language requisite for those who meet the minimum requirement.
Security Clearance: SECRET

18C ENGINEER SERGEANT
REGULATION:
Course No: 011–18C30
Title: Special Forces Engineer Sergeant
Length: 24 Weeks
Location: U.S. Army John F. Kennedy Spec Warfare
Center – SC: 331
Enl MOS: 18C3
Scope: Course effective: 1 Oct 91
Common leader training, pre-engineering subjects, construction, field fortification, land mine warfare, bridging, reconnaissance, demolitions, field training, air operations, general subjects, survival, land navigation, small unit tactics, combat operations, special operations, permission training, basic rifle marksmanship, and a field practical exercise.
Prerequisite: Active and Reserve Components of the armed forces. A male volunteer in the rank of SGT, SSG, or SFC by exception. Possess any MOS in the Army inventory. Meet requirements for Special Forces training contained in AR 614–200. Minimum GT score of 110. Be tested in the TABE (Level D) no later than six months before entry into this course and have the TABE results with him at that time. Be PLDC qualified and airborne qualified. Pass the APRT with minimum of 60 points in each event and an overall score of 206 or above (scored on 17– to 21 year age group IAW FM 21–20). Must have successfully completed the Special Forces Assessment and Selection program. Must pass the Special Forces physical exam IAW AR 40–501, Chapter 5, paragraph 5–3, within one year of class date and must report with medical records on day of inprocessing.
Special Information: Phase 1, MOS qualification and common leader training, and Phase 2, Branch Training (to be taught in the A–Detachment concept) are presented in a 24–week period. Upon completion of the 24–week Special Forces Qualification course, students will enter into a special operations forces basic military language course of instruction. The Commanding General may waive the language requisite for those who meet the minimum requirement.
Security Clearance: SECRET

18D MEDICAL SERGEANT
REGULATION:
Phase One:
Course No: 011–18D30 (2)
Phase: 1
Title: Special Forces Medical Sergeant
Length: 6 Weeks
Location: U.S. Army John F. Kennedy Spec Warfare
Center – SC: 331
Enl MOS: 18D3
Scope: Course effective: 1 Oct 95
Common Leader Training, land navigation, and small unit tactics.
Prerequisite: Active and Reserve component of the Armed Forces. A male volunteer in the rank of Specialist/Corporal, Sergeant, Staff Sergeant, or Sergeant First Class by exception. Possess any MOS in the Army inventory. Meet requirements for Special Forces training contained

in AR 614–200. Minimum GT score of 110. Be tested in the Test of Adult Basic Education (TABE, Level D) no later than six months before entry into this course and have the TABE results with him at that time. Be primary Leadership Development Course qualified and airborne qualified. Pass the Army Physical Readiness Test with a minimum of 60 points in each event and an overall score of 206 or above (scored on 17– to 21 year group IAW FM 21–20). Must pass a swim test of 50 meters, unassisted, while wearing fatigues and combat boots. Must have successfully completed the Special Forces Assessment and Selection (SFAS) program. Must pass the Special Forces physical exam IAW paragraph 5–3, Chapter 5, AR 40–501, within 1 year of class date and must report with medical records on day of inprocessing.
Special Information: MOS 18D, Special Forces Medical Sergeant is awarded upon successful completion of Phase 3, Special Forces Medical Sergeant.
Security Clearance: SECRET

Phase Two:
Course No: 011–18D30
Phase: 2
Title: Special Forces Medical Sergeant
Length: 44 Weeks
Location: U.S. Army John F. Kennedy Spec Warfare
Center – SC: 331
Enl MOS: 18D3
Scope: Course effective: 1 Oct 95
Anatomy and physiology, emergency medical technician–paramedic instruction, advanced cardiac life support, combat trauma management, behavioral, pharmacology, medical diseases, dentistry, radiology, laboratory, veterinary subjects, surgery, anesthesia, field training exercise, and clinical proficiency training.
Prerequisite: Be a Special Forces volunteer 18D candidate. Successfully complete Phase 1, Special Forces Medical Sergeant not more than 3 months prior to starting Phase 2, Special Forces Medical Sergeant.
Special Information: MOS 18D, Special Forces Medical Sergeant, is awarded upon successful completion of Phase 3, Special Forces Medical Sergeant.
Security Clearance: SECRET

Phase Three:
Course No: 011–18D30 (2)
Phase: 3
Title: Special Forces Medical Sergeant
Length: 5 Weeks
Location: U.S. Army John F. Kennedy Spec Warfare
Center – SC: 331
Enl MOS: 18D3
Scope: Course effective: 1 Oct 95
Branch training (air operations, general subjects, survival, combat operations, special operations, permission training, basic rifle marksmanship, and field practical exercise).
Prerequisite: Special Forces volunteer 18D candidate. Successfully complete Phase 2, Special Forces Medical Sergeant not more than 3 months prior to starting Phase 3, Special Forces Medical Sergeant.
Special Information: Branch training (to be taught in the A–Detachment concept) is present in a 5–week

period. Upon completion, students will enter into a Special Operations Forces Basic Military Language course of instruction. The Commanding General may waive the language requisite for those who meet the minimum requirement. Attendance of the first 24 weeks of the Phase 2 is not required for Special Forces volunteer 18D candidates who successfully completed Special Operations Combat Medic course while assigned to a SOF unit, although they must complete Phase 1 prior to attending Phase 2. MOS 18D is awarded upon successful completion of Phase 3.
Security Clearance: SECRET

18E COMMUNICATIONS SERGEANT
REGULATION:

Course No: 011–18E30
Title: Special Forces Communications Sergeant
Length: 24 Weeks
Location: U.S. Army John F. Kennedy Spec Warfare Center – SC: 331
Enl MOS: 18E3
Scope: Course effective: 1 Oct 91
Common leader training, communications training, Special Forces basic skills training in air operations, general subjects, land navigation, small unit tactics, combat operations, special operations, permission training, basic rifle marksmanship, and field training exercise.
Prerequisite: Active and Reserve Component of the armed forces. A male volunteer in the rank of SGT, SSG or SFC by exception. Possess any MOS in the Army inventory. Meet requirements for Special Forces training contained in AR 614–200. Minimum GT score of 110. Be tested in the TABE (Level D) no later than six months before entry into this course and have the TABE results with him at that time. Be PLDC qualified and airborne qualified. Pass the APRT with a minimum of 60 points in each event and an overall score of 206 or above (scored on 17 to 21 year age group IAW FM 21–20). Must have successfully completed the Special Forces Assessment and Selection program. Must pass the Special Forces physical exam IAW AR 40–501, Chapter 5, paragraph 5–3, within one year of class date and must report with medical records on day of inprocessing. Be a graduate of Advanced International Morse Code or capable of passing a verification test at 13/13 groups per minute.
Special Information: Phase 1, MOS qualification and common leader training, and Phase 2, Branch Training (to be taught in the A–Detachment concept) are presented in a 24–week period. Upon completion of the 24–week Special forces qualification course, students will enter into a special operations forces basic military language course of instruction. The Commanding General may waive the language requisite for those who meet the minimum requirement.
Security Clearance: SECRET

SFQC FORWARD:

After a soldier is selected from SFAS he returns to his unit and awaits his slot in the SFQC. There is often a several month waiting period before the soldier begins the course. Soldiers selected for MOS 18B (Weapons) or MOS 18C (Engineer) go directly to the 24 week course at Fort Bragg, North Carolina. Soldiers selected for MOS 18E (Communications) first complete the Advanced International Morse Code (AIMC) course before attending the SFQC.

The SF CMF 18 is subdivided into five accession MOS: 18A, Detachment Commander; 18B, SF Weapons Sergeant; 18C, SF Engineer sergeant; 18D, SF Medical Sergeant; 18E, SF Communications Sergeant. Each SF volunteer receives extensive training in a specialty which prepares him for his future assignment in an SF unit. SF units are designed to operate either unilaterally or in support of and combined with native military and paramilitary forces. Levels of employment for Special Operations Forces include advising and assisting host governments, involvement in continental United States based training and direct participation in combat operations.

Soldiers have two opportunities to indicate their preference for a particular MOS:

♦Soldiers can indicate an MOS preference on their SFAS application, recruiters keep this information in their database;

♦In the early part of SFAS candidates have an opportunity to learn more about the various SF MOSs through presentations or films; at this time, candidates have a chance to submit their written MOS preferences in rank order.

The MOS assignment board has access to both preference statements but gives more weight to the more recent (the more informed) preference.

MOS Assignment:

The assignment decision is based on:

♦Your previous MOS and training;

♦Your aptitude scores;

♦The needs of the force;

♦Your preference.

Most soldiers get their preferred MOS when the preference and aptitudes match; however, there are no guarantees.

All MOSs are infantry oriented (including medics) and everyone cross trains.

SFQC PURPOSE:

The SFQC teaches and develops the skills necessary for effective utilization of the SF sergeant. Duties in CMF 18 primarily involve participation in Special Operations interrelated fields of unconventional warfare. These include foreign internal defense and direct action missions as part of a small operations team detachment. Duties at other levels involve command, control and support functions. Frequently, duties require regional orientation to include foreign language training and in-country experience. SF places emphasis, not only on unconventional tactics, but also on knowledge of conventional light infantry doctrine and low intensity conflict. Missions can include participation in waterborne, desert, jungle, mountain or arctic operations.

SFQC OVERVIEW:

All MOSs:

All soldiers complete the 24 week SFQC at Fort Bragg, North Carolina. Once soldiers receive their SFQC date they are permanently assigned to Fort Bragg.

During the first 2 weeks SFQC soldiers will have some free time but will often work on the weekends. Most weekends after the first 2 weeks are free.

MOS training is geared specifically toward the soldier's MOS.

Phases 1 and 3 of SFQC take place at Camp MacKall, which is about an hour's drive from Fort Bragg. During this training students will be in the field 7 days a week. Phase training culminates with a field training exercise where students perform as part of an SFODA to accomplish an unconventional warfare mission.

Generally, the SFQC requires a great deal of study time. It is helpful if students practice land navigation skills prior to arriving for the course.

Soldiers will be Basic Noncommissioned Officer Course (BNCOC) qualified when they complete SFQC.

18A – SF Detachment Commander:

Training includes: Teaching the officer student the planning and leadership skills he will need to direct and employ other members of his detachment. Training is conducted at Fort Bragg, North Carolina and is 24 weeks long.

18B – SF Weapons Sergeant:

Training includes: Tactics, anti-armor weapons utilization, functioning of all types of U.S. and foreign light weapons, indirect fire operations, man-portable air defense weapons, weapons emplacement and integrated combined arms fire control planning. Training is conducted at Fort Bragg, North Carolina and is 24 weeks long.

18C – SF Engineer Sergeant:

Training includes: Construction skills, field fortifications and use of explosive demolitions. Training is conducted at Fort Bragg, North Carolina and is 24 weeks long.

18D – SF Medical Sergeant:

Training includes: Advanced medical procedures to include trauma management and surgical procedures. Training at Fort Bragg, NC and is approximately 57 weeks long.

18E – SF Communications Sergeant:

Training includes: Installation and operation of SF high frequency and burst communications equipment, antenna theory, radio wave propagation and SF communication operations procedures/techniques. Training is conducted at Fort Bragg, North Carolina and Camp Bullis, Texas, and is 32 weeks long; this includes 8 weeks of Advanced International Morse Code.

SFQC TRAINING:

The SFQC is currently divided into three phases. The phases are: Individual Skills, MOS Qualification and Collective Training. The decision upon which of the four specialties you will receive training will be based on your background, aptitude and desires and the needs of the CMF 18. Your SFQC training will be scheduled upon successful completion of SFAS.

Individual Skills Phase:

During this period soldiers inprocess and are trained on common skills for CMF 18 skill level three. Training is 40 days long and is taught at the Camp Rowe Training Facility. The training covered during this phase includes land navigation (cross country) and small unit tactics. This phase culminates with a special operations overview.

MOS Qualification Phase:

During this phase soldiers are trained in their different specialties. Training for this phase is 65 days and culminates with a mission planning cycle.

Collective Training Phase:

During this 38 day period soldiers are trained in Special Operations classes, Direct Action Isolation, Air Operations, UW classes and Isolation training. Training culminates with an FTX known as "ROBIN SAGE."

SFQC PREREQUISITES:

Upon successful completion of SFAS all enlisted candidates must meet the following prerequisites prior to being scheduled for the SFQC:

♦ Must be in the pay grade of E4-7;

♦ Must have at least an interim SECRET security clearance;

♦ Must have the following minimum remaining service obligation prior to departing losing command:

   1. For MOS 18B and 18C : 19 months remaining service obligation from date of completion of SFQC;

   2. For MOS 18D: 28 months remaining service obligation from date of completion of SFQC;

   3. For MOS 18E: 25 months remaining service obligation from date of completion of SFQC;

♦ Must have completed SFAS no more than 1 year prior to beginning SFQC;

♦ Must meet eligibility under Retention Control Points to graduate SFQC.

SFQC PREPARATIONS:

Although SFAS is a TDY and return course, the SFQC requires the soldier to make a PCS. There will normally be a minimum of 45 days between the completion of SFAS and the start of your next training. It is to your benefit to begin organizing your personal affairs in preparation of this PCS.

Correspondence Courses:

It would be beneficial to each candidate to enroll in the correspondence courses listed in table Special Forces-D to gain an advantage in the MOS selection process, as well as prepare for MOS training.

To order a correspondence course send a DA Form 145 (Army Correspondence Course Enrollment Application) to:

    Institute for Professional Development
    US Army Training Support Center
    Newport News, VA 23628-0001

for 18B, 18C and general correspondence courses.

    For 18D correspondence courses send to:
    Commandant
    Academy of Health Sciences
    Fort Sam Houston, TX 78234-6199.

SFQC REPORTING INFORMATION:

Inprocessing:

The 5 day inprocessing period allows you and your family to get settled before training begins. During this time, wives receive a briefing and the company introduces them to the family support group.

During the inprocessing phase of the SFQC students will have an opportunity to fill out a Group preference form, stating their three choices for SF Group assignment.

LEAVE & PASS POLICY:

You will get at least 1 week of leave between SFQC graduation and the start of language training.

Table: Special Forces-D Correspondence Courses	
COURSE TITLE	COURSE NUMBER
Applicable to all Personnel Attending SFQC	
Troop Leading Procedures	IS 1706
Patrolling, Part I	IN 0404
Basic Tactics	IN 0411
Applicable to 18B, Special Operations Weapons Sergeant	
Military Handguns and Rifles	SF 0746
Sub-machine Guns and Machineguns	SF 0747
60mm Mortar M19	SD 0749
Intro to Mortars	IN 0375
Intro to Mortars Ballistics	IN 0380
Applicable to 18C, Special Operations Engineer Sergeant	
Combat Engineering	EN 0299
Explosives and Demolitions	EN 0053
Roads and Airfields	EN 0064
Field Fortifications	EN 0065
Military Bridges II	EN 0353
Masonry	EN 0535
Frame Structures	EN 0069
Applicable to 18D, Special Operations Medical Sergeant	
Basic Human Anatomy	MED 006
Basic Human Physiology	MED 007
Regional Human Anatomy	MED 009
Basic Medical Terminology	MED 010
Pharmaceutical Calculations	MED 802
Pharmacology I	MED 804
Pharmacology II	MED 805
Pharmacology III	MED 806
Drug Dosage and Therapy	MED 913

FOREIGN LANGUAGE TRAINING:

Everyone who does not already hold a language rating prior to attending SFQC will attend language training upon graduation. For almost everyone, the language training location is Fort Bragg, North Carolina.

Language training ranges from 17-23 weeks, depending on the difficulty of the language. The standards for graduation are 0+, if 0+ is not attained, your SF tab will be revoked.

The training emphasizes basic communication skills for soldiers who will be conducting military training. The focus is on speaking and listening skills; military terminology is emphasized. Students can expect about 6-7 hours of classroom instruction per day plus, homework - part of which may be computer based instruction.

After completing language training all soldiers are authorized 30 days to PCS to their new SF Group assignments. This 30 day PCS authorization applies even to soldiers stationed in 3rd and 7th Groups at Fort Bragg.

SF GROUPS:
FORWARD:

Personnel at the USAJFKSWCS and at the U.S. Total Army Personnel Command are responsible for making SF Group assignments. Their decisions are based on:

- Needs of the Groups;
- Soldier's existing language skills or regional orientation;
- Soldier's language aptitude (Defense Language Aptitude Battery score);
- Soldier's preference.

Group assignments are made first, then language assignments. Students will find out both their Group assignment and their foreign language assignment toward the end of the SFQC.

If you want a certain Group, you can increase your chances by showing proficiency in a language associated with that Group.

It is difficult to change Groups once you are culturally oriented. Most soldiers stay with one Group throughout their SF careers.

As a rule, an SFQC graduate's initial assignment will be to an SFODA. During this period he will enhance his professional development by working with seasoned professionals on a variety of missions in the Group's targeted region of the world.

Each of the five SF Groups is composed of three battalions and a Group support company (which includes Group headquarters). Each of the SF battalions is composed of three line companies (A, B and C) as well as a support company and a battalion headquarters detachment. Each of the three line companies is composed of six SFODAs and one company headquarters.

Every SF Group is capable of performing all types of missions. At any given time, a Group may be focusing on one or two mission types; however, the missions for a Group can quickly change as world events change.

Even within a Group missions vary. Teams sometimes specialize in one or two mission types, depending on their particular skills.

Currently SF soldiers are most commonly involved in foreign internal defense missions and humanitarian activities. These missions require special skills in teaching, negotiating, communication and interpersonal skills as well as technical skills.

SF GROUPS OVERVIEW:

1st Group:

Most of 1st Group is located at Fort Lewis, Washington. Two SF battalions and the 1st Group Headquarters are stationed at this large post. Fort Lewis is also home to the 2/75th Ranger Battalion and the 9th Infantry Division. The post is just minutes south of the town of Tacoma and about 50 miles from Seattle. The cost of living in the area is moderate.

The 1st Battalion of the 1st Group is stationed at Okinawa, the southernmost island of Japan. This small island is also the home of a large U.S. Marine Corps contingent. The cost of living in Okinawa is moderate to high. The climate resembles that found in the Midwestern United States, with cold winters and warm summers.

1st Group's AO covers all countries in the Far East - including Thailand, Korea, Vietnam, Cambodia, Laos, Tagoli, Indonesia and the Philippines, to name a few. The climate and topography in these countries range from extreme heat/humidity and jungle areas (for example, in Thailand) to extreme cold and mountainous regions (for example, in Korea). While Asia is economically the fastest growing region of the world, most of its rural areas are still quite primitive. Generally speaking, the culture differs dramatically in some respects from our Western culture. While Americans like clear decisions, outgoing personalities and clear cut personal victories, Asians value compromise, harmony, respect for each person's status and less overt expressions of opinions. The primary religions include Taoism and Buddhism, but Islam and Hinduism are also prevalent in some areas.

3rd Group:

All of 3rd Group is located at Fort Bragg, North Carolina. Fort Bragg is also the home of the U.S. Army Special Operations Command Headquarters and the USAJFKSWCS. The 7th SF Group is located here, as is the 82nd Airborne Division. The Fort is one of the largest in the world. It is located next to the town of Fayetteville and is about 50 minutes from Raleigh. The cost of living is low. The climate is mild, with a short winter and a long warm summer.

3rd Group's AO covers all countries in Sub-Sahara Africa - including Zaire, Angola, Mozambique and South Africa, to name a few. The climate and topography in many of these countries are characterizes by extreme heat and desert areas, with some heavy rainy seasons. In eastern and central Africa the rainy season is the main seasonal change; however, southern Africa has a relatively mild winter that extends from June to September. Living conditions throughout much of southern Africa are bleak because Africa contains many of the world's poorest countries. Disease and starvation are widespread and there is no government money to help the unemployed, sick or old. Begging is a common practice and giving to beggars is an important value for Muslims.

Roughly half of all Africans are Muslim; however, each of the many ethnic groups in Africa has its own religion. There are literally hundreds of traditional religions in Africa. The main languages spoken are English, French, Portuguese, Arabic and Swahili, although there are other languages widely spoken.

5th Group:

All of 5th Group is located at Fort Campbell, Kentucky. Fort Campbell is also the home of the 101st Airborne Division (Air Assault) and Special Operations Aviation. The Fort is located outside of Clarksville, Tennessee with the Kentucky and Tennessee state lines bisecting it; Nashville is about 45 minutes away. The area around the post has a low cost of living and a full range of seasonal climates.

5th Group's AO covers countries in the Middle East - including Iraq, Egypt, Syria, Jordon and Kuwait, to name a few. The climate and topography in these countries range from extreme heat and desert areas (for example, in Saudi Arabia) to extreme cold and mountainous areas (for example in the mountains of Pakistan). Living conditions are primitive in many areas, although many countries have enjoyed rapid economic growth since World War II. Economically and socially, large status differences exist among various ethnic and religious groups (for example between the Kurds and Arabs, Jews and Muslims) and between rich and poor classes. Religions vary from complete paganism to Christianity, Islam and Judaism. Although Arabic is the dominant language in the Middle East, there are many regions where languages other than Arabic dominate - from Nubian in the Extreme north and Beja in the Red Sea Hills, to the many central African languages of the south.

7th Group:

Most of 7th Group is stationed at Fort Bragg, North Carolina (see 3rd Group). One Company of 7th Group is located at Fort Clayton, Panama. This Fort is located on the Pacific side of the small nation of Panama. The area has a low cost of living and a tropical climate.

7th Group's AO covers all countries in central and South America - including Panama, Honduras, Columbia and Brazil, to name a few. The climate in most of these countries is characterized by extreme heat and humidity; however, some South American countries experience cool winters and dry, pleasant summers. Geography varies from coastal deserts to expansive plains, marshes and swamplands to some of the world's most dense tropical rain forests. Living conditions are generally primitive in rural areas; culturally, the pace of life is much slower than in the United States. The dominant religion is Catholicism, although in many areas pagan deities are worshipped. Spanish is the official language in every country - except Brazil, where Portuguese is spoken and the Guianas, where English, French and Dutch are spoken. The majority of Central and South Americans do not speak English.

10th Group:

Most of the 10th Group is located at Fort Carson, Colorado. Fort Carson is the home of the 4th Infantry Division and is located close to Colorado Springs in the Rocky Mountains. The climate is cool and the cost of living is moderate.

The 1st Battalion is stationed in Stuttgart, Germany. Stuttgart is located in the southern part of Germany. The climate is cool and the cost of living is moderately high.

10th Group's AO covers countries in Eastern and Western Europe - including Germany, Turkey, the Czech Republic and the former Soviet Union. Climate and topography in these countries vary greatly, from heat and desert (for example, in Turkey) to extreme cold and mountainous areas (for example, in Denmark and Siberia). The living conditions in many of the Western European countries are similar to those found in the United States; however, the living conditions in eastern Europe countries are generally poor. Basic necessities such as food, clean drinking water and heat are not available or are very scarce in Eastern European countries, sickness and malnutrition are common. Cultures vary among the many European countries and ethnic differences are a source of great strife among neighboring peoples (for example in Bosnia). Over 20 languages are spoken in Europe, although many Western Europeans understand English. Religious variation in Europe is great; however, most of the religious follow the traditions of Christianity.

SF CONTACT INFORMATION:

Enlisted:

Special Forces In-service Recruiting Commander
U.S. Army John F. Kennedy Special Warfare
Center and School
DSN: 239-1818;
COMM: (910) 432-1637.

Officers:

Special Forces Recruiter

Fort Bragg:
DSN: 239-1818;
COMM: (910) 432-1818.

Fort Campbell:
DSN: 635-9818;
COMM: (502) 439-4390.

Fort Lewis:
DSN: 357-8710;
COMM: (206) 964-1001.

The Special Forces Future Readiness Officer:
U. S. Total Army Personnel Command
DSN: 221-3178;
COMM: (703) 325-3178.

SAMPLE SPECIAL FORCES ASSESSMENT & SELECTION PHYSICAL TRAINING HANDBOOK:

The purpose of this Physical Training Handbook is to assist prospective SFAS candidates to attain and maintain a high state of physical fitness for attendance at the US Army John F. Kennedy Special Warfare Center and School (USAJFKSWCS) Special Forces Assessment and Selection Program (SFAS).

"USAJFKSWCS Assessment and Training Programs are physically demanding because physical and mental toughness are required of Special Forces Soldiers."

Soldiers attending the SFAS course perform physical task that require them to climb obstacles (by use of a rope) 20-30 feet high, swim while wearing boots and fatigues and travel great distances cross country while carrying a rucksack with a minimum of 45 pounds. Upper and lower body strength and physical endurance are required to accomplish physical-oriented goals on a continuous basis for 21 days. You need to be in very good shape and able to carry a rucksack day after day the entire time you are here. SFAS is an assessment of you. This handbook does not teach or coach you to get through SFAS. You will make it on your own strengths.

This handbook outlines a 5 week PT program based on physical requirements set by the USAJFKSWCS.

Do not expect to get "free" time from your unit to complete the program. The responsibility to get in shape is yours and yours alone. Work out on your own time if that is all you have. If you go to the field then work on strengthening drills: pushups, situps, pullups, squats (with extra weight) when ever you can.

Don't delay starting the program. If you have more than 5 weeks until SFAS take advantage of the extra time. The mission is to get in shape. This handbook tells you how.

What to Expect in Physical Training:

"Attaining physical fitness is not an overnight process; the body must go through three stages."

FIRST STAGE -- TOUGHENING:

During the first 2 weeks the body goes through a soreness and recovery period. When a muscle with poor blood supply (such as a weak muscle) is exercised the waste products produced by the exercise collect faster than the blood can remove them. This acid waste builds up in the muscle tissue and irritates the nerve in the muscle fiber causing soreness. As the exercise continues the body is able to circulate the blood more rapidly through the muscles and remove the waste materials, which cause soreness to disappear.

SECOND STAGE -- SLOW IMPROVEMENT:

As the body passes through the toughing stage and continues into the slow improvement stage, the volume of blood circulating in the muscle increases and the body functions more efficiently. In the first few weeks the improvement is rapid, but as a higher level of skill and conditioning is reached, the improvement becomes less noticeable. The body reaches its maximum level of performance between six and ten weeks. The intensity of the program and individual differences account for the variance in time.

THIRD STAGE -- SUSTAINMENT

The sustaining stage is during which physical fitness is maintained. It is necessary to continue exercising at approximately the same intensity to retain the condition developed. Once a high level of physical fitness is attained a maintenance workout program should be applied using the hard/easy workout concept.

Getting the Most out of Your Training:

♦ Do not let bad weather interrupt your conditioning. If you can't do a march, substitute ruck squats, running stairs (with and without a ruck), weight lifting, etc. But remember, there is no "inclement weather" in SFAS;

♦ Utilize map/compass techniques whenever possible during forced march/ cross country workouts;

♦ Practice proper ruck march techniques.

PROPER RUCK MARCH TECHNIQUES:

Weight of body must be kept directly over feet, and sole of shoe must be placed flat on ground by taking small steps at a steady pace.

Knee must be locked on every step in order to rest muscles of the legs (especially when going up hill).

When walking cross country, step over/around obstacles; never step on them.

When traveling up steep slopes, always traverse them; climb in a zig-zag pattern rather than straight up.

When descending steep slopes, keep the back straight and knees bent to take up the shock of each step. Do not lock knees. Dig in with heels and each step.

Practice walking as fast as you can with a rucksack. Do not run with ruck sack. When tested you may have to trot but try not to during training, it may injure you.

A good ruck sack pace is accomplished by continuous movement with short breaks (5 minutes) every 6-8 miles, or every hour in hot weather.

If you cannot ruck sack march then do squats with your rucksack. One hundred (100) repetitions, 5 times or until muscle failure. To avoid injury to your knees, squat only to the point where the upper and lower leg form a 90 degree bend at the knee.

THE HARD/EASY WORKOUT CONCEPT:

Physical workouts should be conducted 6 days a week, alternating hard and easy workout days. For example, do hard workouts Mon/Wed/Sat (using Sat for extra long workouts) and do less strenuous workouts Sun/Tues/Thurs. A hard/easy workout program will allow maximum effort for overloading both the muscle groups and cardiorespiratory system; it will also prevent injury and stagnation in the program.

EASY DAYS:

Easy day workouts are not described in this handbook. Make up your own less strenuous workouts practicing biking, short/slow runs, pullups, pushups, weight lifting and stretching. In addition, swim as often as you can; remember for SFAS you must be able to swim 50 meters wearing boots and fatigues.

HARD DAYS:

On hard days complete the "Hard Workout Day Activities" for weeks 1 through 5. Record the dates of your hard workouts and check the box for each activity you complete; if you change an activity make a note. For ruck marches you can either go along a road or cross country. Strive for the time goals and enter your actual times - be sure to do at least some cross country ruck sack marches.

This Handbook is your guide and your personal record of progress. Be honest with yourself as you track your progress. You are to bring this handbook with you to SFAS. Your entries will not be used to determine your suitability for Special Forces training; your performance in SFAS is the sole criterion for that.

HARD WORKOUT DAY ACTIVITIES:

Week 1
First Day:
♦ APFT (maximum performance in all events, see what you can do). Record your score inside the front cover;
Use 17-21 year old standards
♦ 100 meter swim (nonstop, any stroke do not swim on your back or touch the side or the bottom of the pool);
♦ Forced 3 mile march, 30 pound ruck sack (along a road or cross country); road goal: 45 minutes; cross country goal: 1 hour.
Wear well broken-in boots with thick socks.
Warm up and cool down when you workout.

Second Day:
♦ 3 sets of pushups (1 set = maximum repetitions in 30 seconds);
♦ 3 mile run (moderate pace of 8-9 minutes per mile);
♦ Rope Climb or 3 sets of pullups (as many as you can do);

♦ Forced 5 mile march, 30 pound ruck sack; road goal: 1 hour, 15 minutes; cross country goal: 1 hour, 40 minutes.
Practice proper ruckmarch techniques!

Third Day:
♦ Forced 5 mile march, 30 pound ruck sack; road goal: 1 hour, 15 minutes; cross country goal: 1 hour, 40 minutes.

Week 2
First Day:
♦ Forced 8 mile march, 35 pound ruck sack; road goal: 2 hours; cross country goal: 2 hours, 40 minutes.

Second Day:
♦ 3 sets of pushups, pullups and situps (1 set = maximum repetitions in 35 seconds);
♦ 5 mile run (moderate pace of 8-9 minutes per mile);
♦ 3 sets of squats with 35 pound ruck sack (50 per set).
Squat only to the point where the upper and lower leg form a 90 degree bend at knee. Do not squat any lower or you may injure your knees.

Third Day:
♦ Forced 10 mile march, 35 pound ruck sack; road goal: 3 hours; cross country goal: 4 hours.

WEEK 3
First Day:
♦ 4 sets of pushups, pullups and situps (1 set = maximum repetitions in 40 seconds);
♦ 4 mile run (fast to moderate pace of 7-8 minutes per mile);
♦ 4 sets of squats with 40 pound ruck sack (50 per set).
Squat only to the point where the upper and lower leg form a 90 degree bend at knee.

Second Day:
♦ Forced 12 mile march, 40 pound ruck sack; road goal: 4 hours; cross country goal: 4 hours, 40 minutes.

Third Day:

 ♦ 4 sets of pushups, pullups and situps (1 set = maximum repetitions in 45 seconds);

 ♦ 6 mile run (fast to moderate pace of 7-8 minutes per mile);

 ♦ 4 sets of squats with 40 pound ruck sack (50 per set).

 Remember, only squat to a 90 degree bend.

WEEK 4

First Day:

 ♦ Forced 14 mile march, 50 pound ruck sack; road goal: 4 hours; cross country goal: 4 hours, 40 minutes.

Second Day:

 ♦ 4 sets of pushups, pullups and situps (1 set = maximum repetitions in 1 min);

 ♦ 6 mile run (fast to moderate pace of 7-8 minutes per mile);

 ♦ 4 sets of squats with 50 pound ruck sack (50 per set).

 Remember, only squat to a 90 degree bend.

Third Day:

 ♦ Forced 18 mile march, 50 pound ruck sack; road goal: 4 hours, 45 minutes; cross country goal: 6 hours.

 Drink lots of water when you are training, especially in hot weather.

WEEK 5

First Day:

 ♦ 3 mile run (fast pace of 6-7 minutes per mile);

 ♦ 500 meter swim (nonstop, any stroke but not on your back).

Second Day:

 ♦ APFT. You should be able to achieve a score of at least 240 (minimum of 70 points in any one event) in the 17-21 year age limit.

Third Day:

 ♦ Forced 18 mile march, 50 pound ruck sack; road goal: 4 hours, 45 minutes; cross country goal: 6 hours.

REFERENCE:

1. US Army Formal Schools Catalog. US Army Publishing Agency. DA PAM 351-4, pages 116,117,120,121,169,170, Tables 3-19,3-39. 31 October 1995.
2. In-Service Special Forces Program. USAREC Pamphlet 601-25. 20 May 1991.
3. In-Service Special Forces Recruiting Program (Officer and Enlisted). USAREC Pamphlet 601-25. 26 February 1996.
4. Special Forces Assessment and Selection Physical Training Handbook. US APT 31-210-SWCS.
5. Thinking About Special Forces: Answers to Often-Asked Questions. US Army Publishing Agency.
6. "Special Forces Assessment and Selection." Online. Internet. April 15, 2000. Available: http://users.aol.com/armysof1/sfas.html.
7. "Special Forces Creed." Online. Internet. 15 May 2000. Available: http://www.nightstalkers.com/creed/sfcreed.html.

| Table: Special Forces-Addresses ||
RECRUITING STATION	AREAS OF RESPONSIBILITY
Fort Lewis P.O. Box 33903 Fort Lewis, WA 98433 DSN: 357-8710; COMM: (206) 964-1001	Fort Lewis; Fort Greely; Fort Richardson; Fort Irwin; Hawaii; Korea; Japan; Fort Wainwright; White Sands Missile Range, NM; Sierra Army Depot, CA
Fort Campbell Commander, 101st Airborne Division (AASLT) ATTN: RCRO-SM-SF-FC Fort Campbell, KY 42223 DSN: 635-9818; COMM: (502) 439-4390	Fort Campbell; Fort Leonard Wood; Fort Knox; Fort McCoy; Fort Benjamin Harrison; Fort Drum Fort Polk; Fort Hood; Fort Chaffe
*Fort Bragg Commander USAJFKSWCS ATTN: AOJK-SP-R Fort Bragg, NC 28307 DSN: 239-1818; COMM: (910) 432-1818	Fort Monmouth; Fort Devens; Fort Jackson; Fort McClellen; Redstone Arsenal; Panama/Honduras; Fort Bragg; Fort Lee; Fort Gordon; Fort Dix; Fort Eustis; West Point; Puerto Rico; MDW (Fort Richie, Myer, Meade, Pentagon)
Fort Carson G SC 10th GRP ATTN: SF Recruiting Fort Carson, CO 80913 COMM: (719) 524-1461/62	Fort Bliss; Fort Sam Houston; Fort Riley; Fort Huachuca; APG; Fort Sill; Fort Leavenworth
Fort Benning Bldg. 75B, Rm. 109, World Ave. Fort Benning, GA 31905 COMM: (706) 545-3083	Redstone Arsenal, Fort Rucker, Dahlonega; Fort Gillem, McDill AFB, Hunter Army Air Field; Eglin Air Force Base
Europe Recruiting HHC, 1st PERSCOM ATTN: SF Recruiting APO AE 09081 DSN: 370-8890; COMM: 011-49-6202-806558	Europe; Belgium; Saudi Arabia; Italy

Note: If an applicant wishes to apply, and does not see his post or installation listed above, he may send his completed application to the Fort Bragg Recruiting Station to be processed.

Sample SF Volunteer Statement for Enlisted Applicants

AOJK-SP-R

Memorandum for Commander, USAJFKSWCS, ATTN: AOJK-SP-R, Fort Bragg, NC 28307-5000

SUBJECT: Special Forces Volunteer Statement

1.   I hereby volunteer for Special Forces (SF) training under the provisions of AR 614-200, chapter 6. If not already airborne qualified, I also hereby volunteer for airborne training and understand that failure to successfully complete airborne training will disqualify me from SF training and duty.

2.   I have met all criteria listed in AR 614-200, chapter 6.

3.   Upon successful completion of Special Forces Assessment and Selection (SFAS) and prior to my departure from my losing command, I agree to extend my enlistment or to reenlist, as the case may be, to meet the remaining service obligation as listed in AR 614-200, chapter 6.

4.   I authorize release of data from my files to the SF recruiting team for consideration for training.

5.   I am aware that if so determined by the appropriate SF commander that I may be declared unsuitable
     for further SF training.

6.   Have you ever applied for and/or attended SFAS or qualification courses? (Yes or No) If yes, please explain:

_____

7.   I request reclassification from my present PMOS of _____ to PMOS (list in order of preference: 18E, 18D, 18C, 18B) _____

I REQUEST SFAS   _____
DATE_____   (PRINT AND SIGN NAME)
AND WHY_____   _____
                                        (RANK AND SSN)
                                        _____
                                        (UNIT, POST, AND ZIP CODE)
                                        _____
                                        (DUTY AND HOME TELEPHONE NUMBERS)

DATA REQUIRED BY THE PRIVACY ACT OF 1974

AUTHORITY: Title 10, USC 3013
PRINCIPAL PURPOSE: To serve as application for Special Forces training.
ROUTINE USES: To provide a record of the individual's Special Forces application
MANDATORY OR VOLUNTARY DISCLOSURE AND EFFECT ON INDIVIDUAL NOT PROVIDING
INFORMATION: Voluntary; failure to disclose requested information will have a negative
impact on individual's application for Special Forces training.

Sample SF Volunteer Statement for Officer Applicants

OFFICE SYMBOL

MEMORANDUM FOR Commander, U.S. Total Army Personal Command, ATTN: TAPC-OPE-SF, 200 Stovall Street, Alexandria, VA 22332-0414.

SUBJECT: Special Forces Volunteer Statement

1.   I hereby volunteer for Special Forces (SF) training under the provisions of AR 614-162. If not already airborne qualified, I also hereby volunteer for airborne training and understand that failure to successfully complete airborne training will disqualify me from SF training and duty.

2.   I have met all criteria listed in AR 614-162.

3.   I am aware that if so determined by the appropriate SF command, I may be declared unsuitable for further SF training and/or duty.

4.   I request a branch transfer from _____ Branch to SF Branch upon graduation from the Special Forces Detachment Officer Qualification Course.

_____
(Unit)

_____
(Signature)

_____
(Duty Telephone-DSN/COMM)

_____
(Signature Block)

_____
(Home Address)

_____
(SSN)

_____
(Home Telephone)

_____
(Year Group)

AUTHORITY: Title 44, USC 3103

PRINCIPAL PURPOSE: To serve as application for Special Forces training.

ROUTINE USES: To provide a record of the preparation to the individual's Special Forces application packet.

MANDATORY OR VOLUNTARY DISCLOSURE AND EFFECT ON INDIVIDUAL NOT PROVIDING INFORMATION: Disclosure is voluntary but strongly encouraged. Failure to provide information requested could cause timely and incomplete processing of individual's application.

_____
Home of Record/Leave Address

_____
Telephone Number

_____
Next Assignment (if known)   Reporting Date

Sample Security Clearance Verification

AOJK-SP-R

_____
(Date)

MEMORANDUM FOR Commander, USAJFKSWC, ATTN: AOJK-SPR, Fort Bragg, NC 28307-500
SUBJECT: Security Clearance Verification

NAME:
GRADE:
SSN:
DOB:
POB:
CITIZENSHIP:

1. The above named individual has the following security clearance action:

a. DA Form 873 (Certification of Clearance and/or Security Determination) has been issued with
    the following clearance and investigation:

b. SF 86 (Questionnaire for National Security Positions) was initiated on
    And sent to Central Clearance Facility (CCF) on   -

c. Subject has an ENTNAC/DIS Form 1, however, has no clearance. PCCF Form 5
d. (Request for Security Determination) was sent to CCF for final clearance determination on .
e. Subject has no evidence on an investigation in MPRJ. NAD sent to DIS/PCCF Form 5 sent to
    CCF (cross out the one that does not apply) on   -
f. Other:

2. Point of contact for this command is   -

FOR THE COMMANDER:

DATA REQUIRED BY THE PRIVACY ACT OF 1974

AUTHORITY: Title 44, USC 3101
PRINCIPAL PURPOSE: To verify the security clearance of Special Forces volunteers.

ROUTING USES: Used to provide information on status of security clearance for personnel who have
volunteered for Special Forces.

MANDATORY OR VOLUNTARY DISCLOSURE AND EFFECT ON INDIVIDUAL NOT PROVIDING
INFORMATION: Voluntary; failure to disclose requested information will have a negative impact on
individual's request to attend Special Forces training.

Sample Memorandum Sent to Physical Exam Section

AOJK-SP-R

(Date)

MEMORANDUM FOR physical Exam Section

SUBJECT: Special Forces Physical

1.   Is currently processing a packet for Special Forces Assessment and Selection. It is imperative that his physical be processed expeditiously. With the Army's restructuring, there has become a strong demand for Special Forces (SF) soldiers. This congressionally mandated SF recruiting effort is a demanding one. Historically, the SF physical is our largest obstacle for applicants submitting applications. Your assistance is greatly appreciated.

2.   Please ensure that the applicant is given the original SF 88. SF 93, EKG, Chest X-Ray, and all other supporting documents (i.e., Lab Slips, Results of EKG, and Chest X-Ray). Also, to avoid unnecessary work, please ensure AR 40-501, chapter 2, paragraph 5-3, paragraph 8-26 (3)c, and table 8-1 are used. Below is a list of most commonly missed items on the SF physical:

a. Date of Examination #6
b. Valsalva Results #23
c. Digital Rectal #32
d. Dental ACC or UNACC #44
e. Urinalysis $45
f. Chest X-Ray Results/Date # 46
g. RPR Results $47
h. EKG Results#48
i. Blood Type #49
j. HIV/Sickle Cell Results/Date #50

k. Blood Pressure #57
l. Distant Vision #59
m. Refractive Error #60
n. Near Vision $61
o. Color Vision#64
p. Profile#76
q. Qualification #77
r. Signed by Physician #79, 80, and 81
s. SF93 Missing or Not Signed By Physician

3.   If you have any questions, please feel free to call the SF Officer Recruiter and DSN 239-1818 or 509-83 or the Chief, Medical Training Division at DSN 239-6577.

/signed/
Signature Block

Sample Request for Medical Waiver

_____

(DATE)

MEMORANDUM THRU

Commander, U.S. Army John F. Kennedy Special Warfare Center and School, ATTN: AOJK-SP-R, Fort Bragg, NC 28307-5000

Commander, U.S. Army Special Operations Command, ATTN: AOMD-MT, Fort Bragg, NC 28307-5200

FOR Commander, 1st Special Warfare Training Group, U.S. Army John F. Kennedy Warfare Center and School, ATTN: AOJK-GP, Fort Bragg, NC 28307-5000

SUBJECT: Request for Waiver of Medical Perquisites (Vision), Special Forces Training

1. Request a waiver of the uncorrected vision requirement for Special Forces training. My eyesight uncorrected is _____ / _____ and _____ / _____ .

    1. My eyesight is correctable to _____ / _____ and _____ / _____ .

    2. I have served in (brief background). Convince the Surgeon's Office and the Training Group Commander that you should have these perquisites waived.

NAME
SSN
RANK, BRANCH

Sample DLAB Verification for Officer Applications

MEMORANDUM FOR Commander, U.S. Army John F. Kennedy Special Warfare Center and School, ATTN: AOJK-SP-R, Fort Bragg, NC 28307-5000

SUBJECT: Defense Language Aptitude Battery (DLAB) Test

1.   The individual listed below took the Defense Language Aptitude Battery at the Army Education Center on_____.

2.   The results of the graded test are listed below:

NAME	RANK	UNIT	DLAB SCORE
_____	_____	_____	_____

_____

(VERIFICATION BY EDUCATION CENTER)

Sample Swim Statement and Affidavit for Officer Applicants

MEMORANDUM FOR Commander, U.S. Army John F. Kennedy Special Warfare Center and School, ATTN: AOJK-SP-R, Fort Bragg, NC 28307-5000

SUBJECT: Special Forces Swim test Statement

I certify that _____ successfully completed the Special Forces 50 meter swim test with boots and BDU as prescribed in AR 614-200, paragraph 6-15.

```
                                        _____
                                                        (SIGNATURE)


                                        _____
                                              (TYPE OR PRINT FULL NAME)


                                        _____
                                                  (UNIT AND ADDRESS)
```

NOTE: AFFIDAVIT SED ONLY IF APPLICANT CAN SWIM BUT THERE IS NO POOL AVAILABLE.

Special Forces Swim Affidavit

I certify that I, _____, can successfully complete the Special Forces 50-meter swim test with boots and BDU as prescribed in AR 614-200, paragraph 6-15.

```
                                        _____
                                                        (SIGNATURE)

                                        _____
                                              (TYPE OR PRINT FULL NAME)

                                        _____
                                                  (UNIT AND ADDRESS)
```

Sample Resume Format for Officer Applicants

Unit Address   Rank/Name   Home Address

Duty Phone   SSN   Phone
  DSN:
  COMM:

Objective: Why SF?

Career Highlights: Do not repeat information form ORB. Expound on unique assignments
                        and/or duties

Enlisted Experience: If applicable

Language Training/Proficiency:

Foreign Travel:

Athletics:

Education:

Current Projects:

Hobbies/Interests:

KEEP IN MIND THAT THIS IS JUST A SAMPLE FORMAT. USE WHAT IS APPLICABLE TO YOU AND
TAILOR ACCORDINGLY

SFAS Enlisted Application Checklist

Required Items:	Completed	Date
Attend a Special Forces Briefing	_____	_____
Volunteer Statement	_____	_____
Copy of Your 2A & 2-1 (less than 3 months old)	_____	_____
Security Clearance Status Verification (S2)	_____	_____
APFT & Swim Test -- Administered by Recruiter (All APFT results must be within 6 months of SFAS start date)	_____	_____
Special Forces Physical (less than 2 yrs old)	_____	_____
Airborne School Verification (if ABN qualified and not on 2A or 2-1)	_____	_____
PLDC Verification (If PLDC qualified and not on 2A or 2-1)	_____	_____
SF 88 and SF 93	_____	_____

Strongly Recommended Items (Optional):

	Completed	Date
Defense Language Aptitude Battery (DLAB) (Must hand carry DLAB or DLPT results to SFAS)	_____	_____
T.A.B.E. Test (Version A) (Must hand carry results to SFAS)	_____	_____
Preparatory PT Train-up Pamphlet (PT 31-21-SWCS) (Must hand carry pamphlet to SFAS)	_____	_____
Minimum of 6 Pullups	_____	_____

SFAS Officer Application Checklist

Required Items:	Completed	Date
Volunteer Statement	————	————
Current ORB	————	————
Security Clearance Status Verification (S-2) -- Do not send DA Form 873 if recorded on ORB.	————	————
Swim Test Statement signed by any witness	————	————
SF 88 and SF 93 -- The physical must be within 60 days of application.	————	————
DA Form 705 (APFT) -- Scored at 17-21 age group; PT Test must be completed within 30 days of application.	————	————
DLAB Test Results -- If you already have a DLAB Score and/or a DLPT Score of 1/1 or higher (less than 1 year old) on your ORB, then no additional testing is required.	————	————
Resume -- One page biographical sketch	————	————

Strongly Recommended Items (Optional):

Minimum of 6 Pullups	————	————

W.O.C.S.

WARRANT OFFICER CANDIDATE SCHOOL

REGULATION:
Course No: 911–09W
Title: Warrant Officer Candidate School
Length: 6 Weeks
Location: Warrant Officer Career Center – SC: 020
Scope: Course effective: 1 Oct 87
Leadership, ethics, staff skills, communication skills, personnel
management, military history, employment, tactics, support, structure of
the Army, and common military training.
Prerequisite: Active Army and Reserve Component enlisted personnel.
Selected for training by DA centralized board or enrolled by Chief of
Army Reserve, or Chief, National Guard Bureau.
Security Clearance: None

FORWARD:

The Warrant Officer Education System provides pre-appointment and leadership development training to develop technically and tactically competent Warrant Officers. WOES consists of five levels: pre-appointment (Warrant Officer Candidate School), entry (Warrant Officer Basic Course) and advanced (Warrant Officer Advanced Course), staff (Warrant Officer Staff Course), senior staff (Warrant Officer Senior Staff Course). Technical training is predicated on proponents' identification of required Warrant Officer skill levels.

The TRADOC common core consists of those tasks required of, and common to, all Warrant Officer Military Occupational Specialties. The Warrant Officer Career Center (WOCC) monitors/manages development and execution of Warrant Officer common core training products. WOCC further monitors integration of common core training support products within branch training courses as appropriate.

The Warrant Officer Candidate School (WOCS) is the first level of the five level leadership development training within the Warrant Officer Education System. WOCS is an MOS immaterial course taught in a high stress environment to assess the potential of candidates to become successful Warrant Officers.

Qualified applicants are selected for Warrant Officer Candidate status by centralized U.S. Army Recruiting Command boards, specified branch proponents, or State Adjutants General. Policy governing Warrant Officer selection and appointment is contained in AR 135-100 (Appointment of Commissioned and Warrant Officers of the Army).

All Warrant Officer Candidates (AC and RC) must attend the resident WOCS at Fort Rucker, AL. Course prerequisites must be met prior to graduation.

WARRANT OFFICER CODE:

Willingly render loyal services to superiors, subordinates and peers in every organization of which they are members.

Always set an example in conduct, appearance and performance that will make others proud to know and work with them.

Reliably discharge all duties with which they are confronted whether such duties are expressed or implied.

Readily subordinate their personal interests and welfare to those of their organization and their subordinates.

Accept responsibility at every opportunity and acknowledge full accountability for their actions.

Never knowingly tolerate wrongdoing by themselves or others, whether by commission or omission, design or neglect.

Teach other people in a way the effectively expand and perpetuate the scope of their technical competence.

Obtain breadth of perspective and depth of understanding beyond the limits of their specific responsibility.

Faithfully adhere to their oath of office in all respects, upholding and defending the nation's constitution by both word and deed.

Forcefully take the initiative to stimulate constructive action in all areas requiring or inviting their attention.

Improve themselves both physically and mentally, professionally and personally, to increase their own abilities and the value of their services.

Contribute their past experiences, service and knowledge to a dedicated effort for a betterment of the future.

Earn an ironclad reputation for the absolute integrity of their word.

Reflect credit and inspire confidence in themselves, the Warrant Officer Corps, the military service of the nation and the United States of America.

WARRANT OFFICER MOSs:

Remember, you must meet the minimum prerequisites for the Warrant Officer MOS for which you will apply, or you must request a prerequisite waiver. Waivers are not needed for preferred qualifications.

Refer to Table WOCS-A for a list of Warrant Officer MOS titles and corresponding enlisted MOS feeders.

131A. TARGET ACQUISITION RADAR TECHNICIAN:

Duties:

♦ Plans, organizes, implements, monitors and evaluates operations, threat environ-

ment, unit maintenance and intermediate level support maintenance of Field Artillery radar systems;

♦ Provides advice on technical and tactical aspects of the radar system;

♦ Supervises maintenance of Field Artillery radar system equipment and components;

♦ Ensures that repairs and adjustments are completed and performs final inspection to determine operational status of repaired equipment;

♦ Interprets and implements changes in technical data concerning inspection, repair and test procedures;

♦ Instructs personnel on new or revised radar operation, employment and repair procedures;

♦ Ensures that equipment modifications are completed as required;

♦ Performs other officer level duties essential to the mission of the assigned unit.

Minimum Prerequisites:

♦ Be a SGT (E5) or above;

♦ Hold MOS 13B, 13C, 13D, 13E, 13F, 13P, 13R, 82C or 93F;

♦ One year in a supervisory position documented by NCOER;

♦ Have less than 8 years active federal service;

♦ Have 110 or higher in ASVAB areas of FA and EL;

♦ Have a written recommendation from a CW3-5 who holds the 131A MOS.

Preferred Qualifications:

♦ Have two years in a supervisory position documented by NCOERs;

♦ Six hours of English and six hours of Math from an accredited college or university.

MOS	WARRANT OFFICER TITLE	ENLISTED FEEDER MOS
Table: WOCS-A		
131 A	Target Acquisition Radar Technician	13B, C, D, E, F, P, R; 82C; 93F
140 A	Command and Control Systems Technician	14E; 14J (Male Only)
140 E	PATRIOT System Technician	14E; 14T; 27X
150 A	Air Traffic Control Technician	93C (Reserve Component Only)
151 A	Aviation Maintenance Technician	All CMF 67 MOSs
153 A	Rotary Wing Aviator	All MOSs
180 A	Special Forces Warrant Officer	All CMF 18 MOSs
210 A	Utilities Operation and Maintenance Technician	51B, H, K and R; 52C, D, E and G
215 D	Terrain Analysis Technician	81T (81Q)
250 N	Network Management Technician	31F; 31W and 74C (with ASI Z2)
251 A	Data Processing Technician	74B, G and Z
311 A	CID Special Agent	95D
350 B	All Source Intelligence Technician	96B
350 D	Imagery Intelligence Technician	96D
350 L	Attache Technician	71L (with ASI E4)
351 B	Counterintelligence Technician	97B
351 E	Human Intelligence Collection Technician	97E
352 C	Traffic Analysis Technician	98C
352 D	Emitter Location/Identification technician	98D
352 G	Voice Intercept Technician	98G
352 H	Morse Intercept Technician	98H
352 J	Emanations Analysis Technician	98J
352 K	Non-Morse Intercept Technician	98K
353 A	Intelligence and Electronic Warfare Technician	All CMF 33 MOSs
420 A	Military Personnel Technician	All CMF 75 MOSs
420 C	Bandmaster	All CMF 97 MOSs
880 A	Marine Deck Officer	88K and 88Z
881 A	Marine Engineering Officer	88L and Z; 52E (with ASI S2)
882 A	Mobility Officer	88N
910 A	Ammunition Technician	55B, D and Z
912 A	Land Combat Missile System Technician	27E, M, T and Z; 35B and M
913 A	Armament Repair Technician	45B, G and K; 63E
914 A	Allied Trades Technician	44B and E
915 A	Unit Maintenance Technician (Light)	63B, D, E, H, S, T, W, Y and Z
916 A (AS16D)	High-to-Medium Altitude Air Defense (HIMAD) Direct Support/General Support Maintenance Technician (PATRIOT)	27X
917 A	Maneuver Forces Air Defense Systems Technician	27E, M, T and Z; 35B and M
918 A	Test Measurement Diagnostic Equipment (TMDE) Maintenance Support Technician	35H
918B	Electronic Systems Maintenance Technician	35B,C, D (93D) E, F, H, J, L(68L), N, Q(68Q) and R(68R); 35W and Y; 39B; 68P; 31P; 31S
919 A	Engineer Equipment Repair Technician	52D and X; 62B; 63B
920 A	Property Accounting Technician	92Y
920 B	Supply Systems Technician	92A
921 A	Airdrop Systems Technician	92R
922 A	Food Service Technician	92G

140A. Command & Control Systems Technician:

Duties:

♦ Coordinates the activities of maintenance personnel and manages equipment and site assets for the installation, repair, maintenance and modification of Army Air Defense command and control systems, ancillary equipment and tools;

♦ Develops maintenance SOPs;

♦ Analyzes and interprets technical data employed in the diagnosis of malfunctions, maintenance and repair of equipment;

♦ Advises and instructs repair personnel on specialized tests to isolate causes of equipment failures and malfunctions;

♦ Estimates repair priorities based on mission, type of work to be performed and availability of parts and personnel;

♦ Advises commander or staff officers on command and control system capabilities and limitations;

♦ Makes recommendations of changes to computer software based on mission and operations requirements;

♦ Performs other officer level duties essential to the unit mission.

Minimum Prerequisites:

♦ Be a SGT (E5) or above;

♦ Hold MOS of 14E (24T) or 14J (25L soldiers were reclassified into 14J). Males only in these MOSs;

♦ Four years field experience in MOS;

♦ Physical profile of not less than 111121.

Preferred Qualifications:

♦ An additional year of experience in feeder MOS;

♦ One year in a supervisory position

♦ Twenty or more college credit hours with a minimum of six credit hours of college level English and six credit hours of college level Math;

♦ Written recommendation from a senior Warrant Officer in the same career field.

140E. Patriot System Technician:

Duties:

♦ Supervises unit maintenance;

♦ Advises the commander on march order and emplacement of the PATRIOT system;

♦ Monitors the equipment necessary to detect operator error and/or system malfunctions;

♦ Instructs subordinates in operating procedures, maintenance techniques used in care of special tools and supporting equipment, as well as the Army Maintenance Management System;

♦ Advises the commander on the technical requirements of equipment utilized at battalion or battery level;

♦ Evaluates the effectiveness of maintenance programs and operator training;

♦ Supervises repair operations and isolation procedures as required;

♦ Monitors and coordinates installation of modifications of the PATRIOT system;

♦ Implements proper safety and security procedures applicable to the maintenance support of the PATRIOT system;

♦ Advises commander on all supply and maintenance problems at all levels;

♦ Performs other official duties essential to the mission of the unit.

Minimum Prerequisites:

♦ Be a SGT (E5) or above;

♦ Hold MOS of 14E (24T), 14T (16T) or 27X;

♦ Four years field experience in MOS;

♦ Physical profile of not less than 111121.

Preferred Qualifications:

♦ An additional year of experience in feeder MOS ;

♦ One year in a supervisory position;

♦ Twenty or more college credit hours with a minimum of six credit hours of college level English and six credit hours of college level Math;

♦ Written recommendation from a senior Warrant Officer in the same career field.

150A. AIR TRAFFIC CONTROL TECHNICIAN:

Duties:

♦ Supervises the effective utilization of ATC equipment and ATC personnel at all categories of Army ATC facilities;

♦ Supervises fixed base ATC training and rating programs, combat support training and certification programs, as well as combat support and fixed base facility operations procedures;

♦ Supervises airspace management functions and airspace processing procedures into the National Airspace System (NAS).

Minimum Prerequisites:

♦ Be a SGT (E5) or above in MOS 93C;

♦ Five years experience in MOS 93C, hold facility ratings for both Combat Support Tower and Radar Air Traffic Control (ATC) Facility;

♦ Meet medical fitness standards for air traffic controllers IAW AR 40-501;

♦ Two years experience in air traffic control leadership positions as Tactical Team Leader or Shift Leader as defined in AR 611-201. Leadership experience must be documented on NCOERs.

Preferred Qualifications:

♦ Two years of college credit at an accredited institution;

♦ Experience as a Federal Aviation Agency (FAA) air traffic controller.

NOTE: This MOS is open to reserve components only.

151A. AVIATION MAINTENANCE TECHNICIAN (NON-RATED):

Duties:

♦ Manages personnel, supply, equipment and facility assets to maintain and repair Army rotary and fixed wing aircraft;

♦ Organizes maintenance elements to inspect, service, test, disassemble, repair, reassemble, adjust, replace parts and retest aircraft or aircraft components;

♦ Prepares, implements and maintains standing operating procedures for management of maintenance activities;

♦ Interprets regulations, technical manuals and orders pertaining to maintenance of Army aircraft for commanders and subordinates;

♦ Supervises aviation equipment maintenance and repair shop, section or platoon;

♦ Directs maintenance and accountability of organizational test equipment, supplies and recovery equipment.

Minimum Prerequisites:

♦ Be a SGT (E5) or above;

♦ Hold an MOS in CMF 67 series (includes 68 series MOSs);

♦ Must have worked five of the last eight years in CMF 67;

♦ Be a BNCOC graduate in a feeder MOS;

♦ At least one year experience as a Section Chief or have supervisory experience as defined in AR 611-201. Supervisory experience must be documented in NCOERs.

Preferred Qualifications:

♦ Two years of college credit at an accredited institution;

♦ Hold an Aircraft and Power Plant (A&P) certificate issued by the Federal Aviation Agency (FAA).

153A. ROTARY WING AVIATOR:

Duties:

♦ Pilots and commands utility helicopters under tactical and nontactical conditions;

♦ Operates aircraft during all types of meteorological conditions during day, night and under night vision goggles;

♦ Performs military aircraft operation, rescue hoist operations, air assault operations, aerial mine/flare delivery, internal/external load operations and paradrop/rappelling procedures;

♦ Routinely participates in training operations to include combat, combat support or combat service support operations. Maintains ATM requirements in appropriate aircraft.

Observation/utility helicopters may perform aerial route, zone and area reconnaissance in support of combat maneuver operations. Additionally, observation/utility helicopters may be used in administrative or liaison missions to transport passengers, mail or cargo for military purposes.

Minimum Prerequisites:

♦ Any MOS may apply;

♦ Be at least 18, but not have reached their 29th birthday at the convening of the selection board;

♦ Not have exceeded the age of 30 upon beginning of flight training;

♦ Score 90 or higher on the Alternate Flight Aptitude Selection Test (AFAST);

♦ Successfully pass a Class 1 Flying Duty Medical Examination (FDME) IAW AR 40-501 that has been approved by the Commander, U.S. Army Aeromedical Center;

♦ Interviewed by an Army Aviator in the rank of CW3-5 or Major and above. If the Unit Commander or above is a field grade aviator, the interview may be part of the commander's endorsement. In this case, the commander's endorsement must contain the same statement required for the aviator interview (use a memorandum format and start with the statement, "I have interviewed (your name) and find he/she has the needed personal characteristics, motivation, physical stamina, and qualifications to be appointed a U.S. Army Reserve Warrant Officer and appears acceptable for selection into the WOFT program as a Warrant OFficer Candidate.");

♦ Applicants from other military services may be interviewed by a field grade aviator from their branch of service if an Army aviator is not readily available. Army aviators will conduct the interviews whenever possible.

Preferred Qualifications:

♦ Two years of college credit at an accredited institution;

♦ Federal Aviation Agency (FAA) Private Pilots certificate or higher.

180A. SPECIAL FORCES WARRANT OFFICER:

Duties:

♦ Manages all aspects of Special Forces Operations in all operational environments;

♦ Supports Joint and Army strategic, operational and tactical requirements at all levels of execution as concerns mission planning, development and execution of special operations worldwide;

♦ Is responsible for the conduct of unconventional warfare, intelligence collection and strategic reconnaissance, collective security, strike operations and counter terrorism operations;

♦ Supports psychological operations, civil affairs and deception requirements;

♦ Supports the conduct of other missions, relative to special forces capabilities, as directed.

Minimum Prerequisites:

♦ Be serving as a SSG (E6) or above in CMF 18 MOS and be less than 36 years old;

♦ Graduate from the Special Forces (SF) Operations and Intelligence Sergeants Course (nonresident or resident) or SF Advanced Noncommissioned Officers Course (ANCOC) after October 1994;

♦ Minimum of 3 years experience at the SF Operational Detachment Alpha (SFODA) level or Special Forces;

♦ Current DA Form 330 (within one year) with at least a 1+/1+ language proficiency or a minimum score of 85 on the Defense Language Aptitude Battery (DLAB);

♦ Meet the medical fitness standards for SF duty and the SERE level "C" course according to AR 40-501 and include an SF Warrant Officer Candidate medical screening memorandum completed by the applicant's surgeon;

♦ Pass the Army Physical Readiness Test (APRT) by achieving 70% of the maximum standard for a 17-21 year old male on each event: pushups, situps and the 2 mile run;

♦ Letters of recommendation from Ccompany, Battalion and Group Commanders, the Group Senior Warrant OFficer. Individuals applying from units other than an SF Group must receive letters of recommendation from their current chain of command and letters of recommendation from the previous SF Group chain of command (including the Group Senior Warrant Officer Advisor).

NOTE: Women are not allowed to apply for this field.

210A. UTILITIES OPERATION & MAINTENANCE TECHNICIAN:

Duties:

♦ Develops and provides detailed input to the repair and maintenance of power generation equipment and provides input to command operating budgets;

♦ Develops training strategies and instructional material;

♦ Reviews and writes doctrine and presents formal instruction to Engineer Commissioned Officers, Warrant OFficers and NCOs;

♦ Supervises organizational maintenance of wheeled vehicles, mobile medical support equipment and utility power plants found in the combat support and evacuation hospitals;

♦ Supervises operations, repair and maintenance of facilities and utilities found in a station hospital;

♦ Supervises the Fire Prevention Program and fire fighting efforts in station hospitals;

♦ Repairs, modifies and rehabilitates utilities systems and subsystems, facilities, structures, power plants, station hospitals and mobile hospitals;

♦ Performs Quality Assurance for all work within assigned mission areas;

♦ Supervises preparation of log books, operating reports, malfunction reports, as well as supply and maintenance records;

♦ Prepares formal technical and administrative correspondence.

Minimum Prerequisites:

♦ Be a SGT (E5) or above;

♦ Four years experience in MOS 51B, 51H, 51K, 51R, 52C, 52D, 52E or 52G

♦ Minimum one year experience as a Construction Supervisor, Power Plant Supervisor or Shop Foreman;

♦ BNCOC graduate in feeder MOS.

Preferred Qualifications:

♦ Two years of college credit at an accredited institution;

♦ More than one year experience as a construction supervisor, power plant supervisor or shop foreman.

215D. TERRAIN ANALYSIS TECHNICIAN:

Duties:

♦ Acquires, coordinates, interprets and analyzes terrain data, to include the effects of weather on terrain related capabilities/limitations of enemy and friendly ground forces;

♦ Designs and develops terrain analysis support graphics which will best meet the needs of combat and combat support units;

♦ Supervises the preparation of complex terrain factor overlays and special purpose graphics to be used as decision aids by commanders;

♦ Coordinates graphic/textual analysis and development and supervises the preparation for limited dissemination;

♦ Identifies requirements to support terrain analysis projects;

♦ Analyzes the effects of weather factors affecting terrain mobility/usability for ground forces operation;

♦ Briefs commanders at all levels on analysis results providing recommendations as appropriate;

♦ Develops automated and manual filing and documentation systems for appropriate Military Geographic Information (MGI);

♦ Develops procedures to efficiently store, retrieve and process MGI expediently;

♦ Supervises the use and operation MICROFIX and other computer aided equipment in support of terrain analysis requirements;

♦ Coordinates with Staff Weather Officer (SWO) all requirements for critical weather information;

♦ May be employed as a service school instructor;

♦ Performs other officer level duties essential to mission of assigned unit.

Minimum Prerequisites:

♦ Be a SGT (E5) or above;

♦ Four years experience in MOS 81T (81Q);

♦ One year 81T (81Q) experience at division level;

♦ Two years experience supervising terrain analysis activities;

♦ Must have a Special Background Investigation (SBI) within the last five years;

♦ Be eligible to access Sensitive Compartmented Information prior to admission to WOCS;

♦ Successful completion or construction credit for the Basic and Advanced Terrain Analysis Course.

Preferred Qualifications:

♦ Two years of college credit at an accredited institution;

♦ More than one year experience at division level and more than two years experience supervising terrain analysis activities.

250N. NETWORK TECHNICIAN:

Duties:

♦ Supervises tactical communications switching equipment and personnel at the node level;

♦ Supervises and manages electronic keying equipment and information at the node level;

♦ Plans, manages and troubleshoots tactical switched networks;

♦ Manages electronic keys required to support signal networks;

♦ Develops policy recommendations and provides technical guidance for the planning, managing and troubleshooting of Army, Joint and combined networks;

♦ Advises commanders and staffs on tactical telecommunications network requirements.

Minimum Prerequisites:

♦ Be a SGT (E5) or above;

♦ School trained in MOS 31F, 31W or 74C with ASI Z2. (MOSs 31C, 31L, 31P, 31S and 31U may also qualify if applicant has appropriate practical experience). In some instances practical experience acquired from civilian employment may be acceptable provided the experience can be documented by employee evaluations or performance appraisals and determined to be equivalent to military experience. Waivers of MOS are considered for applicants with significant practical experience beyond the minimum;

♦ Two years practical experience in electronic switching systems (MSE/ TRITAC);

♦ A minimum of six semester hours of college level English (not speech, public speaking, etc). Waivers will not be approved for this requirement. Successful completion of the CLEP general examination in English is the only acceptable alternative;

♦ Attain 12th grade equivalency on the Reading Grade Level portion (vocabulary and comprehension) of the Test of Adult Basic Education (TABE-A or TABE-D) and include a copy of the results authenticated by the Test Control Officer of the Educational Services Office.

Preferred Qualifications:
♦ Be a BNCOC graduate in feeder MOS;
♦ Practical experience in ECB (MSE) and EAC (TRITAC) networks;
♦ 30 semester hours (45 quarter hours) of college.

251A. DATA PROCESSING TECHNICIAN:
Duties:
♦ Manages personnel, facility and equipment at brigade level and above in port authorities, in support commands and selected staff agencies;

♦ Develops computer programs;

♦ Supervises and coordinates activities of military and civilian personnel who operate or program data processing systems;

♦ Advises commanders and staffs on the employment of automation systems and projects, data communications development, as well as the installation and

maintenance of local area networks (LANs) and information systems security.

Minimum Prerequisites:
♦ Be a SGT (E5) or above;

♦ Four years of documented practical experience in computer operations or programming;

♦ School trained in MOS 74B, 74G or 74Z. In some instances practical experience acquired from civilian employment may be acceptable provided the experience can be documented by employee evaluations or performance appraisals and determined to be equivalent to military experience. Waivers of MOS are considered for applicants with significant practical experience beyond the minimum and a bachelor of science degree or higher in a computer intensive discipline. Up to two years of practical experience may be waived if an applicant possesses a bachelor of science degree or higher in a computer intensive discipline;

♦ A minimum of six semester hours of college level English (not speech, public speaking, etc). Waivers will not be approved for this requirement. Successful completion of the CLEP general examination in English is the only acceptable alternative;

♦ Attain 12th grade equivalency on the Reading Grade Level portion (vocabulary and comprehension) of the Test of Adult Basic Education (TABE-A or TABE-D) and include a copy of the results authenticated by the Test Control Officer of the Educational Services Office.

Preferred Qualifications:
♦ Be a BNCOC graduate in feeder MOS;
♦ One year experience in Battlefield Automation Systems (BAS) or tactical Local Area Networks (LANs);
♦ 30 semester hours (45 quarter hours) of college.

311A. CID SPECIAL AGENT:

Duties:

♦ Investigates felony and other significant crime of Army interest as defined by regulation, military and federal law;

♦ Plans, organizes, conducts and supervises overt and covert investigations;

♦ Examines and processes crime scenes;

♦ Collects, preserves and evaluates physical evidence for scientific examination by crime laboratories and use in judicial proceedings;

♦ Obtains and executes arrest and search warrants;

♦ Conducts raids and task force operations;

♦ Interviews and interrogates victims, witnesses, suspects and subjects, as well as obtains written statements executed under oath;

♦ Develops, evaluates and manages informants and other sources of criminal intelligence;

♦ Represents the Army's interest in investigations conducted collaterally with the Department of Defense, Department of Justice, and other federal, state and local investigative agencies;

♦ Maintains close working relationships with attorneys of the Staff Judge Advocate and the United States Attorneys Office;

♦ Testifies at Courts-Martial, Federal District Court and other judiciary tribunals;

♦ Writes, reviews and approves technical investigative reports;

♦ Conducts and supervises technical surveys of Army elements and activities which analyze and detect ongoing crime and recommends actions to prevent crime which could result in significant economic loss and reduced combat effectiveness;

♦ Conducts personnel security vulnerability assessments for designated senior Army officials;

♦ Provides personal security for designated DOD executives, visiting foreign officials and other key officials;

♦ Performs hostage negotiations.

Minimum Prerequisites:

♦ Be a SGT (E5) or above;

♦ Two years criminal investigative experience with USACIDC (serving in MOS 95D);

♦ Demonstrated potential for successful performance under minimal supervision as a Team Chief, Special Agent in Charge or Operations Officer;

♦ Baccalaureate Degree from an accredited institution. Degree requirement may be waived to 60 semesters hours by CID command assuming applicant is otherwise qualified;

♦ Have a TOP SECRET clearance based on a Single Scope Background Investigation (SSBI).

350B. ALL SOURCE INTELLIGENCE TECHNICIAN:

Duties:

♦ Develops order of battle data through the use of information accumulated from maps and intelligence information derived from a variety of sources;

♦ Makes reliability assessments of information received through comparison with previously evaluated information on hand;

♦ Maintains close liaison with other order of battle elements and specialized intelligence activities to include counterintelligence, imagery interpretation, interrogation and language interpretation units;

♦ Ensures compliance with computer interface and operating procedures, concepts and principles as applied to ADP in the development and maintenance of the order of battle data base;

♦ Develops and maintains order of battle maps, overlays and reports to provide complete and accurate intelligence information to users;

♦ Establishes and maintains files as a basis for information to support tactical decisions;

♦ Maintains current information concerning friendly and enemy forces to include identification, disposition, personalities, combat efficiency and history;

♦ Develops and prepares enemy vulnerability studies and evaluates their significance for use in predicting probable enemy courses of action in terms of disposition, capabilities and intentions;

♦ Supervises order of battle operations.

Minimum Prerequisites:

♦ Be a SGT (E5) or above;

♦ Have a minimum of four years operational experience as a working analyst in MOS 96B in at least two assignments;

♦ Have successfully completed course 243-96B10, Intelligence Analyst;

♦ Be a BNCOC graduate;

♦ Have a current Special Background Investigation (SBI) or Single Scope Background Investigation (SSBI);

♦ Be eligible for access to Sensitive Compartmented Information (SCI).

Preferred Qualifications:

♦ Be at least a SGT(P)/E5(P) or above;

♦ Have a minimum of 3 NCOERs with one in a leadership position;

♦ Provide a written recommendation from a senior All Source Intelligence Technician who has direct knowledge of the applicant's technical ability;

♦ Possess an Associate Degree from an accredited college or university.

350D. IMAGERY INTELLIGENCE TECHNICIAN:

Duties:

♦ Provides technical expertise and manages activities engaged in imagery interpretation activities;

♦ Acts as the chief of a platoon, section, detachment or team performing imagery interpretation;

♦ Identifies changes of terrain, equipment locations, troop movements or other information that contributes to intelligence;

♦ Identifies equipment by nomenclature and location to develop assessments of possible threat to U.S. forces;

♦ Develops summaries and prepares reports on imagery interpretation findings;

♦ Establishes and maintains files on imagery interpretation data, findings, records and reports;

♦ Develops map overlays which reflect changed tactical information;

♦ Conducts intelligence briefings based on information obtained.

Minimum Prerequisites:

♦ Be a SGT (E5) or above;

♦ Have a minimum of four years operational experience as an Imagery Analyst in MOS 96D in at least two assignments;

♦ Have successfully completed course 242-96D10, Imagery Analyst;

♦ Be a BNCOC graduate;

♦ Have a current Special Background Investigation (SBI) or Single Scope Background Investigation (SSBI);

♦ Be eligible for access to Sensitive Compartmented Information (SCI).

Preferred Qualifications:

♦ Be at least a SGT(P)/E5(P) or above;

♦ Have a minimum of 3 NCOERs with one in a leadership position;

♦ Provide a written recommendation from a senior Imagery Intelligence Technician who has direct knowledge of the applicant's technical ability;

♦ Possess an Associate Degree from an accredited college or university.

350L. ATTACHE TECHNICIAN:
Duties:
♦ Meets with foreign and U.S. visitors, guests and government representatives ranging to the highest levels of government and civilian structure; must be capable of discussing matters of national level policy interest;

♦ Coordinates operations and operational support of the Defense Attache Office;

♦ Applies regulations, directives and procedures necessary for managing HUMINT collection operations;

♦ Correlates information regarding operational travel, fiscal matters, personnel and materiel resources, collection strategies and HUMINT requirements into a tactical collection management plan;

♦ Serves as a principal advisor to the Defense Attache in matters encompassing Defense Intelligence Agency, Department of State, Army, Navy, Air Force, Marine Corps and policies and procedures of other agencies in the operations and operational support arenas;

♦ Advises other Defense Attache Office personnel and visitors regarding matters of security, protocol, military courtesies and public affairs;

♦ Reads, interprets and prepares intelligence information reports, technical reports, electrical communications and other data;

♦ Authenticates budgets, purchase orders, obligation liquidation documents, requests for supplies and any other correspondence necessary to ensure office support.

Minimum Prerequisites:
♦ Be a SGT (E5) or above;
♦ Hold MOS 71L with an ASI E4;
♦ Be a BNCOC graduate;
♦ Have at least two assignments and a minimum of four years operational experience in the Defense Attache System (DAS);

♦ Applications must be submitted within two years of completion of the last DAS assignment;

♦ Successfully complete course 3A-FB/243-F2, Attache Staff Operations at the Defense Intelligence College, Washington, DC;

♦ Have a current Special Background Investigation (SBI) or Single Scope Background Investigation (SSBI);

♦ Be eligible for access to Sensitive Compartmented Information (SCI);

♦ Provide a written recommendation from a senior Attache Technician who has direct knowledge of the applicant's technical ability.

Preferred Qualifications:
♦ Be at least a SGT(P)/E5(P) or above;
♦ Have a minimum of 3 NCOERs with one in a leadership position;
♦ Possess an Associate Degree from an accredited college or university.

351B. COUNTERINTELLIGENCE TECHNICIAN:
Duties:
♦ Conducts investigations/operations by applying sound judgment and analytical reasoning methods to detect and prevent acts of espionage, sabotage and terrorism directed against Army activities;

♦ Supervises investigative/operational and administrative personnel;

♦ Manages investigative/operational elements of varying size commensurate with skill and experience level;

♦ Prepares, reviews and approves investigative/operational reports of investigations and inspections;

♦ Performs terrorism counteraction analysis and threat analysis;

♦ Investigates national security crimes of Army interest as defined by regulation, the UCMJ or applicable U.S. Code;

♦ Conducts and supervises both overt and covert investigations;

♦ Supervises the technical performance of subordinate military and civilian personnel in related job skills;

♦ Develops, evaluates and manages sources and informants of military intelligence;

♦ Develops and approves investigative plans;

♦ Obtains and executes arrest and search warrants in coordination with the Criminal Investigations Division or the FBI;

♦ Interviews and interrogates witnesses, suspects and subjects, as well as obtains written statements executed under oath;

♦ Represents the Army's interests in investigations conducted collaterally with the DOD, Department of Justice and other federal, state or local investigative agencies.

Minimum Prerequisites:
♦ Be a SGT (E5) or above;

♦ Have a minimum of four years operational experience as a Counter-intelligence Agent in MOS 97B in at least two assignments;

♦ Have successfully completed course 244-97B20, CI Agent;

♦ Be a BNCOC graduate;

♦ Have a current Special Background Investigation (SBI) or Single Scope Background Investigation (SSBI);

♦ Be eligible for access to Sensitive Compartmented Information (SCI).

Preferred Qualifications:
♦ Be at least a SGT (P)/E5 (P) or above;

♦ Have a minimum of 3 NCOERs with one in a leadership position;

♦ Provide a written recommendation from a senior Counterintelligence Technician who has direct knowledge of the applicant's technical ability;

♦ Possess an Associate Degree from an accredited college or university.

NOTE: If the applicant is a Polygraph Institute graduate (ASI 8), 18 months of operational experience as a polygrapher is required.

351E. HUMAN INTELLIGENCE COLLECTION TECHNICIAN:
Duties:
♦ Interrogates, translates and interprets as defined by regulation, the UCMJ and other applicable regulations and agreements;

♦ Conducts and supervises both tactical and strategic interrogation related duties;

♦ Supervises the technical performance of subordinate military and civilian personnel in related job skills;

♦ Develops and approves interrogation, documents translations, plans and missions;

♦ Advises the support element on the best employment of interrogation assets;

♦ Coordinates closely with other intelligence and non-intelligence agencies in the performance of interrogation and debriefing duties;

♦ Writes, reviews and approves interrogation reports which include document translations and limited technical intelligence reports;

♦ Performs language support in the form of translations or interpreter duties when required.

Minimum Prerequisites:
♦ Be a SGT (E5) or above;

♦ Have a minimum of four years operational experience as an Interrogator in MOS 97E in at least two assignments;

♦ Have successfully completed course 241-97E10, Interrogator;

♦ Be a BNCOC graduate;

♦ Be qualified as a linguist with DLPT rating of R2/S2/L2 in one foreign language as verified by a current DA Form 330 (Language Proficiency Questionnaire). Test must have been taken within the past

year and a copy of the DA Form 330 must accompany the application;
♦ DLAB score of 89 or higher;
♦ Final SECRET clearance based on a National Agency Check (NAC).

Preferred Qualifications:
♦ Be at least a SGT(P)/E5(P) or above;
♦ Have a minimum of 3 NCOERs with one in a leadership position;
♦ Provide a written recommendation from a senior Human Intelligence Collection Technician who has direct knowledge of the applicant's technical ability;
♦ Possess an Associate Degree from an accredited college or university;
♦ Obtain an R3/S3/L3 in a foreign language.

352C. TRAFFIC ANALYSIS TECHNICIAN:
Duties:
♦ Manages personnel and equipment to collect, process, locate, identify and analyze SIGINT/EW intercept;
♦ Performs reporting in accordance with SIGINT/EW directives to produce combat information and intelligence;
♦ Establishes priorities of intercept missions for acquisition of desired traffic;
♦ Prioritizes intercept missions for acquisition of desired traffic;
♦ Coordinates SIGINT/EW analytical projects;
♦ Advises and assists commanders and staff officer in formulation plans for SIGINT/EW activities.

Minimum Prerequisites:
♦ Be a SGT (E5) or above;
♦ Have a minimum of four years operational experience as an Interrogator in MOS 98C in at least two assignments;
♦ Have successfully completed course X3ABR20230A, EW/SIGINT Analyst 98C;

♦ Be a BNCOC graduate;
♦ Have a current Special Background Investigation (SBI) or Single Scope Background;
♦ Be eligible for access to sensitive compartmented information (SCI).

Preferred Qualifications:
♦ Be at least a SGT(P)/E5(P) or above;
♦ Have a minimum of 3 NCOERs with one in a leadership position;
♦ Provide a written recommendation from a senior Traffic Analysis Technician who has direct knowledge of the applicant's technical ability;
♦ Possess an Associate Degree from an accredited college or university.

352D. EMITTER LOCATION/ IDENTIFICATION TECHNICIAN:
Duties:
♦ Manages personnel and technical equipment assets engaged in establishment and employment of ELI activities operating or being prepared for operation in a communications and/or electronics intelligence environment;
♦ Performs site surveys incidental to ELI equipment deployment;
♦ Supervises installation, calibration, adjustment and testing of ELI equipment;
♦ Analyzes and evaluates the effectiveness of ELI techniques;
♦ Supervises the operation of communications and cryptologic equipment in support of ELI operations.

Minimum Prerequisites:
♦ Be a SGT (E5) or above;
♦ Have a minimum of four years operational experience in MOS 98D in at least two assignments;
♦ Have successfully completed course 231-98D, EW/SIGINT Emitter Identifier Locator;
♦ Be a BNCOC graduate;

♦ Have a current Special Background Investigation (SBI) or Single Scope Background Investigation (SSBI);

♦ Be eligible for access to Sensitive Compartmented Information (SCI).

Preferred Qualifications:
♦ Be at least a SGT(P)/E5(P) or above;

♦ Have a minimum of 3 NCOERs with one in a leadership position;

♦ Provide a written recommendation from a senior Emitter Location/ Identification Technician who has direct knowledge of the applicant's technical ability;

♦ Possess an Associate Degree from an accredited college or university.

352G. Voice Intercept Technician:
Duties:
♦ Conducts, manages and gives operational direction for use of IEW personnel and equipment;

♦ Performs site selection of OPSEC quality control for deployed EW assets;

♦ Ensures voice intercept operators follow established procedures and techniques;

♦ Supervises intercept, transcription and translation of designated foreign communications;

♦ Advises commanders and staff officers on the employment, deployment and utilization of voice intercept personnel;

♦ Defines and advises the commanders on language problem areas.

Minimum Prerequisites:
♦ Be a SGT (E5) or above;

♦ Have a minimum of four years operational experience in MOS 98G in at least two assignments;

♦ Have successfully completed course X3AZK085ZZ, EW/SIGINT Voice Intercept, 98G;

♦ Be a BNCOC graduate;

♦ Be qualified in at least one foreign language with a DLPT of R2/L2 verified on the DA Form 330. Test must have been taken within the past year and a copy of the DA Form 330 must accompany the application;

♦ DLAB score of 89 or higher;

♦ Have a current Special Background Investigation (SBI) or Single Scope Background Investigation (SSBI);

♦ Be eligible for access to Sensitive Compartmented Information (SCI).

Preferred Qualifications:
♦ Be at least a SGT(P)/E5(P) or above;

♦ Have a minimum of 3 NCOERs with one in a leadership position;

♦ Provide a written recommendation from a senior Voice Intercept Technician who has direct knowledge of the applicant's technical ability;

♦ Obtain a R3/L3 in a foreign language;

♦ Possess an Associate Degree from an accredited college or university.

352H. Morse Intercept Technician:
Duties:
♦ Manages the personnel and technical assets of INSCOM intercept/EW activities;

♦ Coordinates, plans and supervises personnel engaged in intercept activity;

♦ Knows analytical techniques and has training and experience in COMINT and EW;

♦ Conducts training/employment of Morse intercept equipment and personnel;

♦ Establishes work schedules and evaluates training/performance of personnel;

♦ Conducts a continual training program to ensure Morse personnel are adept at their MOS;

♦ Advises the commander and staff officers on employment and deployment of Morse intercept operations;

♦ Conducts studies, analysis and evaluation of collection evaluation statistics and is prepared to present results to commander;

♦ Must know antenna theory and wave propagation.

Minimum Prerequisites:
♦ Be a SGT (E5) or above;
♦ Have a minimum of four years operational experience in MOS 98H in at least two assignments;
♦ Have successfully completed course 231-98H, Morse Interceptor;
♦ Be a BNCOC graduate;
♦ Have a current Special Background Investigation (SBI) or Single Scope Background Investigation (SSBI);
♦ Be eligible for access to Sensitive Compartmented Information (SCI).

Preferred Qualifications:
♦ Be at least a SGT(P)/E5(P) or above;
♦ Have a minimum of 3 NCOERs with one in a leadership position;
♦ Provide a written recommendation from a senior Morse Intercept Technician who has direct knowledge of the applicant's technical ability;
♦ Possess an Associate Degree from an accredited college or university.

352J. EMANATIONS ANALYSIS TECHNICIAN:
Duties:
♦ Manages personnel and technical equipment assets engaged in intercept and analysis of noncommunications electromagnetic emissions;
♦ Plans, organizes and supervises establishment and operation of facilities and units engaged in electronic intelligence activities;
♦ Selects sites for tactical noncommunications intercept/analysis equipment;
♦ Ensures ELINT operators and analysts follow established procedures, techniques and analytical procedures in the intercept/processing equipment, operators and analysts;

♦ Conducts training programs for noncommunications intercept operators and analysts;

♦ May be required to perform ELINT duties at a strategic site or activity.

Minimum Prerequisites:
♦ Be a SGT (E5) or above;
♦ Have a minimum of four years operational experience in MOS 98J in at least two assignments;
♦ Have successfully completed course 233-98J, Noncommunications Interceptor/Analyst;
♦ Be a BNCOC graduate;
♦ Have a current Special Background Investigation (SBI) or Single Scope Background Investigation (SSBI);
♦ Be eligible for access to Sensitive Compartmented Information (SCI).

Preferred Qualifications:
♦ Be at least a SGT(P)/E5(P) or above;
♦ Have a minimum of 3 NCOERs with one in a leadership position;
♦ Provide a written recommendation from a senior Emanations Analysis Technician who has direct knowledge of the applicant's technical ability;
♦ Possess an Associate Degree from an accredited college or university.

352K. NON-MORSE INTERCEPT TECHNICIAN:
Duties:
♦ Manages personnel and equipment assets in establishment and employment of non-Morse intercept activities;
♦ Plans, coordinates and supervises activities of personnel engaged in these operations, establishes work schedules and priorities, and evaluates performance of subordinates;

♦ Coordinates collection activities with applicable traffic analysis and cryptanalysis personnel;

♦ Plans and coordinates procedures for the performance of maintenance, calibration, adjustment and test of non-Morse intercept personnel and equipment;

♦ Establishes, directs and evaluates qualification training programs for non-Morse operations.

Minimum Prerequisites:
♦ Be a SGT (E5) or above;
♦ Have a minimum of four years operational experience in MOS 98K in at least two assignments;
♦ Have successfully completed course A-231-0045-0044, Cryptologic Technician;
♦ Be a BNCOC graduate;
♦ Have a current Special Background Investigation (SBI) or Single Scope Background Investigation (SSBI);
♦ Be eligible for access to Sensitive Compartmented Information (SCI).

Preferred Qualifications:
♦ Be at least a SGT(P)/E5(P) or above;
♦ Have a minimum of 3 NCOERs with one in a leadership position;
♦ Provide a written recommendation from a senior Non-Morse Intercept Technician who has direct knowledge of the applicant's technical ability;
♦ Possess an Associate Degree from an accredited college or university.

353A. INTELLIGENCE/ELECTRONIC WARFARE EQUIPMENT TECHNICIAN:
Duties:
♦ Manages EW/I equipment maintenance activities at organizational, direct support and general support levels;
♦ Manages the EW/I maintenance training program the prescribed load list, repair parts stockpile levels and the Essential Repair Parts Stockage List (ERPSL);

♦ Manages and supervises maintenance and supply personnel;
♦ Manages the Equipment Improvement Report (EIR) Program and Quality Assurance (QA) Program;
♦ Monitors the modification work order program and ensures the work is completed; monitors maintenance requests and the maintenance request register; monitors supply/parts requisitions and the document register, as well as historical records as required;
♦ Prepares or assists in the preparation of the material readiness report;
♦ Acts as the Contracting Officer Representative (COR) or Assistant Contracting Officer Representative (ACOR);
♦ May be assigned as a platoon leader, maintenance facility Officer In Charge (OIC) or Detachment OIC/Commander for general support maintenance detachment activities.

Minimum Prerequisites:
♦ Be a SGT (E5) or above;
♦ Have a minimum of four years operational experience in any CMF 33 MOS in at least two assignments;
♦ Have successfully completed course 102-33S10 EW, Intercept Systems Repair;
♦ Be a BNCOC graduate;
♦ Have a current Special Background Investigation (SBI) or Single Scope Background Investigation (SSBI);
♦ Be eligible for access to Sensitive Compartmented Information (SCI).

Preferred Qualifications:
♦ Be at least a SGT(P)/E5(P) or above;
♦ Have a minimum of 3 NCOERs with one in a leadership position;
♦ Provide a written recommendation from a senior Intelligence and EW Equipment Technician who has direct knowledge of the applicant's technical ability;

♦ Possess an Associate Degree from an accredited college or university.

420A. MILITARY PERSONNEL TECHNICIAN:

Duties:

♦ Manages functions which support the Army's personnel management system;

♦ Performs as Chief of Records Branch/ Personnel Actions Branch or performs similar duties in a Military Personnel Office or Personnel Services Detachment;

♦ Monitors input to the SIDPERS, OMF, EMF and other automated/manual data systems used in personnel management by use of established forms and coding procedures;

♦ Makes decisions based on a variety of information sources, personnel and command requirements;

♦ Initiates and prepares correspondence or messages to other organizations, both military and civilian, and individuals in response to requests for information, policy or guidance;

♦ Oversees word processing activities supporting the personnel activity;

♦ Interprets regulations for individuals, subordinates and commanders;

♦ Counsels individuals on personal and family member affairs, financial matters and career considerations;

♦ Supervises large numbers of military and civilian personnel engaged in specialized personnel and administrative related duties;

♦ Manages the integration of automated personnel systems into the military personnel work center;

♦ Oversees issuance of all types of orders.;

♦ Oversees the overall dispensing of customer services to include management of the personnel services center appointment systems, management of the soldier suspense program and management of the identification card system to include update of the DEERS/RAPIDS data base.

Minimum Prerequisites:

♦ Be a SGT (E5) or above;

♦ Have a minimum of four years operational experience in CMF 75 series MOS;

♦ Be a CMF 75 BNCOC graduate;

♦ Have 6 semester hours of college level English;

♦ Have 18 months experience supervising CMF 75 series soldiers documented on NCOER.

Preferred Qualifications:

♦ Have experience working in both a battalion PAC and a PSD;

♦ Have a minimum of 30 semester hours of college with at least 6 hours training in microcomputer usage and/or core office applications (word processing, spreadsheet, database);

♦ At least three NCOERs;

♦ Have a written recommendation from a senior Military Personnel Technician or Field Grade AG officer.

420C. BANDMASTER:

Duties:

♦ Commands an Army Band, responsible for unit level administration, supply and technical/tactical training;

♦ Conducts or leads instrumental musical groups, including concert bands, marching bands, orchestras and dance bands to support military or official civilian functions;

♦ Selects music to accommodate talents and abilities of musical groups and appropriate for performance to be given;

♦ Positions members within the group to obtain balance among instrumental sections;

♦ Directs groups at rehearsals and performances to achieve desired effects, such as tonal and harmonic balance, dynamics, rhythms, tempos and shadings, utilizing conducting technique, music theory, knowledge or harmony, range, characteristics of instruments and talents of individual performers;

♦ Transcribes musical compositions and melodic lines to adapt them or create a particular style for a group;

♦ Schedules tours and performances and arranges for transportation and lodging;

♦ Participates in domestic and overseas civilian and military community relations functions as a band leader representing the U.S. Army or the U.S. at the highest national and international levels;

♦ Conducts performances for broadcast through national or international television or radio facilities.

Minimum Prerequisites:

♦ Be a SGT (E5) promotable or above;

♦ Have five years musical performance experience in any CMF 97 MOS;

♦ Have one year small group supervisory experience;

♦ Be a BNCOC graduate;

♦ Have a written recommendation from an Army Band Commander or Staff Bands Officer;

♦ Submit a VHS videotape of yourself conducting a band;

♦ Applicant must attain a minimum combined score of 12.0 on the Test of Adult Basic Education (TABE).

Preferred Qualifications:

♦ Have 60 college credit hours towards a Bachelor of Music degree;

♦ Have two years small group experience;

♦ Have three years experience in band administrative activities (i.e. unit administration, operations or supply).

880A. Marine Deck Officer:
Duties:

♦ Commands Army Class A1 vessels operating on lakes, bays, sounds and coastal waters;

♦ Responsible for proper operation of vessel including discipline of crew and seaworthiness of vessel;

♦ Navigates vessel using nautical charts, area plotting sheets, compass, sextant, terrestrial bearings and electronic navigational aids;

♦ Directs course of vessel to avoid surface and underwater hazards, to include areas where ice is seen or reported;

♦ Directs operation of ship to shore radio and visual communication systems;

♦ Directs fueling, ballasting, trimming operations, and cargo stowage.

Minimum Prerequisites:

♦ Be a SGT (E5) or above;

♦ Hold MOS 88K or 88Z;

♦ Have at least three years of documented Marine experience in the Deck Department within the past five years. More years of documented Marine experience may be considered by the proponent in lieu of the five year recency requirement;

♦ Score at the 12th grade level, or above, on the Mathematics portion of the Test of Adult Basic Education (TABE);

♦ Must be certified in CMF 88 to grade per AR 56-9;

♦ Applicants must have a physical profile of not less than 222221, distance visual acuity correctable to at least 20/20 in one eye and 20/40 in the other eye, and have normal color vision based on no more than four errors in reading the pseudoisochromatic plates test.

Preferred Qualifications:

♦ Have one year of the prerequisite experience on board a Class A Army Vessel or equivalent class ship;

♦ Be a BNCOC graduate;

♦ Have a written recommendation from a senior Warrant Officer in either MOS 880A or 881A.

881A. MARINE ENGINEERING OFFICER:

Duties:

♦ Supervises and performs installation and repair of marine power plants, propulsion systems, heating and ventilation systems, as well as other mechanical plumbing and electrical equipment in ships and marine facilities;

♦ Inspects ships' machinery to determine compliance with maintenance standards and/or extent and nature of repairs required;

♦ Maintains maintenance log books and prepares maintenance reports and work orders;

♦ Implements the Army Maintenance Management System (TAMMS) as it applies to Marine material;

♦ Manages on board vessels repair parts supply.

Minimum Prerequisites:

♦ Be a SGT (E5) or above;

♦ Hold MOS 88L or 52E with ASI S2;

♦ Have at least three years of Marine experience in the Engineer Department within the past five years. More years of documented experience may be considered by the proponent in lieu of the five year recency requirement;

♦ Score at the 12th grade level, or above, on the Mathematics portion of the Test of Adult Basic Education (TABE);

♦ Must be certified in CMF 88 to grade per AR 56-9;

♦ Applicants must have a physical profile of not less than 222221, distance visual acuity correctable to at least 20/20 in one eye and 20/40 in the other eye, and have normal color vision based on no more than four errors in reading the pseudoisochromatic plates test.

Preferred Qualifications:

♦ Have one year of the prerequisite experience on board a Class A Army Vessel or equivalent class ship;

♦ Be a BNCOC graduate;

♦ Have a written recommendation from a senior Warrant Officer in either MOS 880A or 881A.

882A. MOBILITY OFFICER:

Duties:

♦ Directs and coordinates the implementation of the following systems: (Global Transportation Network (GTN), Department of the Army Movement Management System Redesign (DAMMS-R), Transportation Coordinator - Automated Command and Control Information System (TC-ACCIS) and TC-ACCIS Air-Load Module (ALM), Transportation Coordinator - Automated Information Management System (TC-AIMS II), Automated Air Load Planning System (AALPS), Air Movement Flow Table (AMFT), Computer Aided Loading and Manifesting System (CALM), Movement Tracking System (MTS), Computerized Movement Planning and Status System (COMPASS), LOGMAR/BARCODE scanners, Combat Service Support Control System (CSSCS), Global Command and Control System - Army (GCCS-A), DAMMS-R (Block III), DAMM-R (Concentrator), World wide Port System (WPS), Frequency tag system, Mobile Suscriber Equipment (MSE) and Tactical Terminal Adapters (TTA);

♦ Plans, assesses, supervises and reports convoy and cargo handling operations at company, battalion, brigade and division levels;

♦ Remains familiar with: constructing road movement/MSR overlays; preparing road movement graphs and tables; preparing traffic circulation/routing plans; use of TB 55-46-1/2; ITO functions, movement of personnel, port call and movement of unit equipment; basic seaport operations; marshaling equipment; inspection standards for sealift; theater opening procedures; US and theater of operation customs procedures; cargo movement documentation; setting up and working out of field locations; scheduling movements within a theater of operation; coordinating transportation plans; facilitating international movement by rail, highway, air and water to, within and from the theater assigned; terminal operating procedures; preparing, supervising and coordinating cargo handling and ensuring its compliance with US Army, contracted and host nation regulatory requirements; planning intra and inter theater movement by any mode of transportation.

Minimum Prerequisites:
♦ Be a SGT (E5) or above;
♦ Hold MOS 88N;
♦ Four years of documented practical experience in movement control operations, with one year in a supervisory capacity;
♦ Attain 12th grade equivalency on the Test of Adult Basic Education - A (TABE-A, Form 5/6) and include a copy of the results authenticated by the Test Control Officer or Educational Services Officer. The TABE-A is not waiverable.

Preferred Qualifications:
♦ One year experience in transportation automation systems;
♦ Be a BNCOC graduate;
♦ Minimum of six semester hours of college level computer science from a regionally accredited academic institution. Courses must be freshman level or higher and progressive (non-repetitive);
♦ Successful completion of the CLEP general examination in English or completion of six semesters of college level English.

910A. AMMUNITION TECHNICIAN:
Duties:
♦ Directs and coordinates the implementation of the following activities: Receipt, storage, issue, surveillance test, maintenance, modification, destruction, demilitarization of conventional ammunition, missile explosive components and non-nuclear items;
♦ Investigates and reports conventional ammunition accidents, failures or malfunctions;
♦ Serves as a Platoon or Section Leader;
♦ Supervises and manages Standard Army Ammunition Systems (SAAS) at unit level and its associated ADP equipment;
♦ Prepares and/or reviews ammunition storage waivers; fire fighting procedures for conventional and special ammunition; emergency destruction of munitions, missiles and special weapons; as well as policies and procedures for surveillance of chemical, biological and nuclear material wastes.

Minimum Prerequisites:
♦ Be a SGT (E5) with six years ammunition field experience in MOS 55B, 55D or 55Z;
♦ BNCOC graduate from a feeder MOS and meet Personnel Reliability Program requirements of AR 50-6;
♦ Enclose a written recommendation from a CW3-5 from within the applicant's organization who holds the WO MOS the applicant is applying for. In organizations where no WO in the correct MOS is available, a letter of recommendation from a senior WO in the correct MOS from a supporting ammunition unit can be substituted.

Preferred Qualifications:
♦ SSG with 7-9 years experience in feeder MOS with three years in a supervisory position;

◆ Have 30 college credit hours with a minimum of six credit hours of college level English.

912A. LAND COMBAT MISSILE SYSTEMS TECHNICIAN:
Duties:

◆ Employs digital switching theory, logic, computer fundamentals and infrared fundamentals applicable to the MLRS, TOW, TOW2, BRADLEY Fighting Vehicle Sub-system (BFVS), DRAGON and associated man-portable common thermal night sights;

◆ Applies theory and fundamentals of solid state devices and optics employed in guidance and sighting systems;

◆ Directs test procedures, diagnostic system analysis and troubleshooting techniques, as well as organizational maintenance responsibilities and unit state reporting requirements for tactical units;

◆ Interprets technical data and instructs subordinates in technical aspects of support missile systems;

◆ Manages the automated Maintenance Reporting and Management System (MRMS), technical supply and shop supply procedures;

◆ Manages supply, equipment, facilities and personnel in the maintenance of supported land combat missile systems, associated equipment and training devices;

◆ Advises commanders on technical aspects of land combat missile system maintenance, support, testing and supply;

◆ May be assigned as the Section Chief of the land combat missile support section of a forward support company or as a Platoon Leader for the land combat platoon section.

Minimum Prerequisites:
◆ Be a SGT (E5) or above;

◆ Six years electronics maintenance shop experience in MOS 27E, 27M, 27T, 27Z, 35B or 35M;

◆ BNCOC graduate from a feeder MOS;

◆ Enclose a written recommendation from a CW3-5 from within the applicant's organization who holds the WO MOS the applicant is applying for. In organizations where no WO in the correct MOS is available, a letter of recommendation from a senior WO in the correct MOS from a supporting maintenance unit can be substituted.

Preferred Qualifications:
◆ SSG with 7-9 years electronics maintenance DS/GS shop experience in a feeder MOS with three years in a supervisory position;

◆ Have 30 college credit hours with a minimum of six credit hours of college level English.

913A. ARMAMENT REPAIR TECHNICIAN:
Duties:

◆ Manages activities and personnel engaged in Forward and Intermediate Direct Support (IDS) maintenance level repair of small arms and forward field artillery weapons;

◆ Directs procedures for the identification and troubleshooting of malfunctions in electrical, hydraulic, fire control and instrument items;

◆ Establishes evacuation and replacement procedures of such items that are unserviceable and beyond the repair capabilities of forward support and IDS companies;

◆ Manages Quality Assurance and production control programs to ensure established work standards are met and repairs are made on a timely basis;

◆ Administers the Army Maintenance Management System (TAMMS) and the

Maintenance Reporting and Management System (MRMS);
♦ Administers regulations and procedures pertaining to physical security, accountability and shipment of weapons;
♦ Directs contact teams in support of field units and activities;
♦ Establishes and directs a shop safety program;
♦ Establishes a technical library and examines, interprets and disseminates technical material, including orders and bulletins.

Minimum Prerequisites:
♦ Be a SGT (E5) or above with six years field experience in MOS 45B, 45D, 45E, 45G, 45K, 45N or 45T;
♦ BNCOC graduate from a feeder MOS;
♦ Enclose a written recommendation from a CW3-5 from within the applicant's organization who holds the WO MOS the applicant is applying for. In organizations where no WO in the correct MOS is available, a letter of recommendation from a senior WO in the correct MOS from a supporting maintenance unit can be substituted.

Preferred Qualifications:
♦ SSG with 7-9 years armament repair Shop experience in a feeder MOS with three years in a supervisory position;
♦ Have 30 college credit hours or vocational training in electronics or computers.

914A. ALLIED TRADES TECHNICIAN:
Duties:
♦ Directs the setup, operation and maintenance of machine tools and welding equipment used to fabricate or repair parts, mechanisms, tools and machinery;
♦ Manages automotive body repair, painting, glass, radiator, canvas and woodworking shop operations;

♦ Supervises and conducts recovery operations and maintenance of tracked and wheeled recovery equipment;
♦ Employs principles of mechanics, metals identification procedures, shop mathematics and shop layout;
♦ Establishes and directs the upkeep of shop stock, repair parts and maintenance related items required per applicable regulations;
♦ Manages Quality Assurance and production control programs to ensure established work standards are met and repairs are made on a timely basis;
♦ Establishes training programs to ensure subordinates are qualified in current maintenance techniques and equipment operation;
♦ Coordinates shop activities with other repair shops to ensure equipment is quickly repaired and returned to user;
♦ Employed in Direct Support (DS)/ General Support (GS) companies and performs additional officer duties as required by unit mission;
♦ Establishes and conducts a shop safety program.

Minimum Prerequisites:
♦ Be a SGT (E5) or above;
♦ Six years field experience in MOS 44B or 44E;
♦ BNCOC graduate from a feeder MOS;
♦ Active military applicants from other services must have received their technical welding or machinist training at the U.S. Army Ordnance Center and School Joint Metalworking Training Department;
♦ Enclose a written recommendation from a CW3-5 from within the applicant's organization who holds the WO MOS the applicant is applying for. In organizations where no WO in the correct MOS is available, a letter of recommendation from a senior WO in the correct MOS from a supporting maintenance unit can be substituted.

Preferred Qualifications:

♦ SSG with 7-9 years allied trades, welding or machine shop experience in a feeder MOS with three years in a supervisory position;

♦ Have 30 college credit hours or vocational training in welding or machine technology.

915A. UNIT MAINTENANCE TECHNICIAN (LIGHT):

Duties:

♦ Plans, organizes and executes unit level maintenance of wheeled vehicles, light track vehicles (less Bradley), self propelled artillery systems, as well as fire control, armament, ground support and power driven chemical equipment;

♦ Diagnoses, tests and analyzes malfunctions of unit equipment;

♦ Directs the establishment and operation of unit prescribed load lists for organizational repair and maintenance related items;

♦ Establishes and enforces shop fire and safety programs;

♦ Manages unit calibration requirements and unit level oil analysis program;

♦ Prepares unit level readiness reports;

♦ Writes and updates internal SOPs for maintenance areas;

♦ Directs emergency recovery and repair for all unit equipment;

♦ Manages the Army Maintenance Management System (TAMMS) at unit level; scheduling of periodic maintenance and services, dispatch of passenger, cargo and combat vehicles, as well as requisitioning and exchange of repair vehicles and disposal of POL products;

♦ Establishes internal procedures to receive, issue and store tools, parts, publications and POL products.

Minimum Prerequisites:

♦ Be a SGT (E5) or above;

♦ Six years field experience in MOS 63B, 63D, 63E, 63H, 63S, 63T, 63Y or 63Z;

♦ BNCOC graduate from a feeder MOS;

♦ Possess a minimum of one year of unit level maintenance (organization maintenance) supervisory experience and have that experience documented on an NCOER;

♦ Enclose a written recommendation from a CW3-5 from within the applicant's organization who holds the WO MOS the applicant is applying for. In organizations where no WO in the correct MOS is available, a letter of recommendation from a senior WO in the correct MOS from a supporting maintenance unit can be substituted.

Preferred Qualifications:

♦ SSG with 7-9 years unit level maintenance (organizational) or DS/GS maintenance shop experience with a minimum of three years supervisory experience at the unit level (organizational) motor pool as a Company, Troop and/or Battery Motor Sergeant or Maintenance Team Chief;

♦ Have 30 college credit hours with an accredited institution, one year of automotive maintenance vocational training or possess current Automotive Service Excellence (ASE) certifications.

916A, ASI-6D. HIGH-TO-MEDIUM ALTITUDE AIR DEFENSE (HIMAD) DIRECT SUPPORT/GENERAL SUPPORT MAINTENANCE TECHNICIAN (PATRIOT):

Duties:

♦ Employs digital switching theory, logic, computer fundamentals and theories, as well as fundamentals applicable to the HIMAD missile systems;

♦ Directs test procedures, diagnostic system analysis and troubleshooting techniques, as well as direct/general support maintenance responsibilities and unit status reporting for missile support units;

♦ Instructs subordinates in operating procedures, maintenance techniques used in care of special tools and supporting equipment, as well as the Army Maintenance Management Systems (TAMMS). Advises the commander on the technical aspects of the HIMAD missile system maintenance, support, testing and supply;

♦ Manages the automated Maintenance Reporting and Management System (MRMS), technical supply and shop supply;

♦ Manages supply, equipment, facilities and personnel in the performance of maintenance of HIMAD missile systems, associated equipment and training devices;

♦ Supervises maintenance and repair of organic tools, test sets and associated training equipment.

Minimum Prerequisites:
♦ Be a SGT (E5) or above;
♦ Six years experience in MOS 27X;
♦ BNCOC graduate from a feeder MOS;
♦ Enclose a written recommendation from a CW3-5 from within the applicant's organization who holds the WO MOS the applicant is applying for. In organizations where no WO in the correct MOS is available, a letter of recommendation from a senior WO in the correct MOS from a supporting maintenance unit can be substituted.

Preferred Qualifications:
♦ SSG with 7-9 years PATRIOT field experience in the feeder MOS with three years in a supervisory position;
♦ Have 30 college credit hours with a minimum of six credit hours of college level English.

917A. MANEUVER FORCES AIR DEFENSE SYSTEMS TECHNICIAN:
Duties:
♦ Employs digital switching theory, logic, computer, as well as theory and fundamentals of solid state devices employed in the MFAD systems;

♦ Directs test procedures, diagnostic system analysis and troubleshooting techniques;

♦ Directs maintenance responsibilities and unit status reporting for missile support units;

♦ Interprets technical data and instructs in technical aspects of support missile systems;

♦ Manages the automated Maintenance and Management Reporting System (MRMS), technical supply and shop;

♦ Manages supply, equipment, facilities and personnel in the maintenance of the MFAD systems, associated equipment and training devices;

♦ Advises commanders on technical aspects of the MFAD system maintenance, support, testing and supply;

♦ Supervises maintenance and repair of organic tools, test sets and associated training equipment;

♦ Supervises the activities of personnel engaged in isolating technical malfunctions and repair of supported missile systems.

Minimum Prerequisites:
♦ Be a SGT (E5) or above;
♦ Six years experience in MOS 27E, 27M, 27T, 27Z, 35B or 35M;
♦ BNCOC graduate from a feeder MOS;
♦ Enclose a written recommendation from a CW3-5 from within the applicant's organization who holds the WO MOS the applicant is applying for. In organizations where no WO in the correct MOS is available, a letter of recommendation from a senior WO in the correct

MOS from a supporting maintenance unit can be substituted.

Preferred Qualifications:
- SSG with 7-9 years electronics maintenance experience in a feeder MOS with three years in a supervisory position;
- Have 30 college credit hours with a minimum of six credit hours of college level English.

918A. TEST, MEASUREMENT, DIAGNOSTIC EQUIPMENT (TMDE) MAINTENANCE SUPPORT TECHNICIAN:

Duties:
- Commands a TMDE Maintenance Support Detachment/Team and is responsible for morale, welfare, training, UCMJ and discipline of assigned personnel;
- Manages activities and personnel engaged in calibration and repair of Test, measurement and Diagnostic Equipment (TMDE), as well as calibration standards and accessories;
- Interprets and analyzes measurement data and specifications, as well as supervises calibration and repair of equipment, instruments or gauges to conform to specified standards;
- Develops procedures for testing and diagnosing malfunctions or implements established guidance to adjust or repair Army materiel requiring calibration and repair maintenance;
- Interprets technical data and schematics on all secondary transfer and secondary reference standards and trains subordinates in the use and operation of this materiel;
- Instructs personnel on metrology skills;
- Certifies accuracy of instrumentation and ensures that accuracy is traceable to higher level standards;
- Performs error analysis on measurement systems;
- Determines calibration and repair requirements and establishes work priorities;
- Assigns work to subordinates and assures proper repair and/or calibration through quality control inspections of in-process work and by final inspections and test of completed work;
- Manages, utilizes and trains assigned support personnel on the Tactical Army Combat Service Support Computer System (TACCS) in support of the Calibration Management Information System (CALMIS) which includes production control operations;
- Develops software applications for TACCS and ensures the system's security;
- Participates with division and higher level staffs in developing contingency/deployment plans, field exercises, maintenance management schemes and other staff actions that relate to TMDE support.

Minimum Prerequisites:
- Be a SGT (E5) or above;
- Six years experience in MOS 35H;
- BNCOC graduate from a feeder MOS;
- Enclose a written recommendation from a CW3-5 from within the applicant's organization who holds the WO MOS the applicant is applying for. In organizations where no WO in the correct MOS is available, a letter of recommendation from a senior WO in the correct MOS from a supporting maintenance unit can be substituted.

Preferred Qualifications:
- SSG with 7-9 years electronics maintenance DS/GS shop experience in a feeder MOS with three years in a supervisory position;
- Have 30 college credit hours with a minimum of six credit hours of college level English.

918B. Electronic Systems Maintenance Technician:

Duties:
♦ Manages personnel, equipment and facility assets for the installation, operation, repair, maintenance and modification of radio, radar, computer, electronic data processing, controlled cryptographic items, television, navigation, avionics and related commu-nications equipment and associated tools, test sets and accessory equipment;

♦ Receives and inspects incoming equipment to determine requirements, assigns work to subordinates and assures proper repair through quality control inspections of in-process work and the final inspections and test of completed work;

♦ Ensures that maintenance programs include regular preventive maintenance;

♦ Plans, coordinates and supervises maintenance activities and programs, develops repair and operating procedures and interprets technical publications and data for use in repair and maintenance functions.

Minimum Prerequisites:
♦ Be a SGT (E5) or above;

♦ Six years experience in MOS 35B, 35C, 35D (93D), 35E, 35F, 35H, 35J, 35L, 35N, 35Q (68Q), 35R (68R), 35W, 35Y, 39B, 68P, 31P or 31S (with 29V or 29Y maintenance background respectively);

♦ BNCOC graduate from a feeder MOS;

♦ Enclose a written recommendation from a CW3-5 from within the applicant's organization who holds the WO MOS the applicant is applying for. In organizations where no WO in the correct MOS is available, a letter of recommendation from a senior WO in the correct MOS from a supporting maintenance unit can be substituted;

♦ Applicants substituting civilian technical training and experience as construction equipment or power generation mechanics must provide documentation that supports their level of technical training and experience as mechanics comparable to that of a feeder MOS, BNCOC graduate.

Preferred Qualifications:
♦ SSG with 7-9 years electronics maintenance DS/GS shop experience in a feeder MOS with three years in a supervisory position;

♦ Have 30 college credit hours with a minimum of six credit hours of college level English;

♦ Obtain a Commercial Electronic Certificate such as Federal Communication Commission (FCC), National Institute for Certification in Engineering Tecnology (NICET) or International Society of Certified Electronic Technicians (ISCET).

919A. Engineer Equipment Repair Technician:

Duties:
♦ Manages, supervises and coordinates the organization and DS/GS maintenance activities for engineer equipment;

♦ Oversees the repair of power generating, earthmoving, earth shaping, earth compacting, earth lifting, earth loading, quarrying, rock crushing, road surfacing, water purification, water distribution, refrigeration, air conditioning, water gap crossing, POL transferring and engineering electronic equipment.

Minimum Prerequisites:
♦ Be a SGT (E5) or above;

♦ Six years experience in MOS 52D, 52X, 62B or 63B;

♦ BNCOC graduate from a feeder MOS;

♦ Enclose a written recommendation from a CW3-5 from within the applicant's organization who holds the WO MOS the applicant is applying for. In organizations where no WO in the correct MOS is available, a letter of recommendation from a senior WO in the correct MOS from a supporting maintenance unit can be substituted.

Preferred Qualifications:
◆ SSG with 7-9 years of unit (organizational) or DS/GS maintenance shop experience in a feeder MOS with three years in a supervisory position;
◆ Have 30 college credit hours or one year of automotive, electronics or power generation related, maintenance vocational technical training or possess current Automotive Service Excellence (ASE) certifications.

920A. PROPERTY ACCOUNTING TECHNICIAN:
Duties:
◆ Supervises the technical aspects of unit property book records per AR 710-2;
◆ Performs in both manual and automated property book accounting environments with the related functions associated with accurate property accountability;
◆ Monitors and performs evaluations of subordinates supply operations per Command Supply Discipline Program (CSDP) and AR 710-2;
◆ Performs financial inventory accounting as applied to the Army's budgeting system. Performs property accounting duties at the unit and organization levels or on division property book teams;
◆ Complies with appropriate regul-ations, forms and procedures pertaining to property books, hand receipts and other property accounting documents.

Minimum Prerequisites:
◆ Be a SGT(P) or above;
◆ Minimum of six years most recent experience in MOS 92Y;

◆ BNCOC or ANCOC graduate in MOS 92Y;
◆ Have documented a minimum of two years experience of serving as a Property Book NCO or Property Book Officer (applicants not meeting this prerequisite must have other documentation indicating their knowledge and skills of property book accounting and management experience);
◆ Have documented a minimum of one year successfully serving in a supervisory and/or leadership position;
◆ Provide a hard (paper) copy of three NCOERs which reflect recent outstanding and exceptional duty performance ratings in MOS 92Y. Copy of three NCOERs must be provided even if already on service member's fiche;
◆ Have completed a minimum of six credit hours of college level English. Successful completion of the English College Level Examination Program (CLEP) is the only acceptable substitute. Speech is not considered an English substitute. No waivers for the above prerequisites will be favorably considered.

Preferred Qualifications:
◆ SGT E5(P) or above with a minimum of 700 promotion points;
◆ Where applicable, it is strongly encouraged that each applicant (especially those with less than 7 years service) enclose a letter of recommendation from a senior Property Accounting Technician.

920B. SUPPLY SYSTEMS TECHNICIAN:
Duties:
◆ Instructs, manages and supervises personnel within a Technical Supply or Supply Support Activity (SSA) concerning supply systems policy and functional procedures;

♦ Responsible for managing the receipt, storage and issuance of supplies and equipment at the technical supply or DSU level in accordance with established policies and regulations;

♦ Plans stockage level requirements for stockage and control based on accumulation of demand data;

♦ Controls management of operational float stocks to ensure compliance with Army policy;

♦ Inspects supported units to ensure stockage levels do not exceed prescribed levels;

♦ Provides technical guidance to personnel of supported units and activities in order to assist, establish and maintain adequate stockage levels for mission accomplishment;

♦ Conducts periodic inventories of stockage supply items, initiates action for disposition of excesses and makes recommendations for changes to the authorized list (ASL);

♦ Develops standard operating procedures and performs administrative duties related to the supply activity.

Minimum Prerequisites:

♦ Be a SGT(P) or above;

♦ Minimum of six years most recent experience in MOS 92A;

♦ BNCOC graduate in MOS 92A;

♦ Have documented a minimum of two years experience in Material and Stock Control Accounting, plus one year of Warehouse Storage Operations;

♦ It is essential that each applicant have documented the formal stock record accounting experience in at least two of the following areas: Stock Control NCO, Material Accounting NCO, Class IX Commodity Manager, Item Manager or Functional Analyst. This entails working with stock record accounts at the COSCOM or Division Material Management Centers (MMC) or nondivisional DSU/SSA;

♦ Have certified and documented training in at least one of the Army's several automated supply systems such as DS4, SAILS, or SARRS-O;

♦ Have documented a minimum of one year successfully serving in a supervisory and/or leadership position;

♦ Provide a hard (paper) copy of three NCOERs which reflect recent outstanding and exceptional duty performance ratings in MOS 92Y. Copy of three NCOERs must be provided even if already on service member's fiche;

♦ Have completed a minimum of six credit hours of college level English. Successful completion of the English College Level Examination Program (CLEP) is the only acceptable substitute. Speech is not considered an English substitute. No waivers for the above prerequisites will be favorably considered.

Preferred Qualifications:

♦ SGT E5(P) or above with a minimum of 700 promotion points;

♦ Where applicable, it is strongly encouraged that each applicant (especially those with less than 7 years service) enclose a letter of recommendation from a senior Supply Systems Technician.

921A. AIRDROP SYSTEMS TECHNICIAN:

Duties:

♦ Provides technical guidance to commanders and staff of activities with the mission of conducting/receiving airborne and/or airdrop operations;

♦ Supervises inspection of parachutes and parachute components to detect flaws in materials and workmanship;

♦ Supervises packing of parachutes;

♦ Ensures that unserviceable, nonrepairable and overage parachutes are retired from inventory;

♦ Supervises airdrop rigging activities and airdrop equipment maintenance activities;

♦ Maintains compliance standards and criteria for life support systems and other airdrop equipment.

Minimum Prerequisites:
♦ Be a SSG or above;

♦ Minimum of eight years most recent experience in MOS 92R;

♦ BNCOC or ANCOC graduate in MOS 92R;

♦ Have documented a minimum of two years experience supervising operations in a packing shed, repair shop, cargo airdrop facility or storage warehouse;

♦ Jumpmaster qualified and completed the Airdrop Load Inspectors Course;

♦ Provide a hard (paper) copy of three NCOERs which reflect recent outstanding and exceptional duty performance ratings in MOS 92R. Copy of three NCOERs must be provided even if already on service member's fiche. Due to the low density and the single annual certification, a significant amount of accession qualifications is placed on enlisted training in MOS 92R, field experience and peer recommendations. Therefore, this specialty is closed for transition of officers;

♦ Have completed a minimum of six credit hours of college level English. Successful completion of the English College Level Examination Program (CLEP) is the only acceptable substitute. Speech is not considered an English substitute. No waivers for the above prerequisites will be favorably considered.

Preferred Qualifications:
♦ Where applicable, it is strongly encouraged that each applicant (especially those with less than 7 years service) enclose a letter of recommendation from a senior Airdrop Systems Technician;

♦ Applicants exceeding 12 years Active Federal Service (AFS) must be approved by HQDA.

922A. FOOD SERVICE TECHNICIAN:
Duties:

♦ Coordinates and supervises the Food Service Program for installations, commands or organizations to include dissemination of information, managing personnel, determining technical training requirements, developing and conducting training for officer, enlisted and civilian personnel, as well as developing management plans for food service;

♦ Develops and coordinates implementation of dining facility modernization and new construction programs;

♦ Develops, coordinates and monitors budget requirements for food service equipment and expendable supplies for both garrison and field requirements;

♦ Plans, trains and implements changes in nutritional awareness programs, modification of menus and implementation of low calorie menus;

♦ Coordinates with Troop Issue Subsistence Activities (TISA) and Class I points to ensure availability of appropriate subsistence for both garrison and field manuals to ensure adequate timely resupply and reconfiguration of non-unitized field rations into nutri-tionally acceptable menus;

♦ Evaluates field feeding requirements and develops milestone plans to support major field exercises;

♦ Reviews and monitors requisitions for Class I, III, and IX supplies to support food service operations and coordinates all planning for food service support for field training;

♦ Evaluates garrison and field feeding operations to ensure food service personnel are complying with food service regulations relative to food preparation, service, accountability and sanitation;

♦ As a contracting officer representative (COR), inspects full food service contract dining facilities to determine if they are in compliance with the terms of the contract.

Minimum Prerequisites:
♦ Be a SGT(P) or above;
♦ Minimum of six years most recent experience in MOS 92G/94B;
♦ Have completed BNCOC or ANCOC in MOS 92G or the new MOS designation of 92G and have documented a minimum of one year successfully serving in a supervisory and/or leadership position;
♦ Provide a hard (paper) copy of three NCOERs which reflect recent outstanding and exceptional duty performance ratings in MOS 92G/94B. Copy of three NCOERs must be provided even if already on service member's fiche;
♦ Have completed a minimum of six credit hours of college level English. Successful completion of the English College Level Examination Program (CLEP) is the only acceptable substitute. Speech is not considered an English substitute. No waivers for the above prerequisites will be favorably considered.

Preferred Qualifications:
♦ SGT E5(P) or above with a minimum of 700 promotion points;
♦ Where applicable, it is strongly encouraged that each applicant (especially those with less than 7 years service) enclose a letter of recommendation from a senior Food Service Technician.

WOCS OVERVIEW:
WOCS trains Warrant Officer Candidates in the fundamentals of leadership and basic military skills. WOCS instills professional ethics, evaluates and develops candidates' leadership potential and prepares those who qualify for appointment as WO1 in the Active Army, the Army National Guard or the U.S. Army Reserve.

The course length is six weeks (30 training days) for Active Army classes, and four weeks (28 training days) for Reserve Component classes.

The academic portion of the course is taught by instructors from the General Studies Branch at the academic complex and by Training, Advising and Counseling (TAC) Officers in the company area and other training sites. Candidates are evaluated academically through performance and written examinations. TAC Officers conduct both objective and subjective evaluations to determine each candidate's potential to become a successful Warrant Officer.

WOCS is divided into three major phases. The centralized selection board that selects candidates to attend WOCS is the first phase; WOCS is the second phase.

Course instruction consists of basic skills, standardized evaluation and training, leadership and ethics, communicative arts, military history, structure of the Army, support functions and other common military subjects. Training, Advising and Counseling (TAC) Officers conduct both objective and subjective eval-uations to determine each candidate's potential to become a successful Warrant Officer. Candidates are academically evaluated through performance and written examinations.

Course curriculum includes the following subjects:
♦ History of the Warrant Officer Corps;
♦ Physical Well Being and Total Fitness;
♦ Military Law;
♦ Stress and Battlefield Leadership;
♦ Risk Assessment;
♦ Special Leadership Issues;
♦ Effective Communication Skills;
♦ Computer Skills;
♦ Military Briefing;
♦ Army Leadership;
♦ Code of Conduct/Survival, Escape and Evasion;
♦ Environmental Awareness;
♦ Military Publications and Record Keeping;
♦ Training Management;
♦ Map Interpretation;

- Ethics and Leadership;
- Threat;
- Military History;
- Structure of the Army;
- Army Operations and Doctrine;
- Signal Operating Instructions;
- Operational Security;
- Nuclear, Biological and Chemical Defense;
- Squad/Platoon Defense;
- Officer and Noncommissioned Officer Evaluations;
- Army Maintenance Management System;
- Personnel Systems;
- Army Supply System;
- Personal Affairs Readiness;
- Customs, Traditions and Courtesies of the Service;
- Officer Professional Development Seminar.

TAC Officers all perform the same basic mission: they train, advise, council, develop, evaluate and make recommendations concerning the progress of each candidate. They demand the maximum performance of which candidates are capable and strive to set an example for the candidates to follow. Candidates must meet the course prerequisites and graduation requirements to move to phase three.

Phase three is the Warrant Officer Basic Course (WOBC) conducted by each candidates proponent school.

WOCS PREREQUISITES:

All applicants must:
- Meet all application and selection prerequisites outlined by the Warrant Officer Procurement Program, the Centralized Selection Board, and DA Circular 601-94-1;
- Be medically qualified IAW chapter 2 of AR 40-501. Candidates cannot possess a profile that limits Army Physical Fitness Test (APFT) or full participation in rigorous physical training;

- Meet the height/weight screening criteria of the Army Weight Control Program. Soldiers who exceed weight standards will be measured for percentage of body fat. Soldiers exceeding body fat standards are eliminated and processed IAW AR 600-9;
- Possess an initial issue of serviceable clothing as outlined in AR 670-1, and AR 700-84. Military clothing is discussed in depth later in this chapter;
- Upon arrival at Fort Rucker, candidates must take and pass an initial standard APFT (pushups, situps and 2 mile run). To pass, candidates must achieve a minimum score of 180 points, with 60 points in each of the three events. No alternate events are allowed. Those who fail are denied enrollment.

PERSONAL CONDUCT & APPEARANCE STANDARDS:

Upon arrival, candidates must present a neat, professional appearance. Report with a fresh haircut and a sharp uniform. The WOCS standard is 1/4 inch on top and 1/8 inch on the sides. As a Warrant Officer Candidate, you must act and look like the officer that you are striving to become.

Finances:

Make sure that your debts are in order before beginning the course. Make arrangements for payments of bills while you are in training. Take extra precautions to ensure that finance has your records in order and that you are paid when and where you specify. Any reports of indebtedness or bad checks may result in your removal from training until the problem is resolved. Recurring problems of this nature may result in elimination.

Alcoholic Beverages and Tobacco Use:

Consumption or possession of alcoholic beverages or tobacco products by students assigned to WOCS is strictly forbidden. This restriction applies from the date of sign in to date of departure, regardless of status (i.e., snowbird, active class, administrative/medical hold, or holdover). If you are a user of tobacco products and believe that you will have severe withdrawal symptoms, it is highly recommended that you see your local medical authorities for help. Violation of this restriction is grounds for immediate elimination.

Static Items:

A static item is anything that duplicates an item that you display for inspections, or an inspectable item that is hidden for the purpose of evading inspection. You can be eliminated from the course for having static items once you begin training. You will have ample opportunity to store extra items in a security room on your first day of active training, so do not throw these duplicate type items away. If you wait until arrival at HHC to purchase the required items, you will avoid purchasing unnecessary items that may be considered "static".

Injuries:

In the event that an injury occurs or you have a profile when arriving at the WOCS report it as soon as possible to cadre for evaluation. The training pace at 1st WOC is fast and an unreported injury may jeopardize your successful completion of WOCS. Candidates placed on medical/administrative hold will perform duties within the limits of their profile, as directed by the unit First Sergeant or Operations Sergeant.

STUDENT RECYCLE:
Academic Recycle:

After coordination with appropriate personnel command and individual's unit, commandants may recycle a student once. Coordination of academic recycling of reserve component students will be through the local reserve component liaison office. Academic recycle should be limited to extraordinary circumstances, i.e., when a student shows significant leadership potential or based on the needs of the Army.

Medical or Emergency Recycles:

Commandants may recycle students who (through illness, injury, emergency leave or other unavoidable training absence) miss a significant portion of training after coordination with appropriate personnel command and individual's unit.

PREPARATIONS:
Clothing & Equipment Requirements:

Verify that you have the military clothing required for the course. Please refer to Tables WOCS-B and WOCS-C for a list of military clothing requirements for males and females, respectively. Refer to Tables WOCS-D and WOCS-E for a list of required items and authorized items, respectively.

If you are reporting from Basic Training and have uniforms that do not fit you (too large, too small, etc.), report to supply for a direct exchange. CTA 50-900 (paragraph 8b) authorizes Reserve Component Warrant Officer Candidates to receive 2 additional sets of BDUs from their unit supply prior to arrival. Candidates attending the WOCS in a TDY or ADT status wear the unit patch of their current or last unit. All others wear the Aviation Center patch. Ensure that all name tapes, patches and authorized badges are properly sewn on in accordance with current requirements of AR 670-1.

Interservice transfers are authorized to have all patches sewn on at government expense. The Clothing Sales store has a deferred payment plan available for purchases over $50.00 and less than a $200.00 unpaid balance.

Wait until you get to HHC to mark your equipment to ensure it is marked IAW the WOC guide.

Unauthorized Items:

Certain clothing items, equipment and products are not permitted to for use during WOCS. These are items that are considered to give candidates an unfair advantage over others. Refer to the Table WOCS-F for a list of unauthorized items.

ITEM	REQUIRED QTY	ADDITIONAL OPTIONAL QTY	REMARKS
Table: WOCS-B			
Inventory Form - Male Personnel			
Bag	0	1	Duffel
Belt	1		Web, black, subdued tip
Belt	1		Web, black, brass tip
Boots	2 pairs	1 pair	Combat, black leather, for the field
Buckle	1		Belt, brass
Buckle	1		Belt, subdued - black
Cap	2		Camouflage, EHWBDU/HWBDU/TBDU (1 cap for each type BDU or 2 if all BDUs the same)
Cap	1		Garrison - AG489
Coat	1		All weather, black, with liner
Coat	1		AG489
Coat	4	2	Camouflage, EHWBDU/HWBDU/TBDU, 6 BDUs are authorized, any type acceptable any type acceptable
Field Jacket	1		Camouflage
Gloves	2 pairs		Wool, inserts
Gloves	1 pair		Black, leather, shell
Gloves	1 pair		Black, leather, unisex, dress
Handkerchief	6		Cotton, white or brown
Necktie	1		Black, not clip on
Shirt	1		Long sleeve, AG415 gray-green
Shirt	2		Short sleeve, AG415 gray-green
Shoes	1 pair		Dress, black, poromeric
Socks	2 pairs		Black, cotton-nylon or polynylon
Socks	7 pairs		Black, cushion sole
CW Bottom,	1	1	PFU, gray
CW Top	1	1	PFU, gray
HW Top	2	2	PFU, gray
HW Bottom	2	2	PFU, Gray
Towel	5	2	Brown, cotton
Trousers	2		Dress, AG489
Trousers	4	2	Camouflage, EHWBDU/HWBDU/TBDU, 6 BDUs are authorized, any type acceptable
Undershirt	2		White, cotton
Undershirt	7		Brown, cotton, for wear under BDU top
Underwear	7		White or brown, Jockey or Boxer
Washcloth	6	4	Brown, cotton
Cap	1		Watch, black, knit (PT)

NOTE: The above list shows military clothing items required to be displayed and/or accounted for throughout the course. Mix and match of above BDUs (EHWBDU or HWBDU) is authorized.

ITEM	REQUIRED QTY	ADDITIONAL OPTIONAL QTY	REMARKS
Table: WOCS-C			
Inventory Form - Female Personnel			
Bag	0	1	Duffel
Belt	1		Web, black, subdued tip
Belt	1		Web, black, brass tip
Boots	2 pairs	1 pairs	Combat, black leather, for the field
Brassieres	5	2	Sports brassieres authorized
Buckle	1		Belt, brass
Buckle	1		Belt, subdued - black
Cap	2		Camouflage, EHWBDU/HWBDU/TBDU (1 cap for each type BDU or 2 if all BDUs the same)
Cap	1		Garrison - AG489
Coat	1		All weather, black, with liner
Coat	1		AG489
Coat	4	2	Camouflage, EHWBDU/HWBDU/TBDU, 6 BDUs are authorized, any type acceptable any type acceptable
Field Jacket	1		Camouflage
Gloves	2 pairs		Wool, inserts
Gloves	1 pair		Black, leather, shell
Gloves	1 pair		Black, leather, unisex, dress
Handkerchief	6		Cotton, white or brown
Necktab	1		Back
Shirt	1		Long sleeve, AG415, gray-green
Shirt	2		Short sleeve, AG415, gray-green
Shoes	1 pair		Dress, black, paromeric
Skirt	1		Female, AG489
Slacks	1		Female, AG489
Socks	2 pairs		Black, cotton-nylon or polynylon
Socks	7 pairs		Black, cushion sole
CW Bottom,	1	1	PFU, gray
CW Top	1	1	PFU, gray
HW Top	2	2	PFU, gray
HW Bottom	2	2	PFU, gray
Towel	5	2	Brown, Cotton
Trousers	2		Dress, AG489
Trousers	4	2	Camouflage, EHWBDU/HWBDU/TBDU, 6 BDUs are authorized, any type acceptable
Undershirt	2		White, cotton
Undershirt	7		Brown, cotton, for wear under BDU top
Underwear	7		White
Washcloth	6	4	Brown, cotton
Cap	1		Watch, black, knit (PT)

NOTE: The above list shows military clothing items required to be displayed and/or accounted for throughout the course. Mix and match of above BDUs (EHWBDU or HWBDU) is authorized.

Table WOCS-D		
Required Items Inventory		
ITEM	QUANTITY	REMARKS
Shoes	1 pair	Civilian, running, serviceable
Socks	6 pairs	White, athletic, crew length
Shoes	1 pair	Shower
Shoe Polish	1 can	2.5 oz
Shoe Brush	1	
Brass Polish	1	Tube / Can
Toothpaste	1	Tube / Container
Toothbrush	1	
Padlock	1	Combination preferable
Shoe Trees	2 pairs	
Scotch Tape	1 roll	Clear, double-stick
Stationary	1 box	Box, with paper, envelopes & lid
Medical Tape	2 rolls	White, 1"
Note cards	2 packs	3" x 5", double-side ruled
Note cards	1 pack	3"x 5", plain on at least one side
Headband	1	Helmet, leather

NOTES:
   In accordance with TRADOC Regulation 351-10, candidates are advised of the required purchase of the above listed items for course attendance.
   The required quantity is also the authorized quantity. Duplicate type items are considered "Static" items and could be grounds for elimination from the program. Prior to purchasing any additional items, verify with your WOCS TAC Officer that you are authorized to possess them.
   Understand that you may purchase required items prior to your arrival at Fort Rucker. However, waiting until you sign in at WOCS to purchase the listed items will better ensure you get the correct items (e.g., color, type, etc).

Table WOCS-E		
Authorized Item Inventory		
ITEM	QTY	REMARKS
"FOR SALE" Sign	4	Plastic, 12" x 8"
"FOR SALE" Sign	4	Plastic, 12" x 7"
Board	1	Sock rolling, wooden
Ruler	1	Metal, sewing type, 6"
Binder Rings	2 to 4	Metal, 2"
Money Clips	4 to 6	4 1/2", stainless steel
Marker / Highlighter	1	
Marker	2	Laundry, black & white
Marker	1	Permanent, black
Emblem Refinisher	2 Bottles	M-NU, Black
Leather Dye	1 Bottle	2.5 oz., plastic bottle only
Lint Brush / Roller	1	
Q-tips	1 Box	
Rags	As Needed	
Knife	1	Small, for paper cutting
Scissors	1	Paper cutting
Iron	1	Steam or dry
Storage box	1	No longer than 10" in height x 10" in width x 15" in length

NOTE: The above list shows items authorized to possess throughout the course.

Table: WOCS-F
Unauthorized Items Inventory
ITEM
Armor All or similar products
Barber clippers
BDU cap stiffeners
Boot blousing weights and forms
Brass box for pre-punching identification cards
Civilian clothes
Commercial cleaners and waxes (not issued by supply)
Computer (other than pocket size or smaller)
Correction tape or fluid (White-out)
Flashlights (other than issued road guard equipment)
Furniture polish
Hair dryers (male only)
Leather luster, Shape-Up or glisten spit shine
Mirrors, personal
Neutral shoe polish, liquid shoe polish or clear liquid waxes
Pre-shined shoe polish lids
QM, Blitz cloth or Never Dull brass cleaners
Sewn-in all weather coat and field jacket liners
Sole and edge dressing
Spray lacquer or poly sealants
Starch, spray or box
Steel wool and scouring pads
Typewriter
Velcro fasteners on uniforms in place of buttons and snaps

NOTES:

The above list indicates those items which have been identified as unauthorized for possession or use while attending WOCS. Possession or use of unauthorized items may result in elimination from the school for attempting to gain an unfair advantage over fellow candidates or for failure to comply with course guidelines and standards.

If you have any questions concerning the use of any products or aids, ask your TAC Officer. If you are not authorized to use an item, it does not mean that you have to throw it away. Storage locations are available. Coordinate with your TAC Officer(s) to place all unauthorized items (except for flammables) in the security room or class amnesty box.

Any questions on items inventories should be addressed to the XO of HHC, WOCC. For further information call
DSN: 558-1287;
COMM: (334) 255-1287.

Applications:
Follow these steps in preparing applications for WOCS.

Step 1:
Review AR 135-100 (Appoint-ment of Commissioned and Warrant Officers of the Army).

Step 2:
Meet the following nonwaiverable requirements:
♦ US Citizenship;
♦ General Technical (GT) score of 110 or higher;
♦ High school graduate or have a GED;
♦ Possess a minimum SECRET security clearance (Interim is acceptable to apply);
♦ Pass the Standard Army APFT (Army Physical Fitness Test);
♦ Pass Appointment/Flight Physical.

Step 3:
Visit the Warrant Officer Recruititng website at http://www.usarec.army.mil/hq/warrant. A sample packet can be viewed and downloaded and all forms can be downloaded for use with Formflow or Adobe Acrobat software.

Step 4:
Ensure you meet the minimum prerequisites listed for the WO Military Occupational Specialty (MOS) for which you will apply. If you do not, you must either wait until you do or request a prerequisite waiver.

Step 5:
Assemble applications, an original and 1 copy. Do not send a partial application with the intention of sending the missing documents later.

Step 6:

Once application is complete, take the application to your Personnel Services Detachment (PSD)/Military Personnel Division (MPD) for review and endorsement. Applications without endorsement will not be processed. Your PSD/MPD will either mail the application to the address in step 12 or give you the endorsement for you to mail with your application. Non-Army personnel can skip this step and submit their application directly to the address indicated in step 12. After mailing, your handling of the application is complete, and personnel at US Army Recruiting Command (USAREC) control the remaining processing.

Step 7:

A WO recruiter screens the application for completeness and accuracy. You will be notified of any discrepancies by phone, email or regular mail using the contact information in blocks 17 & 19 of your DA Form 61.

Step 8:

Application is forwarded to proponent for technical evaluation. 153A (Aviator) applications skip this step unless an age waiver is required. Allow 4-6 weeks. Proponent qualified applications are board ready if no waivers are needed and steps 9 & 10 are skipped. Application is returned if you are not qualified.

Step 9:

Applications requiring a moral waiver (block 26 of the DA Form 61 is answered YES) are forwarded to Army Reserve Personnel Command (AR-PERSCOM), St. Louis, MO. Allow 4-6 weeks.

Step 10:

Applications requiring an Active Federal Service (AFS) waiver (12 or more years active service) or an Age waiver (Aviator applicants who are 29 years of age or older by the convene date of the board) are forwarded to the Deputy Chief of Staff for Personnel (DCSPER) at HQDA. Allow 4-6 weeks.

Step 11:

Accession boards are held bimonthly at USAREC starting in March. At least one WO from your requested WO MOS branch will sit on the board. The board's vote results in one of the following designations:

♦ **Fully Qualified - Selected (FQ-S):** Congratulations you will go to school in approximately 4-6 months;

♦ **Fully Qualified - Not Selected (FQ-NS):** Your application will be considered by one more board;

♦ **Not Competitive - Not Selected (NC-NS):** Considered by 2 boards, not selected, and packet destroyed. If still eligible, you may reapply 1 year from the date you signed original DA Form 61.

Step 12:

You can update your application at any time with awards, NCOERs, transcripts, APFT, resume, letters, etc. Send updates to:

Commander, HQ USAREC
ATTN: RCRO-SM-A
1307 3rd Ave.
Ft. Knox, KY 40121-272

NLT the 1st of the month in which board convenes.

Step 13:

Names of those selected are posted to Warrant Officer Recruiting website NLT the 10th of the month following the board. A complete list of those selected and those considered but not selected is sent to each PSD/MPD.

Application Checklist:

Samples of all statements and waivers listed below are included at the end of the chapter.

1. DA FORM 61 must be completed using the example on the recruiting web page. Pay particular attention to the following areas:

♦ Block 21 - list all colleges attended with either degree/credits and the graduation or expected graduation date;

♦ Block 26 - check your enlistment records for exact information (exclude traffic violations involving a fine of $250.00 or less);

♦ Block 41 - must be in the following format: "I certify that (Applicant's Name) successfully passed the APFT consisting of pushups, situps and the two mile run with a score of (APFT Score) on (APFT Date); the verified height is (Applicant's Height) and verified weight is (Applicant's Weight)." with your data entered and commanders signature block beneath. The Army standard 3 event APFT is the only acceptable test and must have been taken within the past six months. Applicants who do not meet height/weight standards of AR 600-9 must submit a Body Fat Content Worksheet signed by their Commander;

♦ Ensure you sign and date block 42 before forwarding your application;

2. Transcripts are required to verify all education and must show course title, credit hours awarded and grade received, i.e. English 101, 3 hours, A. Copies are acceptable;

3. DA Form 160 must be completed as in the example on the recruiting web page;

4. If required, submit one request for each moral or prerequisite waiver needed. Submit an Active Federal Service (AFS) or age waiver using the prerequisite format at the end of the chapter;

5. Statement of Understanding for appointment as a Warrant Officer, type verbatim;

6. Memorandum from your Security Manager stating security clearance level, the agency that granted it, and the date granted. A copy of your DA Form 873 will not meet this requirement;

7. All applications (other than Flight) require an appointment physical initiated within the last 2 years, IAW AR 40-501, chapter 2. Blocks 5 and 77, or blocks 16 and 46 - depending upon the version of SF88 - must reflect WOC Appointment, WOC School, Warrant Officer Commissioning or similar wording; flight applicants see paragraph 15;

8. The Official Military Personnel File (OMPF), microfiche or hard copy, is required regardless of rank. Any documents missing or deleted from the fiche can be submitted as certified true copies. Include training certificates, transcripts, award certificates, certificates of achievement, evaluations, etc. that are not on the fiche. A copy can be obtained by writing:

Commander, USAREC
ATTN: PCRE-RP
8899 E. 56th Street
Indianapolis, IN 46249-5301;
DSN: 221-3732;
COMM: (703) 325-3732;
DSN: 699-3685 (FAX);
COMM: (317) 510-3685 (FAX).

SGTs or above with NCOERs on file can phone, fax or mail their requests. SGTs and above with no NCOERs on file and SPCs or below must send a written request by mail or fax; include complete name, social security number and signature in the request (visit the PERSCOM website for additional information);

9. DA Form 2A and 2-1, or Enlisted Record Brief (ERB), dated within the past 90 days are required for all applicants. Other services will submit their military personnel service record instead of these documents;

10. An official DA photo (digitized or 4" x 10", color) is required. Other services photos are acceptable as long as they are taken in the Class A uniform (digitized or 4" x 10", color). In exceptional cases, deployed soldiers who do not have a Class A uniform available may have a photo taken in their duty uniform;

11. Company and Battalion Commanders letters of recommendation should be 3-5 paragraphs with specific, quantifiable comments about your character and tactical and technical competence. Use memo format and address to President, Warrant Officer Accession Board. Non-Army personnel will use the first two Commissioned Officers in their UCMJ chain of command. A letter from a Senior Army Warrant Officer (SWO) (CW3-5) from the MOS for which you are applying is the only other letter that will appear in front of the board. If applying for 153A (Aviator), see paragraph 15 below. The letter from the SWO is not required for all applicants (check the WO MOS prerequisites),

but is strongly recommended. Letters must be less than 90 days old. You may use letters from your previous chain of command if you had a recent PCS or change of command;

12. Prepare a resume using the example format at the end of the chapter. You must use this format; however, you can lengthen or shorten the resume as needed. Make sure you sign and date the resume;

13. Take completed application to your PSD/MPD for review and endorsement prior to mailing to USAREC;

14. Non-Army service members have additional requirements and can visit the Warrant Officer Recruiting website for a list of these requirements;

15. Below requirements are for MOS 153A, (Aviator) applicants only:
♦ Class 1 flight physical approved by US Army Aeromedical Center
ATTN: MCXY-AER
Ft Rucker, Alabama 36362-5333.
DSN: 558-7430/2
COMM: (334) 255-7430/20.
Flight physicals cannot be older than 18 months from the date initiated. Reference is AR 40-501, chapter 4;
♦ All flight applicants must be interviewed by an Army Aviator in the rank of CW3-5 or Major and above. If the Unit Commander or above is a field grade aviator, the aviator interview may be part of the commander's endorsement. In this case, the commander's endorsement must contain the same statement required for the aviator interview; use a memorandum format and start with the statement: "I have interviewed (Applicant's Name) and find (he/she) has all the needed personal characteristics, motivation, physical stamina and qualifications to be appointed a U.S. Army Reserve Warrant Officer and appears acceptable for selection into the WOFT program as a Warrant Officer Candidate." Applicants from other

military services may be interviewed by a field grade aviator from their branch of service if an Army aviator is not readily available. Army aviators will conduct the interviews whenever possible;
♦ DA Form 4989-R must be completed and signed by you (block 20) and your Commander (block 21);
♦ DA Form 6256, AFAST Score Worksheet, reflecting a score of 90 or higher (nonwaiverable).

Appointment:

WOCS graduates are appointed to Warrant Officer, grade WO1, contingent upon certification by the MOS proponent that they are technically and tactically qualified for award of an authorized Warrant Officer MOS. Certification follows successful completion of a WOBC or a proponent prescribed alternative certification method.

REPORTING INFORMATION:

Upon arriving at Fort Rucker report to the Headquarters & Headquarters Company (HHC), Building 5910, to inprocess and receive your TA-50 issue, a Warrant Officer Candidate (WOC) guide and your billeting assignment. HHC is where your class is formed and your WOCS orientation begins. Study the WOC guide, pay close attention to the information you receive (listen effectively) and take care of all administrative requirements.

Inprocessing:

Briefings and orientation periods will be conducted the day prior to training day one. You must be completely inprocessed prior to that. You will move as a class to 1st Warrant Officer Company the day prior to training day one.

BILLETING:
Dining Facility:

You will use the Aviation Center Consolidated Dining Facility. You will always march as a unit to the dining facility.

Mail:

You will be issued a mailbox when you inprocess. A sample address is:

WOC John H. Doe
123-45-6789
CMR #3, BOX # _____
Ft. Rucker, AL. 36362.

Telephones:

You may not use military phones for personal business. You may use only the pay phones located in the HHC area while in snowbird status. Once training begins, candidates will not have telephone privileges until the class earns those privileges (usually after the first 2 weeks). You are encouraged to call your family members to inform them of your safe arrival and to advise them of your new address (once you receive your P.O. box assignment). Use of cellular phones is not permitted. Storing of cellular phones in your POV is unauthorized.

Money:

Do not spend excessive amounts of money on items that you think you will need for the course. Wait until you are given your initial orientation during your stay at HHC; you will have time to purchase the items that you need. The average candidate spends $300.00-$500.00 during the six week course on laundry, personal and class expenses. If you arrive by air, one way taxi fee from Dothan Airport is $20.00-$30.00. Once training begins you are limited to a total of $250.00 cash on hand. Additional funds are authorized as needed via personal/travelers checks or ATM cards.

POV:

Park your vehicle in the designated class area. It will remain there during the remainder of your time in the WOCS. If you have a privately owned weapon (shotgun, rifle, handgun), do not store it in your vehicle. You are given time on Sundays to start and idle your vehicle to prevent battery and engine problems. Don't store anything in your POV that is in plain view.

POW:

We recommend that you leave your POW at your place of residence. If you have a POW with you, report it immediately to the HHC cadre (First Sergeant or Commander). If it is after duty hours, have the Candidate Duty Officer call the Crime Prevention Officer. You will register your weapon with the military police and store it in arms room until you complete the course. Ensure you receive a briefing on how you are to draw your weapon from the arms room when it is turned in.

CONTACT INFORMATION:

For more information, contact the recruiter that manages the WO MOS in which you are interested. For a WO MOS not listed below, you can contact any recruiter.

Use the wo-team@usarec.army.mil email address as the primary address because the recruiter may be TDY or on leave. This will ensure your emails are answered promptly.

The toll free number is 1-800-223-3735, EXT 6 and the last four digits of the phone number

Aviation - 151A & 153A:
CW3 Brenda Werner
DSN: 536-0458;
COMM: (502) 626-0458.

Field Artillery and Air Defense - 131A, 140A & 140E:
SFC Donald McConnell
DSN: 536-0457;
COMM: (502) 626-0457.

Military Intelligence - 350B, 350D, 350L, 351B, 351E, 352C, 352G, 352J, 352K and 353A:
CW3 Ronald Duquette
DSN: 536-0716;
COMM: (502) 626-0716.

Ordnance and Quartermaster - 916A, 919A & 921A:
> SFC Shane James
> DSN: 536-1860;
> COMM: (502) 626-1860.

Signal Corps and Criminal Investigation Division - 250N, 251A & 311A:
> SFC Rodney Shepard
> DSN: 536-0466;
> COMM: (502) 626-0466.

Special Forces and Adjutant General - 180A, 420A & 420C:
> CW4 Charles Clayton
> DSN: 536-0478;
> COMM: (502) 626-0478.

Transportation - 880A, 881A & 882A:
> SFC Richard Green
> DSN: 536-0465;
> COMM: (502) 626-0465.

REFERENCE:

1. US Army Formal Schools Catalog. US Army Publishing Agency. DA PAM 351-4, page 29-30, Table 3-2. 31 October 1995.
2. "Warrant Officer Recruiting Team." United States Army Recruiting Command. Online. Internet. 31 May 2000. Available: http://www.usarec.army.mil/hq/warrant.
3. "Warrant Officer Code." Online. Internet. 15 May 2000. Available: http://www.nightstalkers.com/creed/wocreed.html.

Moral Waiver

(Letterhead)

(Office Symbol)   *(Date)*

MEMORANDUM FOR COMMANDER, USAREC, FORT KNOX, KY 40121-2726

SUBJECT: Request for Moral Waiver

1. Request a waiver of the following offense: (State specifically what you were charged with. Do not just list Article 92, Article 32, etc.).

2. Date of offense: *(Month and year)*

3. Place of offense: *(City and State)*

4. Punishment imposed: *(Fine amount, forfeiture amount, extra duty, letter of reprimand, etc.)*

5. Mitigating circumstances surrounding the charge:
       Three points to address:
       (1) Accepting responsibility for your actions,
       (2) The lessons learned, and
       (3) How you now contribute to your unit, community and military service.

(Signature)
(Full Name)
(Rank)
(SSN)

A separate moral waiver request must be submitted for each offense.

Prerequisite Waiver

(Letterhead)

(Office Symbol)   *(Date)*

MEMORANDUM FOR COMMANDER, USAREC, FORT KNOX, KY 40121-2726

SUBJECT: Request for Prerequisite Waiver,
              Request for Age Waiver
              Request for Active Federal Service Waiver (AFS)
              (Select the appropriate one)

1. (State the type of waiver you are requesting)
Example: Request an age waiver.
               Request an Active Federal Service Waiver.
               Request a prerequisite waiver (state the
               prerequisite you wish to waive).

2. Give a detailed explanation why you feel this waiver should be favorably considered. Please note that waivers are approved only in unusual circumstances. Prerequisite waiver requests that do not give adequate justification, i.e. unusual skills, unique talents, special circumstances, etc. will probably be disapproved. With AFS waivers required if you have over 12 years AFS) the same principle applies and requests must be fully justified. Adequate justification might be: unusual circumstances, deployed for past year and unable to submit a packet, unusual skills, or unique talents. Asking for these waivers just because they are a part of the application will not result in approval.

(Signature)
(Full Name)
(Rank)
(SSN)

A separate waiver request must be submitted for each prerequisite.

Statement Of Understanding

(Letterhead)

(Date)

Statement of Understanding for Appointment as a Warrant Officer

      I understand that if I am appointed as a warrant officer in the Reserve of the Army with concurrent active duty, that this appointment is contingent upon technical and tactical certification by successful completion of the appropriate Warrant Officer Basic Course (WOBC) unless I have been pre-certified by the WO MOS proponent.

      I further understand that if I am appointed as a warrant officer in the Reserve of the Army without concurrent active duty, that this appointment is contingent upon technical and tactical certification by successful completion of the appropriate Warrant Officer Basic Course (WOBC) within two years of appointment unless I have been pre-certified by the WO MOS proponent or unless extended by HQDA.

      I also understand that if I am eliminated from, or fail to successfully complete the technical and tactical certification as specified above, I may be subject to discharge, under regulations in effect at that time, from the Reserve of the Army.

(Signature)
(Full Name)
(Rank)
(SSN)

Resume

NAME: WHO, You Are
RANK: Sergeant
SSN: 000-00-0000

ADDRESS: Street Address
City, State ZIP
Telephone Number
email:

UNIT: HHC, III Corps
Fort Hood TX 76544
DSN: 738-7411
email:

OBJECTIVE: To obtain an appointment as a warrant officer, USAR, in MOS 153A, Aviator

CIVILIAN EDUCATION: (This *should agree with Block 21 of the DA Form 61)*

Bachelor of Science, University of Maryland, College Park, MD; Associate of
Arts, Central Texas College, Killeen, TX;
Diploma, Orchard View High School, Muskegon, MI

MILITARY EDUCATION: List in order from most recent to training first attended/completed.

12 Jan 97 - 11 Apr 97
BNCOC
US Army Soldier Support Center
Fort Jackson, SC

List individual accomplishments first.
If distinguished graduate or honor
graduate, then **bold** or <u>underline</u> this
achievement, however, do not use
special effects to excess. Stress MOS
related subjects.
How is school relevant?
Indicating Mid-level management school
or just listing the scope is not very
descriptive.

6 Aug 95 - 1 Sep 95
PLDC
NCO Academy
Camp Jackson, Korea

Resume is very important, shows your
ability to communicate in written form.
Make it reader-friendly; limit acronyms.

1 Feb 93 - 12 Mar 93
Personnel Management Specialist
US Army Soldier Support Center terms.
Fort Jackson, SC terms.

You will have board members unfamiliar
with your MOS so use easily understood
Write at the 12th grade level;
use a thesaurus to help with vocabulary.
Spelling and grammar errors will doom
a packet; ensure you do spell and
grammar checks.

Can list correspondence courses but not sub courses

Resume Continued

MILITARY EXPERIENCE:

Jul 97 - Present
Enlisted Assignments NCO
HHC, III Corps
Fort Hood, TX

Jul 94 - Jun 97
Records NCO
Ft Jackson, SC

Jun 93 - Jun 94
Levy Clerk
A Det. 516th PSB
APO AP 96205, Korea

List **ALL** military assignments

Concise job description focusing on the unique characteristics of your specific position. List outstanding achievements and extra duties while assigned to position.

Can underline or **Bold** any significant achievements, impact awards, receipt of unit coins or certificates of achievement.

Focus on measurements of success. Not a job description, but how well you did the job. Use NCOER bullets as a reference. **Bold** or underline deploy ments or make a separate assignment entry if deployment was for several months.

CIVILIAN EXPERIENCE PERTINENT TO MOS 153A:

Jan 90 - Dec 90
Secretary
Kelly Temporary Services
Grand Rapids, MI

Use same guidance as above. Explain any relevant experience or training you obtained that pertains to the requested warrant officer MOS. if your civilian experience is not relevant the leave this entire section blank.

SUMMARY:

Write a paragraph or two explaining why you are fully qualified to perform the duties of a warrant officer in your skill and how your selection will benefit the Warrant Officer Corps and the United States Army. This is a very important part of the resume. Remember the acronym BLUF for Bottom Line Up Front. Make this a call to action but do so without turning off the reader. State why you should be selected. Mention below-the-zone promotions, impact awards, noteworthy distinctions while in training / schools, deployments, and other significant achievements/ accomplishments. Use these factors in explaining that you should be selected because you are exceptionally qualified and have all the leadership skills needed. it is a good idea to restate all of your significant accomplishments / achievements in your summary of why you should be selected.

SIGNATURE & DATE

NOTE: Use plain white paper, black ink and 12 point font. Use a standard font such as Arial or Times New Roman. Don't go through a big expense. Prepare the resume yourself, but do a quality job. If you are non-Army, the resume takes on increased importance in conveying your qualifications to become an Army Warrant Officer

NOTES

APPENDIX-A

ADDITIONAL INFORMATION

U.S. ARMY JOHN F. KENNEDY SPECIAL WARFARE CENTER; SC: 331 FORT BRAGG, NC 28307–5000

a. Generally, government quarters are available for all student personnel. When students cannot be housed on post, off–post facilities are available in the civilian communities adjacent to Fort Bragg.

b. Government mess is available for enlisted, officer, and civilian students.

c. Transportation information is as follows:
(1) Grannis Airport, Fayetteville, North Carolina, is located 20 miles from Fort Bragg. Commercial limousine service is available to Fort Bragg.
(2) Commercial taxis are available on and off post.
(3) Government transportation is available only for official business.
(4) Commercial air transportation ticket purchasing and reservations office (SATO) is located on main post, Fort Bragg.

d. Uniform: The battle dress uniform is the normal prescribed duty uniform for most courses. The Class A uniform will be required for payday muster formation and graduation upon completion of some courses. Seasonal Class A/B uniform is normally required for certain officer and officer/enlisted courses, although the fatigue uniform is required for selected blocks of instruction and for all Special Forces training. Uniform change dates are the second week in April (to summer) and the third week in October (to winter).

e. Reporting instructions are as follows:
(1) All students, except as indicated below, arriving for training at USAJFKSWCS during duty hours report to the Student Personnel Service Center, Bryant Hall, Building D–3206, Room 105, located on Ardennes Street between Reilly and Community Access Roads, Fort Bragg, NC. After duty hours and holidays, students should report to SDNCO, located in the adjacent building, Kennedy Hall, Bldg D–3004, located on Ardennes Street, between Reilly and Community Access Roads, Fort Bragg, NC.
(a) Combat Diving Qualification, Combat Diving Supervisor and Diving Medical Technician students report to Bldg KW–100, Trumbo Point Annex, Naval Air Station, Key West, FL
DSN: 483–4152;
COMM: (305) 293–4152.
(b) Effective 1 October 1995, students to the Military Free Fall Jumpmaster Course, 2E–F56/011–F15, will report to Building 303, Yuma Proving Grounds, Yuma, AZ
DSN: 899–2880/2768
COMM: (520) 328–2880/2768.
(2) Army students must report with the following documentation:
(a) Active Army PCS students must report with complete 'hard copy' 201 file.
(b) Active Army TDY students report with a current copy of their DD Form 93, SGLI, DA Form 2A, and DA Form 2–1.
(c) Army National Guard and US Army Reserve students, regard-less of travel status, must report with complete 'hard copy' 201 file.
(3) Possession of a current physical examination is required for the following courses: SF Diving Medical Technician, SF Combat Diving Supervisor, SF Combat Diver Qualification, Military Free Fall Parachutist, Military Free Fall Jumpmaster, SERE High Risk (Level C), SF Assessment and Selection, SF Weapons Sergeant, SF Engineer Sergeant, SF Medical Sergeant, SF Communications Sergeant and SF Detachment Officer Qualification. Students to these courses must also bring their complete medical records.
(a) Physical approval authority for SF Diving Medical Technician, SF Combat Diving Supervisor, SF Combat Diver Qualification, Military Free Fall Parachutist, Military Free Fall Jumpmaster, and SERE High Risk (Level C) courses is as follows:
(1) Army students: Surgeon's Office at division, division equivalent, or group level.
(2) Air Force students: Air Education and Training Command.
(3) Other services and agencies: US Army Special Operations Command Medical Training Division. Physical must be

submitted NLT 45 days prior to the start
date of the course.
(b) Physical approval authority for all students
to SF Assessment and Selection, SF Weapons
Sergeant, SF Engineer Sergeant, SF Medic-al
Sergeant, SF Communications Sergeant, and
SF Detachment Officer Qualification is
USASOC Medical Training Division.
Physicals must be submitted NLT 45 days prior
to the start date of the course.
(c) Students should not be permitted to travel
to the school without an approved current
physical examination.
(4) Students attending courses 56 days and longer
will bring a DA Form 705 (APRT card) complete
with the current APRT test score.
(5) Student personnel attending courses that are
required to perform parachute jumps will bring
DA Form 1307 (jump log).
(6) Students attending the 18E (SF Commo Sgt)
or the Advanced International Morse Code
course must have possession of a current audio
perception test filed in their medical records.
(7) Students should check PCS orders prior to
reporting with dependents to ensure concurrent
travel authorization. Failure to do so may result in
hardship and inconvenience.

f. Additional school information may be obtained
from the following:
(1) CMF 18 and AOC 18A course:
Cdr, 1st Bn 1st SWTG (A)
ATTN: AOJK–GPA
Fort Brag, NC 28307–5000.
DSN: 239–4343;
COMM: (910) 432-4343.
(2) Special Forces advanced skills courses:
Cdr, 2nd Bn, 1st SWTG (A)
ATTN: AOJK–GPB
Fort Bragg, NC 28307–5000.
(DSN: 239–5473;
COMM: (910) 432-5473.
(3) Civil Affairs, PSYOPS, and language courses:
Cdr, 3rd Bn, 1st SWTG (A)
ATTN: AOJK–GPC
Fort Bragg, NC 28307–5000.
DSN: 239–6504;
COMM: (910) 432-6504.
(4) Reporting information:
Cdr, Co A, Spt Bn, 1st SWTG (A)
ATTN: AOJK–SPD–SP
Fort Bragg, NC 28307–5000.
DSN: 239–4096;
COMM: (910) 432-4096.

Reference:
US Army Formal Schools Catalog. US Army
Publishing Agency. DA PAM 351-4, page 115, Table
3-19. 31 October 1995.

U.S. ARMY INFANTRY SCHOOL; SC: 071 FORT BENNING, GA 31905–5007

a. Generally, government quarters are available for
student personnel. When on–post quarters are not
available, Off–post quarters are available through
Off–Post Housing Referral Service.

b. Mess facilities are available for enlisted students.
Officer students have access to student messes and
an officer's field ration mess in the 'Follow Me
Dining' facility located in Building 73.

c. Transportation information is as follows:
(1) Columbus Municipal Airport, Columbus,
Georgia, is located approximately 12 miles from
Fort Benning. Commercial taxi service is available
to and from Fort Benning.
(2) Commercial local bus service is available at
the bus stop located on main post. Commercial
long distance bus service is available in Columbus.
(3) Commercial taxis are available on and off–
post.
(4) Government bus service is available on and
off–post.

d. The Battle Dress Uniform is the normal prescribed
uniform for all courses. Seasonal Class A Uniform is
required for selected blocks of instruction and
reporting.

e. Reporting instructions are as follows:
(1) Students arriving at Fort Benning will report
to one of the following locations, depending on
the course they are to attend:
(a) Airborne students report to Building 2747,
Airborne, IRP, on Main Post NLT 1200 hours
on report date.
(b) Ranger students report to Building 5000 in
Harmony Church. Students report NLT 1200
report date.
(c) Sniper students report to BLDG 4475,
Harmony Church, between 0800–1200, in PT
uniform for inprocessing. Additionally, Sniper
students must arrive with the following items of
TA50 equipment for the class: 1 Ruck Sack
with Frame, 1 2–Qt or 2 1–Qt Canteens, 1
Poncho with liner, 1 Entrenching Tool. The
school will provide all other required items.

Reference:
US Army Formal Schools Catalog. US Army
Publishing Agency. DA PAM 351-4, page 43, Table 3-
6. 31 October 1995.

WARRANT OFFICER CAREER CENTER; SC: 020 FORT RUCKER, AL 36362–5000

a. General information applicable to all students attending the Warrant Officer Career Center (WOCC) is identified in this paragraph. Please check supplemental information in paragraphs b, c, and d.

(1) Generally, government quarters are available for all student personnel. When students cannot be housed on post, off–post facilities are available.

(2) Government mess is mandatory for candidates, seven days a week. At present, officer personnel will receive a statement of non–availability for meals.

(3) Transportation: Dothan Airport, Dothan, Alabama, is located 22 miles from Fort Rucker. Taxi/bus service from Dothan Airport to Fort Rucker is available.

(a) Commercial local and long distance bus service is available at bus terminal on Fort Rucker.

(b) Commercial taxis are available on/off post.

(c) Government transportation is available for official business.

(4) Reporting: All students report to 1st Warrant Officer Company, Building 5801, on Andrews Avenue (two blocks west of the Aviation Museum).

(a) Students should check orders upon receipt and verify authorization for dependent travel, POVs, or shipment of household goods. Failure to do so may result in inconvenience and hardship.

(b) Students must meet height/weight standards as specified in AR 600–9 to be eligible for this training.

b. Supplemental instructions for Warrant Officer Candidates (WOCs):

(1) Forward three copies of orders to
        Commander,
        1st Warrant Officer Company,
        Fort Rucker, AL 36362–5000
NLT 30 days prior to class start date.

(2) Hand carry military personnel records jacket and medical records; do not bring dental records. This also applies to USAR and ARNG soldiers ordered to active duty for training or TDY and return status. Failure to bring these records may preclude training and appointment to warrant officer.

(3) Soldier must possess appropriate security clearance/investigation status IAW AR 135–100, paragraph 1–4H, and AR 611–112 (minimum of SECRET).

(4) WOCs must report in Class A uniform with current rank insignia. Clothing and equipment items for the course are identified in the 1st Warrant Officer Company Orientation Packet.

(5) Students will be housed in Buildings 5801/5909.

(6) Soldier must pass the APFT and be found medically qualified for appointment UP AR 135–100 and AR 40–501 prior to departure for WOC training. If soldier possesses a physical profile that precludes participation in the APFT without modification, the candidate is not eligible for entrance into WOC training.

(a) Upon arrival at Fort Rucker, the soldier must successfully complete a standard APFT (three events, no alternates) and start day activities. Failure to satisfactorily complete these events may result in the candidate being returned to the parent unit and loss of WOC status.

(b) If the soldier is not in compliance with any of the above, the commander will immediately notify the appropriate career manager.

(7) Upon arrival at 1st Warrant Officer Company, the WOCC Commandant will appoint active component soldiers as a WOC UP AR 600–200, paragraph 7–46, and AR 310–10, format 304. Reserve component soldiers must be appointed a WOC and promoted to E5 by their component prior to arrival. Soldiers will wear WOC insignia IAW AR 670–1 until eliminated or appointed a warrant officer.

c. Supplemental instructions for Warrant Officer Staff Course (WOSC):

(1) Students must coordinate with Fort Rucker billeting office
        DSN: 558–3780;
        COMM: (205) 598–5216
for rooms or statement/non–availability.

(2) Uniform requirements: Class B uniform for classroom, Class A for graduation, PT uniform for APFT.

(3) Security Clearance: Students should have appropriate clearance level annotated on their orders or have their unit fax verification to WOCC Security Manager
        DSN: 558–1173;
        COMM: (205) 255–1173.

(4) Academic Evaluation Report (AER): An AER will be completed IAW AR 623–1 and AR 623–105. Active component students must receive a close–out OER if 90 days have elapsed since their last OER and course start date. If the AER is to include non–rated time prior to course start date, student must bring conditions and effective dates (e.g., 930623–930821, Chg of Duty; 930822–930901, LV; etc.).

(5) Generally, students will not be authorized a rental car but will receive in–and–around mileage if using a POV.

(6) APFT is a course requirement. If the student has a temporary or permanent profile that precludes completion of the two–mile run or an alternate aerobic event (walk, bike, swim), contact the appropriate career manager for rescheduling.

d. Supplemental instructions for Warrant Officer Senior Staff Course (WOSSC):
(1) Students will have billeting coordinated by the Advanced Studies Branch
DSN: 558–2786;
COMM: (205) 255–2786.
(2) Uniform requirements: class B uniform for classroom, Class A for graduation.
(3) Security clearance: Students should have appropriate clearance level annotated on their orders or have their unit fax verification to WOCC Security Manager
DSN: 558–1173;
COMM: (205) 255–2786.
(4) Academic Evaluation Report (AER): An AER will be completed IAW AR 623–1 and AR 623–105. Active component students must receive a close–out OER if 90 days have elapsed since their last OER and course start date. If the AER is to include non–rated time prior to course start date, student must bring conditions and effective dates (e.g. 930623–930821, Chg of duty; 930822–930901, LV; etc.).
(5) Generally, WOSSC students will not be authorized a rental car but will receive in–and–around mileage if using a POV.

e. Additional school information can be obtained from the following:
(1) Warrant Officer Candidate School:
Commander
1st Warrant Officer Company
ATTN: ATZQ–WCC–C
Fort Rucker, AL 36362–5000.
DSN 558–9686/3379;
COMM: (205) 255–2786/9031.
(2) WOSC and WOSSC:
Director
Warrant Officer Career Center
ATTN: ATZQ–WCC–AS
Fort Rucker, AL 36362–5000.
DSN: 558–2786/9031;
COMM: (205) 255–2786/9031.

Reference:
US Army Formal Schools Catalog. US Army Publishing Agency. DA PAM 351-4, page 29, Table 3-2. 31 October 1995.

U.S. Army Training Center, Fort Jackson; SC: 805
Fort Jackson, SC 29207–7900

a. Reporting instructions are as follows:
(1) Enlisted personnel arriving at Fort Jackson for advanced training, regardless of the day or hour, should report to the Adjutant General Trainee Section (Building 6300).
(2) Trainee personnel should pay close attention to orders regarding reporting with dependent, privately owned vehicles, or household goods.

Failure to do so may result in inconvenience and impose a hardship.

b. Quarters: All soldiers in trainee status, regardless of rank, are housed in company barracks. Trainees will not be permitted to live off–post except in highly unusual hardship circumstances and when approved by the Commander, 4th CST Brigade. Quarters for dependents of trainees are not available. Limited guest house facilities for visitors are available on–post.

c. Mess: Government mess is available for all personnel. All trainees are issued meal cards.

d. Uniform: Battle Dress Uniforms (BDU) and seasonal Class A/B Uniforms are required for training in the 4th CST Brigade. The BDU is the normal duty uniform. Soldiers should arrive at Fort Jackson with a complete basic clothing issue. Running shoes are also recommended.

e. Transportation information is as follows:
(1) Columbia Metropolitan Airport, Columbia, SC, is located 14 miles from Fort Jackson. Commercial bus, limousine, and taxi service are available to and from Fort Jackson. There is a Military Assistance Booth located inside the air terminal; hours of operation are 1200–2200, Monday–Friday (closed Saturday and Sunday). During the period that the Military Assistance Booth is not operational, the individual should call the Staff Duty Officer for assistance
COMM: 751–7611/7612.
(2) Commercial local and long distance bus service is available at the Joint Ticket Office located on Kemper Street (Building 8568).
(3) Government transportation is available only for official business.

Reference:
US Army Formal Schools Catalog. US Army Publishing Agency. DA PAM 351-4, page 192, Table 3-49. 31 October 1995.

U.S. Army Training Center, Fort Benning; SC: 809
Fort Benning, GA 31905–5000

a. Generally, government quarters are available for student personnel. When on–post quarters are not available, off–post quarters are available through Off–Post Housing Referral Service.

b. Mess facilities are available for enlisted students. Officer students have access to student mess and an officer's field ration mess in the 'Follow Me' dining facility located in Building 73.

c. Transportation information is as follows:
(1) Columbus Municipal Airport, Columbus, Georgia, is located approximately 12 miles from

Fort Benning. Commercial taxi service is available to and from Fort Benning.
(2) Commercial local bus service is available at the bus stop located on main post. Commercial long distance bus service is available in Columbus.
(3) Commercial taxis are available on and off–post.
(4) Government bus service is available on–post.

d. The Battle Dress Uniform is the normal prescribed uniform for all courses. Seasonal Class A Uniform is required for selected blocks of instruction and reporting.

e. Reporting instructions are as follows:
(1) Students arriving at Fort Benning will report to one of the following locations, depending on the course they are to attend:
(a) Airborne students report to Building 2747, Airborne, IPR, on main post.
(b) Ranger students report to Building 4827 in Harmony Church.
(c) IOAC students report to Building 2748 on main post.
(d) IOBC students report to Basic Officer Training Battalion (provisional), Building 74, on main post.
(e) ANCOC students report to Building 17E on main post.
(f) BNCOC students report to 5th Student Battalion, Building 2762 on main post.
(g) All other officer students report to unit specified on orders.
(h) All other enlisted students report to unit specified on orders.
(i) Allied students report to Allied Student Training Division, Building 399E on main post.
(2) Students should check their orders prior to reporting with dependents, privately owned vehicles, or household goods. Failure to do so may result in inconvenience and hardship.

f . Additional school information can be obtained from the following:
(1) Orders.
Commander, USAIC and Fort Benning
ATTN: ATZB–AG–PBM (Student Personnel Management, COMPACT)
Fort Benning, Georgia 31905–5000.
(2) Student Enrollment.
Commandant, USAIS
ATTN: ATSH–SE (Academic Records Branch, Office of the Secretary, USAIS)
Fort Benning, Georgia 31905–5000.
DSN: 835–4013;
COMM: (404) 545–4103.
(3) Course Information.
Commandant, USAIS
ATTN: ATSH–I–V–TMDD (Director of Training Developments, USAIS)
Fort Benning, Georgia 31905–5000.
DSN: 835–4013;
COMM: (404) 545–4052.

Reference:
US Army Formal Schools Catalog. US Army Publishing Agency. DA PAM 351-4, page 206, Table 3-55. 31 October 1995.

U.S. ARMY TRAINING CENTER, FORT LEONARD WOOD; SC: 807 FORT LEONARD WOOD, MO 65473–5000

a. Transportation:
(1) Forney Army Airfield is located adjacent to the main cantonment area. Scheduled commercial airlines and chartered flights are available.
(2) Personnel may also fly into Lambert Field, St. Louis International Airport, St. Louis, MO, which is located approximately 120 miles northeast of Fort Leonard Wood.
(3) Commercial bus lines and government shuttle bus service are available. Bus depot is located in the main cantonment area.
(4) Commercial taxis are available on a 24 hour basis.
(5) POV: Basic Training and AIT personnel are not authorized to drive or maintain their POV at Fort Leonard Wood. All other soldiers attending training are authorized to drive and maintain their POV's.

b. Uniform: Battle Dress Uniform (BDU) is the normal prescribed duty uniform for enlisted courses and season Class A/B uniform for graduation ceremony.
(1) In accordance with AR 735–5, Unit Supply Update, Chapter 5–6, Paragraph D, Commanders of USAR personnel participating in split–option training will ensure that when a soldier returns to a training site for subsequent training, a copy of the soldier's clothing record (DA FORM 4886) and all clothing issued previously accompanies the soldier.
(2) Soldiers arriving without previously issued clothing listed in the left column of the above mentioned form will be reissued those items by Directorate of Logistics (DOL). Soldiers arriving without previously issued items listed in the right column will be encouraged to purchase those items. Soldiers will be held monetarily liable for any missing items IAW AR 735–5, Chapter 12–2.
(3) Soldiers scheduled to attend NCOES courses that do not receive a 'Welcome Packet' should contact the Libby MCOA prior to reporting to ensure they bring all required clothing and paperwork.

c. Billeting: Government troop billets and messing are available for all personnel in training status. Officers will be housed in BOQS (Approximately $16.00 per night); ANCOC students will be housed in BEQS (Approximately $9.00 per night). Recommend students report with a minimum of $500.00 for the first month expenses.

d. BT, OSUT, AIT, PLDC, BNCOC, ANCOC and DSS students attending training at this installation will be issued a meal card.

e. Students should check orders prior to reporting with dependents, privately owned vehicles, or household goods. Failure to do so may result in inconvenience and hardship. Due to the limited availability of family housing in the Fort Leonard Wood area, it is highly recommended that dependents not accompany soldier to TDY station.

f. Reporting Procedures:
(1) Personnel reporting for MOS/ASI producing courses during duty hours will report to Building 1378 for inprocessing.
(2) Basic trainee, OSUT and AIT students for 12B10, 12C10 and 12F10 reporting during non–duty hours will report to Building 636, Headquarters, 3rd Training Brigade.
(3) All other OSUT, AIT, Reclass students to include soldiers attending the Sapper Leader course reporting during non–duty hours will report to Building 844, Headquarters, 1st Engineer Brigade.
(4) Officer, warrant officer and ANCOC students will report to Building 315 during duty or non–duty hours.
(5) Drill Sergeant candidates, BNCOC and PLDC students will report to Building 1023, Libby NCOA, during duty and non–duty hours unless otherwise specified in the student's 'Welcome Packet.'
(6) Marine Corps personnel will report with their records to their respective Liaison Officer in Building 1006A during duty hours, and Building 1338 during non–duty hours. Telephone
DSN: 581–7610;
COMM: (314) 596–7610.

g. Class schedules are listed in ATRRS. Confirmation of these dates may be obtained by contacting the Fort Leonard Wood Schools Office
DSN: 676–6083/6084;
or the ATRRS Office
DSN: 676–7182;
COMM: (314) 563–7182.

h. Telephone **prefixes** on Fort Leonard Wood are as follows:
Engineer School
DSN: 676-XXXX;
COMM: (314) 563-XXXX;
all other prefixes on the installation are
DSN: 581-XXXX;
COMM: (314) 596-XXXX;
i. Additional school information can be obtained from the following:
(1) Orders – AIT personnel:

Commander, USAECFLW
ATTN: ATZT–AG–TSM
Fort Leonard Wood, MO 65473–5000.
DSN: 581–6354;
COMM: (314) 596–6354.
Students:
Commander, USAECFLW
ATTN: ATZT–AG–TSP
Fort Leonard Wood, MO 65473–5000.
DSN: 581–3368;
COMM: (314) 596–3368.
(2) Training Information:
Commander, USAECFLW
ATTN: ATT–PTM–TO
Fort Leonard Wood, MO 65473–5000.
DSN: 676–7184/7179;
COMM: (314) 563–7184/7179.
(3) POI/Course Information:
Commander, USAECFLW
ATTN: ATSE–CDE
Fort Leonard Wood, MO 65473–5000.
DSN: 676–7789;
COMM: (314) 563–7789.
(4) Schools Information:
Commander, USAECFLW
ATTN: ATZT–PIM–TS
Fort Leonard Wood, MO 65473–5000.
DSN: 676–6084/6083;
COMM: (314) 563–6084/6083.
(5) Billeting Office: Building 315
DSN: 581–6169;
COMM: (314) 596–6169.
(6) Libby NCOA:
Commandant, Libby NCOA
ATTN: ATZT–NCO
Fort Leonard Wood, MO 65473.
DSN: 581–2419;
COMM: (314) 596–2419.
(7) HQS DSS: Building 1025C,
DSN: 581–3756;
COMM: (314) 596–3756.
(8) HQS ANCOC: Building 1025D,
DSN 581–2716;
COMM: (314) 596–2716.
(9) HQS BNCOC: Building 1025EE,
DSN 581–5832;
COMM: (314) 596–5832.
(10) HQS BNCOC: Building 1006,
DSN 581–5423;
COMM: (314) 596–5423.

Reference:
US Army Formal Schools Catalog. US Army Publishing Agency. DA PAM 351-4, page 202, Table 3-54. 31 October 1995.

APPENDIX-B

GLOSSARY

Accouterment - Items such as medals, ribbons, insignia, badges, emblems, tabs, tapes, authorized for wear on uniforms.

Active Army (AA) - The portion of the U.S. Army in which organizations are comprised of personnel in active military and civilian service of the United States.

Ad Hoc - For specific purpose, case or situation.

Advance Guard (AG) - A security element that precedes and protects the main body of a force, whatever its formation, and covers its deployment for action if enemy contact is made.

Airborne (ABN) - Having the qualification of exiting an aircraft, and landing safely by the use of a parachute.

Air Items - Manned aircraft and aircraft drones, trainers, flight simulators and airborne operations and expendable and non-expendable supplies and equipment in support thereof.

Ancillary - Auxiliary, support.

Anti-Guerrilla Operations (AGO) - Operations conducted by conventional forces against guerrilla forces in rear areas at the same time the conventional force is engaged in conventional combat operations in the forward areas.

Anti-Terrorism (AT) - Defensive measures used to reduce the vulnerability of individuals and property to terrorist acts, to include limited response and containment by local military forces.

Aperture Sight - A lens-less sight by which the target is viewed through a hole, or aperture (as contrasted with an open sight having only a V-cut notch).

Area of Operation (AO) - An area for which training or an operation is taking place.

Area Oriented - Personnel or units whose organization, mission, training, and equipping are based on projected operational deployment to a specific geographic or demographic area.

Armed Reconnaissance - A mission with the primary purpose of locating and attacking targets of opportunity, i.e., enemy material, personnel, and facilities, in assigned general areas or along assigned ground communications routes, and not for the purpose of attacking specific briefed targets.

Armed Services Vocational Aptitude Battery (ASVAB) - A placement test that some take before entering the armed services.

Army Core Values - The seven guidelines for living; LDRSHIP (Loyalty, Duty, Respect, Selfless service, Honor, Integrity, and Personal courage).

Army Special Operations Forces (ARSOF) - Those active and reserve component Army forces designated by the secretary of defense that are specifically organized, trained, and equipped to conduct and support special operations.

Assault - The final step of the attack phase; the rush to close combat with the enemy and to drive him out in hand-to-hand combat with the extensive use of bayonets and hand grenades.

Assault Climber - A highly trained military mountaineer who servers as a guide, advisor, observer, or scout or is involved in special warfare in mountainous terrain.

Assault Echelon - The lead elements of an air-mobile force scheduled for initial assault of the objective area.

Assault Force - Those units charged with the seizure of the objective area.

Attack - A phase of offensive combat; offensive action directed against the enemy with intent to kill, capture, or drive him from his position.

Attack Position - The most forward covered and concealed position in rear of the line of departure occupied by assault units for the minimum amount of time necessary to coordinate final details and preparations for the attack.

Attrition - A gradual lessening of numbers or strengths due to constant stress.

Austere - Stern, severe or extreme.

Authority - The legitimate power of leaders to direct subordinates or to take action within the scope of their responsibility.

Azimuth - A direction in a horizontal plane.

Bacalave - Cold weather hood.

Baccalaureate Degree - The degree of bachelor, conferred on graduates of most US colleges and universities.

Ballasting - Something providing stability in character.

Base of Fire - One or more units that give supporting fire to an attacking unit and serve as the base around which attack operations are carried out.

Battalion - Consisting of several companies.

Battle Dress Uniform (BDU) - Uniform worn during training and working; normally camouflage.

Battle Position - The position on which the main effort of defense is, or is to be made.

Battle Task - A command group, staff, or subordinate organization mission essential task that is so critical that its accomplishment will determine the success of the next higher organization's mission essential task.

Beachhead - A designated area on a hostile shore or territory which, when seized and held, ensures the continuous landing of troops and material, and provides maneuvering space for subsequent projected operations into enemy territory; the physical objective of an amphibious or airborne operation.

Beaten Zone - The pattern formed where rounds or bursts have struck the ground or a target.

Billeting - Boarding and lodging of soldiers.

Bivouac - A temporary, often outside encampment.

BRADLEY – Armored fighting vehicle.

Brigade - Consisting of several battalions.

Cache - A safe place for concealment or a place for hiding strong provisions.

Cadence - A rhythmic rate of march at a uniform step.

Cadre - A small group of trained personnel around which a larger group is commanded.

Campaign Plan - A plan for a series of related military operations aimed at accomplishing a strategic or operational objective within a given time and space.

Capstone - A final task.

Chain of Command - It is the succession of commanders, superior to subordinate, through which command is exercised. It is the most important organizational technique in use in the Army today.

Civil Administration - An administration established by a foreign government in (1) friendly territory, under an agreement with the government of the area concerned, to exercise certain authority normally the function of the local government, or (2) hostile territory, occupied by U.S. Forces, where a foreign government exercises executive, legislative, and judicial authority until an indigenous civil government can be established.

Civil-Military Operations - Group of planned activities in support of military operations that enhance the relationship between the military forces and civilian authorities and populations and which promote the development of favorable emotions, attitudes, or behavior in neutral, friendly, or hostile groups.

Civil-Military Operations Center (CMOC) - An ad hoc organization, normally established by the geographic combatant commander, to assist in the coordination of activities of engaged military forces, and other U.S. Government agencies, non-government organizations, private voluntary organizations, and regional and international organizations. There is no established structure, and its size and composition are situation dependent.

Clandestine - Something kept secret or concealed.

Clandestine (Secret) Operations - An operation sponsored or conducted by government departments or agencies in such a way as to assure secrecy or concealment. A clandestine operation differs from a covert operation in that emphasis is placed on concealment of the operation rather than on concealment of the identity of the sponsor. In special operations, an activity may be both covert and clandestine and may focus equally on operational considerations and intelligence-related activities. Intelligence, counter-intelligence, and other similar activities sponsored or conducted by governmental departments or agencies using secret or illicit means against another nation.

Class I, III, IX - Supplies for support food service operations.

Code of Conduct - It is a set of rules that outline the basic responsibilities and obligations of all members of the Armed Forces of the United States during times of conflict. It is designed to give the U.S. Soldier strength and guidance should they fall into the hands of the enemy. It contains six articles.

Combatant - 1. International Law-Individual members of belligerent forces subject to the laws, rights, and duties of war. 2. Soldier or unit assigned to duty as an active fighter or fighting unit, as distinguished from duty in any of the services, such as administrative, supply or medical.

Combat Search And Rescue (CSAR) - A specific task performed by rescue forces to effect the recovery of distressed personnel during war or military operations other than war.

Combating Terrorism (CBT) - Actions, including anti-terrorism (defensive measures taken to reduce the vulnerability to terrorist acts) and counter-terrorism (offensive measures taken to prevent, deter, and respond to terrorism), taken to oppose terrorism throughout the entire threat spectrum.

Command - The authority a person in the military service lawfully exercises over subordinates by virtue of rank and assignment or position.

Command and Control Warfare (C2W) - The integrated use of operations security, military deception, psychological operations, electronic warfare, and physical destruction, mutually supported by intelligence, to deny information to, influence, degrade, or destroy adversary command and control capabilities against such actions. Command and control warfare is an application of information warfare in military operations and is a subset of information warfare. Command and control warfare applies across the range of military operations and all levels of conflict.

Commander-In-Chief - The President of the United States of America.

Commensurate - Having a common size, scale, extent, scale or length of time.

Common Core - Combination of common military, common leader, and directed/mandated tasks for specific courses, grade levels, or organizational levels regardless of branch or career management field.

Contingency - An emergency involving military forces caused by natural disasters, terrorists, subversives, or required military operations. Due to the uncertainty of the situation, contingencies require plans, rapid response, and special procedures to ensure the safety and readiness of personnel, installations, and equipment.

Counseling - The process of communicating advice, instruction, or judgement with the intent of influencing a person's behavior or performance.

Counter-Drug Activities (CD) - Those active measures taken to detect, monitor, and counter the production, trafficking, and use of illegal drugs.

Counter-Mine Operation - In land mine warfare, an operation to reduce or eliminate the effects of mines or minefields.

Counter-Proliferation (CP) - The activities of the Department of Defense across the full range of U.S. Government efforts to combat proliferation of nuclear, biological, and chemical weapons, including the application of military power to protect U.S. Forces and interests; intelligence collection and analysis; and, support of diplomacy, arms control, and export controls. Accomplishment of these activities may require coordination with other U.S. Government agencies.

Counter-Terrorism (CT) - Offensive measures taken to prevent, deter, and respond to terrorism.

Covert Operation - An operation that is so planned and executed as to conceal the identity of or permit plausible denial by the sponsor. A covert operation differs from a clandestine operation in that emphasis is placed on the concealment of the identity of the sponsor rather than on concealment of the operation.

D-Day - France was liberated when the U.S. and its Allies stormed Normandy beach in 06 June 1944.

Dead Reckoning - A method of estimating the position of a ship or aircraft without any astronomical observations, by using the previous distance traveled and current position.

Defile - A narrow passage in which troops can march only in a file.

Delta - An elite force that trains secretly for classified missions.

Deployment - The relocation of forces and material to desired areas of operation. Deployment encompasses all activities from origin or home station through destination, specifically including intra-continental United States, inter-theater and intra-theater movement legs, staging, and holding areas.

Descender - A rappelling device.

Direct Action (DA) - Short-duration strikes and small-scale offensive actions by special operations forces to seize, destroy, capture, recover, or inflict damage on designated personnel or material. In the conduct of these operations, SOF may employ raid, ambush, or direct assault tactics; emplace mines and other munitions; conduct stand-off attacks by fore from air, ground, or maritime platforms; provide terminal guidance for precision-guided munitions and conduct sabotage.

Doctrine - Fundamental principles derived from theory and concept based on values, beliefs, historical perspective, experience, and research which guide military forces or elements thereof.

Drill Sergeant (DS) - The primary representative of the Army during the formative weeks of an enlistee's training.

Drop Zone (DZ) - Area for which parachutist are dropped from an aircraft.

Employment - The strategic, operational, or tactical use of forces.

Escape - To break free from capture or to succeed in avoiding danger, capture, or harm.

Esprit de corps - The common spirit and feelings of enthusiasm and the devotion and dedication to a cause among a team or members of a group.

Evasion - The act of avoiding or being caught.

Family Advocacy - A family support organization.

Fiche - A piece of microfilm containing a shrunken version of printed text.

Foot march, ruck march, road march - Walking or hiking at an accelerated pace over a long distance on paved, unpaved or rugged surface, carrying a equipment pack.

Force Multiplier - A capability that, when added to and employed by a combat force, significantly increases the combat potential of that force and thus enhances the probability of successful mission accomplishment.

Foreign Internal Defense (FID) - Participation by civilian and military agencies of a government in any of the action programs taken by another government to free and protect its society from subversion, lawlessness, and insurgency.

Ghilley Suit - A camouflage suit worn by Sniper.

Geneva Conference - It provides rules that prisoners of war must be treated humanely. Specifically forbidden are violence to life and person, cruel treatment and torture, out rages on personal dignity; in particular, humiliating and degrading treatment.

Golden Knights - The U.S. Army Parachute Team, Ambassadors of Goodwill, who provide aerial stunts and skills for audiences around the world.

Guerrilla - A member of a irregular military force operating in independent groups capable of moving at a fast rate of speed and mobility.

Guerrilla Warfare (GW) - Military and paramilitary operations conducted in enemy-held or hostile territory by irregular, predominantly indigenous forces.

High Altitude Low Opening (HALO) - Also known as Military Free Fall Parachutist (MFFPC). To train personnel to be qualified military free fall parachutist. Training includes free fall techniques, and maneuvering their parachutes with pinpoint accuracy.

Host Nation - A nation which receives the forces and/ or supplies of allied nations and/or NATO organizations to be located on, to operate in, or to transit through its territory.

Humanitarian Assistance (HA) - Programs conducted to relieve or reduce the results of natural or manmade disasters or other endemic conditions, such as human pain, disease, hunger, or privation, that might present a serious loss of life or that can result in great damage or loss of property. Humanitarian assistance provided by U.S. forces is limited in scope and duration. The assistance is designed to supplement or complement the efforts of the host nation civil authorities or agencies that may have the primary responsibility for providing humanitarian assistance.

Humanitarian De-Mining (HD) - Those operations undertaken to mitigate the effects of landmines on a host nation in a safe, efficient and cost-effective manner. HD activities conducted by U.S. Forces include training host nation personnel to: establish and operate a national de-mining headquarters; locate, identify and destroy landmines in place; and plan and execute a national mine awareness campaign to alert the local population to the dangers of landmines and the procedures for reporting landmine locations and incidents.

Hypothermia - The general lowering of the body core temperature due to heat loss and insufficient heat production.

Infantry - The branch of an army consisting of soldiers trained to fight on foot.

Infiltration - The movement through or into an area or territory occupied by either friendly or enemy troops or organizations. The movement is made, either by small groups or by individuals, at extended or irregular intervals. When used in connection with the enemy, it infers that contact is avoided. In intelligence usage, placing an agent or other person in a target area in hostile territory. Usually involves crossing a frontier or other guarded line.

Information Operations (IO) - Actions taken to affect adversary information and information systems while defending one's own information and information systems.

Information Superiority - The capability to collect, process, and disseminate an uninterrupted flow of information while exploiting or denying an adversary's ability to do the same.

Information Warfare (IW) - Information operations conducted during time of crisis or conflict to achieve or promote specific objectives over a specific adversary or adversaries.

Insurgency - An organized movement aimed at the overthrow of a constituted government through the use of subversion and armed conflict.

Intelligence - The capability of acquiring and applying knowledge and/or information.

Joint Force Commander (JFC) - A general term applied to a combatant commander, a sub-unified commander, or joint task force commander authorized to exercise combatant command (command authority) or operational control over a joint force.

Joint Special Operations Air Component Commander (JSOACC) - The commander within the joint force special operations command responsible for planning and executing joint special air operations and for coordinating and de-conflicting such operations with conventional non-special operations air activities. The joint special air component commander normally will be the commander with the preponderance of assets and/or greatest ability to plan, coordinate, allocate, task, control, and support the assigned joint special operations component commander or to any non-special operations component or joint force commander as directed.

Joint Special Operations Task Force (JSOTF) - A joint task force composed of special operations units from more than one service, formed to carry out a specific special operation or prosecute special operations in support of a joint force commander' campaign or other operations. The joint special operations task force may have conventional non-special operations units assigned or attached to support the conduct of specific missions.

Joint Task Force (JTF) - A joint force that is constituted and so designated by the Secretary of Defense, a combatant commander, a sub-unified commander, or an existing joint task force commander.

Lateral Drift Apparatus - Training aid used to teach airborne students how to conduct a parachute landing fall, while drifting across the drop zone laterally.

Leadership - The process of influencing others to accomplish the mission by providing purpose, direction, and motivation.

Liaison - A person who communicates between groups or units of an organization.

Low-Intensity Conflict (LIC) - Political-military confrontation between contending states or groups below conventional war and above the routine, peaceful competition among states. It frequently involves protracted struggles of competing principles and ideologies. Low-intensity conflict ranges form subversion to the use of armed force. It is waged by a combination of means employing political, economic, informational, and military instruments. Low-intensity conflicts are often localized but contain regional and global security implications.

Military Operations Other Than War (MOOTW) - Operations that en-compass the use of military capabilities across the range of military operations short of war. These military actions can be applied to complement any combination of the other instruments of national power and occur before, during, and after war.

Military Rank - The relative position or degree of precedence granted military personnel marking their situation in military life. It confers eligibility to exercise command or authority in the military within the limits of prescribed law.

Military Time - Time told by using the numbers 00:01 to 24:00 for the 24 hours in a day. A day begins at one minute after midnight and ends at midnight the same day.

Mine Warfare - The strategic and operational use of mines and their counter-measures. Mine warfare is divided into two basic subdivisions: The laying of mines to degrade the enemy's capabilities to wage land, air, and maritime warfare; and the countering of enemy-laid mines to permit friendly maneuver or use of selected land or sea areas.

Moleskin - Material used to protect feet from blisters and reduce friction.

Military Occupational Specialty (MOS) - Job in the U.S. Army.

Noncombatants - All persons participating in military operations or activities are considered combatants. All others are noncombatants. Noncombatants include civilians, medical personnel, chaplains, and other persons captured or detained.

Overt Operations - An operation conducted openly without concealment.

Parameric - Any of several tough, porous substitutes for leather.

Paramilitary - A force designated and organized after a military pattern.

Paramilitary Forces - Forces or groups which are distinct from the regular armed forces of any country but resembling them in organization, equipment, training, or mission.

Peace Operations - A broad term that encompasses peacekeeping operations and peace enforcement operations conducted in support of diplomatic efforts to establish and maintain peace.

Policy - A broad guide or principle, ideally based in doctrine, used to select a definite course or method of action or to guide and determine present and future decisions.

Polypropylene - "Polylpro"; consisting of various thermoplastic resins that are polymers of propylene. Cold weather undergarment.

Post-Strike Reconnaissance - Missions undertaken for the purpose of gathering information used to measure results of a strike.

Predicated - To verbally establish a base, statement or quality.

Promotion Points - The act of promoting through a point system.

Psychological Operations (PSYOP) - Planned operations to convey selected information and indicators to foreign audiences to influence their emotions, motives, objective reasoning, and ultimately the behavior of foreign governments, organizations, groups, and individuals. The purpose of PSYOP is to induce or reinforce foreign attitudes and behaviors favorable to the originator's objectives.

Quarrying - To extract.

Raid - An operation, usually small scale, involving a swift penetration of hostile territory to secure information, confuse the enemy, or to destroy installations. It ends with a planned withdrawal upon completion of the assigned mission.

Rangers - Rapidly deployable, airborne light infantry personnel organized and trained to conduct highly-complex, joint, direct action operations in coordination with, or in support of, other special operations units of all services. Rangers can also execute direct action operations in support of conventional, non-special operations missions conducted by a combatant commander and can operate as conventional light infantry when properly augmented with other elements of combined arms.

Rappel - Method of controlled frictional descent down a rope.

Reconnaissance - The exploration or inspection of an area for military intelligence.

Recovery Operations - Operations conducted to search for, locate, identify, rescue, and return personnel, sensitive equipment, or items critical to national security.

Resistance - A force that opposes a certain element.

Restricted Area - Any area, access to which is subject to special restrictions or controls for reasons of security or safeguarding of property or material.

Rubber duck - Rubber M16 rifle, used in training and demonstrations.

Sabotage - An act or acts with intent to injure, interfere with, or obstruct the national defense of a country by willfully injuring or destroying, or attempting to injure or destroy, any national defense or war material, premises, or utilities, to include human or natural resources.

Security Assistance - Group of programs authorized by the Foreign Assistance Act of 1961, as amended, and the Arms Export Control Act of 1976, as amended, or related statutes by which the United States provides defense-related services by grant, loan, credit, or cash sales in furtherance of national policies and objectives.

Shared Training - Training performed by soldiers from different jobs and/or different skill or organizational levels.

Small Group Instruction (SGI) - A means of delivering training which places the responsibility for learning on the soldier through participation in small groups led by small group leaders who serve as role models throughout the course. SGI uses small group processes, methods, and techniques to stimulate learning.

Small Group Leader (SGL) - An instructor who facilitates role modeling, counseling, coaching, learning, and team building in SGI.

Sorbathane - Synthetic used in the insole of foot ware to reduce shock and friction.

Special Activities - Activities conducted in support of national foreign policy objectives which are planned and executed so that the role of the U.S. Government is not apparent or acknowledged publicly. They are also functions in support of such activities, but are not intended to influence U.S. political processes, public opinion, policies, or media and do not include diplomatic activities or the collection and production of intelligence or related support functions.

Special Forces (SF) - U.S. Army forces organized, trained, and equipped specifically to conduct special operations. Special forces have five primary missions: unconventional warfare, foreign internal defense, direct action, special reconnaissance, and counter-terrorism. Counter-terrorism is a special mission for specially organized, trained, and equipped Special Forces units designated in theater contingency plans.

Special Forces Group (SFG) - A combat arms organization (Army) capable of planning, conducting, and supporting special operations activities in all operational environments in peace, conflict, and war.

It consists of a group Headquarters and Headquarters Company, a support company, and Special Forces battalions. The group can operate as a single unit, but normally the battalions plan and conduct operations from widely separated locations. The group provides general operational direction and synchronizes the activities of subordinate battalions. Although principally structured for unconventional warfare, Special Forces Group units are capable of task organizing to meet specific requirements.

Special Operations (SO) - Operations conducted by specially organized, trained, and equipped military and paramilitary forces to achieve military, political, economic, or psychological objectives by unconventional military means in hostile, denied, or politically sensitive areas. These operations are conducted during war and operations other than war, independently or in coordination with operations of conventional or other non-special operations forces. Political-military considerations frequently shape special operations, requiring clandestine, covert, or low visibility techniques and oversight at the national level. Special operations differ from conventional operations in degree of physical and political risk, operational techniques, mode of employment, independence from friendly support, and dependence on detailed operational intelligence and indigenous assets.

Special Operations Command (SOC) - A subordinate unified or other joint command established by a joint force commander to plan, coordinate, conduct, and support joint special operations within the joint force commander's assigned area of operations.

Special Operations Forces (SOF) - Those active and reserve component forces of the military services designated by the secretary of defense and specially organized, trained, and equipped to conduct and support special operations.

Special Operations-Peculiar - Equipment, material, supplies, and services required for special operations mission support for which there is no broad conventional force requirement. It often includes non-developmental or special category items incorporating evolving technology but may include stocks of obsolete weapons and equipment designed to support indigenous personnel who do not possess sophisticated operational capabilities.

Special Reconnaissance (SR) - Reconnaissance and surveillance actions conducted by SOF to obtain or verify, by visual observation or other collection methods, information concerning the capabilities, intentions, and activities of an actual or potential enemy or to secure data concerning the meteorological, hydrographic, or geographic characteristics of a particular area. It includes target acquisition, area assessment, and post-strike, reconnaissance.

Squad - A small unit of military personnel.

Stabilize - To make permanent or unchanging.

Static Line - Nylon cord that opens the parachute immediately after the jumper exits the aircraft.

Stress - The body's response to a demand placed on it; may be physical or mental.

Sub-Ordinate Unified Command - A command established by commanders of unified commands, when so authorized through the chairman of the Joint Chiefs of Staff, to conduct operations on a continuing basis in accordance with the criteria set forth for unified commands. A subordinate unified commands have functions and responsibilities similar to those of the commanders of unified commands and exercise operational control of assigned joint operations area. Also called sub-unified command.

Subversion - Action designed to undermine the military, economic, psychological, or political strength or morale of a regime.

Surveillance - The act of close observation.

Survival - The process of surviving; continuing to live.

Suspended Harness – Training aid, used to teach Airborne students how to control a parachute, by suspending the student approximately 1 foot off of the ground while simulating steering a parachute.

Swing Landing Trainer – Training aid, used to teach Airborne students how to conduct a proper (PLF) parachute landing fall, from approximately 12 feet above the ground.

Tomb of the Unknowns - A national monument commemorating dead soldiers located in Arlington National Cemetery and guarded year round by the sentinels of The Old Guard.

Total Army - Active Army (both military and civilians), U.S. Army Reserves, and Army National Guard.

Turpitude - A corrupt thought, deed or mind.

Uniform Code of Military Justice (UCMJ) - The law for which any service member, in any branch, is punished for misconduct.

Unconventional Warfare (UW) - A broad spectrum of military and paramilitary operations, normally of long duration, predominately conducted by indigenous forces who are organized, trained, equipped, supported, and directed, in varying degrees, by an external source. UW includes guerrilla warfare and other direct-offensive, low-visibility, covert, or clandestine operations, as well as the indirect activities of subversion, sabotage, intelligence activities, and evasion and escape.

Unified Command - A command with a broad continuing mission under a single commander, composed of significant assigned components of two or more military departments, and which is established and so designated by the president, through the secretary of defense, with the advice and assistance of the chairman of the Joint Chiefs of Staff.

Weapons Of Mass Destruction (WOMD) - In arms control usage, weapons that are capable of a high order of destruction and/or of being used in such a manner as to destroy large numbers of people. Can be nuclear, chemical, biological, and radiological weapons but excludes the means of transporting or propelling the weapon where such means is a separable and divisible part of the weapon.

Wind Chill - The rate at which a man or object cools to the ambient temperature. Wind increases the rate of cooling and adds to the chances of frostbite, hypothermia, and other cold-weather injuries.

World War I - A war fought from 1914 to 1918, in which Great Britain, France , Russia, Belgium, Italy, Japan and the United States defeated Germany, Austria-Hungary, Turkey, and Bulgaria.

World War II - A war fought from 1939 to 1945, in which Great Britain, France, the Soviet Union and the United States, defeated Germany, Italy, and Japan.

Zulu Time - Greenwich Mean Time.

APPENDIX-C

ACRONYMS

A&P - Aircraft and Power Plant
AA - Active Army
AAC - Air Assault Course
AAD - Air Assault Division
AAFES - Army and Air Force Exchange Service
AALPS - Automated Air Load Planning System
AAR - After Action Report / Review
AAS - Air Assault School
AASLT - Air Assault
ABN - Airborne
ABN DIV - Airborne Division
ABQRF - Aviation Brigade's Quick Reaction Force
AC - Active Component
ACCP - Army Correspondence Course Program
ACE - Ammunition, Casualty, and Equipment (report)
ACH - Army Community Hospital
ACOR - Assistant Contracting Officer Representative
ACRC - Army Crime Records Center
ACT - American College Test
AD - Air Defense
ADEPT – Aircraft Departure
ADP - Advance Development Plan
ADR - Adverse Drug Reaction
ADS - Amphibian Discharge Site
ADT - Active Duty for Training
ADW - Aerial Drug Sweep
ADZSO - Assistant Drop Zone Safety Officer
AE - Air Evacuation
AER - Army Emergency Relief
AFAST - Alternate Flight Aptitude Selection Test
AFB - Air Force Base
AFS - Active Federal Service
AFTB - Army Family Team Building
AG - Adjutant General
AG - Advanced Guard
AGO - Anti-Guerilla Operations
AGR - Active Guard and Reserve
AGR/FTS - Active Guard Reserve / Full-Time Support
AI - Additional Identifier
AI - Air Items
AIMC - Advanced International Morse Code
AIQC - Anti-terrorism Instructor Qualification Course
AIRR - Army Investigative Records Repository
AIT - Advanced Individual Training
ALICE - All-purpose Lightweight Carrying Equipment

ALM - Air-Load Module
AMEDDPERSA - U.S. Army Medical Department Personnel Support Agency
AMFFPC - Advanced Military Free Fall Parachutist Course
AMFT - Air Movement Flow Table
Ammo - Ammunition
AMOS - Additional Military Occupational Specialty
AMS - Acute Mountain Sickness
AN - Army/Navy
ANCOC - Advanced Noncommissioned Officer's Course
AO - Area of Operations
APFT - Army Physical Fitness Test
APRT - Army Physical Readiness Test
AR - Armed Reconnaissance
AR - Armor
AR - Army Regulation
ARI - Army Research Institute
ARNG - Army National Guard
AR-PERSCOM - Army Reserve Personnel Command
ARSOF - Army Special Operations Forces
ART - Assessment and Recovery Team
ART - Auto Range Telescope
ARTEP - Army Training and Evaluation Program
ASAP - As Soon As Possible
ASC - Assessment and Selection Course
ASE - Automotive Service Excellence
ASI - Additional Skill Identifier
ASL - Authorized Supply List
ASO - Attache Staff Operations
ASVAB - Armed Services Vocational Aptitude Battery
AT - Anti-Terrorism
ATA - Actual Time of Arrival
ATC - Air Traffic Control
ATD - Actual Time of Departure
ATRRS - Army Training Requirements and Resources System
ATTN - Attention
AUS - Army of the United States
AUSA - Association of the United States Army
AUT - Advance Unit Training
AVN - Aviation
AWACS - Airborne Warning And Control System
AWOL - Absent Without Leave

AZ - Azimuth
BA - Bachelor of Arts
BAC - Basic Airborne Course
BAH - Basic Allowance for Housing
BAQ - Basic Allowance for Quarters
BAQ/OR - Basic Allowance for Quarters/Own Right
BAQ/W - Basic Allowance for Quarters/With dependents
BAS - Battlefield Automation Systems
BAS - Basic Allowance for Subsistence
BASD - Basic Active Service Date
BCT - Basic Combat Training
BDA - Battle Damage Assessment
BDE - Brigade
BDU - Battle Dress Uniform
BDZ - Base Defense Zone
BEAR - Bonus Extension and Reenlistment / Retraining
BEQ - Bachelor Enlisted Quarters
BESD - Basic Enlisted Service Date
BFVS - BRADLEY Fighting Vehicle Subsystem
BLUF - Bottom Line Up Front
BMNT - Beginning Morning Nautical Twilight
BN - Battalion
BNCOC - Basic Noncommissioned Officer Course
BN TAC - Battalion Training Advising Counseling
BOC - Basic Officer Candidate
BOQ - Bachelor Officer Quarters
BOSS - Better Opportunities for Single Soldiers
BP - Battle Position
BPED - Basic Pay Entry Date
BRM - Basic Rifle Marksmanship
BS - Bachelor of Science
CA - Civil Affairs
CA - Combat Arms
CAG - Combat Applications Group
CALM - Computer Aided Loading Movement Tracking System
CALMIS - Calibration Management Information System
CANA - Convulsant Antidote for Nerve Agents
CARP - Computed Air Release Points
CARP - Contingency Alternate Route Plan
CARS - Combat Arms Regimental System
CB - Chemical-Biological
CBT - Combating Terrorism
CC - Chain of Command
CC - Code of Conduct
CCF - Central Clearance Facility
CCT - Combat Control Team
CD - Counter-Drug Activities
CDQC - Combat Diver Qualification Course
CDR - Commander
CDRUSAPT - Commander U.S. Army Parachute Team
CG - Coast Guard
CHAMPUS - Civilian Health and Medical Program of the Uniformed Services

CIA - Central Intelligence Agency
CIB - Combat Infantry Badge
CID - Criminal Investigation Division
CIF - Central Issue Facility
CINC - Commanders In Chief
CIR - Critical Incident Report
CIV - Civilian
CLEP - College Level Examination Program
CLP - Cleaner, Lubricant, Preservative
CLS - Combat Life Saver
CMD - Command
CMF - Career Management Field
CMO - Civil-Military Operations
CMOC - Civil-Military Operations Center
CO - Commanding Officer
Co - Company
COHORT - Cohesion, Operational Readiness, and Training
COMINT - Communications Intelligence
COMM - Commercial phone line
Comm - Communications
COMMEX - Communications Exercise
COMPASS - Computerized Movement Planning and Status System
COMSEC - Communications Security
CONUS - Continental United States
COR - Commander Of the Relief
COR - Contracting Officer Representative
COSCOM - Corps Support Command
CP - Command Post
CP - Counter-Proliferation
CPE - Chemical Protective Equipment
CPL - Corporal
CPMOS - Career Progression Military Occupational Specialty
CPR - Cardiopulmonary Resuscitation
CQ - Charge of Quarters
CQB - Close Quarter Battle
CSA - Chief of Staff of the Army
CSA - Combat Support Arm
CSAR - Combat Search And Rescue
CSDP - Command Supply Discipline Program
CSM - Command Sergeant Major
CSS - Combat Service Support
CSSCS - Combat Service Support Control System
CT - Counter-Terrorism
CTA - Common Table of Allowances
CTT - Common Task Test
C2W - Command and Control Warfare
CW - Cold Weather
CWIE - Cold Weather Individual Equipment
CWST - Combat Water Survival Test
DA - Department of the Army
DA - Direct Action
DACO - Departure Airfield Control Officer
DAIG - Department of the Army Inspector's General
DAMMS-R - Department of the Army Movement Management System Redesign

DAS - Defense Attache System
DBDU - Desert Battle Dress Uniform
DCII - Defense Clearance Investigation Index
DCP - Drill Corporal Program
DCSPER - Deputy Chief of Staff for Personnel
DD - Department of Defense
DDC - Defense Drivers Course
DEA - Drug Enforcement Agency
DEERS - Defense Enrollment Eligibility Reporting System
DEFCON - Defense Readiness Condition
DEP - Delayed Entry Program
DEROS - Date Eligible to Return from Overseas
DET - Detachment
DFAC - Dining Facility
DLAB - Defense Language Aptitude Battery
DLIELC - Defense Language Institute English Language Center
DLIFLC - Defense Language Institute Foreign Language Center
DLPT - Defense Language Proficiency Test
DMOS - Duty Military Occupational Specialty
DMZ - Demilitarized Zone
DOA - Dead On Arrival
DOA - Direction Of Attack
DOB - Date Of Birth
DOCE - Date Of Current Enlistment
DOD - Department Of Defense
DOR - Date Of Rank
DOT - Department Of Transportation
DOT - Directorate of Operation Training
DOW - Died Of Wounds
DPP - Delayed Payment Program
DS - Direct Support
DS - Drill Sergeant
DSN - Defense Switched Network
DSS - Defense Security Service
DSU - Direct Support Unit
DTG - Date Time Group
DUI - Driving Under the Influence
DWI - Driving While Intoxicated
DX - Direct Exchange
DZ - Drop Zone
DZSO - Drop Zone Safety Officer
DZSTL - Drop Zone Support Team Leader
E & E - Escape and Evasion
E & R - Escape/Evade and Resistance
EB - Enlistment bonus
ECLT - English Comprehension Level Test
EDRE - Emergency Deployment Readiness Exercise
EENT - End Evening Nautical Twilight
EEO - Equal Employment Opportunity
EER - Enlisted Evaluation Report
EIB - Expert Infantry Badge
EIR - Equipment Improvement Report
EKG - Electrocardiogram
ELI - Emitter Location and Identification
ELINT - Electronic Intelligence

ELS - Entry Level Separation
EM - Enlisted Member
Email - Electronic Mail
EMF - Enlisted Master File
EMF - Electro-Motive Force
EMP - Electronic Magnetic Pulse
EMPF - Enlisted Military Personnel File
EMT-P - Emergency Medical Technician Paramedic Course
ENTNAC - Entrance National Agency Check
EO - Equal Opportunity
EPW - Enemy Prisoners of War
ERB - Enlisted Record Brief
ERPSL - Essential Repair Parts Stockage List
ETA - Estimated Time of Arrival
ETD - Estimated Time of Departure
ETP - Exception To Policy
ETS - Expiration Term of Service
EW - Electronic Warfare
F - Fahrenheit
FA - Family Advocacy
FA - Field Artillery
FAA - Federal Aviation Administration
FAO - Financial and Accounting Officer
FARP - Forward Arming and Refueling Points
FAST - Flight Aptitude Selection Test
FAX - Facsimile
FBI - Federal Bureau of Investigation
FCC - Federal Communications Commission
FDME - Flying Duty Medical Examination
FDS - Forward Direct Support
FEMA - Federal Emergency Management Agency
FFS - Free Fall Simulator
FID - Foreign Internal Defense
FIST - Fire Support Team
FITT - Frequency, Intensity, Time, Type
FLOT - Forward Line of Troops
FLX - Field Leadership Exercise
FM - Field Manual
FORSCOM - U.S. Army Forces Command
FOUO - For Official Use Only
FPS - Feet Per Second
FQ-NS - Fully Qualified Non-Select
FQ-S - Fully Qualified Select
FRAGO - Fragmentary Order
FRIES - Fast Rope Insertion/Extraction System
FROG - Free Rocket Over Ground
FSA - Family Separation Allowance
FSBAQ - Family Separation Basic Allowance for Quarters
FSE - Fire Support Element
FSG - First Sergeant
Ft - Feet
Ft - Fort
FTX - Field Training Exercise
FW - Fixed Wing
FY - Fiscal Year (unless specific year, FY92)
FYI - For Your Information

GCCS-A - Global Command and Control System-Army
GED - General Equivalency Diploma (High School)
GI - Government Issue
GL - Grid Line
GM - Grid Magnetic
GMRS - Ground Marking Release System
GN - Grid North
GO / NO GO - Pass / Fail grading system
GP - General Purpose
GPS - Global Positioning System
GRE - Graduate Record Examination
GS - General Support
GT - General Technical
GTA - Graphic Training Aid
GTN - Global Transportation Network
GW - Guerrilla Warfare
GZ - Ground Zero
HA - Humanitarian Assistance
HAHO - High Altitude High Opening
HALO - High Altitude Low Opening
HAP INT - High Altitude Parachutist Initial
HD - Humanitarian De-Mining
HF - High Frequency
HHC - Headquarters and Headquarters Company
HIMAD - High to Medium Altitude Air Defense
HIV - Human Immunodeficiency Virus
HLZ - Helicopter Landing Zone
HMMWV - High-Mobility, Multipurpose, Wheeled Vehicle
HN - Host Nation
HQ - Headquarters
HQDA - Headquarters Department of the Army
Hr - Hour
HRT - Hostage Rescue Team
Ht - Height
HUMINT - Human Intelligence
HW - Hot Weather
IAD - Immediate Action Drill
IAW - In Accordance With
ID - Identification
IDS - Intermediate Direct Support
IEDK - Individual Equipment Decontaminating Kit
IET - Initial Entry Training
IEW - Intelligence and Electronic Warfare
IG - Inspector General
IMC - Initial Manifest Call
IN - Infantry
IN DV - Infantry Division
Inf - Infantry
INSCOM - Intelligence and Securities Command
INSEC - Internal Security
IO - Information Operations
IOAC - Infantry Officer Advanced Course
IOBC - Infantry Officer Basic Course
IOC - Intermediate Officer Candidate
IPB - Intelligence Preparation of the Battlefield
IRR - Individual Ready Reserve

ISCET - International Society of Certified Electronic Technicians
ITAC - Individual Terrorism Awareness Course
ITO - Individual Travel Orders
IW - Information Warfare
JAG - Judge Advocate
JFC - Joint Force Commander
JFKSWCS - John F. Kennedy Special Warfare Center and School
JPI - Jumpmaster Personnel Inspection
JROTC - Junior Reserve Officer Training Corps
JRTC - Joint Readiness Training Center
J-SIIDS - Joint Service Interior Intrusion Detection System
JSOACC - Joint Special Operations Air Component Commander
JSOC - Joint Special Operations Command
JSOTF - Joint Special Operations Task Force
JTF - Joint Task Force
JUMPS - Joint Uniform Military Pay System
KIA - Killed In Action
KIM - Keep In Memory
KW - Key West (Florida)
LAAF - Lawson Army Airfield
LANs - Local Area Networks
LAR - Lambert Air Re-breather
LAW - Light Antitank Weapon
Lb (lb) - Pound
LBE - Load Bearing Equipment
LCE - Load Carrying Equipment
LDA - Lateral Drift Apparatus
LDRSHIP - Loyalty, Duty, Respect, Selfless service, Honor, Integrity, Personal Courage (7 Army Values)
LES - Leave and Earnings Statement
LFX - Live Fire Exercise
LIC - Low Intensity Conflict
LITC - Light Infantry Training Center
LOC - Lines Of Communication
LOM - Lack Of Motivation
LOS - Line Of Sight
LRC - Leadership Reaction Course
LRRP - Long-Range Reconnaissance Patrol
LRS - Long Range Surveillance
LRSL - Long-Range Surveillance Leader
LRSLC - Long Range Surveillance Leader Course
LRSU - Long Range Surveillance Unit
LSA - Lubricating oil, weapons, Semi-fluid
LTC - Lieutenant Colonel
LTD - Laser Targeting Devices
LZ - Landing Zone
MAC - Military Airlift Command
MACO - Marshalling Area Control Officer
MACOM - Major Army Command
MASH - Mobile Army Surgical Hospital
MCT - Mobile Contact Teams
MDME - Mock Door Mass Exit
MDW - Military District of Washington
MEDEVAC - Medical Evacuation

Memo - Memorandum
MEPS - Military Entrance Processing Station
METT-T - Mission, Enemy, Terrain (and weather),
Troops (available), and Time (available)
MFAD - Maneuver Forces Air Defense
MFF - Military Free Fall
MFFJMC - Military Free Fall Jumpmaster Course
MFFPC - Military Free Fall Parachutist Course
MFR - Memorandum For Record
MFT - Master Fitness Trainer
MGI - Military Geographic Information
MI - Military Intelligence
MIA - Missing In Action
MIJI - Meaconing, Intrusion, Jamming, and
Interference
MIL - Military
MILCOM - Military Communications
MILES - Multiple Integrated Laser Engagement System
MILPERCEN - Military Personnel Center
MILPO - Military Personnel Office
Min (min) - Minute
MLRS - Multiple Launch Rocket System
MM (mm) - Millimeter
MMC - Material Management Center
MMPI - Minnesota Multi-Phasic Inventory
MOA - Misrepresentation Of Application
MOOTW - Military Operations Other Than War
MOPP - Mission Oriented Protective Posture
MOR – Methods of Release
MOS - Military Occupational Specialty
MOUT - Military Operations on Urbanized Terrain
MP - Military Police
MPA - Military Police Activity
MPD - Military Personnel Division
MPRJ - Military Personnel Records Jacket
MQS - Military Qualifications Standards
MRE - Meal, Ready to Eat
MRMS - Maintenance Reporting and Management
System
MS - Medical Service Corps
MSE - Mobile Susriber Equipment
MSG - Master Sergeant
MSR - Main Supply Route
MTIE - Mock Tower Individual Exit
MTME - Mock Tower Mass Exit
MTOE - Modified Table of Organization and
Equipment
MTP - Mission Training Plan
MTS - Movement Tracking System
MTT - Mobile Training Team
MVT - Movement
N/A - Non-Applicable
NAC - National Agency Check
NAI - Names Areas of Interest
NATO - North Atlantic Treaty Organization
NBC - Nuclear, Biological and Chemical (Warfare)
NC-NS - Not Competitive-Not Selected
NCO - Non-Commissioned Officer

NCOA - Noncommissioned Officer Association
NCOIC - Non-Commissioned Officer In Charge
NICET - National Institute for Certification in
Engineering Technology
NLT - No Later Than
NOD - Night Observation Device
NSA - National Security Agency
NSN - National Stock Number
NVD - Night Vision Devices
OAC - Officer Advanced Course
OBC - Officers Basic Course
OCOKA - Observation and fields of fire, Cover and
concealment, Obstacles and movement, Key terrain,
and Avenues of approach
OCONUS - Outside Continental United States
OCS - Officer Candidate School
OCSSOP - Officer Candidate School Standard /
Standing Operating Procedure (s)
OD - Olive Drab (green)
OER - Officer Evaluation Report
Off SC - Officer Skill Code
OIC - Officer In Charge
OJT - On-the-Job Training
OMF - Officer Master File
OMPF - Official Military Personnel File
OOTW - Operations Other Than War
OP - Observation Post
OPFOR - Opposing Forces
OPNS - Operations
OPORDER - Operation Order
OPS - Operations
OPSEC - Operations Security
ORB - Officer Record Brief
ORP - Objective Rally Point
OSB - Officer Selection Battery
OSS - Office of Strategic Services
OSUT - One Station Unit Training
OTC - Operator Training Course
PA - Physicians Assistant
PAC - Personnel and Administration Center
Pam (pam) - Pamphlet
PANOREX - Panoramic X-Ray
para - paragraph
PB - Patrol Base
PCS - Permanent Change of Station
PDM - Pull Drop Method
PE - Practical Exercise
PEBD - Pay Entry Basic Date
PERSCOM - Personnel Command
PFDR - Pathfinder
PFU - Physical Fitness Uniform
PG - Platoon Guide
PG - Post Graduate
PL - Platoon Leader
PL - Preservative Lubricant
PLAD - Plain Language Address
PLDC - Primary Leadership Development Course
PLF - Parachute Landing Fall

PLT - Platoon
PMCS - Preventive Maintenance Checks and Services
PMOS - Primary Military Occupational Specialty
PO Box - Post Office Box
POC - Point Of Contact
POI - Program of Instruction
POL - Petroleum, Oils, and Lubricants
POV - Privately Owned Vehicle
POW - Privately Owned Weapon
PPT - Pseudoisochromatic Plates Test
PSB - Personnel Services Battalion
PSC - Personnel Service Center
PSD - Personnel Services Detachment
PSG - Platoon Sergeant
psi - pounds per square inch
PSYOP - Psychological Operations
PT - Physical Training
PU - Push-Up
PULHES - Physical capacity, Upper extremities, Lower extremities, Hearing, Eyes, Psychiatric
PVS - Passive Vision Sight
PVT - Private
PW - Prisoner Of War
PX - Post Exchange
PZ - Pickup Zone
QA - Quality Assurance
Q&A - Questions and Answers
QC - Quality Control
RA - Regular Army
R&R - Rest and Recuperation
R&S - Reconnaissance and Security
RAP - Ranger Assessment Phase
RAP - Rocket Assisted Projectile
RAPIDS - Real-time Automated Personnel Identification System
RAWS - Ranger Anti-tank Weapon System
RBC - Rifle Bore Cleaner
RC - Reserve Component
RCA - Riot Control Agent
RECON - Reconnaissance
REGT - Regiment
RHQ - Ranger Headquarters
RI - Ranger Instructor
RICE - Rest, Ice Compression and Elevation
RIF - Reduction In Force
RIP - Ranger Indoctrination Program
ROE - Rules Of Engagement
RON - Remain Over Night
ROP - Ranger Orientation Program
ROTC - Reserve Officer Training Corps
RP - Release Point
RPG - Rocket Propelled Grenade (enemy)
RRF1-3 - Ranger Ready Force One - Three
RSTA - Reconnaissance, Surveillance, Target Acquisition
RTB - Ranger Training Battalion
RTB - Ranger Training Brigade
RTD - Return To Duty

RW - Rotary Wing
RWAC - Rotary Wing Aviator Course
S1 - Adjutant (U.S. Army)
S2 - Intelligence Officer
S3 - Operations and Training Officer
S4 - Supply Officer
S5 - Civil Affairs Officer
SAAS - Standard Army Ammunition Systems
SAILS - Standard Army Integrated Logistic System
SALUTE - Size, Activity, Location, Unit, Time, Equipment
SAM - Statement, Act, and Marriage
SAM - Surface to Air Missile
S&D - Search and Destroy
SAS - Special Air Service (British Special Forces)
SAT - Scholastic Aptitude Test
SAT - Sustained Airborne Training
SAT - Standard Army Training
SAW - Squad Automatic Weapon
SBI - Special Background Investigation
SBP - Survivor Benefit Plan
SC - Signal Corps
SC - School Code
SCH - Scheduling
SCI - Sensitive Compartmented Information
SCUBA - Self-Contained Underwater Breathing Apparatus
SDAP - Special Duty Assignment Pay
SDK - Skin Decontamination Kit
SDNCO - Staff Duty Non-Commissioned Officer
SDT - Self Development Test
SEAL - Sea-Air-Land Team (Navy)
SEO - Sniper Employment Officer
SERE - Survival, Evasion, Resistance, and Escape
Semi - Semiautomatic
SEQ - Senior Enlisted Quarters
SF - Special Forces
SFAS - Special Forces Assessment and Selection
SFC - Sergeant First Class
SFCMF - Special Forces Career Management Field
SFDOQC - Special Forces Detachment Officer Qualification Course
SFG - Special Forces Group
SFGB - Special Forces Green Berets
SFODA - Special Forces Operational Detachment "A" Team
SFOD-D - Special Forces Operational Detachment-Delta
SFQC - Special Forces Qualification Course
SGI - Small Group Instruction
SGL - Small Group Leader
SGLI - Servicemen's Group Life Insurance
SM - Sergeant Major
SGT - Sergeant
SH - Suspended Harness
SIDPERS - Standard Installation / Division Personnel System
SIGIN - Signals Intelligence

SJA - Staff Judge Advocate
SKAs - Skills, Knowledge and Attitudes
SL - Skill Level
SL - Squad Leader
SLT - Swing Landing Trainer
SM - Service Member
SM - Soldiers Manual
SMA - Sergeant Major of the Army
SMCT - Soldiers Manual of Common Tasks
SME - Subject Matter Expert
SMOS - Secondary Military Occupational Specialty
SMRT - Special Missions Recruiting Team
SOAF - Special Operations Academic Facility
SOAR - Special Operations Aviation Regiment
SO - Special Operations
SOC - Senior Officer Candidate
SOCOM - Special Operations Command
SOF - Special Operations Force
SOI - Signal Operating Instructions
SOP - Standard / Standing Operating Procedure (s)
SOQ - Senior Officer Quarters
SOR - Special Observation Report
SOSR - Suppress, Obscure, Secure, and Reduce
SOTIC - Special Operations Target Interdiction Course
SPC - Specialist
SPD - Separation Program Designator
SPORTS - Slap, Pull, Observe, Release, Tap, Shoot
SQD - Squad
SQDN - Squadron
SQ FT - Square Feet
SQI - Special Qualification Identifier
SQT - Skill Qualification Test
SR - Special Reconnaissance
SRB - Selective Re-enlistment Bonus
SR TAC - Senior Training, Advising, Counseling
SSA - Supply Support Activity
SSBI - Single Scope Background Investigation
SSG - Staff Sergeant
SSN - Social Security Number
SSVC - Selective Service
STANO - Surveillance, Target Acquisition, and Night Observation
STD - Sexually Transmitted Disease(s)
STP - Soldier Training Publication
STRAC - Squad Tactical Reaction Assessment Course
STX - Situational Training Exercise
SU - Sit-Up
SWCS - Special Warfare Center and School
SWO - Staff Weather Officer
SWOTC - Senior Warrant Officer Training Course
SWTG - Special Warfare Training Group
TAAS - The Air Assault School
TAB - Target Acquisition Battery
TABE - Test of Adult Basic Education
TAC - Tactical Air Command
TAC - Training, Advising and Counseling

TACCS - Tactical Army Combat Service Support Computer System
TAC NCO - Training, Advising and Counseling Non-Commissioned Officer
TAI - Target Area of Interest
TAMMS - The Army Maintenance Management System
TBA - To Be Announced
TBD - To Be Determined
TBP - To Be Published
TC - Training Circular
TC-ACCIS - Transportation Coordinator-Automated Command and Control Information System
TC-AIMS II - Transportation Coordinator-Automated Information System
TCD - Terrorism Counteraction Department
TD - Tactical Director
TDY - Temporary Duty
TEC - Training Extension Course
T-FFP - Tentative Final Firing Point
TIG - Time In Grade
TIMIG - Time In Military In Grade
TIS - Time In Service
TISA - Troop Issue Subsistence Activities
TL - Team Leader
TLC - Terrorism in Low-intensity Conflict
TM - Technical Manual
TMDE - Test, Measurement, Diagnostic Equipment
TO - Table of Order
TOA - Terms Of Agreement
TOC - Tactical Operations Center
TOD - Time Of Day
TOE - Table of Organization and Equipment
TOF - Time Of Flight
Topo - Topographic
TOT - Time On Target
TOW - Tube-launched, Optically-tracked, Wire-guided missile
TRADOC - U.S. Army Training and Doctrine Command
TRITAC - Tri-service Tactical
TRP - Target Reference Point
TSFO - Training Set Fire Observation
TSOP - Tactical Standing Operating Procedure
TTA - Tactical Terminal Adapters
TTP - Tactics, Techniques, and Procedures
TVD - Tennessee Valley Divide
TZ - Tactical Zone
UA - Uniform Allowance
UCMJ - Uniform Code of Military Justice
UDT - Underwater Demolition Team
UHF - Ultra High Frequency
UN - United Nations
U.S. - United States (of America)
USA - United States Army
USACIDC - United States Army Criminal Investigation Division Command
USAF - United States Air Force

USAIC - United States Army Infantry Center
USAIS - United States Army Infantry School
USAJFKSWCS - United States Army John F. Kennedy Special Warfare Center and School
USAPT - United States Army Parachute Team
USAR - United States Army Reserve
USAREC - U.S. Army Recruiting Command
USASFC - United States of America Special Forces Command
USASOC - United States Army Special Operations Command
USC - United States Code
USMA - United States Military Academy
USMC - United States Marine Corps
USN - United States Navy
USS - United States Ship
UTC - Until Complete
UW - Unconventional Warfare
VA - Veterans Affairs
VB - Vapor Barrier
VD - Venereal Disease
VGLI - Veteran's Group Life Insurance
VHA - Variable Housing Allowance
VHF - Very High Frequency
VIP - Ventilate, Insulate, Protect
VIP - Very Important Person
VIRS - Verbal Initiated Release Point
VOA - Voice Of America
VWT - Vertical Wind Tunnel
WCET - Wind Chill Equivalent Temperature
WCF - Wind Chill Factor
WCT - Water Confidence Test
WIA - Wounded In Action
WIC - Water Infiltration Course
WMD - Weapons of Mass Destruction
WO - Warrant Officer
WOAC - Warrant Officer Advanced Course
WOBC - Warrant Officer Basic Course
WOCC - Warrant Officer Career Center
WOCS - Warrant Officer Candidates School
WOES - Warrant Officer Education System
WOFT - Warrant Officer Flight Training
WOMD - Weapons Of Mass Destruction
WOSC - Warrant Officer Staff Course
WO SQI - Warrant Officer Special Qualification Identifier
WOSSC - Warrant Officer Senior Staff Course
WP -White Phosphorus
WPN - Weapon
Wpn Qual - Weapon Qualification
WPS - World-wide Port System
Wt - Weight
WW - World War
XO - Executive Officer
YPG - Yuma Proving Ground (Arizona)
YTD - Year To Date
ZF - Zone of Fire
ZIP Code - Zone Improvement Plan Code

ZOE - Zone Of Entry
ZOF - Zone Of Fire
Zulu Time - Greenwich Mean Time

APPENDIX-D

MILITARY PUBLICATIONS

AF FORM 1274
Chamber Card
AR 40-5
Preventive Medicine
AR 40-63
Opthamolic Services
AR 40-501
Standards of Medical Fitness
AR 50-6
Chemical Surety
AR 56-9
Watercraft
AR 135-100
Appointment of Commissioned and
Warrant Officers of the Army
AR 135-101
Appointment of Reserve Commissioned
Officers for Assignment to the Army Medical
Department Branches
AR 140-50
Officer Candidate School Army Reserve
AR 140-158
Enlisted Personnel Classification,
Promotion and Reduction
AR 190-11
Physical Security of Arms, Ammunition,
and Explosives
AR 350-15
The Army Physical Fitness Program
AR 350-30
Code of Conduct, Survival, Evasion,
Resistance, and Escape (SERE)
AR 350-41
Nuclear, Biological and Chemical Defense
and Chemical Warfare
AR 351-5
Army Officer Candidate Schools
AR 380-67
The Department of the Army Personnel
Security Program
AR 600-9
The Army Weight Control Program

AR 600-31
Suspension of Favorable Personnel Actions
for Military Personnel
AR 600-37
Unfavorable Information
AR 600-38
Meal Card Management System
AR 600-200
Enlisted Personnel Management System/
Promotions
AR 601-100
Appointment of Commissioned and
Warrant Officers in the Regular Army
Procurement Program
AR 601-210
Regular Army Enlistment Program
AR 601-280
Total Army Retention Program
(Reenlistment)
AR 611-5
Army Personnel Tests
AR 611-201
Enlisted Career Management Fields and
MOSs
AR 614-10
United States Army Personnel Exchange
Program with Armies of other Nations
AR 614-30
Oversea Service
AR 614-110
Assignment of Airborne Officers and
Processing Volunteers for Training
AR 614-200
Enlisted Personnel Selection, Training,
and Assignment System
AR 630-5
Leaves, Passes, Permissive TDY
AR 635-5
Separation Program Designator
AR 635-5-1
Separation Program Designator
AR 635-200
Enlisted Personnel/Separations

AR 640-30
  Photographs for Military Personnel Files
AR 670-1
  Wear and Appearance of the Uniform
AR 700-84
  Issue and Sale of Personal Clothing
AR 710-2
  Inventory management Supply Policy Below
  the Wholesale Level
DA FORM 1A
  Officer Commission Certificate
DA FORM 2-1
  Personnel Qualification Record, Part II
DA FORM 2A
  Personnel Qualification Record, Part I
DA FORM 31
  Request and Authority for Leave
DA FORM 61
  Application for Appointment
DA FORM 71
  Oath of Office-Military Personnel
DA FORM 145
  Army Correspondence Course
  Enrollment Application
DA FORM 160
  Application For Active Duty
DD FORM 214
  Certificate of Release or Discharge from
  Active Duty
DA FORM 330
  Language Proficiency Questionnaire
DA FORM 483
  Officers Assignment Preference
  Statement
DA FORM 705
  Army Physical Fitness Test Scorecard
DA FORM 873
  Certificate of Clearance and/or Security
  Determination
DA FORM 1059
  Service School Academic Evaluation Report
DA FORM 1307
  Jump Record
DA FORM 1610
  Request and Authorization for TDY Travel
DA FORM 3032
  Signature Headcount Sheet
DA FORM 3822-R
  Mental Evaluation
DA FORM 4187
  Personnel Action
DA FORM 4322-R
  Army Officer Candidate Contract and
  Service Agreement

DA FORM 4989-R
  Warrant Officer Flight Training Application
DA FORM 5248-R
  Report of Unfavorable Information for
  Security Determination
DA FORM 5339-R
  Evaluation Sheet
DA FORM 5500-R
  Bodyfat Statement
DA FORM 6256
  (AFAST) Army Flight Aptitude Selection
  Test
DA PAM 351-4
  US Army Formal Schools Catalog
DA PAM 351-20
  Correspondence Course Catalog
DA PAM 600-3
  Commissioned Officer Development and
  Career Management
DA PAM 600-8
  Management and Administrative Procedures
DA PAM 611-5
  Army Personnel Selection and Classification
  Testing
DD FORM 714
  Meal Card
DD FORM 1475
  Basic Allowance for Subsistence Certification
FM 21-20
  Physical Fitness Training
FM 23-9
  M16A1 and M16A2 Rifle Marksmanship
PT31-210-SWCS
  Special Forces Assessment and Selection
  Physical Training Handbook
STANDARD FORM 86
  Questionnaire for National Security Positions
STANDARD FORM 88
  Medical Record Report of Medical
  Examination
STANDARD FORM 93
  Report of Medical History
SH 21-75
  Ranger School Student Handout

APPENDIX-E

MOSs, ASIs & SQIs

MOS Description	
MOS	DESCRIPTION
00B	DIVER
00B	RECRUITER (NG,ER)
00R	RECRUITER AND RETENTION NCO (RA)
00Z	COMMAND SGT. MAGOR
02B	CORNET OR TRUMPET PLAYER
02C	EUPHONIUM PLAYER
02D	FRENCH HORN PLAYER
02E	TROMBONE PLAYER
02F	TUBA PLAYER
02G	FLUTE PLAYER
02H	OBOE PLAYER
02J	CLARINET PLAYER
02K	BASSOON PLAYER
02L	SAXOPHONE PLAYER
02M	PERCUSSION PLAYER
02N	KEYBOARD PLAYER
02S	SPECIAL BAND MEMBER
02T	GUITAR PLAYER
02U	ELECTRIC BASS PLAYER
02Z	BANDS SENIOR SGT.
11B	INFANTRYMAN
11C	INDIRECT FIRE INFANTRYMAN
11H	HEAVY ANTI-ARMOR WEAPONS INFANTRYMAN
11M	FIGHTING VEHICLE INFANTRYMAN
11Z	INFANTRY SENIOR SGT.
12B	COMBAT ENGINEER
12C	BRIDGE CREWMEMBER
12F	ENGINEER TRACKED VEHICLE CREWMAN
12Z	COMBAT ENGINEERING SENIOR SGT.
13B	CANNON CREWMEMBER
13C	TACFIRE OPERATIONS SPEC.
13E	CANNON FIRE DIRECTION SPEC.
13F	FIRE SUPPORT SPEC.

MOS Description	
MOS	DESCRIPTION
13M	MULTIPLE LAUNCH ROCKET SYSTEM (MLRS) CREWMEMBER
13P	MLRS FIRE DIRECTION SPEC.
13R	FIELD ARTILLERY FIREFINDER RADAR OPER.
13Z	FIELD ARTILLERY SENIOR SGT.
14D	HAWK MISSLE SYSTEM CREWMEMBER
14E	PATRIOT MISSLE CREWMEMBER (FORMERLY 16T)
14J	EARLY WARNING SYSTEM (EWS) OPER.
14R	LINE OF SIGHT-FORWARD-HEAVY CREWMEMBER
14S	AVENGER CREWMEMBER
16P	CHAPARRAL CREWMEMBER
16R	VULCAN CREWMEMBER
16S	MAN PORTABLE AIR DEFENSE SYSTEM (MANPADS) CREWMEMBER
16T	PATRIOT MISSLE CREWMEMBER (FORMERLY 16T SEE 14E)
16 Z	AIR DEFENSE ARTILLERY (ADA) SENIOR SGT.
18B	S.F. WEAPONS SGT.
18C	S.F. ENGINEER SGT.
18D	S.F. MEDICAL SGT.
18E	S.F. COMMUNICATIONS SGT.
18F	S.F. ASSIST. OPERATIONS AND INTELLIGENCE SGT.
18Z	S.F. SENIOR SGT.
19D	CAVALRY SCOUT
19E	M60 ARMOR CREWMAN
19K	M1 ARMOR CREWMAN
19Z	ARMOR SENIOR SGT.
23R	HAWK MISSILE SYSTEM MECHANIC
24H	HAWK FIRE CONTROL REPAIRER
24K	HAWK CONTINUOUS WAVE RADAR REPAIRER
24M	VULCAN SYSTEM MECHANIC
24N	CHAPARRAL SYSTEM MECH.
24T	PATRIOT OPER.
25L	AIR DEFENSE ARTILLERY COMMAND AND CONTROL SYSTEMS OPER.
25M	MULTIMEDIA ILLUSTRATOR
25R	VISUAL INFORMATION EQUIPMENT OPERATOR-MAINTAINER
25V	COMBAT DOCUMENTATION/PRODUCTION SPEC.
25Z	VISUAL INFORMATION OPERATIONS CHIEF
27E	LAND COMBAT ELECTRONIC MISSILE SYSTEM REPAIRER
27F	VULCAN REPAIRER
27G	CHAPARRAL AND REDEYE REPAIRER
27H	HAWK FIELD MAINT. EQUIP. AND FIRING SECTION REPAIR
27K	HAWK FIRE CONTROL AND CONTINUOUS WAVE RADAR REPAIR
27M	MLRS REPAIRER
27T	AVENGER SYSTEM REPAIR
27X	PATRIOT SYSTEM REPAIR
27Z	MISSILE SYSTEM MAINT. CHIEF
31C	RADIO OPERATOR/MAINTAINER
31F	NETWORK SWITCHING SYSTEMS OPER/MAINT
31L	CABLE SYSTEMS INSTALLER/MAINT
31P	MICROWAVE SYSTEMS OPER/MAINT

MOS Description	
MOS	DESCRIPTION
31R	MULTICHANNEL TRANSMISSION SYSTEMS OPER/MAINT
31S	SATELLITE COMM. SYSTEMS OPER/MAINT
31T	SATELLITE/MICROWAVE SYSTEMS CHIEF
31U	SIGNAL SUPPORT SYSTEMS SPECIALIST
31W	TELECOMMUNICATIONS OPERATIONS CHIEF
31Z	SENIOR SIGNAL SGT.
33R	AVIATIONS SYSTEMS REPAIRER
33T	ELECTRONIC WARFARE/INTERCEPT TACTICAL SYSTEMS REPAIR
33Y	STATEGIC SYSTEMS REPAIR
33Z	ELECTRONIC WARFARE/INTERCEPT SYSTEMS MAINT. SUPERVISOR
35B	LAND COMBAT SUPPORT SYSTEM (LCSS) TEST SPEC.
35C	SURVEILLANCE RADAR REPAIRER
35E	RADIO AND COMMUNICATIONS SECURITY (COMSEC) REPAIRER
35F	SPECIAL ELECTRONIC DEVICES REPAIRER
35H	TEST, MEASUREMENT, AND DIAGNOSTIC (TMDE) MAINT.SUPPLY SPEC
35J	TELECOMMUNICATIONS TERMINAL DEVICE REPAIR
35M	RADAR REPAIRER
35N	WIRE SYSTEMS EQUIPMENT REPAIRER
35W	ELECTRONIC MAINTENANCE CHIEF
35Y	INTEGRATED FAMILY OF TEST EQUIP. (IFTE) OPER/MAINT
35Z	SENIOR ELECTRONIC MAINTENANCE CHIEF
37F	PSYCHOLOGICAL OPERATIONS SPEC. (PSYOP)
38A	CIVIL AFFAIRS SPEC.
39B	AUTOMATIC TEST EQUIPMENT OPER/MAINT
42E	OPTICAL LABORATORY SPEC.
43E	PARACHUTE RIGGER
43M	FABRIC REPAIR SPEC.
44B	METAL WORKER
45D	SELF-PROPELLED FIELD ARTILLERY TURRET MECHANIC
45E	M1 ABRAMS TANK TURRET MECHANIC
45G	FIRE CONTROL REPAIRER
45K	ARMAMENT REPAIRER
45N	M60A1/A3 TANK TURRET MECHANIC
45T	BRADLY FIGHTING VEHICLE SYS. TURRET (BFVS) MECH.
46Q	JOURNALIST
46R	BROADCAST JOURNALIST
46Z	PUBLIC AFFAIRS CHIEF
51B	CARPENTRY AND MASONRY SPEC.
51H	CONSTRUCTION ENGINEERING SUPERVISOR
51K	PLUMBER
51M	FIREFIGHTER
51R	INTERIOR ELECTRICIAN
51T	TECHNICAL ENGINEERING SPEC.
51Z	GENERAL ENGINEERING SUPERVISOR
52C	UTILLITIES EQUIPMENT REPAIRER
52D	POWER GENERATION EQUIPMENT REPAIRER
52E	PRIME POWER PRODUCTION SPECIALIST
52F	TURBINE ENGINE DRIVEN GENERATOR (TEDG) REPAIRER

MOS Description	
MOS	**DESCRIPTION**
52G	TRANSMISSION AND DISTRUBUTION SPEC.
52X	SPECIAL PURPOSE EQUIP. REPAIR
54B	CHEMICAL OPERATIONS SPEC.
55B	AMMUNITION SPEC.
55D	EXPLOSIVE ORDINANCE DISPOSAL (EOD) SPEC.
55Z	AMMUNITION SUPERVISOR
57E	LAUNDRY AND SHOWER SPEC.
57F	MORTUARY AFFAIRS SPEC.
62B	CONSTRUCTION EQUIP. REPAIRER
62E	HEAVY CONSTRUCTION EQUIPMENT OPERATOR
62F	CRANE OPERATOR
62G	QUARRYING SPEC.
62H	CONCRETE AND ASPHALT EQUIP. OPER.
62J	GENERAL CONSTRUCTION EQUIP. OPER.
62N	CONSTRUCTION EQUIPMENT SUPERVISOR
63B	LIGHT-WHEEL VEHICLE MECH.
63D	SELF-PROPELLED FIELD ARTILLERY SYS. MECH.
63E	M1 ABRAMS TANK SYSTEMS MECH.
63G	FUEL AND ELECTRICAL SYSTEMS REPAIR
63H	TRACK VEHICLE REPAIR
63J	QUARTERMASTER AND CHEMICAL EQUIP. REPAIR
63N	M60A1/A3 TANK SYSTEM MECH.
63S	HEAVY-WHEEL VEHICLE MECHANIC
63T	BRADLEY (BFVS) MECHANIC
63W	WHEEL VEHICLE REPAIR
63Y	TRACK VEHICLE MECHANIC
63Z	MECHANICAL MAINTENANCE SUPERVISOR
67G	UTILITY AIRPLANE REPAIR (ER) reserves only if still available
67H	OBSERVATION AIRPLANE REPAIR
67N	UH-1 (HUEY) HELICOPTER REPAIR (NO LONGER AVAILABLE)
67R	AH-64 (APACHE) HELICOPTER REPAIR
67S	OH-58D (KIOWA) HELICOPTER REPAIR
67T	UH-60 (BLACKHAWK) REPAIR
67U	CH-47 (CHINOOK) HELICOPTER REPAIR
67V	OBSERVATION/SCOUT HELICOPTER REPAIR
67Y	AH-1 (COBRA) HELICOPTER REPAIR
67Z	AIRCRAFT MAINTENANCE SENIOR SGT.
68B	AIRCRAFT POWERPLANT REPAIR
68D	AIRCRAFT POWERTRAIN REPAIR
68F	AIRCRAFT ELECTRICIAN
68G	AIRCRAFT STRUCTURAL REPAIR
68H	AIRCRAFT PNEUDRAULICS REPAIR
68J	AIRCRAFT ARMAMENT/MISSILE SYS. REPAIR
68K	AIRCRAFT COMPONENTS REPAIR SUPERVISOR
68L	AVIONIC COMMUNICATIONS EQUIPMENT REPAIR
68N	AVIONIC MECHANIC
68P	AVIONIC MAINTENANCE SUPERVISOR
68Q	AVIONIC FLIGHT SYSTEMS REPAIR

MOS Description	
MOS	**DESCRIPTION**
68R	AVIONIC RADAR REPAIR
68X	AH-64 (APACHE) ARMAMENT/ELECT. SYSTEMS REPAIR
71 C	EXECUTIVE ADMINISTRATIVE ASSISTANT
71D	LEGAL SPEC.
71G	PATIENT ADMINISTRATION SPEC.
71L	ADMINISTRATIVE SPEC.
71M	CHAPLAIN ASSIST.
73C	FINANCE SPEC.
73D	ACCOUNTING SPEC.
73Z	FINANCE SENIOR SGT.
74B	INFORMATION SYSTEMS OPERATOR/ANALYST
74C	RECORD TELECOMMUNICATIONS OPER/MAINT
74G	TELECOMMUNICATIONS COMPUTER OPER/MAINT.
74Z	TELECOM. SYSTEMS CHIEF
75B	PERSONNEL ADMINISTRATION SPEC.
75C	PERSONNEL MANAGMENT SPEC.
75D	PERSONNEL RECORDS SPEC.
75E	PERSONNEL ACTIONS SPEC.
75F	PERSONNEL INFORMATION SYS. MGMT. SPEC.
75Z	PERSONNEL SGT.
76J	MEDICAL SUPPLY SPECIALIST
77F	PETROLEUM SUPPLY SPECIALIST
77L	PETROLEUM LABORATORY SPEC.
77W	WATER TREATMENT SPEC.
79D	RETENTION NCO
81C	CARTOGRAPHER
81Q	TERRAIN ANALYST
81Z	TOPOGRAPHIC ENGINEERING SUPERVISOR
82C	FIELD ARTILLERY SURVEYOR
82D	TOPOGRAPHIC SURVEYOR
83E	PHOTO AND LAYOUT SPEC.
83F	PRINTING AND BINDERY SPEC.
88H	CARGO SPEC.
88K	WATERCRAFT OPERATOR
88L	WATERCRAFT ENGINEER
88M	MOTOR TRANSPORT OPERATOR (TRUCK DRIVER)
88N	TRANSPORTATION MGMT. COORDINATOR
88P	RAILWAY EQUIPMENT REPAIR (not available for RA)
88T	RAILWAY SECTION REPAIR (not available for RA)
88U	RAILWAY OPERATIONS CREWMEMBER (not available for RA)
88X	RAILWAY SENIOR SGT.
88Y	MARINE SENIOR SGT.
88Z	TRANSPORTATION SENIOR SGT.
91A	MEDICAL EQUIP. REPAIR
91B	COMBAT MEDIC/MEDICAL SPECIALIST
91C	PRACTICAL NURSE
91D	OPERATING ROOM SPEC.
91E	DENTAL SPEC.

MOS Description	
MOS	DESCRIPTION
91F	PSYCHIATRIC SPEC.
91G	BEHAVIORAL SCIENCE SPEC.
91K	MEDICAL LABORATORY SPEC.
91M	HOSPITAL FOOD SERVICE SPEC.
91P	RADIOLOGY SPEC.
91Q	PHARMACY SPEC.
91R	VETERINARY FOOD INSPECTION SPEC.
91S	PREVENTATIVE MEDICINE SPEC.
91T	ANIMAL CARE SPEC.
91V	RESPIRATORY SPEC.
92A	AUTOMATED LOGISTICAL SPEC.
92Y	UNIT SUPPLY SPEC.
92Z	SENIOR NONCOMMISSINED LOGISTICAIN
93B	AEROSCOUT OBSERVER
93C	AIR TRAFFIC CONTROL
93D	ATC EQUIP. REPAIR
93F	FIELD ARTILLERY METEOROLOGICAL CREWMEMBER
93P	AVIATION OPERATIONS SPEC.
94B	FOOD SERVICE SPEC.
95B	MP
95C	CORRECTIONS SPEC.
95D	CID SPECIAL AGENT
96B	INTELLIGENCE ANALYST
96D	IMAGERY ANALYST
96H	IMAGERY GROUND STATION (IGS) OPERATOR
96R	GROUND SURVEILLANCE SYSTEMS OPERATOR
96U	UNMANNED AERIAL VEHICLE OPERATOR
96Z	INTELLIGENCE SENIOR SGT.
97B	COUNTERINTELLIGENCE AGENT
97E	INTERROGATOR
97G	MULTIDISCIPLINE COUNTERINTELLIGENCE (MDCI) ANALYST
97L	TRANSLATOR/INTERPRETOR
97Z	COUNTERINTELLIGENCE SENIOR SGT.
98C	SIGNALS INTELLIGENCE ANALYST
98D	EMITTER LOCATOR/IDENTIFIER
98G	VOICE INTERCEPTOR
98H	MORSE INTERCEPTOR
98J	NONCOMMUNICATIONS INTERCEPTOR
98K	NON-MORSE INTERCEPTOR/ANALYST
98Z	SIGNALS INTELLIGENCE/ELECTRONIC WARFARE CHIEF

ASI	
MOS	DESCRIPTION
A2	AVIATION SAFETY
A3	FORCE DEVELOPMENT (TAADS)
A7	TACTICAL FIRE DIRECTION (TACFIRE) SYSTEMS MAINTENANCE
A8	MASTER GUNNERY M1/M1A1 TANK
B1	ROUGH TERRAIN CONTAINER HANDLING AND OPERATION
B3	ADVANCED ARMY COMPETITIVE SHOOTER
B4	SNIPER
B5	STANDARD ARMY MAINTENANCE SYSTEM (SAMS)
B6	COMBAT ENGINEER HEAVY TRACK
C1	MACOM BAND QUALIFIED
C2	DRAGON GUNNERY
C3	WELL DRILLING
C5	COURT REPORTER
C6	HIGH POWER RADIO OPERATOR/MAINTAINER
C8	TRANSCRIBING/GISTING
C9	MAST AND ELECTRIC POWER PLANT MAINTENANCE
D3	BRADLEY FIGHTING VEHICLE OPERATIONS AND MAINTENANCE
D7	SECONDARY REFERENCE LABORATORY MAINTENANCE
D9	BATTLEFIELD SPECTRUM MANAGEMENT (BSM)
E3	EXECUTIVE ADMINISTRATIVE ASSISTANT
E4	ATTACHE ADMINISTRATIVE SUPPORT
E5	INSTRUMENT MAINTENANCE (POWER STATION)
E9	M901 (ITV) GUNNER/CREW TRAINING
F2	ANTENNA INSTALLATION
F4	POSTAL SUPERVISOR
F5	POSTAL OPERATIONS
F6	CABLE SPLICING
F7	PATHFINDER
F8	FLIGHT SIMULATOR (UH1FS) CONSOLE OPERATIONS
F9	ADVANCED FIELD ARTILLERY TACTICAL DATA SYSTEM
G1	CONTRACTING AGENT
G2	STANDARD ARMY RETAIL SUPPLY SYSTEM(SARSS 2AD/2AC/2B)
G3	STANDARD PROPERTY BOOK SYSTEM-REDESIGN/TACTICAL ARMY COMBAT SERVICE SUPPORT COMPUTER SYSTEM (SPBS-R/TACCS)
G9	DEFENSE AGAINST SOUND EQUIPMENT (DASE)
H1	METEOROLOGICAL EQUIPMENT MAINTENANCE
H3	PHYSICAL SECURITY OPERATIONS
H5	GLOBAL COMMAND AND CONTROL SYSTEM (GCCS) ADMINISTRATOR
H7	PETROLEUM VEHICLE OPERATIONS
H8	RECOVERY OPERATIONS
J1	TELEMETRY COLLECTIONS OPERATIONS
J3	BRADLEY INFANTRY FIGHTING VEHICLE (BIFV)SYSTEM MASTER GUNNER
J5	TECHNICAL ESCORTING
J6	REPRODUCTION EQUIPMENT REPAIR
J7	WHCA CONSOLE CONTROL OPERATIONS
J9	TOW FIELD TEST SET (TFTS),(TOW-GROUND)
K2	ADVANCED SENIOR (SR) ANALYSIS
K4	M1A2 TANK OPERATIONS AND MAINTENANCE

ASI	
MOS	**DESCRIPTION**
K8	MASTER GUNNERY M1A2 TANK
L1	MASTER FOX SCOUT
L4	BIOLOGICAL INTEGRATED DETECTION SYSTEMS (BIDS)
L5	NBC RECONNAISSANCE
M2	CYTOLOGY SPECIALIST
M3	DIALYSIS SPECIALTY
M4	BLOOD DONOR CENTER OPERATIONS
M5	NUCLEAR MEDICINE SPECIALIST
M7	INTERMEDIATE (INTER) ANALYSIS
M8	DRUG AND ALCOHOL COUNSELING
N1	AIRCRAFT CREWMEMBER STANDARDIZATION INSTRUCTION
N2	NONDESTRUCTIVE TEST EQUIPMENT (NDTE)
N3	OCCUPATIONAL THERAPY SPECIALIST
N4	HEALTH PHYSICS SPECIALIST
N5	DENTAL LABORATORY SPECIALIST
N7	STRATEGIC DEBRIEFING AND INTERROGATION
N9	PHYSICAL THERAPY SPECIALTY
P1	ORTHOPEDIC SPECIALIST
P2	EAR, NOSE, AND THROAT SPECIALIST
P3	EYE SPECIALIST
P5	MASTER FITNESS TRAINER
P7	SATELLITE COMMUNICATIONS TERMINAL AN/TSC-85/93 OPERATOR/MAINTAINER
P8	POLYGRAPH OPERATIONS
P9	BIOLOGICAL SCIENCES ASSISTANT
Q2	AVIATION LIFE SUPPORT EQUIPMENT (ALSE)
Q5	SPECIAL FORCES COMBAT DIVING, MEDICAL
Q8	TACTICAL AIR OPERATIONS
Q9	TRAFFIC ACCIDENT INVESTIGATION
S2	MECHANICAL EQUIPMENT MAINTENANCE (POWER STATION)
S3	ELECTRICAL EQUIPMENT MAINTENANCE (POWER STATION)
S6	SPECIAL FORCES COMBAT DIVING, SUPERVISION
S7	FOREIGN COUNTERINTELLIGENCE
S9	DEFENSE SENSOR INTERPRETATION & APPLICATION TRAINING PROGRAM (DSIATP)
T1	ENHANCED POSITION LOCATION AND REPORTING SYSTEM (EPLRS) NET CONTROL STATION (NCS) AND ENHANCED GROUND REFERENCE UNIT (EGRU) OPERATOR
T9	CRYPTANALYSIS
U2	UNMANNED AERIAL VEHICLE-SHORT RANGE (UAV-SR) REPAIR
U4	POWER LINE DISTRIBUTION
U6	FIELD ARTILLERY WEAPONS MAINTENANCE
V5	MILITARY POLICE INVESTIGATION
V7	GUIDANCE COUNSELING
W1	SPECIAL OPERATIONS COMBAT MEDIC
W3	SPECIAL FORCES TARGET INTERDICTION OPERATIONS
W5	OH58D QUALIFICATION
W7	SPECIAL FORCES UNDERWATER OPERATIONS
W8	SPECIAL FORCES MILITARY FREE FALL OPERATIONS
X1	AH-64 MAINTENANCE

ASI	
MOS	DESCRIPTION
X2	PREVENTIVE DENISTRY SPECIALTY
Y1	TRANSITION
Y2	TRANSITION
Y5	TEMPEST INSPECTION
Y6	CARDIOVASCULAR SPECIALTIST
Y7	STERILE PHARMACY SPECIALTY
Z2	AUTOMATIC MESSAGE SWITCHING CENTER OPERATIONS
Z5	ENLISTED AIDE
Z6	DETECTOR DOG HANDLING
Z8	TECHNICAL ELINT COLLECTION AND ANALYSIS
1A	JSTARS E8-A SYSTEMS OPERATOR
1C	SATELLITE SYSTEMS/NETWORK COORDINATOR
1F	ALL SOURCE ANALYSIS SYSTEMS (ASAS) MASTER OPERATIONS
1G	DIRECTION FINDING OPERATOR (CROSSHAIR)
1T	IPDS/TRAC/NIS TENCAP OPERATIONS
2C	JAVELIN GUNNERY
2G	COUNTER-SIGNALS INTELLIGENCE (C-SIGNIT) OPERATIONS
2S	BATTLE STAFF OPERATIONS
2T	TENCAP DATA ANALYST
4A	RECLASSIFICATION TRAINING
4R	TRANSITION NCO
4T	TACTICAL EXPLOITATION OF NATIONAL CAPABILITIES (TENCAP) INTEGRATOR/MAINTAINER)
8A	IDENTIFICATION FRIEND OR FOE (IFF) REPAIRER

SQI	
MOS	DESCRIPTION
B	INSPECTOR GENERAL NONCOMMISSIONED OFFICER
D	CIVIL AFFAIRS OPERATIONS (ACTIVE COMPONENT ONLY)
E	MILITARY MOUNTAINEER
F	FLYING STATUS
*G	RANGER
H	INSTRUCTOR
I	INSTALLER
L	LINGUIST
M	FIRST SERGEANT
N	JOINT PLANNER
O	NO SPECIAL QUALIFICATIONS
P	PARACHUTIST
Q	EQUAL OPPORTUNITY ADVISOR (EOA)
S	SPECIAL OPERATIONS SUPPORT PERSONNEL
T	1ST SFOD-D UNIT OPERATOR
*V	RANGER PARACHUTIST
X	DRILL SERGEANT
2	TRAINING DEVELOPMENT
4	NON-CAREER RECRUITER
6	MOBILIZATION AND DEMOBILIZATION OPERATIONS

NOTES: * - SQI is closed to women; (RC) - Reserve Component. Refer to AR 611-201 for more information.

COMMENTS / CORRECTIONS

It is my intention that "The HOOAH Schools" be as complete and up-to-date as possible. I realize however that in compiling a book with such a diversity of subject areas mistakes can and will be made; there may also be information that has changed without my knowledge.

I believe this reference guide to be one of the most comprehensive, as well as one of the most current, available. I welcome professional comments and / or suggestions for a better reference guide. If you would like to recommend changes / corrections, please use the following format:

(1) Name
(2) Unit / Address
(3) Subject area concerned / page (in reference guide)
(4) Information as it appears
(5) Information as it should appear
(6) Reference source for correction (include page & paragraph)
(7) Additional comments

Send correspondence in care of the following:

PEARLMAN PUBLISHING COMPANY
Serving America's Serviceman
P.O. Box 497
Fort Mitchell, Alabama 36856

All correspondence will receive a reply.

Thank You!

Fold here

From: _____

_____

_____

PLACE
POSTAGE
HERE

To: PEARLMAN PUBLISHING COMPANY
COMMENTS
POST OFFICE BOX 497
FORT MITCHELL AL 36856

Fold here

(1) Name: _____

(2) Unit / Address: _____

                    _____

                    _____

(3) Subject area concerned / page (in reference guide)
     _____ / _____

(4) Information as it appears: _____

_____

_____

_____

_____

(5) Information as it should appear: _____

_____

_____

_____

_____

(6) Reference source for correction (include page & paragraph):
        Page: _____ Para: _____

(7) Additional comments: _____

_____

_____

_____

_____

_____

_____

_____

_____

_____

_____

_____

Fold here

From: _____

_____

_____

PLACE
POSTAGE
HERE

To: PEARLMAN PUBLISHING COMPANY
COMMENTS
POST OFFICE BOX 497
FORT MITCHELL AL 36856

Fold here

(1) Name: _____

(2) Unit / Address: _____

                    _____

                    _____

(3) Subject area concerned / page (in reference guide)
     _____ / _____

(4) Information as it appears: _____

_____

_____

_____

_____

(5) Information as it should appear: _____

_____

_____

_____

_____

(6) Reference source for correction (include page & paragraph):
         Page: _____ Para: _____

(7) Additional comments: _____

_____

_____

_____

_____

_____

_____

_____

_____

_____

_____

_____

Fold here

From: _____

_____

_____

PLACE
POSTAGE
HERE

To: PEARLMAN PUBLISHING COMPANY
ORDERS
POST OFFICE BOX 497
FORT MITCHELL AL 36856

Fold here

DISTRIBUTOR/WHOLESALE ORDERS:

FAX ORDERS: 1 (334) 855-3821. SEND THIS FORM.

TELEPHONE ORDERS: 1 (334) 855-9342

E-MAIL ORDERS: ppc@pearlmanpublishing.com

POSTAL ORDERS: COMPLETE AND SEND THIS FORM TO

PEARLMAN PUBLISHING COMPANY
ORDERS
P.O. BOX 497
FT. MITCHELL, AL 36856

PLEASE SEND ____ COPIES OF THE HOOAH SCHOOLS. I UNDERSTAND THAT I MAY RETURN ANY OF THEM FOR A FULL REFUND -- FOR ANY REASON, NO QUESTIONS ASKED.

PLEASE SEND MORE FREE INFORMATION ON:

___ OTHER AVAILABLE PRODUCTS.

___ FUTURE PRODUCTS.

NAME: _____

ADDRESS: _____

CITY: _____ STATE: _____ ZIP: _____ - _____

TELEPHONE: _____

E-MAIL ADDRESS: _____

ORDER INFORMATION:

ALL ORDERS WILL BE CONFIRMED BY TELEPHONE, FAX, OR EMAIL. INVOICE WILL BE SENT TO SHIPPING ADDRESS, UNLESS A BILLING ADDRESS IS OTHERWISE SPECIFIED. ALL ORDERS ARE SUBJECT TO CREDIT APPROVAL AND AVAILABILITY.

SHIPPING INFORMATION:

ALL ORDERS WILL BE SHIPPED F.O.B. ORIGIN.